Building Quantum Software with Python

Get the eBook FREE!
(PDF, ePub, Kindle, and liveBook all included)

We believe that once you buy a book from us, you should be able to read it in any format we have available. To get electronic versions of this book at no additional cost to you, purchase and then register this book at the Manning website.

Go to https://www.manning.com/freebook and follow the instructions to complete your pBook registration.

That's it!
Thanks from Manning!

Building Quantum Software with Python

A DEVELOPER'S GUIDE

CONSTANTIN GONCIULEA
CHARLEE STEFANSKI
FOREWORD BY HEATHER HIGGINS

MANNING

SHELTER ISLAND

For online information and ordering of this and other Manning books, please visit www.manning.com. The publisher offers discounts on this book when ordered in quantity. For more information, please contact

    Special Sales Department
    Manning Publications Co.
    20 Baldwin Road
    PO Box 761
    Shelter Island, NY 11964
    Email: orders@manning.com

©2025 by Manning Publications Co. All rights reserved.

No part of this publication may be reproduced, stored in a retrieval system, or transmitted, in any form or by means electronic, mechanical, photocopying, or otherwise, without prior written permission of the publisher.

Many of the designations used by manufacturers and sellers to distinguish their products are claimed as trademarks. Where those designations appear in the book, and Manning Publications was aware of a trademark claim, the designations have been printed in initial caps or all caps.

♾ Recognizing the importance of preserving what has been written, it is Manning's policy to have the books we publish printed on acid-free paper, and we exert our best efforts to that end. Recognizing also our responsibility to conserve the resources of our planet, Manning books are printed on paper that is at least 15 percent recycled and processed without the use of elemental chlorine.

The authors and publisher have made every effort to ensure that the information in this book was correct at press time. The authors and publisher do not assume and hereby disclaim any liability to any party for any loss, damage, or disruption caused by errors or omissions, whether such errors or omissions result from negligence, accident, or any other cause, or from any usage of the information herein.

Manning Publications Co. 20 Baldwin Road PO Box 761 Shelter Island, NY 11964	Development editor: Technical editor: Review editor: Production editor: Copy editor: Proofreader: Typesetter: Cover designer:	Dustin Archibald Johan Vos Dunja Nikitović Keri Hales Tiffany Taylor Jason Everett Dennis Dalinnik Marija Tudor

ISBN: 9781633437630
Printed in the United States of America

brief contents

PART 1 FOUNDATIONS 1

- 1 ■ Advantages and challenges of programming quantum computers 3
- 2 ■ A first look at quantum computations: The knapsack problem 19
- 3 ■ Single-qubit states and gates 34
- 4 ■ Quantum state and circuits: Beyond one qubit 69

PART 2 FUNDAMENTAL ALGORITHMS AND PATTERNS 109

- 5 ■ Selecting outcomes with quantum oracles 111
- 6 ■ Quantum search and probability estimation 133
- 7 ■ The quantum Fourier transform 159
- 8 ■ Using the quantum Fourier transform 186
- 9 ■ Quantum phase estimation 218

PART 3 QUANTUM SOLUTIONS: OPTIMIZATION AND BEYOND 251

- 10 ■ Encoding functions in quantum states 253
- 11 ■ Search-based quantum optimization 276
- 12 ■ Conclusions and outlook 304

contents

foreword xiii
preface xv
acknowledgments xvii
about this book xix
about the authors xxiii
about the cover illustration xxiv

PART 1 FOUNDATIONS 1

1 ■ Advantages and challenges of programming quantum computers 3

1.1 Why quantum computing? 4

1.2 Becoming quantum ready 5

1.3 The superpowers of quantum computing 5

The power of quantum parallelism 7 ■ The random nature of quantum measurement 9

1.4 The anatomy of a quantum computation 10

Computing with a single classical bit 10 ■ Computing with a single quantum bit 11 ■ Computing with multiple quantum bits 12 ■ Putting it together 16

vii

CONTENTS

1.5 Patterns of quantum computations 17
Sampling from probability distributions 17 ▪ *Searching for specific outcomes* 17 ▪ *Estimating the probability of specific outcomes* 18

2 A first look at quantum computations: The knapsack problem 19

2.1 A quick overview of optimization problems 20
The knapsack problem 20 ▪ *Problem setup* 21

2.2 The steps of a quantum computation 22
Outcomes as binary strings 22 ▪ *Quantum state and probabilities* 24

2.3 A quantum solution to the knapsack problem 27
Encoding the problem 27 ▪ *Knapsack problem solution* 29

2.4 Tools for programming a quantum solution 31

3 Single-qubit states and gates 34

3.1 Single-qubit state: A pair of complex numbers 35
Visualizing single-qubit states with tables 35 ▪ *The general form of a single-qubit state* 38 ▪ *Programmatically encoding single-qubit states with lists* 39 ▪ *Implementing a single-qubit quantum computing simulator in Python* 43

3.2 Changing amplitudes with single-qubit gates 45
Rotation is multiplication 45 ▪ *Basic single-qubit gates* 46 *The general form of a single-qubit gate* 52 ▪ *More basic single-qubit gates* 53 ▪ *Single-qubit gate inverses* 55

3.3 Simulating changing amplitudes with gates 57
Printing and visualizing the state 58 ▪ *Transforming a single-qubit state* 58 ▪ *Single-qubit circuits* 60

3.4 Simulating measurement of single-qubit states 61
Encoding the uniform distribution in a single-qubit quantum state 63

3.5 Applications of single-qubit computations 64
Encoding a Bernoulli distribution in a single-qubit quantum state 64 ▪ *Encoding a number with a single qubit* 65

4 Quantum state and circuits: Beyond one qubit 69

4.1 Computing with more than one qubit 70
Measurement counts 70 ▪ *Sampling from a probability distribution* 71 ▪ *Understanding quantum computations with a simple Python simulator* 71

CONTENTS

4.2 A quantum state is a list of complex numbers 72
Two-qubit states 72 ▪ Multi-qubit states 78 ▪ Simulating multi-qubit states in Python 83

4.3 Changing amplitudes with quantum transformations 84
Selecting pairs of amplitudes based on the target qubit 84 Pair selection in Python 86 ▪ Simulating amplitude changes 87 Encoding a uniform distribution in a multi-qubit quantum system 90

4.4 Controlled quantum transformations 92
Simulating controlled gate transformations in Python 94 Simulating multicontrol gate transformations in Python 95

4.5 Simulating quantum circuits 96
Simulating measurement of multi-qubit states 96 ▪ Quantum registers and circuits in code 97 ▪ Reimplementing the uniform distribution with registers and circuits 102 ▪ Encoding the binomial distribution in a multi-qubit state 103 ▪ Implementing the Bell states 106

PART 2 FUNDAMENTAL ALGORITHMS AND PATTERNS 109

5 Selecting outcomes with quantum oracles 111

5.1 Describing outcomes with quantum oracles: Intuition and classical implementation 113
Phase oracles 113 ▪ Bit oracles 115

5.2 Quantum implementation of oracles 117
Creating quantum circuits from building blocks 117 Phase oracle 119 ▪ Bit oracle 122

5.3 Converting between phase and bit quantum oracles 124
Converting a phase oracle to a bit oracle 124 ▪ Converting a bit oracle to a phase oracle 126

5.4 Fibonacci numbers and the golden ratio with good outcomes 128

6 Quantum search and probability estimation 133

6.1 Amplitude amplification: Intuition and classical implementation 134
Finding good outcomes with oracles 135 ▪ Computing similarity with inner products 137 ▪ The inversion operator 139

Putting it together: The Grover iterate 144 ▪ *A classical but quantum-friendly implementation of the inversion operator* 150

6.2 Magnitude amplification: Quantum circuit implementation 152

Quantum oracle 153 ▪ *The inversion operator* 153 ▪ *Grover iterate* 155 ▪ *Putting it all together: Grover's algorithm* 155

7 The quantum Fourier transform 159

7.1 Periodic patterns in sound waves and quantum states 160

Periodic patterns in sound waves 161 ▪ *Periodic patterns in quantum states* 164 ▪ *Roots of unity and their geometric sequences* 168

7.2 Converting from phase to magnitude encoding with the Hadamard gate 169

7.3 From classical to quantum Fourier transforms 171

The classical (discrete) Fourier transform 171 ▪ *Introducing the QFT and IQFT* 174

7.4 Quantum circuits for the QFT and IQFT 179

Understanding the effect of the IQFT on a geometric sequence state 181

8 Using the quantum Fourier transform 186

8.1 The single-slit experiment: Wave diffraction 187

Introducing the discrete sinc function 189

8.2 Encoding a periodic signal using discrete sinc quantum states 189

Phase-to-magnitude frequency encoding with the IQFT 195 *Some useful numerical forms of the frequency encoding pattern* 198 *Reversed qubit implementation of phased discrete sinc quantum states* 202

8.3 Discrete sinc as a sequence of coin flips 205

8.4 Encoding trigonometric distributions in a quantum state 208

Raised cosine 209 ▪ *Other trigonometric functions* 213

9 Quantum phase estimation 218

9.1 Estimating the frequency of a periodic quantum state 219

Getting better angle estimates with more qubits 222 ▪ *Reading between the ticks: Getting better estimates with interpolation* 225

- 9.2 Quantum circuits as rotations with eigenstates and eigenvalues 228
- 9.3 The quantum phase estimation algorithm 232
- 9.4 Circuit-level implementation of the quantum phase estimation algorithm 237
- 9.5 An alternative implementation of the phase estimation circuit without qubit swaps 238
- 9.6 Amplitude estimation and quantum counting 242

  Amplitude estimation 243 • Estimating the number of good outcomes with quantum counting 245 • Estimating the probability of good outcomes with amplitude estimation 247

PART 3 QUANTUM SOLUTIONS: OPTIMIZATION AND BEYOND 251

10 Encoding functions in quantum states 253

- 10.1 Encoding function inputs and outputs 254

  Encoding a simple function 255 • Encoding the knapsack problem 259 • Encoding polynomials of binary variables 263 Complexity of polynomial-encoding circuits 266 • Representing negative values 267

- 10.2 Searching for function values 268
- 10.3 Finding zeros of polynomial functions 272

11 Search-based quantum optimization 276

- 11.1 Finding desired outcomes with Grover adaptive search 277
- 11.2 Finding optimal outcomes with the Grover optimizer 283
- 11.3 Solving the knapsack problem with a Grover optimizer 297

  Preparing the state 297 • Encoding constraints 298 Defining the parameters of the Grover optimizer 300

12 Conclusions and outlook 304

- 12.1 Quantum concepts in review 305

  Quantum readiness 305 • Quantum advantage and its limitations 305

12.2   Building quantum software and running on real quantum computers   306

The importance of a fast, flexible quantum simulator   306
Source-level compatibility between Hume and Qiskit   306
Running on real quantum hardware   308 ▪ *Quantum assistant   311*

12.3   Revisiting quantum gates and the butterfly pattern   312

Another look at single-qubit gates and the butterfly pattern   313

12.4   Quantum states as an image   315

Visualizing quantum state evolution   317

12.5   Combinatorial optimization problems   318

Encoding polynomials with noninteger coefficients   318
Shor's factorization algorithm   320

appendix A   *Math refresher   322*
appendix B   *More about quantum states and gates   334*
appendix C   *Outcome pairing strategies   338*

index   341

foreword

We are on the cusp of the most disruptive revolution in modern-day computation history: the arrival of quantum computing and its integration into quantum-centric supercomputing architectures. Quantum computation is an entirely new branch of computing based on the ability to represent and manipulate data in entirely different ways.

Quantum computations unlock vast solution spaces with unique abilities to use quantum effects, including entanglement, to empower users with a rich set of probabilistic information to extract insights from highly complex datasets. Another key difference from classical computing is that these calculations can be performed at the same time, increasing computational power and efficiency.

With the arrival of useful quantum computing, industries will be able to solve complex problems that are unsolvable or impractical today. These new computational capabilities will fundamentally change business workflows, discover products, and create new business models. To unlock this value, organizations will need quantum skills and expertise.

Early-adopter organizations, poised to capture a disproportionate share of value, are shaping a new quantum-aware workforce while fiercely competing to secure globally scarce quantum talent. This workforce of the future will include a broad set of roles requiring varying degrees of quantum expertise. There is an emerging need for quantum-aware software and application developers to work alongside researchers and computational scientists with deep quantum theory and algorithm expertise.

Quantum-aware developers with a solid foundational understanding and working knowledge of quantum technologies will be able to create commercial applications with unparalleled capabilities. Despite a global need for industry to accelerate and broaden workforce development efforts, today's educational materials and skill-building tools are often designed for advanced mathematicians and/or scientists with a deep understanding of quantum mechanics, creating a steep hurdle for a broader audience.

This book, *Building Quantum Software with Python: A Developer's Guide*, bridges the learning chasm. Coauthors, Constantin Gonciulea and Charlee Stefanski, introduce readers to the foundational building blocks for understanding quantum computation with a conversational tone that instills confidence using multimodal reinforcements.

Basic concepts are introduced and reintroduced throughout the guided conversation with engaging visuals and contextual tips to reinforce readers' foundational understanding of:

- Essential quantum computing concepts
- Fundamental algorithms and patterns
- How to apply basic concepts and run experiments on real quantum computers

Learners at all levels will establish a stronger foundation for understanding quantum computation's basic concepts and unique application benefits.

Developers are encouraged to progress their learning journey from a conceptual understanding of basic building blocks to more complex applications with hands-on learning tools, including:

- Reusable code snippets
- Interactive exercises
- AI assistance

As a rising software engineer, new to the field of quantum computing, Charlee's influence, based on her personal learning experience, is the perfect complement to Constantin's deep expertise in math and science as a research scientist and chief technology officer for advanced technology, including quantum computing.

Together, the coauthors have established an intuitive, game-changing framework for developers to quickly build and learn to apply quantum computing concepts in a highly consumable, contextual, and actionable manner.

—HEATHER HIGGINS, Executive Partner, IBM Quantum

preface

The future of quantum computing lies not just in the hands of quantum physicists but also in those of software developers who will integrate quantum solutions into mainstream applications. The motivation for this book grew from experiences at two financial institutions, where it became clear that developers will be central to the creation and adoption of practical, real-world quantum computing applications. A common misconception is that quantum computing requires an advanced physics or mathematics background. In reality, developers already possess much of the knowledge needed to understand and work with quantum computing. The challenge is not mathematical complexity but connecting familiar computing concepts to quantum computing's "strange" principles. This is the core message of this book.

We build this bridge through extensive visual representations and by focusing on computational structures that showcase quantum computing's unique advantages. Wave-like structures with periodic patterns, in particular, demonstrate where quantum approaches dramatically outperform classical ones. These periodic signals enable "embarrassingly parallel" quantum implementations, where a maximum number of operations occur simultaneously. The Fourier transform—a fundamental tool for working with periodic signals—is the cornerstone of many quantum algorithms, including Shor's famous factorization algorithm.

Although we don't cover Shor's algorithm, this book guides you toward similar principles through encoding polynomial functions as quantum states and extracting information from them. This capability opens the door to solving optimization problems that appear across many domains. Along the way, you'll master quantum computing foundations, fundamental algorithms, and implementations of various probability distributions for efficient random sampling.

To ensure the book's longevity, we've avoided tying it to any particular quantum computing framework. Instead, we build our own minimal framework in a few hundred lines of code. This approach serves two purposes: it deepens your understanding of quantum concepts, and it provides a practical implementation that's interface-compatible with IBM's Qiskit, the most popular quantum computing framework. We maintain this compatibility in our repositories, ensuring that the skills you learn remain relevant as quantum computing evolves.

acknowledgments

Writing a book, especially one that simplifies a complex subject like quantum computing, requires substantial time and effort. We would like to express our heartfelt thanks to the team at Manning Publications for their support throughout this project. Our development editor, Dustin Archibald, deserves special recognition for his invaluable feedback and relentless dedication to refining our manuscript. We'd also like to thank the entire editorial and production teams who helped shepherd this book into its final form.

We are also deeply grateful to our technical editor, Johan Voss, cofounder of Gluon, whose expert insights significantly improved the technical accuracy of the book; and to Filip Wojcieszyn, our technical proofreader, for his thorough review of the book's codebase.

This book was greatly enhanced by Paul Stefanski's work on refining the narrative, correcting errors, and enhancing clarity; Claudia Gonciulea's content review and initial development and testing of the quantum simulator code; Nick Gonciulea for the initial implementation of the AI assistant; Vitaliy Dorum for containerizing some of the tools; and Naren Satishkumar's creation and refinement of additional applications and tools for the book's ecosystem.

We extend our gratitude to all our reviewers, including Brian Hanaffe, Alex Khan, Kelvin Meeks, Saveliy Yusufov, Aatmaj Rajesh, Alain Couniot, Alasdair Collinson, Bhavesh Dave, Biswanath Chowdhury, Brandon Darlington-Goddard, Calvin Tang, Christophe Pere, David Drummond, Dennis Delali Kwesi Wayo, Dylan Shields, Frank Zickert, Gary Pass, Gregory Varghese Manalumbhagath, Jared Duncan, Jean-François

Morin, Jonathan Owens, Jort Rodenburg, Julia Varigina, Keith Kim, Kelum Prabath Senanayake, Krzysztof Kamyczek, Lewis Van Winkle, Marcel van den Brink, Mikolaj Pawlikowski, Piero Giacomelli, Potito Coluccelli, Renaud Béchade, Richard Barnes, Sagar Kumar, Satej Kumar Sahu, Shivani Mayekar, Sleiman Salameh, Steven Fernandez, Tony Holdroyd, and William E. Wheeler, whose insightful critiques and suggestions have significantly improved the quality of this work.

Finally, we would like to thank Chintan Mehta for his support and encouragement.

about this book

Building Quantum Software with Python: A Developer's Guide was written to help software developers and technology professionals unlock the potential of quantum computing. The book builds on well-known classical computing concepts at the foundation of quantum computing while emphasizing additional distinctive characteristics that combine into a quantum advantage (from classical to quantum computing). We teach quantum computing using a visual, hands-on approach that requires only basic knowledge of programming and math (a visual approach for developers).

The book begins with the fundamentals of quantum computations: quantum states, transformations, and measurement. Each of these concepts is explained visually and with code. The second part of the book covers essential quantum algorithms. Throughout all the chapters are implementations of basic applications. By the end of this book, you will have a deep understanding of quantum computations and how to design and implement quantum solutions.

Who should read this book

This book is for software developers, machine learning professionals, computer science students, and, broadly, anyone with a background in computation or information science. You do not need deep knowledge of quantum mechanics to develop quantum solutions. However, you do need a basic understanding of fundamental classical computing concepts and patterns that will translate to quantum computing. Additionally, some basic math concepts are required, including trigonometry and complex numbers. We include math concept refreshers in appendix A for readers who need them.

This book is not linked to a specific quantum library or hardware provider. It provides an agnostic foundation to help you use any quantum library or platform. In chapters 3 and 4, a quantum simulator called Hume is developed from scratch in Python. Therefore, to understand the code in this book, you should have knowledge of Python programming.

How this book is organized: A road map

This book has 12 chapters grouped into three parts. Example applications are included throughout all the chapters.

The first part covers fundamentals:

- Chapter 1 provides a high-level introduction to quantum computations and discusses the advantages and challenges of quantum computing.
- Chapter 2 goes through a quantum approach to solving a real-world optimization problem (the knapsack problem).
- Chapter 3 introduces single-qubit quantum states and introduces basic quantum computing instructions called quantum gates.
- Chapter 4 covers multi-qubit systems.

Part 2 covers fundamental quantum algorithms:

- Chapter 5 covers quantum oracles.
- Chapter 6 uses oracles to implement a quantum solution to search. It covers a very important quantum algorithm (Grover's algorithm) and amplitude amplification.
- Chapter 7 covers the quantum Fourier transform, which is one of the sources of quantum advantage. It is used in many quantum programs.
- Chapter 8 explores several applications of the quantum Fourier transform.
- Chapter 9 introduces another essential quantum algorithm: quantum phase estimation. It also covers quantum counting.

Part 3 includes implementations of more complex quantum solutions, specifically quantum optimization:

- Chapter 10 brings together concepts from the first two parts of the book to implement an essential pattern in quantum computing: encoding functions in quantum states.
- Chapter 11 introduces a method called Grover adaptive search that uses Grover's algorithm to solve optimization problems. The chapter includes an implementation of a Grover optimizer.
- Chapter 12 discusses some concepts that are beyond the scope of this book but that are natural continuations of the book's material.

About the code

This book contains many examples of source code both in numbered listings and in line with normal text. In both cases, source code is formatted in a `fixed-width font like this` to separate it from ordinary text.

In many cases, the original source code has been reformatted; we've added line breaks and reworked indentation to accommodate the available page space in the book. In rare cases, even this was not enough, and listings include line-continuation markers (➥). Additionally, comments in the source code have often been removed from the listings when the code is described in the text. Code annotations accompany many of the listings, highlighting important concepts.

The book's companion code is on GitHub at https://github.com/learnqc/code. The repository contains Jupyter notebooks to accompany each chapter. There is a directory for each chapter that contains a Jupyter notebook with the code snippets and examples in the chapter, as well as Python scripts that contain the source code required from previous chapters. The repository also contains Jupyter notebooks with the exercise solutions for each chapter. In addition, the repository provides resources and examples for working with Hume, including a notebook that demonstrates how to run examples from the book on IBM quantum computers.

We have developed some interactive applications and tools to enhance your learning experience. You can find these tools in the GitHub repository at https://github.com/learnqc/code_plus. This repository also contains an AI assistant that will evolve in time.

In addition, you can get executable snippets of code from the liveBook (online) version of this book at https://livebook.manning.com/book/building-quantum-software-with-python. The complete code for the examples in the book is available for download from the Manning website at https://www.manning.com/books/building-quantum-software-with-python.

liveBook discussion forum

Purchase of *Building Quantum Software with Python* includes free access to liveBook, Manning's online reading platform. Using liveBook's exclusive discussion features, you can attach comments to the book globally or to specific sections or paragraphs. It's a snap to make notes for yourself, ask and answer technical questions, and receive help from the authors and other users. To access the forum, go to https://livebook.manning.com/book/building-quantum-software-with-python/discussion. You can also learn more about Manning's forums and the rules of conduct at https://livebook.manning.com/discussion.

Manning's commitment to our readers is to provide a venue where a meaningful dialogue between individual readers and between readers and the authors can take place. It is not a commitment to any specific amount of participation on the part of the authors, whose contribution to the forum remains voluntary (and unpaid). We suggest you try asking the authors some challenging questions lest their interest stray!

The forum and the archives of previous discussions will be accessible from the publisher's website as long as the book is in print.

Other online resources

All the code repositories related to the book can be found at https://github.com/learnqc. More materials, including videos and tutorials, can be found at https://learnqc.com.

about the authors

CONSTANTIN GONCIULEA leads the Advanced Technology group at Wells Fargo. He holds advanced degrees in mathematics and computer science. Over the last 25 years, he has delivered major server-side, web, and mobile online banking platforms and products. He has worked in quantum computing since 2018.

CHARLEE STEFANSKI is a senior software engineer in the Advanced Technology group at Wells Fargo, where she leads the development of the internal quantum computing platform. She holds a BS from the University of Michigan and a Masters from UC Berkeley.

about the cover illustration

The figure on the cover of *Building Quantum Software with Python*, titled "Femme d'Ile de Tine," or "Woman from the Isle of Tinos," is taken from the book *Album of Turkish Costume Paintings*, published in 1867. The book belongs to the George Arents Collection, a part of the New York City Public Library Digital Collections. Each illustration is finely drawn and colored by hand.

In those days, it was easy to identify where people lived and what their trade or station in life was just by their dress. Manning celebrates the inventiveness and initiative of the computer business with book covers based on the rich diversity of regional culture centuries ago, brought back to life by pictures from collections such as this one.

Part 1

Foundations

Traditional programming has evolved to use high-level abstractions that protect developers from the intricacies of hardware, but quantum computing still largely involves low-level programming tasks. Today's quantum developers must work closely with basic quantum computing instructions, much like early classical programmers worked directly with assembly code. This is not likely to change soon, and that is why understanding quantum computing fundamentals is crucial for anyone wanting to develop quantum software.

Don't let this intimidate you. You won't need complex physics or mathematics to master quantum programming. With basic programming experience and high school trigonometry, you can build a strong foundation in quantum computing. Our approach centers on hands-on learning: you'll implement quantum concepts in Python, building a quantum simulator that lets you experiment directly with quantum states and operations.

This part of the book builds your quantum computing knowledge from the ground up. Chapter 1 introduces core quantum computing concepts and explores their potential advantages and challenges. In chapter 2, you'll see these concepts in action through a practical optimization problem that demonstrates quantum computing's unique strengths. Chapter 3 dives into single-qubit quantum states and gates, teaching you to implement basic quantum operations in Python. Chapter 4 expands to multi-qubit systems and shows you how to prepare quantum states corresponding to useful probability distributions for random sampling.

Advantages and challenges of programming quantum computers

This chapter covers
- Why quantum computing is a promising tool, and what developers need to know to use it
- The main sources of quantum advantage
- High-level differences between quantum and classical computing
- An overview of the anatomy of quantum computations

Quantum computing opens the door to new ways to solve problems. For specific computational tasks, quantum computers can be much faster than traditional computers.

For some computations, the speedup is significant. One such computation is Fourier transforms, a topic we will cover in depth in chapters 7 and 8. Fourier transforms are essential for analyzing and processing signals and data in various fields such as engineering, physics, image processing, and telecommunications. Computing Fourier transforms more efficiently could enable high-frequency trading algorithms to detect market patterns faster, reducing latency in trade execution. Also, it can accelerate the filtering and compression of computer graphics.

One of the best classical algorithms for computing Fourier transforms is called the fast Fourier transform (FFT), which some consider one of the most important algorithms of all time. The FFT algorithm requires exponentially more operations than its quantum implementation, as shown in figure 1.1.

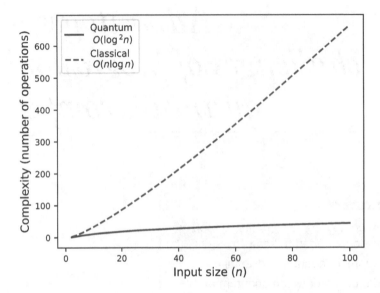

Figure 1.1 Comparison of the increase in computational complexity relative to the input size for computing (fast) Fourier transforms with classical and quantum computers

Popular physicist Brian Cox commented on the physical nature of quantum mechanics by explaining that "particles hop from place to place with a particular probability." The outcomes of a quantum computation are similar to the places a particle can hop to. Each outcome has a probability of occurring. In this chapter, we will look at the high-level components of quantum computing, how they compare to classical computing, and common patterns in quantum computations.

1.1 Why quantum computing?

The public interest in quantum computing kicked off in the 1980s. Notable physicists like Richard Feynman and Yuri Manin proposed that computing hardware based on quantum processes could radically outperform classical hardware for some types of problems.

As hardware and manufacturing continue to advance in the quantum computing space, we expect that the adoption of quantum computing will accelerate, and the demand will grow for software developers who know how to develop and implement solutions with quantum computing resources. This book focuses less on the physics of quantum computing and more on the mathematical and programming techniques of applied quantum computing. With this knowledge, you will have a solid foundation for applying quantum computing to real-world business and scientific problems.

The benefit of quantum computing is often referred to as *quantum advantage*. Quantum advantage can be any improvement compared to using a classical computer for the same computation. Understanding the sources of quantum advantage will enable you to assess the utility of quantum computing, classical computing, and hybrid approaches in specific scenarios. We want our readers to build the knowledge necessary to create quantum, quantum-inspired, or hybrid quantum–classical applications.

1.2 Becoming quantum ready

The developmental stage of quantum computing technology in the 2020s may be comparable to classical computing in the late 1940s and early 1950s, but the culture and adoption surrounding quantum computing are very different. Not everyone believed in the potential of early computers, and not all governments and businesses chose to invest in them at first. Contemporary culture is far quicker to adopt new technologies at industrial scales, and quantum computing for business and research is generally well-funded and met with intrigue rather than skepticism.

Even though the field is still in its infancy, there is already a growing demand for developers who can build quantum-based solutions. This book will help you develop a strong foundation in quantum computing, leading you to become "quantum ready." You will learn how to identify problems that can benefit from a quantum approach and develop quantum solutions at a small scale. We start with the fundamentals of quantum programming and algorithms. Then, we move on to implementing small-scale examples.

This book is designed for software developers, machine learning professionals, computer science students, and, broadly, anyone with a background in computation or information science. You do not need deep knowledge of quantum mechanics to develop quantum solutions. However, you do need a basic understanding of the classical computing concepts and patterns that will translate to quantum computing. We will cover the concepts and techniques used in quantum computations in reference to familiar computer science concepts like arrays and binary strings. We also include visualizations to help illustrate difficult concepts and create useful representations to help you build your intuition for applying quantum solutions. This book is not linked to any specific quantum library or hardware provider. It provides an agnostic foundation to help you use other quantum libraries or platforms.

1.3 The superpowers of quantum computing

To speed up and scale classical computations, we can use larger hardware configurations and distributed workloads. For some problems, increasing the classical computing resources will provide a respective increase in performance. For other problems, when the input size increases linearly, the necessary classical computing resources (such as time and memory) increase exponentially. In contrast, for some types of problems, quantum computers may require only a polynomial increase in the resources needed. This means that as the input increases, the gap in resource requirements between classical and quantum algorithms widens significantly, which allows for more efficient and scalable solutions to complex problems.

Furthermore, quantum computers are expected to perform some computations that classical computers cannot, like simulations of chemical or physical processes and random sampling from useful probabilistic distributions. We look for computational problems with these properties when deciding where to apply quantum computing solutions.

From a computing point of view, two key computational properties—quantum parallelism and measurement—are primarily responsible for quantum advantage. To explain these properties, we can use outcome–probability pairs. Table 1.1 shows an example dataset that could be used in a quantum computation. The outcome–probability pairs feature eight possible outcomes and the respective probability of each outcome. The probabilities of all possible outcomes must add up to one.

Table 1.1 Eight outcome–probability pairs

Outcome	Probability
0	0.05
1	0.11
2	0.13
3	0.02
4	0.34
5	0.17
6	0.06
7	0.12

> **Quantum superposition and entanglement**
> These quantum mechanics concepts are crucial to building quantum computers but are not directly relevant to writing software for quantum computing. *Quantum superposition* captures the notion that a quantum system can exist in multiple states. This translates into the uncertainty of what outcome will be observed in a measurement. Computationally, the state of a quantum system contains the probabilities of all possible outcomes, and these probabilities change instantly and simultaneously (in parallel, from a computing point of view). Throughout this book, we will use the term *quantum parallelism* to refer to this computational benefit that arises from quantum superposition.
>
> *Quantum entanglement* refers to the fact that qubits (quantum bits) can be connected to the extent that their state cannot be described independently of each other, and

1.3 The superpowers of quantum computing

> therefore individual qubit measurements are not always independent of each other. It is the implementation mechanism for conditional transformations. Without conditional transformations, we could not implement any nontrivial computation. As such, quantum entanglement is an enabler of quantum computing.

1.3.1 The power of quantum parallelism

Suppose that we want to swap the consecutive values corresponding to even and odd indices (i.e., those corresponding to 0 and 1, 2 and 3, and so on) in table 1.1. For a classical implementation, we can write out all the operations or use a `for` loop. Either way, the machine-level instructions are executed sequentially. Figure 1.2 illustrates the serial steps required to perform the swaps.

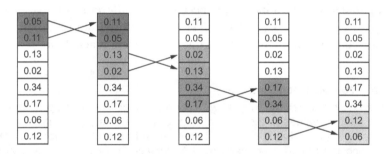

Figure 1.2 A visualization of the classical implementation for swapping consecutive values

On a classical computer, the number of operations necessary will grow linearly with the number of swaps we want to perform. If we had twice as many values to swap, we would need twice as many operations. The increase is linear even if single-instruction multiple-data (SIMD) processing is available, as a limited and typically small number of entries are processed in parallel.

If all swaps could occur simultaneously, it would speed up the computation without interfering with the outcome—and that's where the superpowers of quantum computing come in. The quantum implementation of the same process performs all the swaps with one quantum computing instruction, shown in figure 1.3. This means a quantum implementation requires only one instruction to swap as many pairs in the system as we want. This ability to execute unlimited parallel elementary operations is quantum parallelism. In practice, we can think of quantum parallelism as an unlimited form of SIMD.

> **NOTE** SIMD is a computing concept where one instruction can be performed on multiple data points simultaneously, allowing for faster parallel processing of operations like vector calculations.

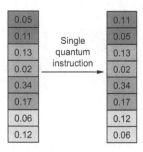

Figure 1.3 A visualization of the quantum implementation for swapping consecutive values

Quantum parallelism is a powerful tool for achieving quantum advantage, but it can be like painting with a broad brush. Depending on the problem, using the same instruction for many pairs of values may not be desirable. To limit and correct unwanted effects of quantum parallelism, we need additional steps that may counter the benefit.

Quantum parallelism seems like magic because it is different from parallelism in classical computing. The values (probabilities) are not stored but represent internal quantities that change when the underlying quantum system is acted on.

The butterfly computational model

Instead of swapping a pair of values, we can recombine them using a formula. Recombining pairs of values is the general form of all elementary quantum instructions. It is also a pattern that is common in nature and other fields, from how DNA works to how account transfers are performed. Making changes in pairs is also at the heart of making Fourier transforms fast.

The computational building block of this pattern can be illustrated with a *butterfly diagram*, which shows a pair of values that are recombined using a formula to update the values with new ones. The butterfly pattern is a fundamental part of various applications, including these:

- *Signal processing*—Uses the FFT algorithm, which relies on the butterfly pattern
- *Machine learning*—Uses structured linear maps like butterfly matrices to compress neural networks

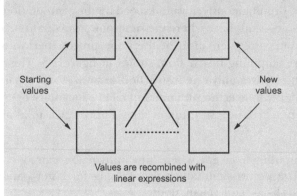

Single-pair butterfly diagram

1.3 The superpowers of quantum computing

> In a quantum system, the recombination of value pairs happens simultaneously for all affected pairs, leading to the advantage in computing Fourier transforms that we discussed at the beginning of the chapter.

1.3.2 The random nature of quantum measurement

The second key feature of quantum computing is measurement. When we measure a quantum system, we get one of a defined set of outcomes. The outcome is nondeterministic, but it does follow a certain probability distribution. If we repeat the same computation, we may get a different measurement outcome. Depending on the problem we are trying to solve, we may need to do this a few times to get useful information from the distribution of outcomes.

> **NOTE** In computer science, a *deterministic algorithm* is one that, given the same input, will produce the same output with each execution. A *nondeterministic algorithm* is one that, given the same input, can produce different outputs with each execution.

The result of a computation on a quantum computer is usually represented as a binary string, which is a sequence of zeros and ones. We can interpret binary strings in various ways, but it is most common to interpret them as their integer (decimal form) value. In this chapter, we will use this interpretation for the possible outcomes of a computation. Later chapters will cover other methods of interpretation.

We can visualize the randomness of a measurement using a circle divided into equal sectors, as shown in figure 1.4. Each sector corresponds to a possible measurement outcome. We can think of this circle as a wheel of fortune; we spin the wheel, and when it stops, one sector is selected.

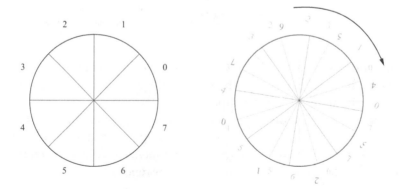

Figure 1.4 A circle divided into equal sectors, where each sector represents a possible outcome of a certain quantum computation

The values of the quantum state define the probability of selecting each outcome. We cannot directly inspect the values of a quantum state; to figure out what they are, we must perform measurements. For example, suppose we do not know the probability of each outcome (sector) on the circle in figure 1.4. By spinning the wheel and noting how often we land on a sector, we can infer the probability of each outcome. Quantum measurement is like sampling from a probability distribution with a tremendous advantage over classical sampling: the samples are genuinely nondeterministic, and the sampling is highly efficient.

Measurement can be beneficial for many problems. In some cases, it can even enable computations that are not possible using a classical computer, like generating truly random numbers. It is important to understand the concepts of parallelism and measurement to determine which problems can benefit from a quantum approach.

1.4 The anatomy of a quantum computation

To understand the anatomy of a quantum computation, we will compare and contrast it with classical computing. Classical software programs consist of a sequence of instructions that manipulate variables to generate outputs. Registers, or groups of bits, can define more complex variables, such as the binary representation of an integer or character. Programming has become more intuitive through layers of abstraction, like high-level languages, which offer control over the type and number of variables. They also provide more intuitive instructions to change their values. At the lowest level, all these layers of abstraction translate to instructions that operate on bits.

1.4.1 Computing with a single classical bit

A classical bit has one of two possible states labeled 0 and 1. It works like a toggle or switch between two values, as shown in figure 1.5.

Figure 1.5 A classical bit works like a toggle or switch between 0 and 1.

In its simplest form, a single-bit computation involves changes to the bit value. When the computation is complete, we read the value of the bit, as shown in figure 1.6. The last written value is the result of the computation.

As previously mentioned, the outcome of a classical computation is deterministic. No matter how many times we repeat the same computation, the result will be the same. This is not true for the quantum version of a single-bit computation, which can have a different result when the same computation is repeated.

1.4 The anatomy of a quantum computation

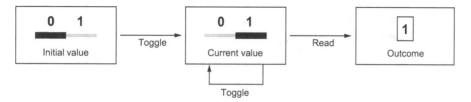

Figure 1.6 The stages of a computation using a classical bit. In this example, the initial value of the bit is 0. The value is changed to 1 during the computation. When the value is read, the result is the last written value, 1.

1.4.2 Computing with a single quantum bit

A quantum bit, or *qubit*, is the fundamental unit of a quantum computing system. In a quantum computer, a qubit can be encoded by a property of a particle like a photon or an electron. In this book, we will not focus on the physical components of quantum computers or complex mathematical models. Instead, we will compare and contrast the applied uses of qubits and classical bits from a programming perspective.

Let's first look at a simpler version of a quantum bit. Imagine that we can change the probability of a coin landing heads or tails. Such a coin can be called a *variable-bias coin* or a *probabilistic bit*. We cannot predict the outcome (heads or tails) of any given toss; we can only predict the expected frequency of the possible outcomes. In figure 1.7, we visualize changing the probability of the outcomes with a slider that moves some probability from one outcome to the other. The state of the probabilistic bit consists of the probabilities of its two outcomes at any given moment.

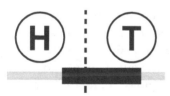

Figure 1.7 A probabilistic bit, or variable-bias coin, works like a slider that changes the probability of getting heads or tails.

To compute using a probabilistic bit, we change the probability of the outcomes and then measure to get one of the outcomes. The diagram in figure 1.8 shows these steps. We are changing the probabilities of the outcomes instead of just switching between the outcomes as we would with a classical bit. At the end of the computation, we get one outcome, heads or tails, which we can interpret as 0 or 1. If we repeat the same computation, we may get a different outcome.

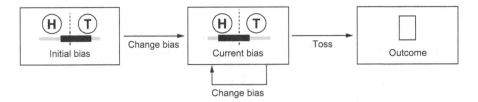

Figure 1.8 The stages of a computation with a probabilistic bit. In this example, the initial probability that the outcome will be tails is 0.7. During the computation, the probability that the outcome will be tails is changed to 0.3. For example, each time the same computation is repeated (the coin is tossed), we get one outcome according to these encoded probabilities. If we perform 10 repetitions (tosses), we expect to see roughly 7 heads and 3 tails. The more tosses we perform, the closer we expect the distribution of outcomes to be to the encoded probabilities.

> **Probabilities with direction**
>
> We mentioned that each possible outcome of a quantum computation has an associated probability of occurring. However, there is more to this story. Each such probability is the squared length of a planar vector. Richard Feynman informally calls these vectors "arrows." Formally, they are called *amplitudes*, and mathematically, they are best described as *complex numbers*.
>
> The direction of amplitudes is essential in how the state of quantum systems changes but not in the frequency of the computation outcomes they are associated with. We will go into more detail regarding the direction of probabilities in later chapters.

1.4.3 *Computing with multiple quantum bits*

When we perform a computation with one quantum bit, we have two possible measurement outcomes: 0 and 1. Similarly, when we use multiple quantum bits, each qubit represents one binary digit of the outcome. Therefore, the number of qubits in a quantum system determines the number of possible outcomes of a computation. For example, if we perform a computation with two qubits, there are four possible outcomes: 00, 01, 10, and 11. We can refer to these outcomes with a positive integer interpretation of the binary strings: in this case, 0 through 3.

Figure 1.9 shows a model of the steps of a specific quantum computation. We will go over the details of this model in the following subsections. As discussed, the outcome will consist of a binary string, with a digit for each qubit in the computation. In the example in figure 1.9, the measured outcome is 100, which we can interpret as the integer 4. We will use this model to understand the core concepts of quantum computations. To understand each step, let's take a closer look at three quantum computing concepts: quantum state, its evolution, and its collapse through quantum measurement.

1.4 The anatomy of a quantum computation

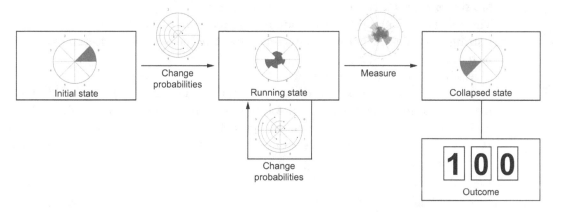

Figure 1.9 The steps of a quantum computation using quantum bits (qubits). The example in the diagram uses three qubits, so there are eight possible outcomes, each with a certain measurement probability represented by the filled part of the sectors. When a measurement is performed, we get one result according to the probabilities. The result is interpreted as a binary string.

THE STATE OF A QUBIT-BASED QUANTUM SYSTEM

The state of a quantum system consists of a list of values (probabilities with direction), one for each possible outcome. Intuitively, the probabilities must add up to 1. Remember, a two-qubit system has four possible outcomes: 00, 01, 10, and 11. Thus, the state of a two-qubit system consists of four values.

Typically, the default state of a quantum system, before any operations are applied to it, is one where only the outcome with all qubits being measured as 0 is possible. All the other outcomes have a probability of 0. In figure 1.10, we visualize the initial state of a three-qubit system. If we measure the state, there is a 100% probability of getting the outcome 000 (or 0, if we are using the integer form of the binary string outcomes).

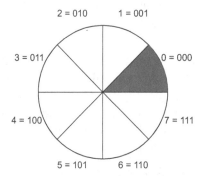

Figure 1.10 A wheel representation of a three-qubit quantum state in its initial state

MEASURING THE STATE OF A QUBIT-BASED QUANTUM SYSTEM

The result of a computation using an n-qubit quantum system can be represented as a string of 0s and 1s that is n characters long. The measurement of each qubit will be 0 or 1.

Each time a computation is repeated and a measurement is performed, we get one of the possible outcomes according to the corresponding probability. To illustrate measuring a quantum state, we can use the wheel from the previous section, where each sector represents an outcome. In figure 1.11, we use a *rose chart* (or *polar area chart*) where the proportion of a sector covered by its "petal" is the probability of measuring the sector's corresponding outcome.

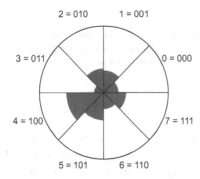

Figure 1.11 A rose chart representation of the probabilities associated with the outcomes of a three-qubit quantum system

NOTE The rose chart was first popularized by Florence Nightingale in 1858. As a nurse and statistician, she used this type of diagram to concisely represent the complex statistics for the causes of mortality of British soldiers during the Crimean War. Today, with modern visualization software like `matplotlib`, this diagram is the polar version of bar charts.

Before measurement, a quantum system is said to be in a *superposition* of all its possible outcomes. After measurement, the state of the system "collapses," so the probability of the measured outcome is 1 and the probabilities of the other possible outcomes are 0. The measured outcome is the only information we get from a quantum computation.

EVOLVING THE STATE OF A QUBIT-BASED QUANTUM SYSTEM

The state of a quantum bit system is modified using elementary quantum instructions that change pairs of values. Each operation changes the values of each pair while keeping the total probability in each pair the same. In other words, the sum of the probabilities of the two outcomes of the pair stays the same. The target qubit of the operation determines the pairing of the values. The binary representation of indices in a pair differs only in the position of the target qubit.

NOTE A complete theoretical description of quantum state evolution requires advanced knowledge of linear algebra. Such a description considers more general state transformations that need to be decomposed into elementary

1.4 The anatomy of a quantum computation

quantum instructions before being executed on a quantum-bit system. Because this book focuses on building applications that can be run on quantum hardware, we will generally use elementary transformations called *gates* that recombine pairs of values (amplitudes).

When using the wheel representation for the state of a quantum system, we can show how the pairing is done using arcs that join the sectors or outcomes whose values are being recombined. Figure 1.12 shows the pairing process for each of the three possible target qubits of a three-qubit system.

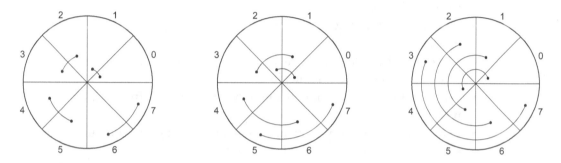

Figure 1.12 The three possible pair combinations of a three-qubit system. The indices differ in the last, middle, or first binary digit when the target qubit is 0, 1, or 2, respectively.

The arcs represent pairwise updates that happen simultaneously (in parallel). No matter how large the number of possible outcomes is, their probabilities (with direction) are all updated simultaneously when a quantum instruction is applied. The number of outcomes and the number of pairs doubles with the addition of a qubit. Figure 1.13 shows the pairing process for all four possible target qubits of a four-qubit system.

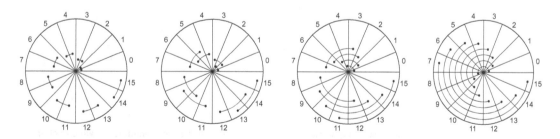

Figure 1.13 The four possible pair combinations of a four-qubit system. The indices differ in the binary digit corresponding to the target qubit, 0, 1, 2, or 3, respectively.

All quantum operations, no matter how complex, are sequences of elementary quantum operations. As mentioned, elementary quantum operations consist of a target

16 CHAPTER 1 *Advantages and challenges of programming quantum computers*

qubit and a formula for recombining two probabilities with direction. It's like a money transfer between two accounts: the total balance stays the same.

1.4.4 Putting it together

The most common quantum computing model, as captured in figure 1.14, is simple: *pairs of probabilities are changed simultaneously, and computation outcomes are selected according to these probabilities.* We can summarize the core concepts required to understand a quantum computation as follows:

- The state of a quantum computation consists of a probability with direction for each possible outcome.
- Elementary computing instructions change pairs of probabilities with direction in parallel.
- The probabilities determine the frequency of corresponding measurement outcomes when the same computation is repeated.
- The measurement outcome is the only available data from a quantum computation.
- Before measurement, the quantum system encoding the computation is in a state of superposition of possible outcomes.
- After a measurement, the state of the system collapses into a state where the measured outcome has a probability of 1 and the other outcomes have a probability of 0.

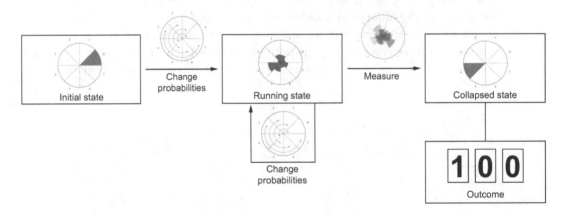

Figure 1.14 The steps of a quantum computation using three qubits. During the computation, we can change the probabilities by applying quantum computing instructions. When a measurement is performed, we get one outcome according to the encoded probabilities.

1.5 Patterns of quantum computations

In this book, we will learn about quantum computing through examples. These examples will follow three main patterns, each of which utilizes the superpowers of quantum computing in a specific way. Let's look at high-level descriptions of these three patterns.

1.5.1 Sampling from probability distributions

Sampling from probability distributions using classical methods can be inefficient or intractable. Quantum measurement can help with such cases.

Remember that the result of measuring a quantum system is one outcome. The frequency of each outcome follows the probability distribution defined by the quantum state. Repeated measurements will provide a list of samples from the associated probability distribution. Measurement is one of the main benefits of quantum computing; it is useful for sampling from distributions that are hard to build using classical methods. A Galton board, where many marbles fall into various bins (see figure 1.15), is like repeated quantum measurements: each marble is like one repetition of a quantum computation.

Figure 1.15 A Galton board showing physical pegs driving marbles into bins according to the binomial distribution

1.5.2 Searching for specific outcomes

As we have discussed, the result of measuring a qubit system is one of many possible outcomes, where each qubit can be measured as 0 or 1. The 0s and 1s in the outcome can encode information that is relevant in the context of a problem of interest. This encoding is referred to as *digital encoding*. For example, in a portfolio optimization scenario, a binary digit of an outcome can indicate whether an investment instrument is included in a portfolio.

Solving a problem can be framed as a search for the outcomes that encode a solution. Quantum searches can potentially be more efficient on a quantum computer, using Grover's algorithm, discussed in chapter 6.

1.5.3 Estimating the probability of specific outcomes

In other quantum computations, the answer is encoded in the probability of an outcome or the combined probability of more outcomes. This is referred to as *analog encoding*. Calculating these probabilities requires a carefully chosen and potentially large number of repeated quantum state preparations and measurements called *shots*. This can be done using the Quantum Amplitude Estimation algorithm, which we will discuss in chapter 9.

As we will see, analog encoding can be converted to digital encoding (but the cost can be prohibitive depending on the available hardware). We will explore different ways to estimate probabilities of outcomes and the classes of problems that can benefit from this approach.

Summary

- To be "quantum ready," you need to understand the sources of quantum advantage and which types of problems quantum computing can solve more efficiently than classical computing.
- Quantum parallelism and measurement can provide a quantum advantage over classical methods.
- In a quantum computation, pairs of probabilities are changed simultaneously, and computation outcomes are selected according to these probabilities. Quantum computations have the following distinct characteristics:
  - The state of a quantum computation consists of amplitudes (probabilities with direction) for each possible outcome.
  - Elementary computing instructions change pairs of amplitudes in parallel (using the butterfly computational model/pattern).
  - Quantum measurement is like sampling all possible outcomes according to their probabilities by repeating the same computation.
- We will focus on three quantum computing patterns: sampling from probability distributions, searching for optimal values (desired outcomes), and estimating the probability of certain computation outcomes.

A first look at quantum computations: The knapsack problem

This chapter covers

- Introducing a quantum solution to an optimization problem: the knapsack problem
- Examining the steps of a quantum computation, including quantum state evolution and measurement
- Tools for programming a quantum solution

The material in this book does not depend on any knowledge of quantum mechanics or how to build a quantum computer. Programming quantum computers requires familiarity with a few mathematical concepts, specifically *binary strings*, *complex numbers*, and some basic trigonometry and probabilities. We provide an overview of these concepts for readers who are unfamiliar or want a refresher.

> **NOTE** Elementary quantum computing instructions can be represented with simple trigonometric expressions. The instructions used for quantum computing are very different from those used in classical software development. For that reason, it's important to understand the foundational mathematical concepts—complex numbers and basic trigonometry—that are at the core of quantum theory.

CHAPTER 2 A first look at quantum computations: The knapsack problem

In this chapter, we will look at a quantum solution applied to a simple optimization problem. We will cover the relevant concepts as we go through the computation step by step. We will also use this example to familiarize you with some tools used throughout the book.

2.1 A quick overview of optimization problems

Optimization problems have a simple goal: find the "optimal" value given some constraints. The definition of "optimal" depends on the problem—it could be the highest value, the lowest value, or a value that meets some other criteria. To solve an optimization problem, we typically perform several steps that get us incrementally closer to the optimal value.

A common type of optimization problem called *binary optimization* involves a set of variables with binary choices (like yes or no, in or out, on or off, etc.). The goal is to find the combination of binary choices that is the optimal solution to the specific problem. A practical limitation of solving binary optimization problems in classical computing is that as the number of variables increases linearly, the number of possible combinations increases exponentially. This exponential growth quickly becomes computationally demanding and challenging to solve, even with the most sophisticated, efficient classical algorithms. With this in mind, we will look at how a quantum approach can more efficiently solve optimization problems.

2.1.1 The knapsack problem

If you are familiar with computing algorithms, you may have encountered the *knapsack problem*. It is a straightforward, fun example of a binary optimization problem. Imagine that you have a knapsack with a defined maximum weight capacity. You also have a set of items, each with a weight and a value (or price). The goal is to maximize the value of the items that fit in the knapsack without exceeding its weight capacity (see figure 2.1).

Each item in the knapsack problem comes with a binary choice: put the item in the knapsack or do not put the item in the knapsack. If you select an item, the weight of

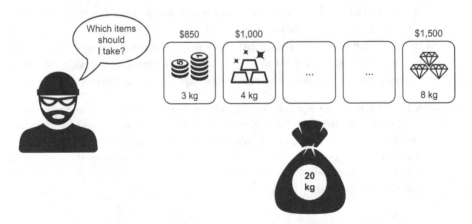

Figure 2.1 The knapsack problem is a binary optimization problem where the optimal solution is the collection of items with the highest value that does not exceed the weight limit.

that item counts toward the total weight of the knapsack, and the value of that item counts toward the total value. We encode this problem using binary variables, one for each item, with a value of 1 if it is included in the knapsack or 0 if it is not.

2.1.2 Problem setup

Let's define the knapsack problem we are going to solve. We have a capacity of at most 4 weight units, such as kilograms or pounds. We have three items (see table 2.1) with 3, 2, and 1 units of weight, respectively. The values of the items are $2,000, $3,000, and $1,000, respectively. To make the calculations easier, we can reduce the value of each item by a factor of 1,000, resulting in the values 2, 3, and 1. Table 2.2 shows the value and weight of each possible combination of items.

Table 2.1 The items, weights, and values for the example knapsack problem

Item label	Value	Weight
0	2 ($2,000)	3
1	3 ($3,000)	2
2	1 ($1,000)	1

Exercise 2.1
Can you work out the optimal solution in your head?

NOTE For n binary variables, there are 2^n possible combinations. We use a simple example (with $n = 3$ variables and $2^3 = 8$ possible combinations) to make it easier to understand, but in real-world problems, there can be a large number of items. For example, if there were 41 items, there would be 2^{41} (over 1 trillion!) possible combinations.

Table 2.2 A table with each possible selection of items and the corresponding value and weight

Item selection	Value	Weight
None	0	0
Item 0	2	3
Item 1	3	2
Items 0 and 1	5	5
Item 2	1	1
Items 0 and 2	3	4
Items 1 and 2	4	3
Items 0, 1, and 2	6	6

2.2 The steps of a quantum computation

In chapter 1, we used figure 2.2 to visualize the steps of executing a quantum computation. It is important to understand that each execution (or run) of a quantum computation results in one of potentially many possible outcomes. Multiple runs of the same computation result in a collection of measured outcomes. In figure 2.2, we show an example distribution of measured outcomes from multiple runs of a computation.

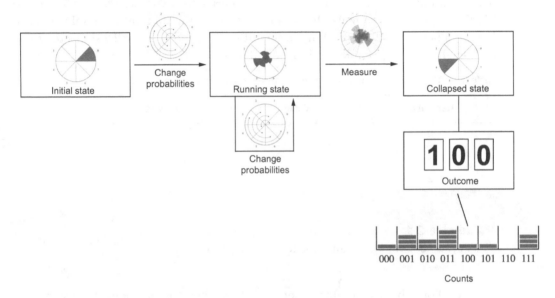

Figure 2.2 The steps of a quantum computation using quantum bits (qubits)

What exactly is a *run* of a quantum computation? Each run consists of three main parts:

1. The system of qubits used to run the program is set up in an initial state.
2. We change the state of the system using a specific set of instructions.
3. We perform a system measurement that collapses the state and produces one of the possible outcomes.

We repeat these steps or run the computation as many times as required to obtain the information we need. The goal for many quantum computations is to increase the probability of measuring desired outcomes.

2.2.1 Outcomes as binary strings

The only information we can get from a quantum computation run is a measurement outcome. A measurement outcome of a quantum computation is represented as a *binary string*: a sequence of 0s and 1s. Each digit in the binary string corresponds to a qubit in the *quantum system* running the computation. In this book, we assume that all qubits are measured at the end of a computation unless specified otherwise.

2.2 The steps of a quantum computation

DEFINITION Quantum systems used for computing are typically composed of quantum bits or qubits.

In this book, when we refer to a quantum system, we are referring to a qubit system. There are several types of quantum computers, each of which uses different technologies to physically implement qubits. We will not discuss quantum computing hardware in this book beyond the concepts you need to understand to write software for them.

In figure 2.3, we use empty boxes to represent the binary digits. Each time we run a quantum program, we get one outcome.

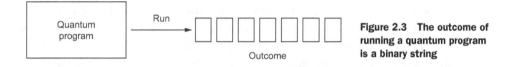

Figure 2.3 The outcome of running a quantum program is a binary string

Representing outcomes with binary strings

There are 2^n binary strings with length n, where $n > 0$ is the number of digits. Each qubit in a quantum system corresponds to one binary digit in the measurement outcome. Therefore, a quantum system with n qubits has 2^n possible outcomes.

As mentioned in chapter 1, we often talk about measurement outcomes using decimal form (base 10 integers). The following tables show the decimal (base 10) values of binary strings of lengths one, two, and three.

One-qubit outcomes

Binary form	Decimal form
0	0
1	1

Two-qubit outcomes

Binary form	Decimal form
00	0
01	1
10	2
11	3

Three-qubit outcomes

Binary form	Decimal form
000	0
001	1
010	2
011	3
100	4
101	5
110	6
111	7

The decimal (base 10) value of binary strings of length one, two, and three

(continued)
If you are unfamiliar with binary strings and converting between binary and decimal values, check out the review in appendix A.

Exercise 2.2
What can be said about integers whose binary representation ends in 0?

Similar to a classical computer, we can use groups of qubits, called *quantum registers*, to represent different variables. In the knapsack problem example, we will use three registers to represent three variables: item selection, selection value, and selection weight. Figure 2.4 shows these three registers. The size of the registers for each variable is determined by how large the variables need to be in a specific problem (number of items, weights, and values).

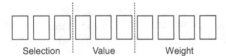

Figure 2.4 Three registers encoding an item selection, its total value, and its total weight for solving the knapsack problem

2.2.2 Quantum state and probabilities

As mentioned in chapter 1, each possible outcome of a quantum computation has a certain probability of occurring. A quantum system's state, called a *quantum state*, consists of a value for each possible outcome, called an *amplitude* (or *probability amplitude*), which determines the outcome probability. Remember that an amplitude is a two-dimensional entity that has a magnitude (length) and direction. The probability of each outcome is equal to the squared magnitude of its associated amplitude.

Why are probabilities the squares of magnitudes?
This is one of the features of quantum mechanics that is accepted in practice without proof. For this reason, these features are called *postulates*. Once formulated, the postulates are not hard to understand and represent in code like we do in this book. In different versions of quantum theory, some postulates may be replaced by others, and the old postulates can be derived from new ones. A full discussion of postulates is beyond the scope of this book.

The postulates of quantum mechanics were derived after a long process of trial and (mostly) error, which involved a considerable amount of guessing and fumbling by the originators of the theory.

—Michael A. Nielsen and Isaac L. Chuang

2.2 The steps of a quantum computation

Complex numbers are the most convenient way to represent amplitudes. We will look closely at amplitudes in the next chapter.

In chapter 1, we used a wheel with sectors to represent the state of a quantum system. The wheel in figure 2.5 represents the state of a three-qubit system, where each side is an outcome and the shaded parts represent the probabilities.

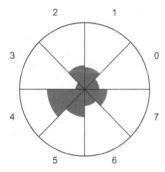

Figure 2.5 A rose chart representation of the probabilities associated with the outcomes of a three-qubit quantum system

The wheel representation is an intuitive way to visualize the setup of a quantum computation, but in many cases, it is useful to present additional information. We will "unwrap" the wheel into a table, where we can add columns to include more information. In this book, we will use table visualizations called *state tables* to visualize quantum states. In this chapter, we will use simplified state tables. In the next chapter, we will add more columns to the tables.

Figure 2.6 is the corresponding table visualization of the state shown in figure 2.5. Similar to the sectors of the wheel, the probability is represented by the length of the bar relative to the total length of the column.

Outcome	Binary	Probability bar
0	000	
1	001	
2	010	
3	011	
4	100	
5	101	
6	110	
7	111	

Figure 2.6 The possible outcomes of a three-qubit system and the corresponding probabilities

Deep dive: Ket notation

Ket notation is the formal mathematical expression of quantum states. We will not rely on this notation, but we will include explanations and examples throughout the book for interested readers.

A *ket*, $|\psi\rangle$, denotes a column vector of complex numbers representing a quantum state. Consider a quantum state with $n = 3$ qubits. The state will consist of $2^n = 8$ amplitudes, each corresponding to a possible outcome. We can express the state with ket notation:

$$|\psi\rangle = \begin{bmatrix} z_0 \\ z_1 \\ z_2 \\ z_3 \\ z_4 \\ z_5 \\ z_6 \\ z_7 \end{bmatrix}$$

where z_i for $0 \leq i < 2^n = 8$ is a complex number.

We can also express this state in terms of the standard (computational) basis:

$$|\psi\rangle = \begin{bmatrix} z_0 \\ z_1 \\ z_2 \\ z_3 \\ z_4 \\ z_5 \\ z_6 \\ z_7 \end{bmatrix} = z_0 \begin{bmatrix} 1 \\ 0 \\ 0 \\ 0 \\ 0 \\ 0 \\ 0 \\ 0 \end{bmatrix} + z_1 \begin{bmatrix} 0 \\ 1 \\ 0 \\ 0 \\ 0 \\ 0 \\ 0 \\ 0 \end{bmatrix} + z_2 \begin{bmatrix} 0 \\ 0 \\ 1 \\ 0 \\ 0 \\ 0 \\ 0 \\ 0 \end{bmatrix} + z_3 \begin{bmatrix} 0 \\ 0 \\ 0 \\ 1 \\ 0 \\ 0 \\ 0 \\ 0 \end{bmatrix} + z_4 \begin{bmatrix} 0 \\ 0 \\ 0 \\ 0 \\ 1 \\ 0 \\ 0 \\ 0 \end{bmatrix} + z_5 \begin{bmatrix} 0 \\ 0 \\ 0 \\ 0 \\ 0 \\ 1 \\ 0 \\ 0 \end{bmatrix} + z_6 \begin{bmatrix} 0 \\ 0 \\ 0 \\ 0 \\ 0 \\ 0 \\ 1 \\ 0 \end{bmatrix} + z_7 \begin{bmatrix} 0 \\ 0 \\ 0 \\ 0 \\ 0 \\ 0 \\ 0 \\ 1 \end{bmatrix}$$

The basis vector with all zero entries except a single 1 in the kth row is denoted by $|k\rangle$, also representing the kth outcome. Using this notation, we can express the same quantum state with

$$|\psi\rangle = z_0|0\rangle + z_1|1\rangle + z_2|2\rangle + z_3|3\rangle + z_4|4\rangle + z_5|5\rangle + z_6|6\rangle + z_7|7\rangle$$

Depending on the context, we can also use the binary expansion of outcomes:

$$|\psi\rangle = z_0|000\rangle + z_1|001\rangle + z_2|010\rangle + z_3|011\rangle + z_4|100\rangle + z_5|101\rangle + z_6|110\rangle + z_7|111\rangle$$

For a system with *n* qubits, we typically use a sum notation:

$$|\psi\rangle = \sum_{k=0}^{2^n - 1} z_k |k\rangle$$

To change the amplitudes of a quantum state and therefore the outcome probabilities, we use instructions called *quantum gates*. An elementary quantum gate is the basic building block of a quantum computation that recombines a pair of amplitudes using a specific formula. In the field of signal processing, the combination of a pair of complex numbers is visually represented with a "butterfly" diagram like the one shown in figure 2.7. We will look at the common elementary gates and their formulas in the next chapter.

Figure 2.7 An elementary quantum instruction (gate) recombines pairs of amplitudes. The two inputs, *a* and *b*, are recombined according to a formula to compute two outputs, creating a shape that resembles butterfly wings.

To solve optimization problems using a quantum computation, the goal is to increase the probability of the outcomes that satisfy the problem criteria. In the case of the knapsack problem, this means increasing the probability of the optimal item configuration with the highest value and weight not exceeding the allowed maximum.

2.3 A quantum solution to the knapsack problem

Let's get into more detail about how to implement a quantum program to solve the knapsack problem. Don't worry; you are not expected to understand all the details of the implementation at this point. By the end of the book, you will be able to implement the solution to the problem yourself and much more.

2.3.1 Encoding the problem

Returning to our three quantum registers shown in figure 2.8, we can set up our knapsack problem. The selection register will have three qubits, one for each item (see figure 2.9). If an item is included in the selection, the corresponding digit in the outcome will have a value of 1. If an item is not included, the corresponding digit will have a value of 0.

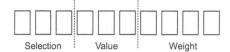

Figure 2.8 Three registers encoding an item selection, its total value, and its total weight for solving the knapsack problem

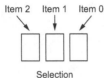

Figure 2.9 The register for encoding item selections. Each qubit corresponds to an item.

We will use two registers to encode the corresponding value and weight of each selection. Table 2.3 shows the value and weight of each possible selection of items.

Table 2.3 Each possible selection of items and the corresponding value and weight

Selection	Value	Weight
000	0	0
001	2	3
010	3	2
011	5	5
100	1	1
101	3	4
110	4	3
111	6	6

We can express the value and weight of each selection using linear functions of binary variables:

$$v(x_0, x_1, x_2) = 2x_0 + 3x_1 + x_2$$
$$w(x_0, x_1, x_2) = 3x_0 + 2x_1 + x_2$$

where x_0, x_1, and x_2 are the binary digits of the selection register (indexed from right to left, as shown in figure 2.9). For example, if the selection outcome is 110, then $x_0 = 0$, $x_1 = 1$, and $x_2 = 2$. We can find the weight and value of this selection using the functions we just defined:

$$v(x_0, x_1, x_2) = 3 + 1 = 4$$
$$w(x_0, x_1, x_2) = 2 + 1 = 3$$

This representation is useful for encoding the weight and value of each selection in a quantum state. The method of encoding is the subject of a later chapter.

> **Linear functions of binary variables**
>
> Consider the case where the inputs of a function are a list of *n* binary variables (0 or 1) for a positive integer *n*. A linear function of binary variables is a mathematical expression of the form
>
> $$f(x_0, x_1, \ldots, x_{n-1}) = c + c_0 x_0 + c_1 x_1 + \cdots + c_{n-1} x_{n-1} = c + \sum_{k=0}^{n-1} c_k x_k$$
>
> where $x_0, \ldots, x_{n-1}$ are either 0 or 1 and $c, c_0, \ldots, c_{n-1}$ are constant real numbers.
>
> For example, we can express the function $y = x + 3$ as a linear function of $n = 2$ binary variables
>
> $$f(x_0, x_1) = 3 + x_0 + 2x_1 = c + \sum_{k=0}^{1} c_k x_k$$
>
> where $c = 3$, $c_0 = 1$, and $c_1 = 2$.

2.3.2 Knapsack problem solution

To find the solution to our example knapsack problem, we will use the `solve_knapsack` function from the chapter's companion code. We are running this function using our Python simulator, which we will discuss in more detail in the next section.

> **NOTE** A Jupyter notebook with the complete implementation of the example from this chapter can be found in the src/ch02 folder in the source code on the book's website (www.manning.com/books/building-quantum-software-with-python) and in the book's companion repository (https://github.com/learnqc/code).

This function has three parameters: a list of item values, a list of item weights, and the maximum weight of selections we are looking for. We define the inputs for our example as follows:

```
values = [2, 3, 1]
weights = [3, 2, 1]
max_weight = 4
```

Let's perform one function call with these inputs:

```
solve_knapsack(values, weights, max_weight)
```

The following output shows the optimal selection that satisfies the given weight constraint:

```
Optimal selection consists of items 1, 2. The combined value is 4, and the
    combined weight is 3.
```

Let's go into more detail about what this function does. The solution relies on two important patterns in quantum computing:

- Efficiently recognizing nonnegative outcomes within a certain register
- Increasing the probability of measuring desired outcomes

The first pattern refers to having an efficient *oracle* and the second to the *amplitude amplification* algorithm, which uses an oracle in its implementation. The combination of these two patterns, discussed in later chapters, allows us to increase the probability of measuring selections that have a minimum value and a maximum weight through quantum measurement.

The implementation starts by looking for selections with the given maximum weight parameter, 4, and a minimum value defined as the highest value of a single item: in this case, item 1, with a value of 3. We use this as the starting minimum value because we know that the optimal outcome should have the same or greater value than putting only the highest-value item in the knapsack.

> **NOTE** If you already solved the problem in your head, you know the most optimal outcome has a greater value than item 1 by itself. We are simply using the value of item 1 to set a minimum value for the parameters of the computation. Doing this does not indicate or dictate that item 1 must be included in the most optimal outcome, only that any outcome with lesser value than item 1 can be ignored.

The probability of selections that meet these criteria is increased. In figure 2.10, we can see that these outcomes have a higher probability than the outcomes that do not meet these requirements.

Selection	Value	Weight	Probability	Probability bar
000	0	0	0.03	
001	2	3	0.03	
010	3	2	0.28	▇
011	5	5	0.03	
100	1	1	0.03	
101	3	4	0.28	▇
110	4	3	0.28	▇
111	6	6	0.03	

Figure 2.10 The probability of outcomes when looking for selections with a maximum weight of 4 and a minimum value of 3

Next, the function simulates one or more measurements. There is an equal probability of getting any of the three selections identified in this step: it is possible that we will get the best selection, but it is equally likely that we will get one of the other non-optimal outcomes. The most frequent selection and its weight and value are recorded.

Assume that the most frequent measurement outcome is 101 (selection of the first and third items). Next, we want to see if we can find a solution with a higher value. We can increase the minimum value from 3 to 4 and perform the same operations to search for the selections with this minimum value (and a maximum weight of 4).

As shown in figure 2.11, only one selection is identified, and the probability of that outcome is increased. Once again, the function simulates a measurement of this state. We get the selection outcome 110 (items 1 and 2).

Selection	Value	Weight	Probability	Probability bar
000	0	0	0.03	
001	2	3	0.03	
010	3	2	0.03	
011	5	5	0.03	
100	1	1	0.03	
101	3	4	0.03	
110	4	3	0.78	▇▇▇▇
111	6	6	0.03	

Figure 2.11 The selection register outcome probabilities after looking for selections with a maximum weight of 4 and a minimum value of 4

Next, we will try to increase the minimum value again, this time to 5. However, the function will not yield a solution that meets this requirement, so the search is done. The best solution identified in the previous steps is returned.

2.4 Tools for programming a quantum solution

In the ecosystem of quantum computing software packages, Qiskit, Cirq, and PennyLane are among the most popular as of this writing (2025). These packages enable you to compile and run code on quantum computers (when and if one is available to you), and they often include a simulator for testing code before committing to using quantum computing time.

Quantum computing programmers spend most of their time using simulators; simulators are crucial to the process of becoming "quantum ready." In chapters 3 and 4, we will go through the step-by-step process of implementing a simulator. Writing a simulator from scratch requires only a couple of hundred lines of code and is a great way to familiarize yourself with foundational quantum computing concepts.

The Python simulator we use in this book, called *Hume*, is designed for learning, flexibility, and efficiency. The building blocks of Hume covered in this book can easily be translated into other languages. The book is meant to provide the necessary knowledge for organizations to adopt quantum computing and build quantum computing platforms; we believe this requires tools that are flexible and that can evolve.

> **NOTE** A complete implementation of Hume can be found in the source code on the book's website (www.manning.com/books/building-quantum-software-with-python) and in the book's companion repository (https://github.com/learnqc/code). A JavaScript version of Hume can be found at https://github.com/learnqc/code_js.

The diagram in figure 2.12 shows the general structure of the quantum concepts we will cover in the book and implement in the simulator.

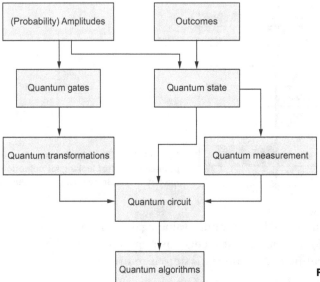

Figure 2.12 Map of quantum concepts implemented in Hume

The syntax for writing quantum circuits in Hume closely matches that of Qiskit. This is intentional, as Qiskit is among the most popular quantum computing SDKs. As part of Hume, we created tools to seamlessly convert to Qiskit so that we can run on IBM quantum backends, both simulators and real quantum computers. For example, to convert a circuit to a Qiskit circuit object, we use the `to_qiskit` function:

```
qiskit_circuit = to_qiskit(hume_circuit)
```

The function returns a Qiskit `QuantumCircuit` instance. We also include a function to run a circuit using Qiskit's state vector simulator. These tools also allow you to run code written in Hume on real quantum hardware.

Summary

- Binary optimization problems are good candidates for efficient quantum computing solutions.
- The output of one execution (run) of a quantum computation can be interpreted as a binary string, with one digit for each qubit in the system.
- The state of a quantum system (quantum state) consists of a value called an amplitude for each possible outcome. The corresponding amplitude determines the probability of an outcome.
- We change the amplitudes, and therefore the probabilities, using elementary quantum instructions called quantum gates.
- To solve several types of problems—including optimization problems—using quantum computations, the goal is to increase the probability of desired outcomes. We do this using a process called amplitude amplification.

Single-qubit states and gates

This chapter covers
- Single-qubit quantum states and introducing state tables
- Basic single-qubit quantum gates and single-qubit quantum circuits
- Simulating single-qubit quantum systems in Python

In this chapter, we look at the state of a single-qubit system with programmatic and visual representations. We also cover how a qubit can be used as a computational tool. In the next chapter, we will generalize these concepts to any number of qubits.

The simplest representation of a quantum state in code is a list of *complex numbers*. This list is often called a *state vector*. We will use state tables like the ones introduced in chapter 2 to visualize quantum states.

This chapter also introduces the basics of applying programming instructions, called *quantum gates*, to a single-qubit system and combining them into a *quantum circuit*. We will look at some ways to visualize gates and circuits. Finally, we will examine a few simple single-qubit circuits with practical applications. Figure 3.1 shows the structure of the concepts introduced in this chapter.

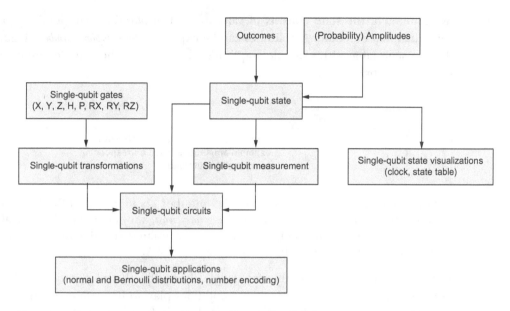

Figure 3.1 A dependency diagram of concepts introduced in this chapter

NOTE The source code, examples, and exercise answers can be found on the book's website (www.manning.com/books/building-quantum-software-with-python) and in the book's companion repository (https://github.com/learnqc/code).

3.1 Single-qubit state: A pair of complex numbers

A single-qubit quantum system has two possible outcomes, denoted by 0 and 1. Its state consists of a pair of amplitudes, one for each outcome. We will look at the properties of a single-qubit state in detail using both visualizations and code.

3.1.1 Visualizing single-qubit states with tables

Throughout this book, we use state tables to describe and visualize quantum states. The columns in a state table contain relevant properties of a quantum state.

Each qubit in a quantum system corresponds to a binary digit in the measurement outcomes. For a single-qubit system, we need only one binary digit to represent its outcomes. For single-digit outcomes, the decimal and binary expressions are the same, as shown in figure 3.2, but this will not be the case for larger systems.

Outcome	Binary
0	0
1	1

Figure 3.2 A single-qubit state has two possible outcomes.

As mentioned, the state consists of values called *amplitudes* corresponding to each computational outcome. Amplitudes can be expressed as *complex numbers*. Figure 3.3 shows a state table with example amplitudes; in this case, the complex numbers are shown in algebraic form.

Outcome	Binary	Amplitude
0	0	−0.34 + 0.43i
1	1	0.68 + 0.49i

Figure 3.3 A single-qubit state with two example amplitudes, each corresponding to a possible outcome

NOTE The algebraic form of a complex number z is $z = x + iy$. In this form, x and y are real numbers, and i is the *imaginary unit*, a number with the special property that its square is -1, $i^2 = -1$. If you are unfamiliar with complex numbers or need a refresher, please refer to appendix A.

It is also useful to include in the state table columns for the magnitude and direction of each amplitude. The directions of amplitudes play an important role in quantum computations and will be explored in more detail in future chapters.

NOTE Given a complex number $z = x + iy$, we can find its magnitude $|z|$ with the formula $|z| = \sqrt{x^2 + y^2}$ and its direction θ using trigonometric expressions. Conveniently, the Python math library function atan2(y, x) takes care of all the necessary computational details and gives the direction in radians. If you are unfamiliar with these concepts, you can find more details in appendix A.

The example amplitudes in figure 3.3 have magnitudes $\sqrt{0.3}$ and $\sqrt{0.7}$:

$$-0.3415 + 0.4282i = \sqrt{0.3}\left(\cos\frac{5\pi}{7} + i\sin\frac{5\pi}{7}\right)$$

$$-0.6769 + 0.4918i = \sqrt{0.7}\left(\cos\frac{\pi}{5} + i\sin\frac{\pi}{5}\right)$$

Remember that the squared magnitudes of the amplitudes in a quantum state must add up to 1, so each magnitude will be at most 1. This makes it easy to illustrate the values in a state table with an *amplitude bar*, where the length of the bar is proportional to the length of its cell (e.g., a magnitude of 0.5 would be a bar that covers half of the cell). The color of the bar corresponds to the amplitude's direction. In figure 3.4, we add amplitude bars to the state table to visualize the magnitude and direction of the amplitudes.

3.1 Single-qubit state: A pair of complex numbers

Outcome	Binary	Amplitude	Direction	Magnitude	Amplitude bar
0	0	−0.34 + 0.43i	128.6°	0.55	
1	1	0.68 + 0.49i	36.0°	0.84	

Figure 3.4 A single-qubit state has two amplitudes. Each amplitude has a magnitude and direction.

Amplitudes as colored bars

As mentioned, amplitudes have a magnitude and direction. We know that each amplitude of a quantum state will have a magnitude less than or equal to 1. So, we can plot amplitudes within the unit circle. The left side of the following figure shows a graphical representation of the two amplitudes of this state inside a unit circle. We use the color wheel on the right side of the figure to find the corresponding hue of each amplitude direction to color our amplitude bars.

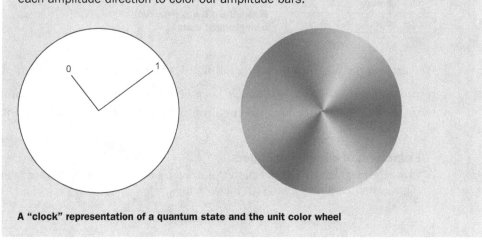

A "clock" representation of a quantum state and the unit color wheel

Next, we can add a column with the probability of each outcome and one containing a bar whose length reflects the probability. The probability of an outcome is the square of the magnitude of its amplitude. Figure 3.5 shows the probabilities as numerical values and colored bars.

NOTE The probability of an outcome with amplitude z is $p = |z|^2$.

Outcome	Binary	Amplitude	Direction	Magnitude	Amplitude bar	Probability	Probability bar
0	0	−0.34 + 0.43i	128.6°	0.55		0.30	
1	1	0.68 + 0.49i	36.0°	0.84		0.70	

Figure 3.5 The probability of each outcome is the squared magnitude of the corresponding amplitude.

Figure 3.5 is an example of an "expanded" state table for a single-qubit state. Depending on the need, we will use a more compact or expanded version of the state table.

3.1.2 The general form of a single-qubit state

A single-qubit state is captured by two amplitudes whose squared magnitudes add up to 1. We denote the amplitude corresponding to outcome 0 by z_0 and the amplitude corresponding to outcome 1 by z_1. If the probability of outcome 0 is p, then the probability of outcome 1 is $1 - p$. The directions θ_0 and θ_1 can be any two angles.

For a single-qubit state, if we know the probability p of the outcome 0 and the directions of the amplitudes (θ_0 and θ_1), we can derive the corresponding amplitudes. Let's start with the general form single-qubit state in figure 3.6.

Outcome	Direction	Probability
0	θ_0	p
1	θ_1	$1 - p$

Figure 3.6 The general form of a single-qubit state

We can find the magnitudes of the amplitudes by taking the square roots of the corresponding probabilities: $\sqrt{p}$ and $\sqrt{1-p}$. Then we can express the amplitudes in terms of their magnitude and direction using the *polar form* of complex numbers.

> **Polar form of complex numbers**
> Given the magnitude r and direction θ of a complex number $z = x + iy$, we can express the real and imaginary parts with these formulas:
>
> $$x = r \cos \theta$$
> $$y = r \sin \theta$$
>
> This leads to the polar form of z:
>
> $$z = r(\cos \theta + i \sin \theta)$$

Now we can add columns to the state table for the amplitudes and their magnitudes, as shown in figure 3.7. We can also denote the probabilities of outcomes 0 and 1 with p_0 and p_1, respectively (see figure 3.8). This is useful when we want the notation to reflect the outcome the probability corresponds to.

3.1 Single-qubit state: A pair of complex numbers

Outcome	Amplitude	Direction	Magnitude	Probability
0	$\sqrt{p}(\cos\theta_0 + i\sin\theta_0)$	θ_0	$\sqrt{p}$	p
1	$\sqrt{1-p}(\cos\theta_1 + i\sin\theta_1)$	θ_1	$\sqrt{1-p}$	$1-p$

Figure 3.7 The general form of a single-qubit state with amplitudes in polar form where the probabilities of outcome 0 is p and therefore the probability of outcome 1 is 1 – p.

Outcome	Amplitude	Direction	Magnitude	Probability
0	$\sqrt{p_0}(\cos\theta_0 + i\sin\theta_0)$	θ_0	$\sqrt{p_0}$	p_0
1	$\sqrt{p_1}(\cos\theta_1 + i\sin\theta_1)$	θ_1	$\sqrt{p_1}$	p_1

Figure 3.8 The general form of a single-qubit state with amplitudes in polar form where the probability of outcomes 0 and 1 are denoted by p_0 and p_1

> **Ket notation**
>
> As mentioned in chapter 2, ket notation is often used in the field of quantum computing to express quantum states. A single-qubit state can be expressed in terms of the standard (computational) basis
>
> $$|\psi\rangle = \begin{bmatrix} z_0 \\ z_1 \end{bmatrix} = z_0 \begin{bmatrix} 1 \\ 0 \end{bmatrix} + z_1 \begin{bmatrix} 0 \\ 1 \end{bmatrix} = z_0|0\rangle + z_1|1\rangle$$
>
> where z_0 and z_1 are complex numbers satisfying
>
> $$|z_0|^2 + |z_1|^2 = 1$$

> **Exercise 3.1**
> What directions correspond to amplitudes that are real numbers?

3.1.3 Programmatically encoding single-qubit states with lists

A single-qubit quantum state can be expressed as a list of two amplitudes, where the index of an amplitude is the corresponding outcome. Let's start by encoding the example single-qubit state from the previous section. Note that Python represents the imaginary unit, i, in a complex number with the symbol j:

```
state = [0.2958+0.51235j, -0.40311+0.69821j]
```
⟵ In Python, we use j for the imaginary unit.

The index of each amplitude is the corresponding outcome. Let's look at the item at index 0:

```
print(state[0])
```

The output is the amplitude corresponding to outcome 0:

```
(0.2958+0.51235j)
```

Let's look at some other single-qubit quantum states:

```
from math import sqrt

state1 = [1, 0]

state2 = [0, 1]

state3 = [sqrt(1/2), sqrt(1/2)]

state4 = [sqrt(0.3), sqrt(0.7)]
```

These example states have positive real numbers as amplitudes (the imaginary part is 0). If an amplitude is a positive real number, its direction must be a 0 angle.

For example, let's look at the real and imaginary parts of the amplitude corresponding to outcome 0 in the following example state:

```
state = [1, 0]
print(state[0].real, state[0].imag)
```
⬅ We can use the built-in attributes .real and .imag to get the real and imaginary parts of a complex number.

The output is

```
1 0
```

To verify that the previous examples are valid single-qubit quantum states, we can check that the sum of the squared magnitudes is 1. In Python, you can find the magnitude of a complex number with the `abs` function. We can use this list comprehension to get the sum of the squared magnitudes:

```
state = [1, 0]
assert sum([abs(k)**2 for k in state]) == 1

state1 = [sqrt(0.3), sqrt(0.7)]
assert sum([abs(k)**2 for k in state1]) == 1
```

The following state shows an example of an amplitude that is a negative real number, whose direction is 180°, or π radians:

```
state = [sqrt(0.3), -sqrt(0.7)]
```

3.1 Single-qubit state: A pair of complex numbers

Note that all odd integer multiples of 180° (or π if radians are used) are valid representations for the same direction.

As mentioned, in Python, we can find the direction of a complex number in radians using the atan2 function from the math library:

```
from math import atan2

state = [sqrt(0.3), -sqrt(0.7)]
direction = atan2(state[1].imag, state[1].real)
print(direction)
```

> Remember, the direction (in radians) is atan2(y, x). We can use .real and .imag to get x and y, respectively.

The output is the direction in radians:

```
3.141592653589793
```

We can convert from radians to degrees with the following expression:

```
from math import pi

direction * (180/pi)
```

The output is the direction in degrees:

```
180.0
```

The following is a state with amplitude directions $\pi/7$ and $\pi/5$ radians:

```
from math import cos, sin

state = [sqrt(0.3) * (cos(5 * pi / 7) + 1j * sin(5 * pi / 7)),
         sqrt(0.7) * (cos(pi / 5) + 1j * sin(pi / 5))]

print(state)
```

> Remember, in Python, j is used to represent the imaginary unit in a complex number.

The output is

```
[(-0.34149942885245477+0.42822673911544473j),
 (0.6768721799802616+0.4917764247793589j)]
```

Although this list is an efficient, compact representation, it is useful to explicitly include each index (which is the same as the outcome in this representation):

```
table = [[k, state[k]] for k in range(len(state))]
for row in table:
    print(row)
```

The output is

```
[0, (-0.34149942885245477+0.42822673911544473j)]
[1, (0.6768721799802616+0.4917764247793589j)]
```

To make the table more readable, we can use fewer decimal places for the real and imaginary parts of the amplitudes. For example, let's format them using five digits after the decimal point:

```
formatted_table = [
    [
        round(x.real, 5) + 1j * round(x.imag, 5) if isinstance(x, complex) else x
        for x in table[k]
    ]
    for k in range(len(table))
]

for row in formatted_table:
    print(row)
```

The output is

```
[0, (-0.3415+0.42823j)]
[1, (0.67687+0.49178j)]
```

Next, we will add the other properties we want in the state table: direction, magnitude, and probability. We can get the magnitude of a complex number using the built-in Python function `abs`:

```
abs(state[0])
```

To get the probability, we square the magnitude:

```
abs(state[0])**2
```

We can put everything together to get all the values in the state table shown in figure 3.9.

```
expanded_table = [
    [
        k,
        state[k],
        atan2(state[k].imag, state[k].real) * (180 / pi),
        abs(state[k]),
        abs(state[k]) ** 2
    ]
    for k in range(len(state))
]

formatted_expanded_table = [
    [
        round(x, 5) if isinstance(x, float)
        else round(x.real, 5) + 1j * round(x.imag, 5) if isinstance(x, complex)
        else x
        for x in expanded_table[k]
    ]
    for k in range(len(expanded_table))
]
```

3.1 Single-qubit state: A pair of complex numbers

```
for row in formatted_expanded_table:
    print(row)
```

Outcome	Binary	Amplitude	Direction	Magnitude	Amplitude bar	Probability	Probability bar
0	0	−0.34 + 0.43i	128.6°	0.55		0.30	
1	1	0.68 + 0.49i	36.0°	0.84		0.70	

Figure 3.9 The expanded state table for the example state encoded in Python

The output is a row for each outcome with the corresponding amplitude, direction, magnitude, and probability:

```
[0, (-0.3415+0.42823j), 128.57143, 0.54772, 0.3]
[1, (0.67687+0.49178j), 36.0, 0.83666, 0.7]
```

3.1.4 Implementing a single-qubit quantum computing simulator in Python

The diagram in figure 3.10 illustrates the components of a quantum computation using a single-qubit system. We can simulate each part of a quantum computation using a classical computer. Writing a quantum computing simulator is not as difficult as you may think; it requires only a couple of hundred lines of code in any programming language. We are going to build the components of a quantum simulator from scratch using Python. We will use a functional programming approach for our simulator and wrap it in an object-oriented style that reflects the syntax used by Qiskit, one of the most popular quantum computing frameworks. This way, the code examples can be run with our simulator or Qiskit. Our approach is meant to provide a blueprint for implementing a simulator in the programming language of your choice.

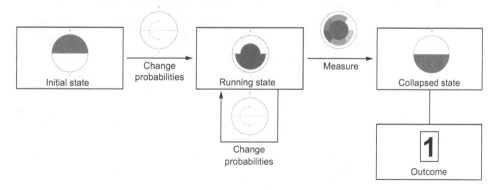

Figure 3.10 The steps of a single-qubit quantum computation

CHAPTER 3 *Single-qubit states and gates*

INITIAL STATE

Typically, qubit systems start in a default state where the only possible outcome is for every qubit to be 0. In other words, the probability of getting the outcome 0 from the default state is 100%.

In our single-qubit simulator, we implement a function called `init_state` that returns a list representation of a default single-qubit quantum state.

Listing 3.1 Function to create a default single-qubit state

```
def init_state():
    state = [0 for _ in range(2)]    ← Creates a list with two 0 entries
    state[0] = 1    ← Changes the first value (index 0) to 1 because
                      in a default single-qubit state, the probability
    return state     of outcome 0 is 1
```

Let's use this function to initialize a single-qubit state:

```
state = init_state()
print(state)
```

The output is a state where the amplitude corresponding to outcome 0 is 1:

```
[1, 0]
```

PREPARING A SINGLE-QUBIT STATE

When using quantum computers, we cannot write the state of a program directly. We have to apply a set of instructions, called *gates*, to change the amplitudes. Programming a quantum computer to have a desired quantum state is the subject of many of the coming chapters in the book. However, in a classical simulator, we can write amplitudes directly into a list.

To make sure the classical simulations mimic the behavior of a real quantum computer, we need to remember that a single-qubit state consists of two amplitudes, and the sum of the squared magnitudes of those amplitudes must be 1. To that end, let's create a function, `prepare_state`, that creates the state and validates these constraints. We can use the `is_close` function (defined in the chapter code) to check that the sum of the magnitudes is 1.

Listing 3.2 Checking that a list of complex numbers is a valid single-qubit state

```
from util import is_close
                                            ← Creates a new state list using the
def prepare_state(*a):                        values passed to the function
    state = [a[k] for k in range(len(a))]   ←
    assert(len(state) == 2)                 ← Checks that the state
                                              has two amplitudes
    assert(is_close(sum([abs(state[k])**2 for k in range(len(state))]), 1))   ←
    return state
                                            Checks that the sum of the
                                            squared magnitudes is 1
```

For example, let's check that the example state we used previously is a valid quantum state:

```
list = [0.2958+0.51235j, -0.40311+0.69821j]
state = prepare_state(*list)
```

3.2 Changing amplitudes with single-qubit gates

Now that we have implemented the simulation code for initializing a quantum state, let's move on to the next part of a quantum computation: changing amplitudes. This section will focus on basic quantum instructions, called gates, which alter pairs of amplitudes in quantum systems with any number of qubits. Changing the state of a single-qubit system can be thought of as changing the probabilities of the sides of a coin. The pairs of combined amplitudes are determined by the target qubit of the gate. Note that all the gates preserve the combined probability of the outcomes in the pair. In the case of a single-qubit quantum system, there is only one option for the target qubit and only one pair of amplitudes. In the next chapter, we will explain how pairs are selected when there is more than one qubit. In this section, we will focus on the definitions of common single-qubit gates and the result of applying them to a single-qubit state. We will use the state table representation whenever it's helpful for understanding.

3.2.1 Rotation is multiplication

A few gates rely on rotating amplitudes. Given a complex number with magnitude r and direction θ (measured counterclockwise from the positive x axis), we can express it as

$$r(\cos\theta + i\sin\theta)$$

If we multiply it by a complex number with magnitude 1

$$\cos\varphi + i\sin\varphi$$

we get

$$r(\cos(\theta + \varphi) + i\sin(\theta + \varphi))$$

Effectively, the result is the counterclockwise rotation of the initial complex number by an angle φ.

> **Multiplying complex numbers in polar form**
> Given two complex numbers in polar form
> $$z = r(\cos\theta + i\sin\theta)$$
> $$c = s(\cos\varphi + i\sin\varphi)$$

> *(continued)*
> their product is
>
> $$rs(\cos(\theta + \varphi) + i \sin(\theta + \varphi))$$
>
> In words, magnitudes are multiplied, and directions are added.

In code implementations of rotations, we will use the shortcut function in listing 3.3. This function is named for the shorthand *cis notation* defined by

$$\operatorname{cis} \varphi = \cos \varphi + i \sin \varphi$$

Listing 3.3 Shortcut function for rotations

```
def cis(theta):
    return cos(theta) + 1j*sin(theta)
```

NOTE You may be familiar with the exponential notation $e^{i\varphi} = \cos \varphi + i \sin \varphi$, an equality known as Euler's formula. We prefer to use the `cis` function, which is concise and developer friendly.

3.2.2 Basic single-qubit gates

In this section, we will look at eight common single-qubit gates in detail. You will notice that some gates change the outcome probabilities, some change the directions, and some change both. We will show the effect of a gate transformation using whichever form of the state best captures the transformation.

THE X GATE

Also called the NOT gate, the X gate swaps the amplitudes corresponding to a pair of outcomes. In the state table, the data in the rows corresponding to those outcomes are swapped, as shown in figure 3.11.

Outcome	Amplitude
0	z_0
1	z_1

$\xrightarrow{X}$

Outcome	Amplitude
0	z_1
1	z_0

Figure 3.11 The general form of the effect of the X gate on a pair of amplitudes

To simulate an X gate applied to a single-qubit state in code, we just need to swap the items in the pair of amplitudes:

```
state = [state[1], state[0]]
```

3.2 Changing amplitudes with single-qubit gates

Figure 3.12 shows an example of applying an X gate to a single-qubit state.

Out	Bin	Ampl	Dir	Mag	Ampl bar
0	0	0.30 − 0.17i	−30.3°	0.35	
1	1	−0.71 + 0.62i	138.9°	0.94	

$\xrightarrow{X}$

Out	Bin	Ampl	Dir	Mag	Ampl bar
0	0	−0.71 + 0.62i	138.9°	0.94	
1	1	0.30 − 0.17i	−30.3°	0.35	

Figure 3.12 The effect of the X gate on an example pair of amplitudes

THE Z GATE

This gate multiplies the 1 side of a pair of amplitudes by −1. It changes the signs of both the real and the imaginary parts of the amplitude of the 1 side of the pair. Figure 3.13 shows the effect of the Z gate on the amplitudes of a single-qubit state.

Outcome	Amplitude
0	z_0
1	z_1

$\xrightarrow{Z}$

Outcome	Amplitude
0	z_0
1	$-z_1$

Figure 3.13 The general form of the effect of the Z gate on a pair of amplitudes

The magnitude of that amplitude does not change (and therefore its probability does not change), but the direction is reversed (changed by 180°). Figure 3.14 shows the effect of the Z gate on the probabilities with directions representing a single-qubit state.

Outcome	Direction	Probability
0	θ_0	p_0
1	θ_1	p_1

$\xrightarrow{Z}$

Outcome	Direction	Probability
0	θ_0	p_0
1	$180° + \theta_1$	p_1

Figure 3.14 The general form of the effect of the Z gate on a pair of probabilities with direction

The effect of the Z gate on a single-qubit state is straightforward to simulate. The transformation can be simulated with the following code:

```
state = [state[0], -state[1]]
```

Figure 3.15 shows an example of the result of the application of the Z gate on an example single-qubit state in state table and clock form.

Out	Bin	Ampl	Dir	Mag	Ampl bar
0	0	0.30 − 0.17i	−30.3°	0.35	
1	1	−0.71 + 0.62i	138.9°	0.94	

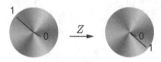

Out	Bin	Ampl	Dir	Mag	Ampl bar
0	0	0.30 − 0.17i	−30.3°	0.35	
1	1	0.71 − 0.62i	−41.1°	0.94	

Figure 3.15 The effect of the Z gate on an example pair of amplitudes

Exercise 3.2
Write code that verifies that multiplying the 1 side of the following example state by −1 reverses its direction:

```
state = [sqrt(0.3), -sqrt(0.7)]
```

THE PHASE GATE

The phase gate rotates the 1 side of a pair of amplitudes by a given angle. We denote by $P(\varphi)$ the Phase gate that uses φ as a rotation angle in radians. Remember that rotation is multiplication, as shown in figure 3.16.

Outcome	Amplitude
0	z_0
1	z_1

$\xrightarrow{P(\varphi)}$

Outcome	Amplitude
0	z_0
1	$\text{cis}(\varphi)z_1$

Figure 3.16 The effect of the $P(\varphi)$ gate on a pair of amplitudes

When a phase gate is applied, the direction of the amplitude on the 1 side of the pair changes by φ, as shown in figure 3.17. The probabilities are not changed.

Outcome	Direction	Probability
0	θ_0	p_0
1	θ_1	p_1

$\xrightarrow{P(\varphi)}$

Outcome	Direction	Probability
0	θ_0	p_0
1	$\varphi + \theta_1$	p_1

Figure 3.17 The general form of the effect of the $P(\varphi)$ gate on a pair of probabilities with direction

Given what we know about rotating an amplitude by a given angle, we can use the following code to get the new value of the 1 side of a single-qubit amplitude pair after applying a phase gate:

```
phi = pi/3
state = [state[0], cis(phi)*state[1]]
```
Uses the cis shortcut function from listing 3.3

Figure 3.18 shows an example of the result of the application of the $P(\pi/3)$ gate on an example single-qubit state. Note that an angle of $\pi/3$ radians is the same as 60°.

Out	Bin	Ampl	Dir	Mag	Ampl bar
0	0	0.30 − 0.17i	−30.3°	0.35	
1	1	−0.71 + 0.62i	138.9°	0.94	

$P(\frac{\pi}{3})$ →

Out	Bin	Ampl	Dir	Mag	Ampl bar
0	0	0.30 − 0.17i	−30.3°	0.35	
1	1	−0.89 − 0.30i	−161.1°	0.94	

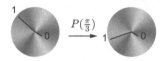

Figure 3.18 The effect of the $P(\pi/3)$ gate on our example state

THE HADAMARD GATE

The Hadamard gate (or H gate), named after the famous mathematician Jacques Hadamard, replaces an amplitude pair with their sum and difference divided by the square root of 2, as shown in figure 3.19. Note that dividing by the square root of 2 is the same as multiplying by the square root of 1/2.

Outcome	Amplitude
0	z_0
1	z_1

H →

Outcome	Amplitude
0	$\frac{1}{\sqrt{2}}(z_0 + z_1)$
1	$\frac{1}{\sqrt{2}}(z_0 - z_1)$

Figure 3.19 The general form of the effect of the H gate on a pair of amplitudes

Adding and subtracting vectors

The addition and subtraction of two given vectors in a plane produce the diagonals of a parallelogram formed from these vectors. The Parallelogram Law states that the sum of the squares of the diagonals' lengths is twice the sum of the squares of the original vectors' magnitudes. The Hadamard gate replaces the original vectors with the parallelogram diagonals scaled down by $\sqrt{2}$, resulting in new vectors whose squared magnitudes add to the same value as the original vectors' squared magnitudes.

Addition and subtraction of two vectors in a plane produces the diagonals of a parallelogram.

50 CHAPTER 3 *Single-qubit states and gates*

To simulate a Hadamard gate application on a single-qubit state, we can use the following code:

```
state = [sqrt(0.5)*(state[0] + state[1]), sqrt(0.5)*(state[0] -state[1])]
```

Figure 3.20 shows an example of the result of the application of the H gate on our example single-qubit state.

Out	Bin	Ampl	Dir	Mag	Ampl bar
0	0	0.30 − 0.17i	−30.3°	0.35	
1	1	−0.71 + 0.62i	138.9°	0.94	

$\xrightarrow{H}$

Out	Bin	Ampl	Dir	Mag	Ampl bar
0	0	−0.29 + 0.31i	132.8°	0.42	
1	1	0.71 − 0.56i	−38.2°	0.91	

Figure 3.20 The effect of the H gate on our example pair of amplitudes

The Hadamard gate can be used to assign equal probabilities to the two outcomes when starting with a state where the total probability is assigned to one of them. Figure 3.21 shows how this is done.

Out	Bin	Ampl	Dir	Mag	Ampl bar
0	0	1	0.0°	1	
1	1	0		0	

$\xrightarrow{H}$

Out	Bin	Ampl	Dir	Mag	Ampl bar
0	0	0.71	0.0°	0.71	
1	1	0.71	0.0°	0.71	

Figure 3.21 The effect of the H gate on the default single-qubit state

THE R_Z GATE

For a given angle θ, the $R_Z(\theta)$ gate rotates the 0 side of a pair of amplitudes clockwise by $\theta/2$ and the 1 side of the pair counterclockwise by $\theta/2$. Figure 3.22 shows a $R_Z(\theta)$ rotation as the multiplication of complex numbers. Applying an $R_Z(\theta)$ gate changes both directions but does not change the probability of either outcome, as shown in figure 3.23.

Outcome	Amplitude
0	z_0
1	z_1

$\xrightarrow{R_Z(\theta)}$

Outcome	Amplitude
0	$\text{cis}(-\frac{\theta}{2})z_0$
1	$\text{cis}(\frac{\theta}{2})z_1$

Figure 3.22 The general form of the effect of the R_Z gate on a pair of amplitudes

3.2 Changing amplitudes with single-qubit gates

Outcome	Direction	Probability
0	θ_0	p_0
1	θ_1	p_1

$\xrightarrow{R_Z(\theta)}$

Outcome	Direction	Probability
0	$\theta_0 - \frac{\theta}{2}$	p_0
1	$\theta_1 + \frac{\theta}{2}$	p_1

Figure 3.23 The general form of the effect of the R_Z gate on a pair of probabilities with direction

To simulate the application of an R_Z gate on a single-qubit quantum state, we need to change the direction of both amplitudes:

```
theta = pi/3
state = [cis(-theta/2)*state[0], cis(theta/2)*state[1]]
```

Figure 3.24 shows an example of the result of the application of the R_Z gate on our example single-qubit state.

Out	Bin	Ampl	Dir	Mag	Ampl bar
0	0	0.30 − 0.17i	−30.3°	0.35	
1	1	−0.71 + 0.62i	138.9°	0.94	

$\xrightarrow{R_Z(\frac{\pi}{3})}$

Out	Bin	Ampl	Dir	Mag	Ampl bar
0	0	0.17 − 0.30i	−60.3°	0.35	
1	1	−0.92 + 0.18i	168.9°	0.94	

Figure 3.24 The effect of the $R_Z(\pi/3)$ gate on our example pair of amplitudes

THE Y GATE

The effect of the Y gate on the amplitudes in a pair is equivalent to carrying out the following two steps:

1. Rotate the amplitude on the 0 side counterclockwise by 90° and the amplitude on the 1 side clockwise by 90°.
2. Swap the two amplitudes.

The effect of applying a Y gate on the amplitudes of a single-qubit state is shown in figure 3.25. Applying a Y gate to a single-qubit state changes both directions and swaps the probabilities, as shown in figure 3.26.

Outcome	Amplitude
0	z_0
1	z_1

$\xrightarrow{Y}$

Outcome	Amplitude
0	$-iz_1$
1	iz_0

Figure 3.25 The general form of the effect of the Y gate on a pair of amplitudes

CHAPTER 3 *Single-qubit states and gates*

Outcome	Direction	Probability
0	θ_0	p_0
1	θ_1	p_1

$\xrightarrow{Y}$

Outcome	Direction	Probability
0	$\theta_1 - 90°$	p_1
1	$\theta_0 + 90°$	p_0

Figure 3.26 The general form of the effect of the Y gate on a pair of probabilities with direction

We can simulate a Y gate transformation on a single-qubit state with the following code:

```
state = [-1j*state[1], 1j*state[0]]
```

Figure 3.27 shows an example of the result of applying the Y gate on a concrete single-qubit state.

Out	Bin	Ampl	Dir	Mag	Ampl bar
0	0	0.30 − 0.17i	−30.3°	0.35	
1	1	−0.71 + 0.62i	138.9°	0.94	

$\xrightarrow{Y}$

Out	Bin	Ampl	Dir	Mag	Ampl bar
0	0	0.62 + 0.71i	48.9°	0.94	
1	1	0.17 + 0.30i	59.7°	0.35	

Figure 3.27 The effect of the Y gate on our example pair of amplitudes

3.2.3 The general form of a single-qubit gate

We were able to describe the effect of the X, Y, Z, H, P, and R_Z gates on the amplitudes of a qubit in plain language. We saw that they can move some probability from one outcome to the other, but the total probability of the outcomes is still 1.

They have another property in common: they are linear transformations. This means their effect can be defined by a two-by-two matrix that is used to recombine the amplitudes in a pair to obtain new ones:

$$\begin{bmatrix} a & b \\ c & d \end{bmatrix} \begin{bmatrix} z_0 \\ z_1 \end{bmatrix} = \begin{bmatrix} az_0 + bz_1 \\ cz_0 + dz_1 \end{bmatrix}$$

The recombination of amplitudes for a single-qubit state can be implemented with variations of the following code. This snippet simulates applying the Hadamard gate to a single-qubit state:

```
(a, b, c, d) = (1/sqrt(2), 1/sqrt(2), 1/sqrt(2), -1/sqrt(2))
state = [a*state[0] + b*state[1], c*state[0] + d*state[1]]
```

3.2 Changing amplitudes with single-qubit gates

Exercise 3.3

Find the values a, b, c and d for which the following is true for any pair of amplitudes z_0, z_1:

$$\begin{bmatrix} a & b \\ c & d \end{bmatrix} \begin{bmatrix} z_0 \\ z_1 \end{bmatrix} = \begin{bmatrix} z_0 \\ z_1 \end{bmatrix}$$

Figure 3.28 shows the two-by-two matrices corresponding to the gates discussed so far.

Gate	Matrix
X	$\begin{bmatrix} 0 & 1 \\ 1 & 0 \end{bmatrix}$
Y	$\begin{bmatrix} 0 & -i \\ i & 0 \end{bmatrix}$
Z	$\begin{bmatrix} 1 & 0 \\ 0 & -1 \end{bmatrix}$
H	$\frac{1}{\sqrt{2}} \begin{bmatrix} 1 & 1 \\ 1 & -1 \end{bmatrix}$
$P(\varphi)$	$\begin{bmatrix} 1 & 0 \\ 0 & \cos\varphi + i\sin\varphi \end{bmatrix}$
$R_Z(\theta)$	$\begin{bmatrix} \cos\frac{\theta}{2} - i\sin\frac{\theta}{2} & 0 \\ 0 & \cos\frac{\theta}{2} + i\sin\frac{\theta}{2} \end{bmatrix}$

Figure 3.28 Two-by-two matrix representations for the X, Y, Z, H, P, and R_Z gates

Exercise 3.4

Show that YX = –XY, ZX = –XZ, and ZY = –YZ.

3.2.4 More basic single-qubit gates

In this section we will introduce two more single-qubit gates, the R_X gate and the R_Y gate. These gates are not at easy to describe intuitively, so we will rely on their two-by-two matrix representation.

THE R_X GATE

For a given angle θ, the $R_X(\theta)$ gate is defined by the matrix

$$\begin{bmatrix} \cos\frac{\theta}{2} & -i\sin\frac{\theta}{2} \\ -i\sin\frac{\theta}{2} & \cos\frac{\theta}{2} \end{bmatrix}$$

Depending on the angle used, the R_X gate can change the magnitude and direction of both sides of an amplitude pair. Therefore, it is helpful to examine several examples of R_X gate applications. In the chapter code, you will find examples of R_X gate applications with different angles. Figure 3.29 shows an example of the result of applying a R_X gate with angle parameter $\pi/3$ on our example single-qubit state.

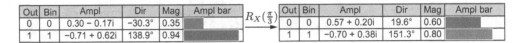

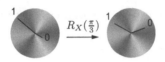

Figure 3.29 The effect of the $R_X(\pi/3)$ gate on our example pair of amplitudes

THE RY GATE

For a given angle θ, the $R_Y(\theta)$ gate is defined by the matrix

$$\begin{bmatrix} \cos\frac{\theta}{2} & -\sin\frac{\theta}{2} \\ \sin\frac{\theta}{2} & \cos\frac{\theta}{2} \end{bmatrix}$$

The R_Y gate may be hard to understand with pure intuition. When applied to the default state, the R_Y gate keeps the amplitudes real. You can think of it as a dial, effectively modeling a (biased) coin. There are several examples of R_Y-gate applications in the chapter code. Figure 3.30 shows an example of the result of applying the R_Y gate with angle parameter $\pi/3$ on our example single-qubit state.

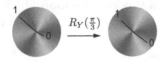

Figure 3.30 The effect of the $R_Y(\pi/3)$ gate on our example pair of amplitudes

> **Exercise 3.5**
> Check that rotations of the same type compose by adding rotation angles. For example, $R_Y(\theta_2)R_Y(\theta_1) = R_Y(\theta_1 + \theta_2)$.

> **Where do rotation names come from?**
>
> Rotations are standard in controlling the flight of an object, as they allow it to maneuver in the air and change its direction. Typically, these rotations are composed of three axes: roll (X), pitch (Y), and yaw (Z).
>
>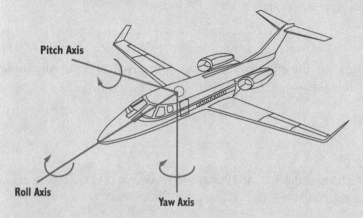
>
> **Rotations of a flying object**
>
> Roll is the rotation around the X, or longitudinal (front-to-back), axis. It is the movement of the object banking left or right.
>
> Pitch is the rotation around the Y, or lateral (side-to-side), axis. It is the movement of the object's front up or down.
>
> Yaw is the rotation around the Z, or vertical (up-and-down), axis. It is the movement of the object's nose from side to side.

3.2.5 Single-qubit gate inverses

Each quantum gate has an inverse, which reverses its effect on a pair of amplitudes. This is a general property of quantum system evolution, where any transformation can be reversed. Take the X gate, for example. This gate swaps the two amplitudes in a pair. Applying it again reverses the first swap, thus undoing its effect.

We use the power of -1 to represent the inverse of a gate, the same way we do with numbers. In the case of the X gate, $X^{-1} = X$.

We can verify this with code. First, let's apply an X gate to the default single-qubit state:

```
state = init_state()           ◁──┤ Creates a single-qubit
                                    default state
state = [state[1], state[0]]   ◁──┐ Applies an X gate
                                    to the state
print(state)
```

The output is a state where the amplitudes are swapped:

```
[0, 1]
```

If we apply another X gate, we get the initial amplitudes:

```
state = [state[1], state[0]]

print(state)
```

In the resulting state, the effect of the X gate is reversed, and the amplitudes are the same as in the initial state:

```
[1, 0]
```

> **Exercise 3.6**
> Use the definitions of the Y, Z, and H gates to prove that they are their own inverses.

Figure 3.31 shows the inverses of the basic single-qubit gates.

Gate	Inverse
X	X
Y	Y
Z	Z
H	H
$P(\phi)$	$P(-\phi)$
$R_X(\theta)$	$R_X(-\theta)$
$R_Y(\theta)$	$R_Y(-\theta)$
$R_Z(\theta)$	$R_Z(-\theta)$

Figure 3.31 Gate inverses

> **The general form of inverse gates**
> It can be proven that the inverse of a single-qubit gate defined by a two-by-two matrix
>
> $$U = \begin{bmatrix} a & b \\ c & d \end{bmatrix}$$

(continued)

is the gate corresponding to the matrix

$$\begin{bmatrix} \bar{a} & \bar{c} \\ \bar{b} & \bar{d} \end{bmatrix}$$

Recall that the bar above a complex number denotes its conjugate. This matrix is called the *adjoint* of U and is denoted by $U^\dagger$. This means $U^{-1} = U^\dagger$.

3.3 Simulating changing amplitudes with gates

We now know how to simulate several of the components of a single-qubit computation in figure 3.32 using simple Python code. In section 3.1, we discussed how in most quantum computers, the system's initial state is one where the probability of measuring 0 for every qubit is 100%. We defined the `init_state` function to create a list that represents the initial state of a single-qubit state.

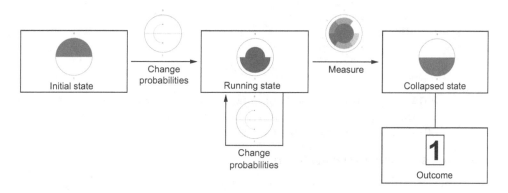

Figure 3.32 The steps of a single-qubit quantum computation, starting with the initial state and ending with a measurement

On a classical computer, we can also just write values to the list representing the state. We do need to check that the list represents a valid single-qubit state using the `prepare_state` function.

3.3.1 Printing and visualizing the state

We will use the following function to read and help visualize a quantum state.

> **Listing 3.4 Visualizing a quantum state with a state table**

```
def to_table(s, decimals=5):
    table = [
        [k, s[k], atan2(s[k].imag, s[k].real) / (2 * pi) * 360, abs(s[k]),
        abs(s[k]) ** 2] for k in range(len(s))]

    table_r = [[round(x, decimals) if isinstance(x, float) else round(
        x.real) + 1j * round(x.imag, decimals) if isinstance(x,complex) else
        x for x in table[k]] for k in range(len(table))]

    return table_r

def print_state(state, decimals=5):
    print(*to_table(state, decimals),sep='\n')
```

Creates nested lists with outcome, amplitude, direction, magnitude, and probability

Rounds the values (the default number of digits is five)

Creates a function that prints the state table for a given state

Let's initialize a single-qubit state and then visualize it:

```
state = init_state()
print_state(state)
```

The output is

```
[0, 1, 0.0, 1, 1]
[1, 0, 0.0, 0, 0]
```

> **NOTE** In the Jupyter notebooks that accompany each chapter, we most often use the `print_state_table` function to visualize quantum states. The output of this function includes the colored amplitude bars.

3.3.2 Transforming a single-qubit state

In a qubit-based quantum computer, we use quantum gates to change the amplitudes of the state. In the previous section, we simulated single-qubit gate transformations using short, gate-specific code snippets. In this section, we will define each gate in its general form so that we can use one function to simulate the application of any gate. This will make for a smoother transition to multi-qubit gate computations in the next chapter. Remember that the general mathematical form of a single-qubit gate is a two-by-two matrix:

$$\begin{bmatrix} a & b \\ c & d \end{bmatrix}$$

We can use nested lists to encode the four values of a gate:

```
gate = [[a, b], [c, d]]
```

3.3 Simulating changing amplitudes with gates

We can get the value of a with `gate[0][0]`, and so on.

The following listing defines several single-qubit gates that we will use to simulate state evolution in a real quantum computer.

Listing 3.5 Code implementations of basic single-qubit gates

```
x = [[0, 1], [1, 0]]

z = [[1, 0], [0, -1]]

def phase(theta):
    return [[1, 0], [0, complex(cos(theta), sin(theta))]]

h = [[1/sqrt(2), 1/sqrt(2)], [1/sqrt(2), -1/sqrt(2)]]

def rz(theta):
    return [[complex(cos(theta / 2), -sin(theta / 2)), 0],
            [0, complex(cos(theta / 2), sin(theta / 2))]]

y = [[0, complex(0, -1)], [complex(0, 1), 0]]

def rx(theta):
    return [[cos(theta/2), complex(0, -sin(theta/2))],
            [complex(0, -sin(theta/2)), cos(theta/2)]]

def ry(theta):
    return [[cos(theta/2), -sin(theta/2)], [sin(theta/2), cos(theta/2)]]
```

We also know that we can compute the amplitudes after applying a gate with the formula:

$$\begin{bmatrix} a & b \\ c & d \end{bmatrix} \begin{bmatrix} z_0 \\ z_1 \end{bmatrix} = \begin{bmatrix} az_0 + bz_1 \\ cz_0 + dz_1 \end{bmatrix}$$

In code, we will not use matrices to find the new amplitudes. Instead, we can compute the new amplitude for outcome 0 with

`gate[0][0]*state[0] + gate[0][1]*state[1]`

and the new amplitude for outcome 1 with

`gate[1][0]*state[0] + gate[1][1]*state[1]`

We will use the `transform` function shown in listing 3.6 to apply gates to a single-qubit state. When we pass the state to the `transform` function, we use the first element in the array as the 0 side of the pair and the second element as the 1 side of the pair. In later chapters, we will discuss quantum systems with more than one qubit and how to select the amplitude pairs depending on the target qubit of the gate.

Listing 3.6 Simulating applying gate transformations to a single-qubit gate

```
def transform(state, gate):
    assert(len(state) == 2)           ◁── Checks that the state has two values
    z0 = state[0]
    z1 = state[1]
    state[0] = gate[0][0]*z0 + gate[0][1]*z1   ◁── Finds the new value of the first amplitude
    state[1] = gate[1][0]*z0 + gate[1][1]*z1   ◁── Finds the new value of the second amplitude
```

3.3.3 Single-qubit circuits

A single-qubit *quantum circuit* is a sequence of one or more single-qubit quantum gates. The following is an example of initializing a single-qubit state, followed by a series of transformations to change the amplitudes of the state:

```
s = init_state()
transform(s, ry(2*pi/3))
transform(s, x)
transform(s, phase(pi/3))
transform(s, h)
```

We can write this sequence of gates as an expression: $HP(\pi/3)\ XR_Y(2\pi/3)$. Note that the gates are listed in the reverse order of application, with gates added to the left of the expression.

It is very common to visualize circuits using a circuit diagram. We represent a qubit as a horizontal line, or wire, and the gates applied to it by boxes on the line from left to right in the order of their application, as shown in figure 3.33.

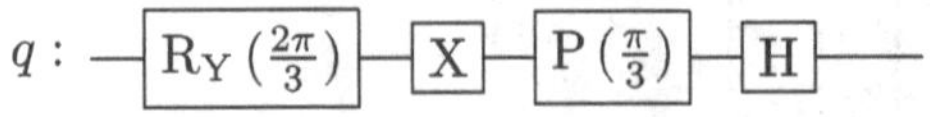

$q: \ —\boxed{R_Y\left(\tfrac{2\pi}{3}\right)}—\boxed{X}—\boxed{P\left(\tfrac{\pi}{3}\right)}—\boxed{H}—$

Figure 3.33 A circuit diagram representation of the gate sequence $HP(\pi/3)\} XR_Y(2\pi/3)$

Let's use the `print_state` function to look at the single-qubit state after these transformations:

```
print_state(s)

[0, (0.78915+0.30619j), 21.20602, 0.84647, 0.71651]
[1, (0.4356-0.30619j), -35.10391, 0.53244, 0.28349]
```

We can use a state table to display the single-qubit quantum state, as shown in figure 3.34.

Outcome	Binary	Amplitude	Direction	Magnitude	Amplitude bar	Probability	Probability bar
0	0	0.79 + 0.31i	21.2°	0.85		0.72	
1	1	0.44 − 0.31i	−35.1°	0.53		0.28	

Figure 3.34 The state table of a single-qubit state after the transformations in figure 3.33

3.4 Simulating measurement of single-qubit states

To get any information from a computation on a quantum computer, we need to perform a measurement. Therefore, in a quantum computation, a measurement is performed after the instructions to change the amplitudes have been applied. Quantum measurements are nondeterministic: given the same inputs, the output is not always the same.

Each possible outcome has a certain probability of occurring, and these probabilities must add up to 1. We call the probabilities of a set of possible outcomes a *probability distribution*. Measuring a single-qubit state is like tossing a biased coin.

Let's look at the state created in the previous example using the circuit in figure 3.35. Using our simulator, we get the following state:

```
[0, (0.78915+0.30619j), 21.20602, 0.84647, 0.71651]
[1, (0.4356-0.30619j), -35.10391, 0.53244, 0.28349]
```

We can see in the printed statements that the probability of outcome 0 is 0.71651, and the probability of outcome 1 is 0.28349.

$q:\ -\boxed{R_Y\left(\frac{2\pi}{3}\right)}-\boxed{X}-\boxed{P\left(\frac{\pi}{3}\right)}-\boxed{H}-$

Figure 3.35 Example single-qubit circuit

If we run this circuit on a real quantum device, we will repeat the computation multiple times. As we know, measurement is the last step for each execution, or run, of the computation. When a measurement is performed, the quantum state collapses, and one of the amplitudes becomes 1. The outcome corresponding to that amplitude is the measured outcome. Figure 3.36 illustrates repeated executions of the single-qubit circuit in figure 3.35. The visualization captures a measurement where the outcome is 1, but we can see in the recorded counts that previous measurements produced other outcomes.

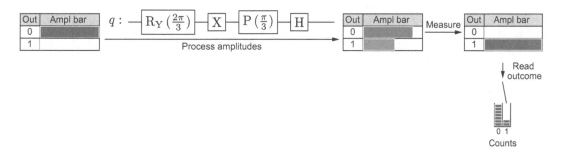

Figure 3.36 The steps of running the single-qubit circuit in figure 3.35, with counts of the outcomes from previous executions of the computation

We can use classical computers to simulate the nondeterminism of quantum measurement. When we simulate measurement with Python, we do not need to repeat the computation as we would on a quantum computer. Instead, we can just use the probabilities of outcomes to select samples. In our Python simulator, we can use the `choices` function from the `random` Python library, which takes the possible outcomes and the probabilities of each outcome and returns a list of samples. Now, let's simulate 10 measurements by getting 10 samples from the probability distribution determined by the state:

```
from random import choices
from collections import Counter

samples = choices(range(len(s)), [abs(s[k])**2 for k in range(len(s))], k=10)
print(samples)
```

Uses a list comprehension to find the respective probabilities

We get a list of the generated samples:

```
[0, 0, 0, 1, 0, 0, 1, 1, 0, 0]
```

Let's count the resulting samples:

```
for (k, v) in Counter(samples).items():
    print(str(k) + ' -> ' + str(v))

0 -> 7
1 -> 3
```

In figure 3.37, we visualize the last step of the computation (measurement) six times. This shows us what it might look like to perform six executions of the circuit on a quantum computer.

The resulting outcome frequency reflects the expected probabilities. If we take more samples, we expect the frequencies to get closer to the exact probabilities. Let's try 1,000 samples:

```
samples = choices(range(len(s)), [abs(s[k])**2 for k in range(len(s))], k=1000)

for (k, v) in Counter(samples).items():
    print(str(k) + ' -> ' + str(v))
```

The counts of the samples are

```
0 -> 726
1 -> 274
```

3.4 Simulating measurement of single-qubit states

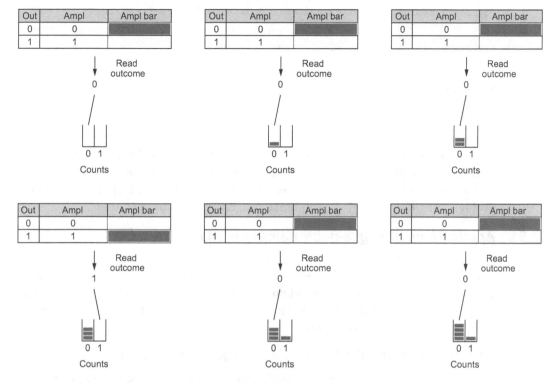

Figure 3.37 **Six measurements and the resulting outcome counts**

3.4.1 Encoding the uniform distribution in a single-qubit quantum state

The uniform distribution with two outcomes is the mathematical version of a fair coin, where both outcomes have equal probability. Let's use our simulator to create a single-qubit state with equal outcome probabilities. With a single qubit in its initial state, all we need to do is apply one of the following gates: H, $R_Y(\pi/2)$, $R_X(\pi/2)$.

For example, let's initialize a single-qubit state and apply a Hadamard gate:

```
state = init_state()

transform(state, h)

print_state(state)
```

We can see that the amplitudes of the state are equal, and therefore we know the probabilities will be equal:

```
[0, '0', 0.70711, 0.0, 0.70711, 0.5]
[1, '1', 0.70711, 0.0, 0.70711, 0.5]
```

Let's take 10 samples of this state:

```
samples = choices(range(len(state)), [abs(state[k])**2 for k in
    range(len(state))], k=10)

for (k, v) in Counter(samples).items():
    print(str(k) + ' -> ' + str(v))
```

The counts of the samples are

```
0 -> 4
1 -> 6
```

When running on real quantum hardware, we have to decide how many times to repeat the computation so that we can get the information we want from the frequency of outcomes. This number depends on several factors, including the type of problem, the desired level of confidence, and error rates, among others.

3.5 Applications of single-qubit computations

A single-qubit state has just two amplitudes, so quantum parallelism does not offer any benefit over classical implementations of the same computations. Nonetheless, a single qubit still offers an advantage when it comes to using quantum measurement for sampling from probability distributions with two outcomes. Let's look at a few use cases related to such distributions.

3.5.1 Encoding a Bernoulli distribution in a single-qubit quantum state

The *Bernoulli distribution* models the probability of an event with only two possible outcomes (a binary event). A Bernoulli distribution can be described by a single parameter p, where the probability of getting one outcome is p and the other is $1 - p$. For example, if we flip a fair coin, the probability of getting heads is 0.5 and the probability of getting tails is 0.5. In this example, the coin flip follows a Bernoulli distribution with $p = 0.5$. If we flip a biased coin, the parameter p will be a different value. Figure 3.38 shows a vertical bar graph representation of the Bernoulli distribution for $p = 0.8$.

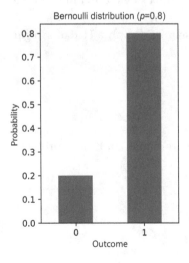

Figure 3.38 The Bernoulli distribution for $p = 0.8$

3.5 Applications of single-qubit computations

You can think of a Bernoulli distribution as the mathematical version of a coin, biased or not. Applying $R_Y(\theta)$ for an angle θ to the default qubit state results in a state with amplitudes $\cos \theta/2$ and $\sin \theta/2$. If we choose our angle θ such that $\cos^2 \theta/2 = p$ and therefore $\sin^2 \theta/2 = 1 - p$, the probabilities of the outcomes match those of the desired Bernoulli distribution. A solution is $\theta = 2\arccos(\sqrt{p})$.

Let's simulate encoding the Bernoulli distribution for $p = 0.7$:

```
from math import acos

p = 0.7
theta = 2*acos(sqrt(p))      ◁── Finds θ according to the value of p

s = init_state()
transform(s, ry(theta))       ◁── Applies the R_Y(θ) gate

print_state(s)
```

The resulting state is

```
[0, '0', 0.83666, 0.0, 0.83666, 0.7]
[1, '1', 0.54772, 0.0, 0.54772, 0.3]
```

In these printed results, we see that the probability of outcome 0 is 0.7.

3.5.2 Encoding a number with a single qubit

Given a nonnegative real number $x < 1{,}000$, how can we encode it using a single qubit? In this chapter, we will look at two options:

- The magnitude of one of the amplitudes (e.g., the magnitude of the amplitude corresponding to outcome 0)
- The angle (or phase) of one of the amplitudes (e.g., the angle of the amplitude corresponding to outcome 0)

ENCODING A NUMBER AS THE MAGNITUDE OF A (REAL) AMPLITUDE

Say we want to encode the value $x = 273.5$. We know that the magnitude of an amplitude must be between 0 and 1, so we adjust our value to fit within this range: $x/1000 = 0.2735$. We want to create a single-qubit state where the magnitude of one of the outcomes is 0.2735.

We start with a single qubit in its initial state, where the amplitudes of the state are $z_0 = 1$ and $z_1 = 0$. If we apply an $R_Y(\theta)$ gate to a single-qubit state in its initial state, we know the resulting amplitudes will be

$$\begin{bmatrix} \cos \frac{\theta}{2} & -\sin \frac{\theta}{2} \\ \sin \frac{\theta}{2} & \cos \frac{\theta}{2} \end{bmatrix} \begin{bmatrix} 1 \\ 0 \end{bmatrix} = \begin{bmatrix} \cos \frac{\theta}{2} \\ \sin \frac{\theta}{2} \end{bmatrix}$$

The resulting amplitude corresponding to outcome 0 will be $z_0 = \cos\theta/2$. The magnitude of z_0 will be $|z_0| = \sqrt{\cos^2\frac{\theta}{2}} = \left|\cos\frac{\theta}{2}\right|$. Using this knowledge, we can define the angle θ according to the value we would like to encode. In this case, we define θ as $\theta = 2 \arccos(0.2735)$.

The following code creates a single-qubit state and encodes the value $x = 273.5$ in the magnitude of the amplitude corresponding to outcome 0:

```
x = 273.5
theta = 2*acos(x/1000)
assert is_close(cos(theta/2), x/1000)

state = init_state()
transform(state, ry(theta))

print_state(state)
```

- `theta = 2*acos(x/1000)` — Finds θ according to the value of x
- `assert is_close(...)` — Checks that θ is close the value to be encoded
- `transform(state, ry(theta))` — Applies the $R_Y(\theta)$ gate

The printed state table is as follows:

```
[0, '0', 0.2735, 0.0, 0.2735, 0.0748]
[1, '1', 0.96187, 0.0, 0.96187, 0.9252]
```

The resulting state table is shown in figure 3.39. As we can see, the magnitude of the amplitude of outcome 0 reflects the encoded value.

Outcome	Binary	Amplitude	Direction	Magnitude	Amplitude bar	Probability	Probability bar
0	0	0.27	0.0°	0.27	▪	0.07	▪
1	1	0.96	0.0°	0.96	▬	0.93	▬

Figure 3.39 The state table after encoding the value $x = 273.5$ in a single-qubit state in the magnitude of outcome 0

ENCODING A NUMBER IN THE ANGLE OF AN AMPLITUDE

To encode a value in the angle, or phase, of an amplitude, we start with a single-qubit state in its initial state. We know that when we apply a Hadamard gate to an initial single-qubit state, the amplitudes of the state will change as follows:

$$\begin{bmatrix} \frac{1}{\sqrt{2}} & \frac{1}{\sqrt{2}} \\ \frac{1}{\sqrt{2}} & -\frac{1}{\sqrt{2}} \end{bmatrix} \begin{bmatrix} 1 \\ 0 \end{bmatrix} = \begin{bmatrix} \frac{1}{\sqrt{2}} \\ \frac{1}{\sqrt{2}} \end{bmatrix}$$

If we apply a phase gate next, the resulting amplitudes will be

$$\begin{bmatrix} 1 & 0 \\ 0 & \cos\varphi + i\sin\varphi \end{bmatrix} \begin{bmatrix} \frac{1}{\sqrt{2}} \\ \frac{1}{\sqrt{2}} \end{bmatrix} = \begin{bmatrix} \frac{1}{\sqrt{2}} \\ \frac{1}{\sqrt{2}}\cos\varphi + i\frac{1}{\sqrt{2}}\sin\varphi \end{bmatrix}$$

3.5 Applications of single-qubit computations

If we apply a phase gate with angle parameter $\varphi = \pi v$, where $0 \leq v < 0.5$, the direction (or phase) of the amplitude corresponding to the outcome 1 (θ_1) will also be πv.

If we want to encode the value $x = 273.5$ in the phase of the amplitude corresponding to outcome 1, we will use $v = x/1000$. We can use the Hadamard gate followed by a phase gate with the angle πv: $P(\pi x/1000) H$.

The following code implements this example:

```
x = 273.5
theta = pi*x/1000          ◀──┤ Finds θ according
                                 to the value of x

state = init_state()
transform(state, h)            │ Applies an H gate followed
transform(state, phase(theta)) │ by a P(θ) rotation

print_state(state)
```

The printed state table is

```
[0, '0', 0.70711, 0.0, 0.70711, 0.5]
[1, '1', (0.46176+0.53552j), 49.23, 0.70711, 0.5]
```

Let's check that θ_1 in the resulting state reflects our encoded value. We know that $\theta_1 = \pi x/1000$, so we need to find θ_1 and then solve for x:

```
direction_1 = atan2(state[1].imag, state[1].real)   ◀── Gets θ₁
round(direction_1/pi*1000, 1)                       ◀──┤ Solves for x
```

The output is

```
273.5
```

The resulting state table is shown in figure 3.40. Note that the phase of amplitude 1 in our resulting state is $\theta_1 = \pi (x/1000)$, so we will need to adjust for those factors to get our encoded value.

Outcome	Binary	Amplitude	Direction	Magnitude	Amplitude bar	Probability	Probability bar
0	0	0.71	0.0°	0.71		0.50	
1	1	0.46 + 0.54i	49.2°	0.71		0.50	

Figure 3.40 The state table after encoding the value x = 273.5 in a single-qubit state in the phase of the amplitude corresponding to outcome 1

Summary

- Single-qubit computations are the simplest form of quantum computing. They are comparable to tossing a coin and have two possible outcomes.
- You can simulate a one-qubit computation using a two-element list of complex numbers. This list is initialized at the start and then undergoes simple transformations (known as single-qubit gates).
- The most common single-qubit gates are X, Y, Z, P, H, and rotational gates (denoted as R_X, R_Y, and R_Z). These rotational gates require an angle parameter.
- You can visualize the state of a single-qubit system with state tables that include amplitudes and other useful derived properties (directions, magnitudes, probabilities).
- Sequences of gates are called quantum circuits.
- Quantum computations are nondeterministic. When repeated, they yield different outcomes with distributions that reflect the state of the quantum system.
- The outcomes of a repeated quantum computation are aggregated into counts, which compose the typical output of a quantum computer.
- Single-qubit computations can be used to generate truly random numbers from Bernoulli distributions.

Quantum state and circuits: Beyond one qubit

This chapter covers

- Understanding multi-qubit quantum states (using state tables)
- Using quantum gates to change amplitudes of multi-qubit states
- Using quantum circuits and registers to model quantum computations with Python
- Examples of preparing useful quantum states (encoding uniform and binomial distributions, Bell states)

In chapter 3, we introduced key concepts such as quantum states and quantum gates in a single-qubit context. To solve consequential problems using a quantum computer, we usually require more than one qubit.

In this chapter, we will explore methods to represent multiple qubits programmatically and visually, as we did for one qubit in chapter 3. We will learn how the state of a multi-qubit system evolves via quantum transformations. We will then use Python to create a quantum computing simulator that works with any number of qubits. Finally, we will look at a couple of examples of useful quantum computations using this simulator. The concept map in figure 4.1 illustrates the quantum computing concepts covered in this chapter and how these concepts relate to and build on each other.

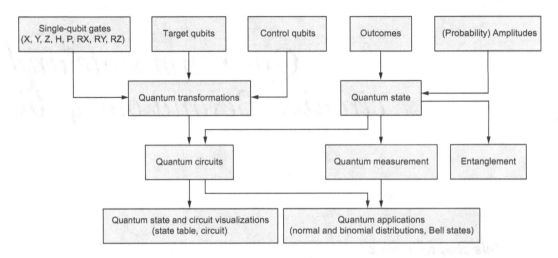

Figure 4.1 A dependency diagram of concepts introduced in this chapter

4.1 Computing with more than one qubit

The power of quantum computing is fully realized when we use multiple qubits together. By using more than one qubit, we can take advantage of the unique properties of quantum computers and perform more intricate computations. In this chapter, we will explore the effects of quantum phenomena such as quantum measurement and *parallelism* and review examples to help illustrate these concepts. Before diving into those topics, let's first discuss the fundamental components involved in a quantum computation, as we did in chapter 3.

4.1.1 Measurement counts

When running a quantum computation, the only output is a *measurement result*. A measurement result is a binary string with a digit for each measured qubit. In this book we will assume we are measuring all qubits unless specified otherwise. We repeat the same computation several times and analyze the frequencies of the outcomes, often referred to as *counts*. This allows us to extract relevant information from a quantum state and find a solution for a given problem.

The way we interpret measurement counts depends on the problem. In chapter 1, we discussed three main patterns for quantum computations:

1. Sampling from probability distributions
2. Searching for specific outcomes
3. Estimating the probability of specific outcomes

Let's start with an example of the first pattern.

4.1.2 Sampling from a probability distribution

Each repetition of a quantum computation produces one nondeterministic outcome. We can use quantum measurements to get random samples from a probability distribution. Measurement is useful for sampling from distributions that are hard to handle using classical methods. We know that the frequencies, or counts, of each outcome reflect the probabilities determined by the amplitudes of the state. Therefore, we need to change the amplitudes of the state to match the probability distribution we would like to sample from.

For example, there are many applications for random sampling from a *uniform distribution*. In a uniform distribution, each value in a given set has an equal probability of being selected. Samples from a uniform distribution are used for random number generation or to generate random inputs for simulations and modeling. Quantum computations produce randomly generated numbers, unlike the pseudorandom numbers generated by classical computing.

In this chapter, we show how to encode a uniform distribution and other useful distributions in a quantum system with any number of qubits. Once we know how to do that, we can perform truly random sampling from a uniform distribution on a quantum computer.

4.1.3 Understanding quantum computations with a simple Python simulator

To get a better understanding of how a quantum state evolves, we can use simulators that run on classical computers. These simulators encode the fundamental principles of quantum computing, making them useful for preparing and testing code intended to run on a real quantum computer.

To simulate the application of an elementary quantum operation, a classical computer has to sequentially process updates to the state (typically using a `for` loop). Every additional qubit doubles the processing power needed to complete the simulation. Therefore, simulating quantum computations on a classical computer can be very computationally expensive. There are approaches to help make the process more efficient, but for the purpose of understanding, we won't focus on those methods in our Python simulator. On the other hand, a simulator allows us to both inspect and directly modify the state, unlike on a quantum computer.

In chapter 3, we looked at how to simulate the stages of a single-qubit quantum computation using simple Python code. The components of the computation are the same for a single qubit and multiple qubits. In this chapter, we will write the code for simulating quantum computations with any number of qubits; we will use this code throughout the rest of the book. The first thing to know is how to represent the state of a multi-qubit system in Python.

4.2 A quantum state is a list of complex numbers

As we learned, we can describe the state of a single-qubit system with two complex numbers, one for each of the two possible outcomes. The state of a multi-qubit system also consists of a complex number for each possible outcome. We will start by exploring two-qubit states. Then we will expand our understanding to states with any number of qubits. We will continue to use state tables to visualize these multi-qubit states and Python lists to encode quantum states in our simulator.

4.2.1 Two-qubit states

Each qubit represents a binary digit in a computational outcome. Therefore, a quantum system with two qubits has four possible measurement outcomes: 0, 1, 2, and 3, or '00', '01', '10', and '11' in binary form. Similar to single-qubit states, we represent the state of two qubits with a list of four complex numbers (one for each outcome), which is often called the *state vector*. For the list to be a valid quantum state, the squared magnitudes of the four complex numbers must add to 1.

THE GENERAL FORM OF A TWO-QUBIT STATE

Remember that we can define the general form of a single-qubit state with probabilities and directions. Similarly, we can define a two-qubit state table with four probabilities (p_0, p_1, p_2, p_3) that add to 1 and any four angles (θ_0, θ_1, θ_2, θ_3) defining the direction for each of them. We can derive the amplitudes (complex numbers) from the direction and probability associated to each outcome the same way we did in chapter 3. We are given the direction, and we know the magnitude of the corresponding amplitude will be the square root of the probability. With this information, we can express the polar form of the amplitude corresponding to an outcome k (with $0 \leq k < 4$) as $z_k = \sqrt{p_k}(\cos \theta_k + i \sin \theta_k)$. For example, the amplitude corresponding to outcome 0 will be $z_0 = \sqrt{p_0}(\cos \theta_0 + i \sin \theta_0)$.

ENCODING A TWO-QUBIT STATE WITH A LIST OF COMPLEX NUMBERS

Again, a two-qubit quantum state can be represented as a list of four complex numbers, where the list index of an amplitude is the corresponding outcome. We can encode the general form of a two-qubit state, as shown in figure 4.2, using the following Python list:

```
from math import sqrt, cos, sin

[p0, p1, p2, p3] = [1, 0, 0, 0]
[theta0, theta1, theta2, theta3] = [0, 0, 0, 0]

state = [sqrt(p0) * (cos(theta0) + 1j * sin(theta0)),
         sqrt(p1) * (cos(theta1) + 1j * sin(theta1)),
         sqrt(p2) * (cos(theta2) + 1j * sin(theta2)),
         sqrt(p3) * (cos(theta3) + 1j * sin(theta3))]
```

4.2 A quantum state is a list of complex numbers

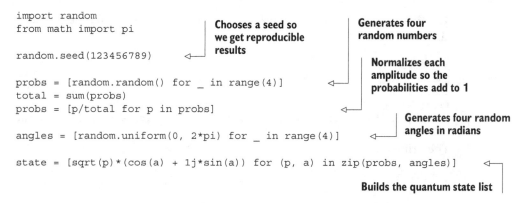

Figure 4.2 The general form of a two-qubit state

We can use the built-in `random` package in Python to generate example probabilities and directions:

```
import random
from math import pi                    Chooses a seed so          Generates four
                                       we get reproducible        random numbers
random.seed(123456789)                 results
                                                                  Normalizes each
probs = [random.random() for _ in range(4)]                       amplitude so the
total = sum(probs)                                                probabilities add to 1
probs = [p/total for p in probs]

                                                                  Generates four random
angles = [random.uniform(0, 2*pi) for _ in range(4)]              angles in radians

state = [sqrt(p)*(cos(a) + 1j*sin(a)) for (p, a) in zip(probs, angles)]

                                                                  Builds the quantum state list
```

Figure 4.3 shows the full state table for a quantum state generated with this code.

Outcome	Binary	Amplitude	Direction	Magnitude	Amplitude bar	Probability	Probability bar
0	00	0.17 − 0.43i	−67.8°	0.46		0.21	
1	01	−0.34 + 0.26i	143.0°	0.42		0.18	
2	10	0.53 − 0.22i	−22.6°	0.57		0.33	
3	11	−0.20 − 0.49i	−111.9°	0.53		0.28	

Figure 4.3 The state table for a random two-qubit quantum state

PRODUCT STATES: COMPOSING A STATE FROM TWO INDEPENDENT SINGLE-QUBIT STATES

In earlier chapters, we talked about imagining a single qubit system as a (biased) coin. Now, consider tossing two biased coins at the same time. After tossing the two coins, there are four possible results: heads-heads, heads-tails, tails-heads, or tails-tails. This is similar to composing a two-qubit quantum state from two single-qubit quantum states, as we will see in the following example.

Figure 4.4 shows two single-qubit states in general form. Using probabilities with direction is the same as using the polar form for the amplitudes of a quantum state.

Figure 4.4 State tables for two single-qubit states

First state

Outcome	Direction	Probability
0	θ_0	p
1	θ_1	$1-p$

Second state

Outcome	Direction	Probability
0	φ_0	q
1	φ_1	$1-q$

Note that we can use the shortcut function introduced in chapter 3:

```
def cis(theta):
    return cos(theta) + 1j*sin(theta)
```

The first state has probability $p = 0.75$ for outcome 0 and amplitude directions $\theta_0 = 0°$ and $\theta_1 = 60°$:

```
p = 0.75
theta0 = 0
theta1 = 60/(180/pi)                                           ◁── Converts to radians
first_state = [sqrt(p)*cis(theta0), sqrt(1-p)*cis(theta1)]
print([round(amp.real, 5)+1j*round(amp.imag, 5) for amp in first_state])
```

The printed output is

```
[(0.86603+0j), (0.25+0.43301j)]
```

The second state has $q = 0.5$ as the probability for outcome 0 and amplitude directions $\varphi_0 = 0°$ and $\varphi_1 = -120°$:

```
q = 0.5
phi0 = 0
phi1 = -120/(180/pi)
second_state = [sqrt(q)*cis(phi0), sqrt(1-q)*cis(phi1)]
print([round(amp.real, 5)+1j*round(amp.imag, 5) for amp in second_state])
```

The printed output is

```
[(0.70711+0j), (-0.35355-0.61237j)]
```

If we create a product two-qubit state from these two single-qubit states, the new amplitudes will be all the possible products of the two pairs of amplitudes.

> **Product of two complex numbers in polar form**
> When multiplying complex numbers in polar form, we multiply the magnitudes and add the directions of the two numbers:
>
> $$r_0(\cos\theta_0 + i\sin\theta_0)r_1(\cos\theta_1 + i\sin\theta_1) = r_0 r_1(\cos(\theta_0 + \theta_1) + i\sin(\theta_0 + \theta_1))$$

4.2 A quantum state is a list of complex numbers

The product of two amplitudes with directions θ and φ will have the direction $\theta + \varphi$. Figure 4.5 shows the general form of the combined state.

Outcome	Binary	Direction	Probability
0	00	$\theta_0 + \varphi_0$	pq
1	01	$\theta_0 + \varphi_1$	$p(1-q)$
2	10	$\theta_1 + \varphi_0$	$(1-p)q$
3	11	$\theta_1 + \varphi_1$	$(1-p)(1-q)$

Figure 4.5 State table for the product state of the two single-qubit states in figure 4.4

Let's create a two-qubit state from the two single-qubit states:

```
new_state = [first_state[0]*second_state[0], first_state[0]*second_state[1],
             first_state[1]*second_state[0], first_state[1]*second_state[1]]
print([round(amp.real, 5)+1j*round(amp.imag, 5) for amp in new_state])
```

The printed output is

```
[(0.61237+0j), (-0.30619-0.53033j), (0.17678+0.30619j), (0.17678-0.30619j)]
```

If we write the combined state using the definitions in figure 4.4, we get the same result:

```
new_state = [sqrt(p*q)*cis(theta0 + phi0), sqrt(p*(1-q))*cis(theta0 + phi1),
             sqrt((1-p)*q)*cis(theta1 + phi0), sqrt((1-p)*(1-q))*cis(theta1
    + phi1)]
print([round(amp.real, 5)+1j*round(amp.imag, 5) for amp in new_state])
```

The printed output is

```
[(0.61237+0j), (-0.30619-0.53033j), (0.17678+0.30619j), (0.17678-0.30619j)]
```

Not all two-qubit states are product states, where the measurement outcomes of each qubit are independent. To unlock the advantages of quantum computing and benefit from its unique features, we must use nonproduct states, where the two qubits become *entangled*. We can think of two independent coins as a product two-qubit state, and two dependent coins as a nonproduct state consisting of two entangled qubits, as visualized in figure 4.6.

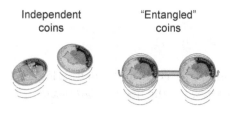

Figure 4.6 We can think of two coins with independent bias as a product state and two dependent coins as a nonproduct state.

> **Quantum entanglement**
>
> Quantum entanglement is a physical phenomenon that occurs when qubits or particles such as photons, electrons, or atoms become linked together so that the quantum state of each particle cannot be described independently of the others, even when the particles are separated by large distances. This means the particles remain connected even when they are separated spatially and can have an (apparently) instantaneous influence on each other.
>
> The *Bell states*, the topic of the next section, are the perfect example of how two qubits can be entangled: their measurement values are linked. Entanglement is an incredible phenomenon, but it comes at a cost in terms of processing power and system coherence. Without entanglement, we would not be able to do any meaningful quantum computing. To summarize, entanglement is essential in quantum computing, but it isn't always efficient.

EXAMPLES OF NONPRODUCT STATES: BELL STATES

Let's look at computations where only the two outcomes with matching digits ('00' and '11') are possible and have equal probability. This means $p_1 = p_2 = 0$ and $p_0 = p_3 = 0.5$. This is similar to tossing two coins at the same time and getting the same result (two heads or two tails) with an equal chance of either outcome. Later in the chapter, we will show how to build this state, but for now, we will focus on its structure.

We can prove that such a state cannot be a product of two single-qubit states. Let's take two single-qubit states in general form: one with probability p for outcome 0 and one with probability q for outcome 0. If we composed a two-qubit state from these single-qubit states, the new state would have the following probabilities:

$$p_0 = pq$$
$$p_1 = p(1-q)$$
$$p_2 = (1-p)q$$
$$p_3 = (1-p)(1-q)$$

For the outcomes '01' and '10' to have probability 0 ($p_1 = p_2 = 0$), p and q must have the same value, 0 or 1. If $p = 0$ and $q = 0$, then $p_0 = 0$ and $p_3 = 1$. If $p = 1$ and $q = 1$, then $p_0 = 1$ and $p_3 = 0$. Neither of these cases satisfies the requirement that $p_0 = p_3 = 0.5$.

The following two-qubit quantum states have the properties we are looking for:

```
bell_state1 = [sqrt(0.5), 0.0, 0.0, sqrt(0.5)]

bell_state2 = [sqrt(0.5), 0.0, 0.0, -sqrt(0.5)]
```

We see that p_1 and p_2 are 0 and that p_0 and p_3 are equal and sum to 1. Figure 4.7 shows the state tables of these states. They are known as the first two *Bell states*.

4.2 A quantum state is a list of complex numbers

Outcome	Binary	Amplitude	Direction	Magnitude	Amplitude bar	Probability	Probability bar
0	00	0.71	0.0°	0.71		0.50	
1	01	0.00		0.00		0.00	
2	10	0.00		0.00		0.00	
3	11	0.71	0.0°	0.71		0.50	

Outcome	Binary	Amplitude	Direction	Magnitude	Amplitude bar	Probability	Probability bar
0	00	0.71	0.0°	0.71		0.50	
1	01	0.00		0.00		0.00	
2	10	0.00		0.00		0.00	
3	11	−0.71	180.0°	0.71		0.50	

Figure 4.7 State tables for the first two Bell states

Similarly, the following two states also have only two possible outcomes with equal probabilities ('01' and '10'):

```
bell_state3 = [0.0, sqrt(0.5), sqrt(0.5), 0.0]

bell_state4 = [0.0, sqrt(0.5), -sqrt(0.5), 0.0]
```

They are the last two Bell states, shown in figure 4.8.

Outcome	Binary	Amplitude	Direction	Magnitude	Amplitude bar	Probability	Probability bar
0	00	0.00		0.00		0.00	
1	01	0.71	0.0°	0.71		0.50	
2	10	0.71	0.0°	0.71		0.50	
3	11	0.00		0.00		0.00	

Outcome	Binary	Amplitude	Direction	Magnitude	Amplitude bar	Probability	Probability bar
0	00	0.00		0.00		0.00	
1	01	0.71	0.0°	0.71		0.50	
2	10	−0.71	180.0°	0.71		0.50	
3	11	0.00		0.00		0.00	

Figure 4.8 State tables for the last two Bell states

> **Exercise 4.1**
>
> The famous mathematician John von Neumann proposed a method for getting fair results by tossing a biased coin. The solution is succinctly described like this:
>
> 1. Toss the coin twice.
> 2. If the results match (HH or TT), start over, forgetting both results.
> 3. If the results differ (HT or TH), use the first result, forgetting the second.
>
> Which Bell state offers a quantum solution to von Neumann's problem?

4.2.2 Multi-qubit states

Now we can expand to quantum states with any number of qubits. A quantum system with n qubits will have n binary digits in a measurement outcome. We know that there are 2^n binary strings of length n. This means there are 2^n possible outcomes when running a computation using n qubits. The system's state is represented by a complex number for each possible outcome.

THE GENERAL FORM OF A MULTI-QUBIT STATE

For n qubits, we can express each amplitude as $z_k = a_k + ib_k$, where a_k and b_k are real numbers, and k is the corresponding outcome, where $0 \leq k < 2^n$. Figure 4.9 shows a compact, general state table with these amplitudes. Note that in many cases it is easier to define the state by specifying probabilities and directions for the outcomes, as shown in figure 4.10.

Outcome	Amplitude
k	$a_k + ib_k$

Figure 4.9 The amplitudes of an *n*-qubit quantum state with outcomes $0 \leq k < 2^n$

Outcome	Direction	Probability
k	θ_k	p_k

Figure 4.10 The probabilities and directions of a quantum state with *n* qubits with outcomes $0 \leq k < 2^n$

ENCODING A MULTI-QUBIT STATE WITH A LIST OF COMPLEX NUMBERS

A list or array of 2^n complex numbers is the simplest and often the most efficient way to describe a quantum state. The list's indices match the integer representation of the outcome. For a list of complex numbers to be a valid quantum state, it must have a length that is a power of 2, and the sum of the squares of the magnitudes must equal 1.

Note that we cannot directly set the state of a quantum system when running on real quantum hardware. However, in a simulator, we can directly update the amplitudes in a list. For example, let's define an example state with the following eight complex numbers:

4.2 A quantum state is a list of complex numbers

```
amplitude_list = [(0.09858+0.03637j),
                  (0.07478+0.06912j),
                  (0.04852+0.10526j),
                  (0.00641+0.16322j),
                  (-0.12895+0.34953j),
                  (0.58403-0.6318j),
                  (0.18795-0.08665j),
                  (0.12867-0.00506j)]
```

In our simulator, we allow setting amplitudes directly after validating the constraints for a quantum state. This function, prepare_state, is defined in the following listing.

> **Listing 4.1 Function to check whether a list is a valid quantum state**

```
from math import log2, ceil, floor
from util import is_close

def is_power_of_two(m):
    return ceil(log2(m)) == floor(log2(m))

def prepare_state(*a):
    state = [a[k] for k in range(len(a))]
    assert(is_power_of_two(len(state)))          ◁— Checks that the length of the list is a power of 2
    assert (is_close(sum([abs(state[k]) ** 2 for k in range(len(state))]),
                     1.0))                        ◁— Checks that the squared magnitudes add to 1
    return state                                  ◁— If the conditions are met, we return the state.
```

Let's check that the state we defined is a valid quantum state:

```
state = prepare_state(*amplitude_list)
```

We will use this state as an example throughout this section.

BUILDING STATE TABLES WITH PYTHON LIST COMPREHENSIONS

Let's look at the general form of a quantum state with n qubits shown in figure 4.11. We will call figure 4.11 a *table comprehension*, referencing the fact that we can express the same values in Python using the following list comprehension:

```
print([[k, state[k]] for k in range(len(state))])
```

Outcome	Amplitude
k	$a_k + ib_k$

Figure 4.11 The amplitudes of an *n*-qubit quantum state with outcomes $0 \leq k < 2^n$

The printed output is

```
[[0, (0.09858+0.03637j)],
 [1, (0.07478+0.06912j)],
 [2, (0.04852+0.10526j)],
```

```
    [3, (0.00641+0.16322j)],
    [4, (-0.12895+0.34953j)],
    [5, (0.58403-0.6318j)],
    [6, (0.18795-0.08665j)],
    [7, (0.12867-0.00506j)]]
```

As we saw with single-qubit states, we can go from the amplitude form in figure 4.11 ($z_k = a_k + ib_k$) to probabilities (p_k) and directions (θ_k) using the following formulas:

$$p_k = |z_k|^2 = a_k^2 + b_k^2$$

$$\theta_k = \text{atan2}(b_k, a_k)\frac{180}{\pi}$$

Note that because atan2 returns values in the interval [−π, π], the direction in degrees will be in the interval [−180°, 180°]. We can also express this representation as a table comprehension, as shown in figure 4.12.

Outcome	Amplitude	Direction	Magnitude	Probability
k	$a_k + ib_k$	$\text{atan2}(b_k, a_k)\frac{180}{\pi}$	$\sqrt{a_k^2 + b_k^2}$	$a_k^2 + b_k^2$

Figure 4.12 Table comprehension for a quantum state with *n* qubits with outcomes $0 \le k < 2^n$

In Python, we can use the following list comprehension to add probabilities and directions, derived from amplitudes:

```
from math import atan2

table1 = [
    [
        k,
        round(atan2(state[k].imag, state[k].real) / (2 * pi) * 360, 5),
        round(abs(state[k]) ** 2, 5)
    ]
    for k in range(len(state))
]

for row in table1:
    print(row)
```

The printed output shows each outcome with the magnitude and direction of the corresponding amplitude:

```
[0, 20.25098, 0.01104]
[1, 42.74755, 0.01037]
[2, 65.25248, 0.01343]
```

```
[3, 87.75103, 0.02668]
[4, 110.25023, 0.1388]
[5, -47.25, 0.74026]
[6, -24.75097, 0.04283]
[7, -2.25202, 0.01658]
```

We can build an expanded version of the state table that includes the direction and magnitude of amplitudes, as well as the probability of the outcomes:

```
expanded_table = [
    [
        k,
        state[k],
        round(atan2(state[k].imag, state[k].real) / (2 * pi) * 360, 5),
        round(abs(state[k]), 5),
        round(abs(state[k]) ** 2, 5)
    ]
    for k in range(len(state))
]

for row in expanded_table:
    print(row)
```

The printed output shows each outcome and the corresponding amplitude, magnitude, direction, and probability:

```
[0, (0.09858+0.03637j), 20.25098, 0.10508, 0.01104]
[1, (0.07478+0.06912j), 42.74755, 0.10183, 0.01037]
[2, (0.04852+0.10526j), 65.25248, 0.1159, 0.01343]
[3, (0.00641+0.16322j), 87.75103, 0.16335, 0.02668]
[4, (-0.12895+0.34953j), 110.25023, 0.37256, 0.1388]
[5, (0.58403-0.6318j), -47.25, 0.86038, 0.74026]
[6, (0.18795-0.08665j), -24.75097, 0.20696, 0.04283]
[7, (0.12867-0.00506j), -2.25202, 0.12877, 0.01658]
```

Conversely, starting with probabilities and directions, we can get the amplitudes of the state using the following formulas:

$$a_k = \sqrt{p_k} \cos \theta_k, \, b_k = \sqrt{p_k} \sin \theta_k$$
$$z_k = a_k + ib_k$$

In Python, we can use the following list comprehension to get amplitudes from directions and probabilities:

```
table2 = [
    [
        row[0],
        (
            round(sqrt(row[2]) * cos(row[1] / (180 / pi)), 5) +
            round(sqrt(row[2]) * sin(row[1] / (180 / pi)), 5) * 1j
```

)
        ]
        for row in table1
]

for row in table2:
    print(row)
```

The printed output shows each outcome and the corresponding amplitude:

```
[0, (0.09858+0.03637j)]
[1, (0.07478+0.06912j)]
[2, (0.04851+0.10524j)]
[3, (0.00641+0.16321j)]
[4, (-0.12895+0.34953j)]
[5, (0.58403-0.6318j)]
[6, (0.18794-0.08665j)]
[7, (0.12866-0.00506j)]
```

If we use probabilities and directions, the expanded table is shown in figure 4.13.

Outcome	Amplitude	Direction	Magnitude	Probability
k	$\sqrt{p_k}(\cos\theta_k + i\sin\theta_k)$	θ_k	$\sqrt{p_k}$	p_k

Figure 4.13 Table comprehension for a quantum state with *n* qubits with outcomes $0 \le k < 2^n$

Finally, as we did for single-qubit states, we can use a more visually informative representation of the state table, shown in figure 4.14, that includes amplitude bars and probability bars. Remember, the colors of the amplitude bars reflect the phases of the associated amplitude using the color wheel method discussed in chapter 3.

Outcome	Binary	Amplitude	Direction	Magnitude	Amplitude bar	Probability	Probability bar
0	000	0.10 + 0.04i	20.3°	0.11		0.01	
1	001	0.07 + 0.07i	42.7°	0.10		0.01	
2	010	0.05 + 0.11i	65.3°	0.12		0.01	
3	011	0.01 + 0.16i	87.8°	0.16		0.03	
4	100	−0.13 + 0.35i	110.3°	0.37		0.14	
5	101	0.58 − 0.63i	−47.2°	0.86		0.74	
6	110	0.19 − 0.09i	−24.8°	0.21		0.04	
7	111	0.13 − 0.01i	−2.3°	0.13		0.02	

Figure 4.14 Table comprehension for a quantum state with *n* qubits with outcomes $0 \le k < 2^n$
```

> **Deep dive: Ket notation from list comprehensions**
>
> Using ket notation, we can express a quantum state as a mathematical sum
>
> $$|\psi\rangle = \sum_{k=0}^{2^n-1} z_k |k\rangle$$
>
> $$= \sum_{k=0}^{2^n-1} (a_k + ib_k)|k\rangle$$
>
> $$= \sum_{k=0}^{2^n-1} \sqrt{p_k}(\cos\theta_k + i\sin\theta_k)|k\rangle$$
>
> where *n* is the number of qubits. This notation is similar to the table comprehensions and list comprehensions discussed in this section. State tables visually bridge math and code.

4.2.3 Simulating multi-qubit states in Python

We know we can represent multi-qubit states with Python lists. Now we can write the Python code we need for simulating the first step of a quantum computation: initializing the state.

INITIALIZING A MULTI-QUBIT STATE

Most qubit-based quantum computers start with all qubits in a default state with a 100% probability of measuring the outcome 0. In our simulator, we define a function called `init_state` that takes the number of qubits as an argument and returns a list representing the initial state.

Listing 4.2 Function to create a default quantum state

```
def init_state(n):
    state = [0 for _ in range(2 ** n)]
    state[0] = 1
    return state
```

- `state = [0 for _ in range(2 ** n)]` — Given n qubits, the state will contain 2^n complex numbers.
- `state[0] = 1` — The amplitude corresponding to outcome 0 (the first amplitude in the list) will have a value of 1.

For example, we can initialize a two-qubit state:

```
state = init_state(2)
print(state)
```

The output is

```
[1, 0, 0, 0]
```

4.3 Changing amplitudes with quantum transformations

In a quantum computation, we use gate transformations to change the amplitudes of a quantum state and therefore the probabilities of the possible outcomes. When applying a gate to a single-qubit state, we recombine its two amplitudes using two equations. When we apply a gate to a multi-qubit state, the same equations are used to recombine all amplitudes in pairs. Quantum gate transformations are applied to a selected qubit in a system called the *target qubit*, which determines the pairs of amplitudes to be recombined. When we looked at single-qubit states in the previous chapter, there was only one option for the target qubit and only one pair to recombine. In this chapter, we will look at what happens when we apply gates to various qubits in a multi-qubit system.

4.3.1 Selecting pairs of amplitudes based on the target qubit

The target qubit determines how we pair the amplitudes for recombination. To select pairs, we look at the possible outcomes in binary form. The pairs are the amplitudes of the outcomes that differ only in the digit of the target qubit.

For example, if we apply a gate to one of the qubits of a three-qubit state, there are three options for the target qubit, which we will denote by t: $t = 0$, $t = 1$, and $t = 2$. Note that qubits are indexed right to left, so the rightmost digit in the binary string outcome represents qubit 0. As we know, there are eight possible outcomes for a three-qubit system, '000', '001', '010', '011', '100', '110', '101', and '111'. If we apply a single-qubit gate with target $t = 0$, the pairs will be the amplitudes of outcomes that differ only in position $t = 0$. The pairs are highlighted in figure 4.15. We show the pairs sequentially, like they are processed when we simulate the transformation. When running on a real quantum computer, applying a transformation does not involve sequential steps.

Outcome	Binary		Outcome	Binary		Outcome	Binary		Outcome	Binary
0	000		0	000		0	000		0	000
1	001		1	001		1	001		1	001
2	010		2	010		2	010		2	010
3	011		3	011		3	011		3	011
4	100		4	100		4	100		4	100
5	101		5	101		5	101		5	101
6	110		6	110		6	110		6	110
7	111		7	111		7	111		7	111

Figure 4.15 The pairs of outcomes for applying a single-qubit gate to a three-qubit system with the target qubit in position 0

As discussed in chapter 2, when converting from binary (base 2) form to decimal (base 10) form, each digit in a binary number is multiplied by a power of 2, starting

4.3 Changing amplitudes with quantum transformations

with 2^0 for the rightmost digit. This means if the binary forms of two numbers differ only in position t, the decimal values of the numbers differ by 2^t. Given a transformation with a target t, we can find the outcomes whose binary representation has 0 in the position t and add 2^t to them to identify the other amplitude in the pair.

In the previous example, where $t = 0$, the decimal values of the outcomes of each pair differ by 1. In this case, the rows of each pair are next to each other.

If we apply a gate to a three-qubit system with target qubit $t = 1$, the binary form of the outcomes differ only in position 1 and the decimal forms of the outcomes differ by 2, as shown in figure 4.16. Finally, if the target qubit is $t = 2$, the first digit in the binary outcomes, the decimal values of the outcomes differ by 4, as shown in figure 4.17.

Outcome	Binary	Outcome	Binary	Outcome	Binary	Outcome	Binary
0	000	0	000	0	000	0	000
1	001	1	001	1	001	1	001
2	010	2	010	2	010	2	010
3	011	3	011	3	011	3	011
4	100	4	100	4	100	4	100
5	101	5	101	5	101	5	101
6	110	6	110	6	110	6	110
7	111	7	111	7	111	7	111

Figure 4.16 The pairs of outcomes for applying a single-qubit gate to a three-qubit system with the target qubit in position 1

Outcome	Binary	Outcome	Binary	Outcome	Binary	Outcome	Binary
0	000	0	000	0	000	0	000
1	001	1	001	1	001	1	001
2	010	2	010	2	010	2	010
3	011	3	011	3	011	3	011
4	100	4	100	4	100	4	100
5	101	5	101	5	101	5	101
6	110	6	110	6	110	6	110
7	111	7	111	7	111	7	111

Figure 4.17 The pairs of outcomes for applying a single-qubit gate to a three-qubit system with the target qubit in position 2

We can use a table comprehension to show the outcome and amplitudes of pairs before and after a gate transformation with target qubit t. This is illustrated in figure 4.18.

86 CHAPTER 4 *Quantum state and circuits: Beyond one qubit*

Outcome	Amplitude
k_0	z_{k_0}
$k_1 = k_0 + 2^t$	z_{k_1}

$\begin{bmatrix} a & b \\ c & d \end{bmatrix} \longrightarrow$

Outcome	Amplitude
k_0	$az_{k_0} + bz_{k_1}$
$k_1 = k_0 + 2^t$	$cz_{k_0} + dz_{k_1}$

Figure 4.18 The pairs of outcomes and amplitudes of an *n*-qubit state (with outcomes $0 \le k < 2^n$) before and after applying a gate transformation to the target qubit *t*

4.3.2 Pair selection in Python

To simulate gate transformations, we need to select the pairs of amplitudes to be recombined. Several strategies can be used to find the pairs in code. Each method has advantages and disadvantages in terms of caching and resource consumption. In this chapter, we will discuss only one strategy; two more strategies are discussed in appendix C.

PAIRING CHUNKS OF AMPLITUDES

Given a target qubit position *t*, we can identify pairs of outcomes utilizing what we call *chunks*. There is a pattern for the location of the 0 side and 1 side of pairs: chunks of 2^t outcomes with 0 in the target position are followed by a chunk of 2^t outcomes with 1 in that position. Therefore, we can traverse the outcomes in chunks of 2^t. If we traverse the first chunk, 0, through $2^t - 1$, we know the 1 sides of the pairs will be 2^t through $2^{t+1} - 1$. The chunks for three-qubits and the target qubit $t = 1$ are visualized in figure 4.19.

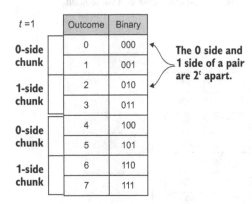

Figure 4.19 Pair generating strategy using chunks of outcomes for a three-qubit system and the target qubit *t* = 1

The Python implementation of this method is shown in the following listing.

Listing 4.3 Traverse-by-chunk method for selecting pairs

```
def pair_generator_pattern(n, t):
    distance = int(2 ** t)
```
◁┘ Distance is the size of each chunk.

4.3 Changing amplitudes with quantum transformations

```
for j in range(2**(n-t-1)):
    for k0 in range(2*j*distance, (2*j+1)*distance):
        k1 = k0 + distance
        yield k0, k1
```

- Gets the 0 side of each pair
- Gets the 1 side of the pair by adding the distance (2^t)

Let's take the example of three qubits (n = 3) and the target qubit 0 (t = 1) and generate the pairs using this method:

```
for (k0, k1) in pair_generator_pattern(3, 1):
    print(k0, k1)
```

The generated pairs of outcomes are printed:

```
0 2
1 3
4 6
5 7
```

The pairs match the highlighted rows discussed earlier and shown in figure 4.16.

4.3.3 Simulating amplitude changes

Remember that when applying a general single-qubit quantum gate (a two-by-two matrix with entries *a*, *b*, *c*, *d*) to a pair of amplitudes z_0 and z_1, the new amplitudes are

$$\begin{bmatrix} a & b \\ c & d \end{bmatrix} \begin{bmatrix} z_0 \\ z_1 \end{bmatrix} = \begin{bmatrix} az_0 + bz_1 \\ cz_0 + dz_1 \end{bmatrix}$$

In Python code, we can define a function `process_pair` that computes the new amplitudes of a pair of outcomes. To simulate a gate transformation on a multi-qubit state, we will use the `transform` function, which takes a state, a target qubit, and a gate (as a two-by-two list) and then simulates a gate transformation by selecting the pairs and calling `process_pair` to compute the new amplitudes. The definitions of these functions are shown in the next listing. Note that the `pair_generator` function can be any pair-selecting strategy, including that in listing 4.3.

> **Listing 4.4 Functions to simulate a gate transformation on a multi-qubit state**

```
def process_pair(state, gate, k0, k1):
    x = state[k0]
    y = state[k1]
    state[k0] = x * gate[0][0] + y * gate[0][1]
    state[k1] = x * gate[1][0] + y * gate[1][1]
```

- Gets the original amplitudes of the pair
- Computes the amplitudes given the gate definition and replaces the old amplitudes in the state list

CHAPTER 4 Quantum state and circuits: Beyond one qubit

```
def transform(state, t, gate):
    n = int(log2(len(state)))           ◄──── Gets the number of
    for (k0, k1) in pair_generator(n, t):      qubits in the state
        process_pair(state, gate, k0, k1)  ◄──── Calls pair_generator, which
                                                 returns pairs as tuples given
                      For each pair, calls       a number of qubits (n) and
                   process_pair to compute       the target qubit (t)
                         the new amplitudes
```

Let's look at some examples of gate transformations on a multi-qubit state. If we apply an X gate to the qubit in position 0 ($t = 0$), the amplitudes of each pair will be swapped. In figure 4.20, we start with an example three-qubit state and show how each pair of amplitudes is processed (recombined).

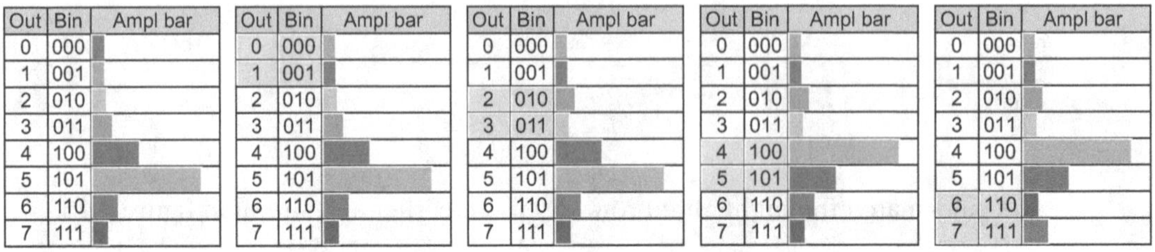

Figure 4.20 Amplitude pair processing for the X gate applied to target qubit 0 in a three-qubit system

Let's use the example state from figure 4.20 as a list:

```
state = [(0.09858+0.03637j),
         (0.07478+0.06912j),
         (0.04852+0.10526j),
         (0.00641+0.16322j),
         (-0.12895+0.34953j),
         (0.58403-0.6318j),
         (0.18795-0.08665j),
         (0.12867-0.00506j)]
```

Now we can use the `transform` function to apply an X gate to target qubit 0:

```
from sim_gates import *      ◄──── Imports the gate definitions
                                   added to the source code
transform(state, 0, x)             from chapter 3
print(state)
```

The resulting output is

```
[(0.07478+0.06912j),
 (0.09858+0.03637j),
 (0.00641+0.16322j),
 (0.04852+0.10526j),
 (0.58403-0.6318j),
 (-0.12895+0.34953j),
```

```
(0.12867-0.00506j),
(0.18795-0.08665j)]
```

We can see that the amplitudes of each pair are swapped, and the final state matches the last state table in figure 4.21.

Out	Bin	Ampl bar
0	000	
1	001	
2	010	
3	011	
4	100	
5	101	
6	110	
7	111	

Out	Bin	Ampl bar
0	000	
1	001	
2	010	
3	011	
4	100	
5	101	
6	110	
7	111	

Out	Bin	Ampl bar
0	000	
1	001	
2	010	
3	011	
4	100	
5	101	
6	110	
7	111	

Out	Bin	Ampl bar
0	000	
1	001	
2	010	
3	011	
4	100	
5	101	
6	110	
7	111	

Out	Bin	Ampl bar
0	000	
1	001	
2	010	
3	011	
4	100	
5	101	
6	110	
7	111	

Figure 4.21 Amplitude pair processing for the X gate applied to target qubit 2 in a three-qubit system

Let's apply an X gate to the same example three-qubit state, but this time we will apply the gate to the qubit in position 2 ($t = 2$), as shown in figure 4.21. The outcome (amplitude) pairing pattern shown here is native to qubit-based computing but is also used in classical computing. In particular, the fast Fourier transform algorithm uses it to drastically improve the performance of computing Fourier transforms.

We will discuss the quantum version of Fourier transforms in chapter 7. *Butterfly diagrams*, shown in figure 4.22, are used to represent this pairing pattern. We can also indicate which pairs of outcomes are paired by using circular diagrams, shown in figure 4.23, where each sector represents an outcome.

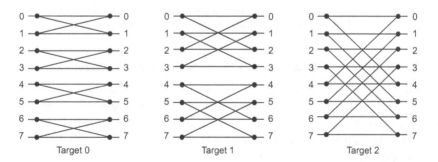

Figure 4.22 Butterfly diagrams of the pairs of outcomes in a three-qubit system for targets 0, 1, and 2

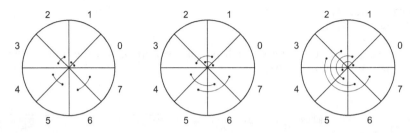

Figure 4.23 Butterfly diagrams of the pairs of outcomes in a three-qubit system for targets 0, 1, and 2

> **Quantum superposition and parallelism**
>
> A quantum system is said to be in superposition when it is in an "undetermined" or "uncertain" state. This can be thought of as being in multiple states at once. Mathematically, superposition is expressed as a summation of all possible states of the system. In a state-table representation, multiple rows with nonzero amplitudes indicate a system in superposition.
>
> Quantum parallelism, enabled by superposition, is often considered the most powerful feature of quantum computing. When a quantum gate is applied, the result is immediate in a quantum system. In contrast, a simulator can only achieve the same result by processing pairs one at a time.
>
> Quantum parallelism is similar to SIMD (single instruction, multiple data) processing. This type of parallel processing allows one instruction to be applied to multiple data elements simultaneously, improving the performance of CPUs by executing multiple instructions at the same time.
>
> SIMD processing can be used to make certain tasks faster. For example, if the same operation needs to be applied to multiple pieces of data, SIMD can help speed up the process. Quantum parallelism can be thought of as unlimited SIMD.

4.3.4 Encoding a uniform distribution in a multi-qubit quantum system

In a uniform distribution, each outcome has an equal probability. In a quantum state, this means all the amplitudes must have equal magnitudes. We already encoded a uniform distribution in a single qubit in the previous chapter. With the concepts introduced in this chapter, we can encode a uniform distribution in a state with any number of qubits.

Let's use our simulator to encode a uniform distribution in a three-qubit system. First we initialize a three-qubit state:

```
state = init_state(3)
```

We know that each time we apply a gate, it will process all the amplitudes in pairs. Also, all the amplitudes in the initial state are 0 except the first one:

4.3 Changing amplitudes with quantum transformations

```
print(state)
```

```
[1, 0, 0, 0, 0, 0, 0, 0]
```

Thus, when we apply the first Hadamard gate (to any target qubit in the state), we will only see the amplitudes of the pair with '000' in it change. For example, if we choose target qubit 0, the amplitudes corresponding to outcomes '000' and '001' (which differ only in the target qubit position) will be paired. Let's see this in our simulator:

```
transform(state, 0, h)
print(state)
```

In the printed output, we can see that the amplitudes corresponding to outcomes '000' and '001' are recombined:

```
[0.7071067811865475, 0.7071067811865475, 0.0, 0.0, 0.0, 0.0, 0.0, 0.0]
```

Similarly, if we choose target qubit 1, the amplitudes corresponding to outcomes '000' and '010' will be paired:

```
state = init_state(3)
transform(state, 1, h)
print(state)
```

In the printed output, we can see that the amplitudes corresponding to outcomes '000' and '010' are recombined:

```
[0.7071067811865475, 0.0, 0.7071067811865475, 0.0, 0.0, 0.0, 0.0, 0.0]
```

If we use a Hadamard gate on each qubit in a system in its default state, the amplitudes for all the outcomes will all be real numbers and have an equal magnitude. This creates a state where each outcome has an equal probability. Thus, the state will have a uniform probability distribution:

```
state = init_state(3)
transform(state, 0, h)
transform(state, 1, h)
transform(state, 2, h)
print(state)
```

We can see that all the amplitudes are real numbers, and the magnitudes are equal:

```
[0.3535533905932737,
 0.3535533905932737,
 0.3535533905932737,
 0.3535533905932737,
 0.3535533905932737,
 0.3535533905932737,
 0.3535533905932737,
 0.3535533905932737]
```

In the state table in figure 4.24, we can see that the probabilities are uniformly distributed.

Outcome	Binary	Amplitude	Direction	Magnitude	Amplitude bar	Probability	Probability bar
0	000	0.35	0.0°	0.35		0.12	
1	001	0.35	0.0°	0.35		0.12	
2	010	0.35	0.0°	0.35		0.12	
3	011	0.35	0.0°	0.35		0.12	
4	100	0.35	0.0°	0.35		0.12	
5	101	0.35	0.0°	0.35		0.12	
6	110	0.35	0.0°	0.35		0.12	
7	111	0.35	0.0°	0.35		0.12	

Figure 4.24 The state table for the uniform probability distribution on eight outcomes

4.4 Controlled quantum transformations

Every time we apply a quantum gate to a quantum state, all the amplitudes can be changed at once. This is called *quantum parallelism*. As discussed, quantum parallelism is one of the main sources of advantage in quantum computations. Although it can be used to create efficient computations, it also limits the types of states we can create. We can use *controlled transformations* to limit the effect of gate transformations to certain pairs.

> **NOTE** In a real quantum system, controlled transformations are usually computationally more expensive than noncontrolled ones, and they typically decrease the coherence of the system. But in a simulator, each control qubit (position) cuts the number of pairs to recombine in half.

When applying a controlled transformation, the pairs of amplitudes to be recombined correspond to outcomes that differ only in the target position and have a 1 in the *control qubit* position(s). For example, if we apply a controlled gate transformation to a three-qubit state with target qubit 0 and control qubit 2, the pairs of amplitudes that are recombined correspond to the outcomes that differ only in position 0 and have the digit 1 in position 2. In figure 4.25, outcomes that do not have 1 in the control qubit position are grayed out, and the selected pairs are highlighted.

Figure 4.26 shows another example. This time, the target qubit is in position 2 and the control qubit is in position 1. Once again, the outcomes with 0 in the control qubit position are grayed out and the target pairs are highlighted.

When we apply a controlled gate transformation, the effect of the gate on a pair of amplitudes remains the same, but the number of pairs is limited by the control qubit. For example, if we apply a controlled X gate to a three-qubit state with the target qubit

4.4 Controlled quantum transformations

Outcome	Binary
0	000
1	001
2	010
3	011
4	100
5	101
6	110
7	111

Outcome	Binary
0	000
1	001
2	010
3	011
4	100
5	101
6	110
7	111

Figure 4.25 The pairs of outcomes for applying a controlled single-qubit gate to a three-qubit system with target qubit 0 and control qubit 2

Outcome	Binary
0	000
1	001
2	010
3	011
4	100
5	101
6	110
7	111

Outcome	Binary
0	000
1	001
2	010
3	011
4	100
5	101
6	110
7	111

Figure 4.26 The pairs of outcomes for applying a controlled single-qubit gate to a three-qubit system with target qubit 2 and control qubit 1

in position 0 and the control qubit in position 2, the pairs highlighted in figure 4.27 will be swapped. Similarly, figure 4.28 shows a controlled X gate applied to a three-qubit state with target qubit 2 and control qubit 1.

Out	Bin	Ampl	Ampl bar
0	000	0.10 + 0.04i	
1	001	0.07 + 0.07i	
2	010	0.05 + 0.11i	
3	011	0.01 + 0.16i	
4	100	−0.13 + 0.35i	
5	101	0.58 − 0.63i	
6	110	0.19 − 0.09i	
7	111	0.13 − 0.01i	

Out	Bin	Ampl	Ampl bar
0	000	0.10 + 0.04i	
1	001	0.07 + 0.07i	
2	010	0.05 + 0.11i	
3	011	0.01 + 0.16i	
4	100	0.58 − 0.63i	
5	101	−0.13 + 0.35i	
6	110	0.19 − 0.09i	
7	111	0.13 − 0.01i	

Out	Bin	Ampl	Ampl bar
0	000	0.10 + 0.04i	
1	001	0.07 + 0.07i	
2	010	0.05 + 0.11i	
3	011	0.01 + 0.16i	
4	100	0.58 − 0.63i	
5	101	−0.13 + 0.35i	
6	110	0.13 − 0.01i	
7	111	0.19 − 0.09i	

Figure 4.27 Pair processing for applying a controlled X gate to a three-qubit state with target qubit 0 and control qubit 2

Out	Bin	Ampl	Ampl bar
0	000	0.10 + 0.04i	
1	001	0.07 + 0.07i	
2	010	0.05 + 0.11i	
3	011	0.01 + 0.16i	
4	100	−0.13 + 0.35i	
5	101	0.58 − 0.63i	
6	110	0.19 − 0.09i	
7	111	0.13 − 0.01i	

Out	Bin	Ampl	Ampl bar
0	000	0.10 + 0.04i	
1	001	0.07 + 0.07i	
2	010	0.19 − 0.09i	
3	011	0.01 + 0.16i	
4	100	−0.13 + 0.35i	
5	101	0.58 − 0.63i	
6	110	0.05 + 0.11i	
7	111	0.13 − 0.01i	

Out	Bin	Ampl	Ampl bar
0	000	0.10 + 0.04i	
1	001	0.07 + 0.07i	
2	010	0.19 − 0.09i	
3	011	0.13 − 0.01i	
4	100	−0.13 + 0.35i	
5	101	0.58 − 0.63i	
6	110	0.05 + 0.11i	
7	111	0.01 + 0.16i	

Figure 4.28 Pair processing for applying a controlled X gate to a three-qubit state with target qubit 2 and control qubit 1

4.4.1 Simulating controlled gate transformations in Python

To apply a controlled gate transformation with one control qubit in our simulator, we will use the `c_transform` function defined in listing 4.5. We can use the same pair-generation strategies as in `transform`, but we need to add a condition to check whether the digits in the control qubit positions are 1 before we recombine the values in a pair. For each possible outcome, we check if the target qubit in the binary form of an outcome is 1 in a given position using the `is_bit_set` function.

Listing 4.5 Applying controlled gate transformations to a state

```
def is_bit_set(m, k):
    return m & (1 << k) != 0

def c_transform(state, c, t, gate):
    n = int(log2(len(state)))
    for (k0, k1) in filter(lambda p: is_bit_set(p[0], c),
                           pair_generator(n, t)):
        process_pair(state, gate, k0, k1)
```

Uses the same pair-generation function as for regular transforms but adds a filter to check if the control position is 1

Once we get the right subset of pairs, we recombine the amplitudes according to the gate.

Let's use the example state in figure 4.27 and figure 4.28:

```
state = [(0.09858+0.03637j),
         (0.07478+0.06912j),
         (0.04852+0.10526j),
         (0.00641+0.16322j),
         (-0.12895+0.34953j),
         (0.58403-0.6318j),
         (0.18795-0.08665j),
         (0.12867-0.00506j)]
```

We can apply a controlled X gate to target qubit 2 with control qubit 1 using the `c_transform` function:

```
c_transform(state, 1, 2, x)
print(state)
```

4.4 Controlled quantum transformations

The output is

```
[(0.09858+0.03637j),
 (0.07478+0.06912j),
 (0.18795-0.08665j),
 (0.12867-0.00506j),
 (-0.12895+0.34953j),
 (0.58403-0.6318j),
 (0.04852+0.10526j),
 (0.00641+0.16322j)]
```

We can see that in the resulting state, the amplitudes corresponding to outcomes 2 and 6 are swapped, and the amplitudes corresponding to outcomes 3 and 7 are swapped. The resulting state matches that in figure 4.28.

4.4.2 Simulating multicontrol gate transformations in Python

Controlled transformations can have one or more control qubits. If there is more than one control qubit, the pairs are further limited to outcomes where each control qubit position has the digit 1.

To simulate multicontrolled gate transformation in our simulator, we will use the `mc_transform` function in the next listing. Similar to the `c_transform` function, we get the pairs of outcomes that differ only in the target qubit position and then check whether they have the value 1 in each of the control qubit positions.

Listing 4.6 Applying multicontrolled gate transformations to a state

```
def mc_transform(state, cs, t, gate):
    assert not t in cs
    n = int(log2(len(state)))
    for (k0, k1) in filter(
            lambda p: all([is_bit_set(p[0], c) for c in cs]),
            pair_generator(n, t)):
        process_pair(state, gate, k0, k1)
```

- `assert not t in cs` — The target qubit cannot be the same as the control qubits.
- `lambda p: all([is_bit_set(p[0], c) for c in cs])` — Checks that the pairs have 1 in all the control qubit positions
- `process_pair(state, gate, k0, k1)` — Recombines the amplitudes of the selected pairs

Let's apply a multicontrolled transformation to our example state:

```
state = [(0.09858+0.03637j), (0.07478+0.06912j), (0.04852+0.10526j),
         (0.00641+0.16322j), (-0.12895+0.34953j), (0.58403-0.6318j),
         (0.18795-0.08665j), (0.12867-0.00506j)]
```

If we apply a controlled transformation with two control qubits to a three-qubit state, there will be only one pair to recombine. For example, if the target qubit is 0 and the control qubits are 1 and 2, the pair selected will be '110' and '111' (outcomes 6 and 7):

```
mc_transform(state, [1, 2], 0, x)
print(state)
```

The output is

```
[(0.09858+0.03637j),
 (0.07478+0.06912j),
 (0.04852+0.10526j),
 (0.00641+0.16322j),
 (-0.12895+0.34953j),
 (0.58403-0.6318j),
 (0.12867-0.00506j),
 (0.18795-0.08665j)]
```

We can see in this printed state that only the last two amplitudes (6 and 7) are swapped.

4.5 Simulating quantum circuits

We have been using a functional programming style for the simulator, passing the state to processing functions as an argument. However, when implementing a circuit, it is better to wrap the functionality in an object that keeps the state as an attribute. The interface of our simulator closely matches Qiskit's interface. This is helpful because Qiskit code can be used to run computations on many real quantum computers. This also allows us to easily transition from simulation to running on a real computer.

> **NOTE** In the book's repository, an additional Jupyter notebook in the chapter folder contains code to run the examples from this chapter using a Qiskit simulator backend.

4.5.1 Simulating measurement of multi-qubit states

As we know, each time we repeat a quantum computation, we get one outcome non-deterministically. We know that the frequency, or counts, of each outcome will reflect the probabilities determined by the amplitudes of the state. We can simulate quantum measurement using the `choices` function from the built-in `random` Python package. We will use the `measure` function, defined in the next listing, which takes the state vector and a number of samples (`shots`). The function calculates the probabilities using the amplitudes of the given state and returns a dictionary with the counts of each outcome.

Listing 4.7 Simulating measurement of a quantum state

```
from random import choices
from collections import Counter

def measure(state, shots):
    samples = choices(
        range(len(state)),
        [abs(state[k])**2 for k in range(len(state))],
        k=shots)
    counts = {}
    for (k, v) in Counter(samples).items():
        counts[k] = v
    return counts
```

4.5 Simulating quantum circuits

For example, let's take the example state we used earlier:

```
state = [(0.09858+0.03637j), (0.07478+0.06912j), (0.04852+0.10526j),
         (0.00641+0.16322j), (-0.12895+0.34953j), (0.58403-0.6318j),
         (0.18795-0.08665j), (0.12867-0.00506j)]
```

Let's use a list comprehension to look at the probability of each outcome:

```
probabilities = [[k, abs(state[k])**2] for k in range(len(state))]

for i in probabilities:
    print("probability of outcome", i[0], ": ", round(i[1], 3))
```

The printed output is

```
probability of outcome 0 :  0.011
probability of outcome 1 :  0.01
probability of outcome 2 :  0.013
probability of outcome 3 :  0.027
probability of outcome 4 :  0.139
probability of outcome 5 :  0.74
probability of outcome 6 :  0.043
probability of outcome 7 :  0.017
```

Now, let's use our `measure` function to simulate the outcomes of 100 executions of the computation that creates our example state:

```
samples = measure(state, 100)
print(samples)
```

The printed samples are

```
{4: 17, 5: 73, 7: 1, 6: 5, 3: 2, 1: 2}
```

The frequency of each outcome in the resulting samples reflects the outcome probabilities. For example, outcome 5 has a probability of about 74%, and in our experiment, 73 of the 100 samples were outcome 5, closely reflecting the expectation.

On a real quantum computer, we get one measurement outcome after each execution of a computation. Figure 4.29 visualizes one measurement outcome being added to the measurement counts from previous executions. In the figure, the outcome is 4, so the amplitude of outcome 4 is 1 in the state table after measurement.

4.5.2 Quantum registers and circuits in code

A quantum circuit consists of a sequence of transformations (quantum gates applied to a target qubit). As we know, in addition to a target qubit, each transformation can also have control qubits. We apply a circuit to a set of qubits. Sometimes it is convenient to group qubits in *registers* that have their own index starting at 0.

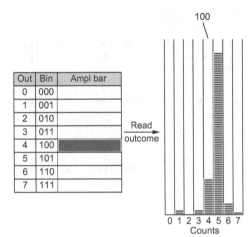

Figure 4.29 One measurement and the counts of previous measurement outcomes. In this example, the measurement outcome is 100, or 4.

The `QuantumRegister` class keeps track of a list of qubits. When an instance of the class is created, we specify the `size` parameter, which is the number of qubits in that register. The methods of the class allow for the right target and control qubits to be selected when executing the transformations in a circuit.

Listing 4.8 QuantumRegister class

```
class QuantumRegister:
    def __init__(self, size, shift=0):
        self.size = size
        self.shift = shift

    def __getitem__(self, key):
        if isinstance(key, slice):
            return [self[ii] for ii in range(*key.indices(len(self)))]
        elif isinstance(key, int):
            if key < 0:
                key += len(self)
            assert(0 <= key < self.size)
            return self.shift + key

    def __len__(self):
        return self.size

    def __iter__(self):
        return list([self.shift + i for i in range(self.size)])

    def __reversed__(self):
        return list([self.shift + i for i in range(self.size)[::-1]])
```

In our simulator, we use the `QuantumTransformation` class for each transformation in a circuit. Each transformation consists of a gate (a two-by-two list), a target qubit, and optional control qubits (for controlled gate transformations).

Listing 4.9 QuantumTransformation class

```
class QuantumTransformation:
    def __init__(self, gate, target, controls=[], name=None, arg=None):
        self.gate = gate
        self.target= target
        self.controls = controls
        self.name = name
        self.arg = arg

    def __str__(self):
        return rf'{self.name} {round(self.arg, 2) if self.arg is not None 
    else ""} ' \
               f'{self.controls} {self.target}'

    def __copy__(self):
        return QuantumTransformation(
            self.gate,
            self.target,
            self.controls,
            self.name,
            self.arg
        )
```

The `QuantumCircuit` class consists of two main attributes: a state variable and a list of `QuantumTransformation` entries. When we create a new circuit, we pass one or more registers of qubits. Then, we create an internal variable for the state amplitudes. The `QuantumCircuit` class includes a method for each gate. In listing 4.10, we only include the X gate, the Hadamard gate, the R_Y gate, the controlled X gate, and the multicontrolled X gate.

The complete implementation can be found in the companion code repository (https://github.com/learnqc/code). When we call the `run` method on a circuit object, we iterate through the transformations and apply the appropriate transform function to the state. Note that after we apply the transformations, we set the transformations attribute of the class to an empty list.

Listing 4.10 Partial implementation of the QuantumCircuit class

```
class QuantumCircuit:
    def __init__(self, *args):
        bits = 0
        regs = []
        for register in args:
            register.shift = bits
            bits += register.size
            regs.append(register.size)

        self.state = init_state(bits)
        self.transformations = []
        self.regs = regs
        self.reports = {}
```

```python
    def initialize(self, state):
        self.state = state

    def x(self, t):
        self.transformations.append(
            QuantumTransformation(x, t, [], 'x'))

    def h(self, t):
        self.transformations.append(
            QuantumTransformation(h, t, [], 'h'))

    def ry(self, theta, t):
        self.transformations.append(
            QuantumTransformation(ry(theta), t, [], 'ry', theta))

    def cx(self, c, t):
        self.transformations.append(
            QuantumTransformation(x, t, [c], 'x'))

    def mcx(self, cs, t):
        self.transformations.append(
            QuantumTransformation(x, t, cs, 'x'))

    def measure(self, shots=0):
        state = self.run()
        samples = measure(state, shots)
        return {'state vector': state, 'counts': samples}

    def run(self):
        for tr in self.transformations:
            cs = tr.controls
            if len(cs) == 0:
                transform(self.state, tr.target, tr.gate)
            elif len(cs) == 1:
                c_transform(self.state, cs[0], tr.target, tr.gate)
            else:
                mc_transform(self.state, cs, tr.target, tr.gate)
        self.transformations = []
        return self.state
```

In later chapters, we will continue to add methods to the `QuantumCircuit` class as needed.

NOTE As mentioned in chapter 2, we can run examples using our simulator or Qiskit backends. In the code base, we added a `run` method to the `QuantumCircuit` class in Qiskit to make the syntax for running circuits identical. Examples of running a circuit using a Qiskit simulator backend are in the book's companion repository.

In chapter 3, we visualized a couple of example single-qubit quantum circuits with circuit diagrams. Figure 4.30 shows a three-qubit circuit diagram; there is a line for each qubit. Each transformation in the circuit is shown as a box on the respective target qubit and labeled with the gate type. The third transformation in this circuit is

4.5 Simulating quantum circuits

a multicontrolled X gate: the target qubit is shown with an open circle, and the control qubits are shown with closed circles.

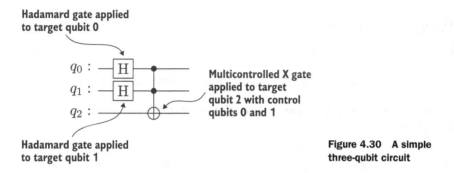

Figure 4.30 A simple three-qubit circuit

Let's implement the simple circuit in figure 4.30 using our QuantumCircuit class. First we initialize a state with three qubits. Then we apply each gate in the circuit to the respective target (and control) qubits:

```
q = QuantumRegister(3)
qc = QuantumCircuit(q)

qc.h(q[0])
qc.h(q[1])
qc.mcx([q[0], q[1]], q[2])
```

When we call the run function, the respective transformations are applied to the state object, and the transformed state is returned:

```
state = qc.run()
```

The resulting state table is shown in figure 4.31.

Outcome	Binary	Amplitude	Direction	Magnitude	Amplitude bar	Probability	Probability bar
0	000	0.50	0.0°	0.50		0.25	
1	001	0.50	0.0°	0.50		0.25	
2	010	0.50	0.0°	0.50		0.25	
3	011	0.00		0.00		0.00	
4	100	0.00		0.00		0.00	
5	101	0.00		0.00		0.00	
6	110	0.00		0.00		0.00	
7	111	0.50	0.0°	0.50		0.25	

Figure 4.31 The state table after applying our simple circuit

We can simulate measurement on the resulting state with the `measure` function:

```
samples = measure(state, 1000)
print(samples)
```

The printed samples are

```
{2: 240, 7: 280, 0: 253, 1: 227}
```

As we expect, we see similar counts for the outcomes 0, 1, 2, and 7.

4.5.3 Reimplementing the uniform distribution with registers and circuits

We can encode the uniform distribution in a quantum state by applying a Hadamard gate to each qubit (starting with the default state). Figure 4.32 shows a circuit diagram for encoding a uniform distribution in a three-qubit system.

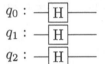

Figure 4.32 Circuit for encoding a uniform distribution in a three-qubit state

We can implement this circuit with our quantum simulator:

```
q = QuantumRegister(3)
qc = QuantumCircuit(q)

for i in range(len(q)):
    qc.h(q[i])

state = qc.run()
```

The resulting state table is shown in figure 4.33.

Outcome	Binary	Amplitude	Direction	Magnitude	Amplitude bar	Probability	Probability bar
0	000	0.35	0.0°	0.35		0.12	
1	001	0.35	0.0°	0.35		0.12	
2	010	0.35	0.0°	0.35		0.12	
3	011	0.35	0.0°	0.35		0.12	
4	100	0.35	0.0°	0.35		0.12	
5	101	0.35	0.0°	0.35		0.12	
6	110	0.35	0.0°	0.35		0.12	
7	111	0.35	0.0°	0.35		0.12	

Figure 4.33 The state table for the uniform probability distribution on eight outcomes

4.5 Simulating quantum circuits

To create the circuit for encoding the uniform distribution in a state with more (or fewer) qubits, we can use the `uniform` function defined next.

Listing 4.11 Encoding the uniform distribution in a quantum state

```
def uniform(n):
    q = QuantumRegister(n)
    qc = QuantumCircuit(q)

    for i in range(len(q)):
        qc.h(q[i])

    return qc
```

4.5.4 Encoding the binomial distribution in a multi-qubit state

The *binomial probability distribution* models the number of successes of a binary event for n trials. The probability of one outcome (success) is p, and the probability of the other is $1 - p$. The probability of getting k successes in a sequence of n events is

$$\binom{n}{k} p^k (1-p)^{n-k}.$$

We can encode a binomial distribution in a quantum state using R_Y rotations.

NOTE When modeling a probability p with an R_Y rotation, its angle θ is typically chosen so that $p = \cos^2 \theta/2$, and therefore $1 - p = \sin^2 \theta/2$.

Given an angle θ, if we apply a $R_Y(\theta)$ rotation to each qubit in a system in its initial state, all the amplitudes will be real, and each magnitude will depend on the number of 1s in the binary representation of the corresponding outcome. In chapter 3, we saw examples of the effect of applying the R_Y gate with various rotation angles. Figure 4.34 shows the circuit corresponding to $\theta = \pi/3$ and a three-qubit state.

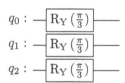

Figure 4.34 The quantum circuit that applies an $R_Y(\pi/3)$ rotation to all three qubits of the system

We can implement this circuit with our quantum simulator:

```
q = QuantumRegister(3)
qc = QuantumCircuit(q)

for i in range(len(q)):
    qc.ry(pi/3, q[i])

state = qc.run()
```

104 CHAPTER 4 *Quantum state and circuits: Beyond one qubit*

The resulting state table is shown in figure 4.35.

Outcome	Binary	Probability	Probability bar
0	000	$\sin^0 \frac{\pi}{6} \cos^6 \frac{\pi}{6}$	
1	001	$\sin^2 \frac{\pi}{6} \cos^4 \frac{\pi}{6}$	
2	010	$\sin^2 \frac{\pi}{6} \cos^4 \frac{\pi}{6}$	
3	011	$\sin^4 \frac{\pi}{6} \cos^2 \frac{\pi}{6}$	
4	100	$\sin^2 \frac{\pi}{6} \cos^4 \frac{\pi}{6}$	
5	101	$\sin^4 \frac{\pi}{6} \cos^2 \frac{\pi}{6}$	
6	110	$\sin^4 \frac{\pi}{6} \cos^2 \frac{\pi}{6}$	
7	111	$\sin^6 \frac{\pi}{6} \cos^0 \frac{\pi}{6}$	

Figure 4.35 The three-qubit state prepared by applying $R_Y(\pi/3)$ gates to every qubit

Note that this is not exactly the binomial distribution, as the outcomes with the same number of 1s (successes) are not grouped. This grouping needs to be done as a post-measurement processing step. The result of the outcome grouping for $\theta = \pi/3$ is in figure 4.36.

# of 1s	Outcome	Binary	Probability	Probability bar
0	0	000	$\binom{3}{0} \sin^0 \frac{\pi}{6} \cos^6 \frac{\pi}{6}$	
1	1, 2, 4	001, 010, 100	$\binom{3}{1} \sin^2 \frac{\pi}{6} \cos^4 \frac{\pi}{6}$	
2	3, 5, 6	011, 101, 110	$\binom{3}{2} \sin^4 \frac{\pi}{6} \cos^2 \frac{\pi}{6}$	
3	7	111	$\binom{3}{3} \sin^6 \frac{\pi}{6} \cos^0 \frac{\pi}{6}$	

Figure 4.36 The binomial distributions for $p = \cos^2 \pi/3$

Generally, we can use the following code to apply an $R_Y(\theta)$ rotation to each of n qubits in a system.

Listing 4.12 Encoding the binomial distribution in a quantum state

```
def binomial(n, theta):
    q = QuantumRegister(n)
    qc = QuantumCircuit(q)

    for i in range(len(q)):      ◁── Iterates through each
        qc.ry(theta, q[i])            qubit in the register and
                                      applies an R_Y gate
    return qc
```

4.5 Simulating quantum circuits

The resulting state can be represented by the table comprehension in figure 4.37.

Outcome	Probability
k	$\sin^{2o(k)} \frac{\theta}{2} \cos^{2n-2o(k)} \frac{\theta}{2}$

Figure 4.37 The state table for the circuit that applies an $R_Y(\theta)$ rotation to n qubits. Here, $o(k)$ denotes the number of 1s in the binary expansion of k.

If we apply the circuit to a three-qubit state for a given θ, the resulting amplitudes are those in figure 4.38. To get a true binomial distribution, we can group outcomes, as shown in figure 4.39.

Outcome	Binary	Probability
0	000	$\sin^0 \frac{\theta}{2} \cos^6 \frac{\theta}{2}$
1	001	$\sin^2 \frac{\theta}{2} \cos^4 \frac{\theta}{2}$
2	010	$\sin^2 \frac{\theta}{2} \cos^4 \frac{\theta}{2}$
3	011	$\sin^4 \frac{\theta}{2} \cos^2 \frac{\theta}{2}$
4	100	$\sin^2 \frac{\theta}{2} \cos^4 \frac{\theta}{2}$
5	101	$\sin^4 \frac{\theta}{2} \cos^2 \frac{\theta}{2}$
6	110	$\sin^4 \frac{\theta}{2} \cos^2 \frac{\theta}{2}$
7	111	$\sin^6 \frac{\theta}{2} \cos^0 \frac{\theta}{2}$

Figure 4.38 The general form of the three-qubit state prepared by applying $R_Y(\theta)$ to every qubit

# of 1s	Outcome	Binary	Probability
0	0	000	$\binom{3}{0} \sin^0 \frac{\theta}{2} \cos^6 \frac{\theta}{2}$
1	1, 2, 4	001, 010, 100	$\binom{3}{1} \sin^2 \frac{\theta}{2} \cos^4 \frac{\theta}{2}$
2	3, 5, 6	011, 101, 110	$\binom{3}{2} \sin^4 \frac{\theta}{2} \cos^2 \frac{\theta}{2}$
3	7	111	$\binom{3}{3} \sin^6 \frac{\theta}{2} \cos^0 \frac{\theta}{2}$

Figure 4.39 The result of grouping outcomes with the same number of 1s

For three qubits and $\theta = \pi/2$, we get the uniform distribution, as shown in figure 4.40. The result of the outcome grouping for $\theta = \pi/2$ is shown in figure 4.41.

Outcome	Binary	Probability	Probability bar
0	000	$\sin^0 \frac{\pi}{4} \cos^6 \frac{\pi}{4}$	■
1	001	$\sin^2 \frac{\pi}{4} \cos^4 \frac{\pi}{4}$	■
2	010	$\sin^2 \frac{\pi}{4} \cos^4 \frac{\pi}{4}$	■
3	011	$\sin^4 \frac{\pi}{4} \cos^2 \frac{\pi}{4}$	■
4	100	$\sin^2 \frac{\pi}{4} \cos^4 \frac{\pi}{4}$	■
5	101	$\sin^4 \frac{\pi}{4} \cos^2 \frac{\pi}{4}$	■
6	110	$\sin^4 \frac{\pi}{4} \cos^2 \frac{\pi}{4}$	■
7	111	$\sin^6 \frac{\pi}{4} \cos^0 \frac{\pi}{4}$	■

Figure 4.40 The uniform distribution prepared by applying $R_Y(\pi/2)$ gates to every qubit

# of 1s	Outcome	Binary	Probability	Probability bar
0	0	000	$\binom{3}{0} \sin^0 \frac{\pi}{4} \cos^6 \frac{\pi}{4}$	
1	1, 2, 4	001, 010, 100	$\binom{3}{1} \sin^2 \frac{\pi}{4} \cos^4 \frac{\pi}{4}$	
2	3, 5, 6	011, 101, 110	$\binom{3}{2} \sin^4 \frac{\pi}{4} \cos^2 \frac{\pi}{4}$	
3	7	111	$\binom{3}{3} \sin^6 \frac{\pi}{4} \cos^0 \frac{\pi}{4}$	

Figure 4.41 The binomial distributions for $p = \cos^2 \pi/2$

NOTE This approach uses the same number of qubits as the number of trials. This is sometimes referred to as a *unary implementation*, as opposed to a binary implementation where the number of trials is a power of 2 (2^n) for n qubits. A unary implementation is very straightforward, as there are no complex gates, but it is not as efficient as a binary implementation in terms of the number of qubits needed to perform a certain number of trials.

4.5.5 Implementing the Bell states

Earlier in this chapter, we used the Bell states as examples of nonproduct states. Now, let's look at how we can encode these states.

THE FIRST BELL STATE

The first Bell state we looked at was a two-qubit state where only the outcomes '00' and '11' are possible. We can use the following circuit to encode this state:

```
q = QuantumRegister(2)
qc = QuantumCircuit(q)

qc.h(q[0])
qc.cx(q[0], q[1])

state = qc.run()
```

The resulting state table is shown in figure 4.42.

Outcome	Binary	Amplitude	Direction	Magnitude	Amplitude bar	Probability	Probability bar
0	00	0.71	0.0°	0.71		0.50	
1	01	0.00		0.00		0.00	
2	10	0.00		0.00		0.00	
3	11	0.71	0.0°	0.71		0.50	

Figure 4.42 The first Bell state table

THE THIRD BELL STATE

In this two-qubit state, only the outcomes '01' and '10' are possible. We can encode it with the following code:

4.5 Simulating quantum circuits

```
q = QuantumRegister(2)
qc = QuantumCircuit(q)

qc.h(q[0])
qc.x(q[1])
qc.cx(q[0], q[1])

state = qc.run()
```

The resulting state table is shown in figure 4.43.

Outcome	Binary	Amplitude	Direction	Magnitude	Amplitude bar	Probability	Probability bar
0	00	0.00		0.00		0.00	
1	01	0.71	0.0°	0.71		0.50	
2	10	0.71	0.0°	0.71		0.50	
3	11	0.00		0.00		0.00	

Figure 4.43 The third Bell state table

Exercise 4.2
Implement circuits that encode the remaining two Bell states.

Exercise 4.3
The geometric distribution models the number of times a process must be repeated before a successful outcome is achieved. If the probability of success is p, then the probability of having k failures before the first success is $(1-p)^k p$.

Verify that the following circuit

```
q = QuantumRegister(n)
qc = QuantumCircuit(q)

for i in range(len(q)):
    qc.ry(theta, q[i])

for i in range(len(q) - 1):
    qc.cry(pi - theta, q[i], q[i+1])

z = qc.run()
```

prepares a quantum state z with the following properties:

1. The amplitudes in the state z at indices $2^n - 2^k$ for $0 \leq k < n$ (which start with $n-k$ digits of 1, and end with k digits of 0) are $z_{2^n - 2^k} = \cos^k \frac{\theta}{2} \sin \frac{\theta}{2}$ and the

(continued)

probabilities: $|z_{2^n - 2^k}|^2 = \cos^{2k}\frac{\theta}{2} \sin^2\frac{\theta}{2} = (1-p)^k p$, matching the geometric distribution probabilities.

1 Amplitude z_0 is the "leftover" amplitude accounting for the infinite tail of the geometric distribution.
2 All other amplitudes are 0.
3 The state table representation for $n = 3$ and $\theta = 0.8\pi$ matches the following state table:

Outcome	Binary	Amplitude	Amplitude bar
0	000	0.0295	
1	001	0.0000	
2	010	0.0000	
3	011	0.0000	
4	100	0.0908	
5	101	0.0000	
6	110	0.2939	
7	111	0.9511	

The state prepared using the circuit created with the previous function for $n = 3$ and $\theta = 0.8\pi$

Summary

- A quantum system made up of n qubits can be represented by an array of 2^n complex numbers, where the sum of squared magnitudes of the complex numbers is 1.
- State tables provide a visual way of understanding quantum states, connecting the mathematical and programmatic models.
- A quantum transformation applies a quantum gate to one qubit (the target qubit). It can also be controlled by using other qubits as control qubits.
- A quantum transformation recombines pairs of amplitudes determined by the target and control qubits according to the specific gate formula.
- Quantum circuits use quantum transformations to create useful states and probability distributions.
- Qubits can be organized into registers to make it easier to represent logical variables.
- We can write a simple Python simulator to simulate the basic principles of quantum computing.

Part 2

Fundamental algorithms and patterns

With a solid grasp of quantum states and operations, you're ready to implement and apply fundamental quantum algorithms and computing patterns. These aren't just theoretical constructs—they're the building blocks used in real quantum applications, including search and optimization problems.

Chapter 5 introduces quantum oracles and their role in algorithm design. Chapter 6 shows how oracles enable Grover's search algorithm, a quantum approach that quadratically speeds up unstructured search problems. Chapter 7 develops your understanding of the quantum Fourier transform, and Chapter 8 puts it to work in various applications. Chapter 9 brings these concepts together with quantum phase estimation and quantum counting, completing your toolkit of fundamental quantum algorithms.

Selecting outcomes with quantum oracles

This chapter covers
- Specifying "good" outcomes of quantum computations with quantum oracles
- Implementing phase and bit quantum oracles
- Converting between phase and bit quantum oracles

In chapter 1, we discussed three main patterns of quantum computations:

- Sampling from probability distributions
- Searching for specific outcomes
- Estimating the probability of specific outcomes

We explored several examples of the first pattern: sampling from probability distributions encoded into quantum states. In this chapter, we will learn how to identify specific outcomes of a quantum computation. This is an essential component for implementing solutions to problems that involve searching for certain outcomes or estimating the probabilities of certain outcomes.

Depending on the problem context, the possible outcomes of a quantum computation may represent items in an unstructured database, choices in a binary optimization problem, or the possible prices of a stock at a specific point in time. To search for an item in a database, find an optimal selection, or estimate the probability of a price, we need to specify desired outcomes in each context. To specify desired outcomes, we will use a quantum *oracle*. An oracle is a quantum circuit that recognizes desired outcomes and "tags" or marks them in some way.

You may be familiar with using SQL queries to retrieve data from a database. In a SQL query, the WHERE clause can be used to filter for records that fulfill a specific condition. You can think of an oracle like the WHERE clause in a SQL query: it identifies data entries that satisfy a condition.

In a typical database search, specifying the WHERE clause is easy, but the actual search performed by the database engine may be time-consuming—for example, if a full table scan is required in a large database. In a quantum search, the situation is reversed. Implementing an efficient oracle is typically hard, whereas the actual search is easy with quantum measurement. This comparison is shown in table 5.1.

Table 5.1 Comparison of the difficulty of classical and quantum approaches to unstructured search

	Search Specification	Search Execution
Classical	Easy (e.g., a SQL WHERE clause)	Typically hard (table scan)
Quantum	Hard (efficient oracles)	Easy (with Grover's algorithm)

> **Looking ahead: Oracles are everywhere in quantum computing**
>
> In this chapter, we will cover how quantum oracles work and how to implement them. As you design and implement quantum solutions, you will need quantum oracles.
>
> Quantum oracles perform a critical function in quantum computing. Oracles are required to implement Grover's algorithm, which we will cover in the next chapter. Oracles (and Grover's algorithm) are used in various quantum computing solutions, including optimization problems and quantum machine learning algorithms. Oracles are used for searching and sampling within many quantum algorithms. Therefore, designing efficient quantum oracles is essential in order to develop quantum solutions that outperform their classical counterparts.
>
> For example, when searching for the minimum or maximum values of a function, it would be ideal, but virtually impossible, to implement an oracle selecting those values. Instead, we can use a simple oracle that searches for negative (or non-negative) values and incrementally reduce the search space until we reach the desired values.

In this chapter, we will introduce two types of oracles and look at examples of each. We will learn how to implement these oracles using our Python simulator so that we can use them in applications in future chapters (see figure 5.1).

5.1 Describing outcomes with quantum oracles: Intuition and classical implementation

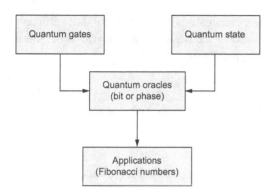

Figure 5.1 A dependency diagram of concepts introduced in this chapter. Oracles are also an essential building block of Grover's algorithm, covered in the next chapter.

As mentioned, in a quantum computation, we can use an oracle to recognize certain outcomes and "tag" them in some way. We will refer to the outcomes we want to recognize as "good" outcomes and all the others as "bad" outcomes. There are different ways an oracle can identify or tag an outcome. The most common tagging effects are as follows:

- The amplitudes of the good outcomes are rotated by 180°. Oracles that do this are called *phase oracles*.
- Outcomes are entangled with an additional qubit in such a way that the good ones are associated with its measurement of 1 and the bad ones with its measurement of 0. Oracles that do this are called *bit oracles*.

The implementation of an oracle is independent of how it is used (hence the name "oracle"). Note that a phase oracle is straightforward to implement on top of a bit oracle, because the good outcomes are already tagged by the bit oracle. Let's look at phase oracles first.

5.1.1 Phase oracles

After the phase oracle is applied, the amplitudes of the good outcomes are rotated by 180°. In figure 5.2, we denote good outcomes with g and bad outcomes with b. Rotating a complex number by 180° is the same as multiplying it by –1.

Outcome	Amplitude
b	s_b
g	s_g

$\xrightarrow{O}$

Outcome	Amplitude
b	s_b
g	$-s_g$ or $\operatorname{cis}(\pi)s_g$

Figure 5.2 The effect of a phase oracle on the amplitudes of a state with good outcomes g and bad outcomes b

CHAPTER 5 *Selecting outcomes with quantum oracles*

The good outcomes can be specified classically with a predicate that returns `True` for a good outcome and `False` otherwise. For example, in a scenario with one good outcome, 3, we can define the following predicate:

```
predicate = lambda k: True if k == 3 else False
```

Say we have eight possible outcomes ($n = 3$ qubits). We can use the `predicate` function to list the good outcomes:

```
n = 3
print(f'\nGood outcomes: {[k for k in range(2**n) if predicate(k)]}')
```

The output is

```
Good outcomes: [3]
```

We can use this predicate to classically simulate an oracle that takes any state and multiplies the amplitudes of the good outcomes by –1:

```
def classical_phase_oracle(state, predicate):
    for item in range(len(state)):
        if predicate(item):
            state[item] *= -1
```

Let's start with a state with $n = 3$ qubits in a uniform superposition where the magnitudes of all amplitudes are equal:

```
from math import sqrt

n = 3
state = [1/sqrt(2**n) for _ in range(2**n)]
```

We can apply the classical phase oracle to this state with the following code:

```
classical_phase_oracle(state, predicate)
```

The state tables before and after the oracle is applied are illustrated in figure 5.3.

Out	Bin	Ampl	Dir	Mag	Ampl bar
0	000	0.35	0.0°	0.35	
1	001	0.35	0.0°	0.35	
2	010	0.35	0.0°	0.35	
3	011	0.35	0.0°	0.35	
4	100	0.35	0.0°	0.35	
5	101	0.35	0.0°	0.35	
6	110	0.35	0.0°	0.35	
7	111	0.35	0.0°	0.35	

$\xrightarrow{O}$

Out	Bin	Ampl	Dir	Mag	Ampl bar
0	000	0.35	0.0°	0.35	
1	001	0.35	0.0°	0.35	
2	010	0.35	0.0°	0.35	
3	011	–0.35	180.0°	0.35	
4	100	0.35	0.0°	0.35	
5	101	0.35	0.0°	0.35	
6	110	0.35	0.0°	0.35	
7	111	0.35	0.0°	0.35	

Figure 5.3 The effect of a phase oracle on a three-qubit state prepared with amplitudes in equal superposition and a single good outcome, 3

5.1 Describing outcomes with quantum oracles: Intuition and classical implementation

In the second state table in figure 5.3, the phase of the amplitude of the good outcome is rotated by 180°.

> **Exercise 5.1**
> Start with $n = 4$ qubits in a uniform superposition:
>
> ```
> n = 4
> state = [1/sqrt(2**n) for _ in range(2**n)]
> ```
>
> Use the classical predicate definition for good outcomes 2 and 9 to create a classical phase oracle, apply it to the state, and check whether the amplitudes of the good outcomes are rotated by 180°:
>
> ```
> predicate = lambda k: True if k in [2, 9] else False
> ```

5.1.2 Bit oracles

Now let's look at bit oracles. A bit oracle entangles the outcomes with an additional qubit, which we will call the *tag bit*. In figure 5.4, the good outcomes (denoted by g) will have a nonzero probability when the tag bit has the value 1. The tag bit can then be used to find the good outcomes.

Outcome	Amplitude
b	s_b
g	s_g

$\xrightarrow{O}$

Tag bit	Outcome	Amplitude
0	b	s_b
1	g	s_g

Figure 5.4 The effect of a bit oracle on the amplitudes of a state with good outcomes g and bad outcomes b

The function `classical_bit_oracle` is a classical implementation of a bit oracle. Remember, when a qubit is added to a quantum system, the digit in the binary outcome corresponding to the last qubit added is the leftmost digit. If we add a tag bit to an n-qubit state representing $N = 2^n$ items, there will be $2^{n+1} = 2N$ possible outcomes. The first N outcomes will have 0 in the tag bit position, and the second N outcomes will have 1 in the tag bit position. Therefore, we can find the amplitude corresponding to the item with 1 in the tag bit position by adding N to the index of the item with 0 in the tag bit position:

```
def classical_bit_oracle(state, predicate):
    N = len(state)
    state = state + [0 for _ in range(N)]
    for item in range(N):
        if predicate(item):
            state[N + item] = state[item]
```

- Adding a qubit doubles the number of possible outcomes and therefore the number of amplitudes.
- Finds the amplitude corresponding to the outcome with 1 in the tag bit position by adding N to the amplitude index

```
            state[item] = 0
    return state
```

Let's apply this oracle to a state with $n = 3$ qubits, where 3 is the good state:

```
predicate = lambda k: True if k == 3 else False

n = 3
state = [1/sqrt(2**n) for _ in range(2**n)]

tag_state = classical_bit_oracle(state, predicate)
```

In the second state table in figure 5.5, the good outcome is the only outcome with 1 in the tag bit position and a corresponding amplitude whose magnitude is greater than zero.

Out	Bin	Ampl	Dir	Mag	Ampl bar
0	000	0.35	0.0°	0.35	
1	001	0.35	0.0°	0.35	
2	010	0.35	0.0°	0.35	
3	011	0.35	0.0°	0.35	
4	100	0.35	0.0°	0.35	
5	101	0.35	0.0°	0.35	
6	110	0.35	0.0°	0.35	
7	111	0.35	0.0°	0.35	

$\xrightarrow{O}$

Out	Bin	Ampl	Dir	Mag	Ampl bar
0	0000	0.35	0.0°	0.35	
1	0001	0.35	0.0°	0.35	
2	0010	0.35	0.0°	0.35	
3	0011	0		0	
4	0100	0.35	0.0°	0.35	
5	0101	0.35	0.0°	0.35	
6	0110	0.35	0.0°	0.35	
7	0111	0.35	0.0°	0.35	
8	1000	0		0	
9	1001	0		0	
10	1010	0		0	
11	1011	0.35	0.0°	0.35	
12	1100	0		0	
13	1101	0		0	
14	1110	0		0	
15	1111	0		0	

Figure 5.5 The effect of a bit oracle on a three-qubit state prepared with amplitudes in equal superposition and a single good outcome, 3

We can also apply this oracle to a random state generated using our `generate_state` function:

```
from util import generate_state

n = 3
state = generate_state(n, seed=777)
state = classical_bit_oracle(state, predicate)
```

In the state tables in figure 5.6, we can see that the amplitude corresponding to the good outcome with 1 in the tag bit position has a nonzero magnitude, and the amplitudes corresponding to the bad outcomes with 1 in the tag bit position are zero.

5.2 Quantum implementation of oracles

Out	Bin	Ampl	Dir	Mag	Ampl bar
0	000	−0.17 − 0.16i	−136.0°	0.23	
1	001	−0.25 + 0.21i	140.3°	0.32	
2	010	−0.07 + 0.29i	104.0°	0.29	
3	011	0.25 − 0.01i	−2.5°	0.25	
4	100	0.25 − 0.12i	−25.5°	0.28	
5	101	−0.15 − 0.39i	−110.9°	0.42	
6	110	0.36 − 0.30i	−40.3°	0.47	
7	111	0.37 + 0.28i	37.3°	0.46	

→ O →

Out	Bin	Ampl	Dir	Mag	Ampl bar
0	0000	−0.17 − 0.16i	−136.0°	0.23	
1	0001	−0.25 + 0.21i	140.3°	0.32	
2	0010	−0.07 + 0.29i	104.0°	0.29	
3	0011	0		0	
4	0100	0.25 − 0.12i	−25.5°	0.28	
5	0101	−0.15 − 0.39i	−110.9°	0.42	
6	0110	0.36 − 0.30i	−40.3°	0.47	
7	0111	0.37 + 0.28i	37.3°	0.46	
8	1000	0		0	
9	1001	0		0	
10	1010	0		0	
11	1011	0.25 − 0.01i	−2.5°	0.25	
12	1100	0		0	
13	1101	0		0	
14	1110	0		0	
15	1111	0		0	

Figure 5.6 The effect of a bit oracle on a random three-qubit state with a single good outcome, 3

> **Exercise 5.2**
> Create a random state with $n = 4$ qubits, and apply a bit oracle for good outcome 11.

Now that we understand how these two types of oracles work, let's look at quantum circuits that implement oracles.

5.2 Quantum implementation of oracles

The classical implementation of phase oracles and bit oracles is helpful for understanding their effects. In this section, we will look at quantum implementations of oracles.

5.2.1 Creating quantum circuits from building blocks

As we work with more and more complex circuits, it is essential to be able to combine reusable circuits the same way we do gates. In listing 5.1, we introduce a method of the `QuantumCircuit` class called `append` that allows us to combine circuits. The implementation applies the individual gates in the circuit to a register in another circuit with the same number of qubits.

Listing 5.1 Method to append a quantum circuit to a register in another circuit instance

```
def append(self, circuit, reg):
    assert(reg.size == sum(circuit.regs))
    for tr in circuit.transformations:
        self.transformations.append(
            QuantumTransformation(
                tr.gate,
                reg.shift + tr.target,
                tr.controls,
```

For example, let's create a three-qubit register and a circuit with one X gate applied to target qubit 0:

```
from sim_circuit import *

n = 3
q = QuantumRegister(n)
qc = QuantumCircuit(q)
qc.x(0)
```

Next, we will use the `uniform` function from chapter 4. This function creates a circuit for encoding the uniform distribution in a state with n qubits:

```
def uniform(n):
    q = QuantumRegister(n)
    qc = QuantumCircuit(q)

    for i in range(len(q)):
        qc.h(q[i])

    return qc
```

We can apply the circuit defined by the function `uniform` to our three-qubit register using the `append` method:

```
n = 3
uniform_qc = uniform(n)       ◁─── Applies the circuit
qc.append(uniform_qc, q)           to the register q
```

We can also append a circuit that is controlled on qubits in other registers with the `c_append` method defined in the next listing. The implementation adds the additional control qubits to the existing control qubits (if any) of each gate in the circuit to be appended.

Listing 5.2 Method to append a circuit with control qubits

```
def c_append(self, circuit, c, reg):
    assert(c not in range(reg.shift, reg.shift + reg.size))
    for tr in circuit.transformations:
        self.transformations.append(
            QuantumTransformation(
                tr.gate,
                reg.shift + tr.target,
                [c] + [reg.shift + t for t in tr.controls],
                tr.name,
                tr.arg
            )
        )
```

Unitary transformations

The action of a circuit on m qubits is mathematically represented by the action of a matrix with 2^m rows and 2^m columns. The matrix has to preserve the squared magnitudes of the set of m amplitudes it acts on. Such matrices are a more general form of the two-by-two matrices that represent single-qubit gates. And just like single-qubit gates changing all amplitudes in pairs, an m-qubit unitary changes all amplitudes in groups of 2^m.

We can use a butterfly-style diagram similar to the one we use for pairs to indicate that groups of amplitudes are recombined using a unitary transformation.

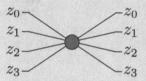

Butterfly-style diagram for the action of two-qubit transformation on a group of four amplitudes

We can also use the circular version of the diagram that shows how the grouping of amplitudes (outcomes) is done. Each arc in the diagram represents a group.

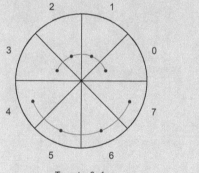

Circular butterfly diagrams showing groups of four outcomes whose amplitudes are transformed by a two-qubit transformation

Our simulator includes support for appending multi-qubit circuits represented by unitaries.

5.2.2 Phase oracle

Using a list of good outcomes `items`, we can use the function in listing 5.3 to create a circuit that multiplies the amplitudes corresponding to the good outcomes by -1.

> **NOTE** Following the convention in Qiskit, the `mcp` method applies a multi-controlled phase gate transformation.

Listing 5.3 Function to create a phase oracle circuit

```
from math import pi

def is_bit_not_set(m, k):
    return not (m & (1 << k))

def phase_oracle_match(n, items):
    q = QuantumRegister(n)
    qc = QuantumCircuit(q)

    for m in items:
        for i in range(n):
            if is_bit_not_set(m, i):
                qc.x(q[i])

        qc.mcp(pi, [q[i] for i in range(len(q) - 1)], q[len(q) - 1])
        for i in range(n):
            if is_bit_not_set(m, i):
                qc.x(q[i])
    return qc
```

Multi-controlled transformation

Let's use this function to create a phase oracle circuit for $n = 3$ qubits and a single good outcome, 3:

```
n = 3
items = [3]

oracle_circuit = phase_oracle_match(n, items)
```

This oracle circuit is illustrated in figure 5.7.

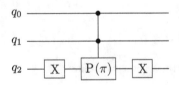

Figure 5.7 The phase oracle circuit for $n = 3$ qubits and a single good outcome, 3

We can create a state in equal superposition (uniform distribution) by applying a Hadamard gate to each qubit:

```
q = QuantumRegister(n)
qc = QuantumCircuit(q)

for i in range(n):
    qc.h(q[i])
```

5.2 Quantum implementation of oracles

Then we can apply the oracle circuit:

```
qc.append(oracle_circuit, QuantumRegister(n))
```

The circuit created is illustrated in figure 5.8.

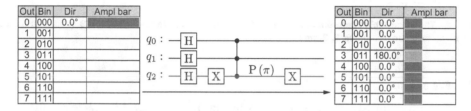

Figure 5.8 The state tables before and after applying a circuit that applies a Hadamard gate to each of n = 3 qubits followed by the phase oracle for a single good outcome, 3

Let's create an oracle for $n = 3$ qubits and associated with good outcomes 1, 3, and 5:

```
n = 3
items = [1, 3, 5]

oracle_circuit = phase_oracle_match(n, items)
```

Let's create a circuit that applies a Hadamard gate to each qubit and then applies the oracle defined above:

```
q = QuantumRegister(n)
qc = QuantumCircuit(q)

for i in range(n):
    qc.h(q[i])

qc.append(oracle_circuit, QuantumRegister(n))
```

The circuit and the resulting state are shown in figure 5.9. In the second state table in the figure, the amplitudes corresponding to each of the three good outcomes have been rotated by 180°.

122   CHAPTER 5 *Selecting outcomes with quantum oracles*

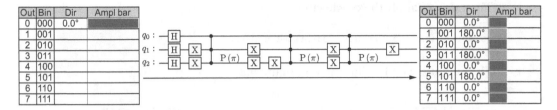

Figure 5.9 The state tables before and after applying a Hadamard gate to each of *n* = 3 qubits followed by the phase oracle for good outcomes 1, 3, and 5

5.2.3 Bit oracle

The function `bit_oracle_match` in listing 5.4 creates a bit oracle circuit for a state with n qubits and a list of good outcomes items.

> **NOTE** We use an additional qubit, often called an *ancilla* or *ancillary* qubit.

Listing 5.4 Function to create a bit oracle circuit

```
def bit_oracle_match(n, items):
    q = QuantumRegister(n)
    a = QuantumRegister(1)
    qc = QuantumCircuit(q, a)

    for m in items:
        for i in range(n):
            if is_bit_not_set(m, i):
                qc.x(q[i])

        qc.mcx([q[i] for i in range(len(q))], a[0])    ◁─── Multi-controlled transformation

        for i in range(n):
            if is_bit_not_set(m, i):
                qc.x(q[i])
    return qc
```

Let's create the bit oracle circuit and apply it to our familiar example where a state with *n* = 3 qubits is prepared using Hadamard gates and the good item is 3.

```
n = 3
items = [3]

oracle_circuit = bit_oracle_match(n, items)

q = QuantumRegister(n)
a = QuantumRegister(1)
qc = QuantumCircuit(q, a)

for i in range(n):
    qc.h(q[i])

qc.append(oracle_circuit, QuantumRegister(n + 1))    ◁─── The circuit created by bit_oracle_match adds an ancilla qubit, so we need to pass a register with n+1 qubits when we append the circuit.
```

5.2 Quantum implementation of oracles

The circuit created and the state tables before and after its application are illustrated in figure 5.10.

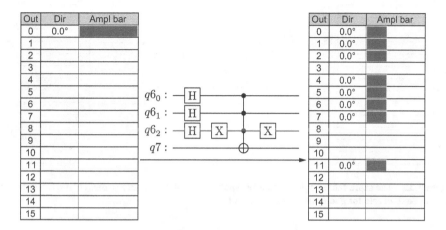

Figure 5.10 The state tables before and after applying a Hadamard gate to each of *n* = 3 qubits followed by a bit oracle for a single good outcome 3

Next, let's create a bit oracle for the same state with three good outcomes:

```
n = 3
items = [1, 3, 5]

oracle_circuit = bit_oracle_match(n, items)

q = QuantumRegister(n)
a = QuantumRegister(1)
qc = QuantumCircuit(q, a)

for i in range(n):
    qc.h(q[i])

qc.append(oracle_circuit, QuantumRegister(n+1))
```

The oracle circuit created and the state tables before and after its application are illustrated in figure 5.11. In the second state table in the figure, the outcomes with 1 in the tag bit position (located in the lower half of the state table) have amplitudes with a magnitude of 0 if they correspond to a bad outcome and a magnitude greater than 0 if they correspond to a good outcome.

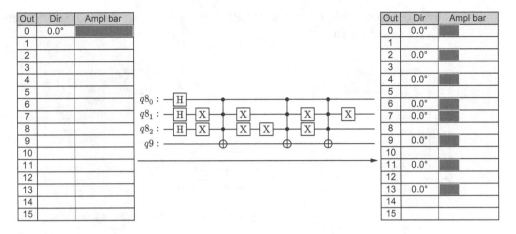

Figure 5.11 The state tables before and after applying a Hadamard gate to each of $n = 3$ qubits followed by the phase oracle for good outcomes 1, 3, and 5

5.3 Converting between phase and bit quantum oracles

In some cases, we may want to create an oracle using an oracle of a different type. In this section, we will learn how to convert from a phase oracle to a bit oracle and vice versa.

5.3.1 Converting a phase oracle to a bit oracle

If we have a phase oracle circuit for a set of good outcomes and n qubits, we can create a bit oracle circuit. The circuit diagram in figure 5.12 illustrates the circuit to create a bit oracle using a phase oracle circuit O_P.

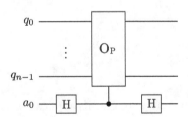

Figure 5.12 Circuit diagram of a bit oracle using the corresponding phase oracle O_P

If we have a phase oracle circuit defined using the `QuantumCircuit` class in our simulator, we can use it to implement the circuit in figure 5.12 using the following function:

```
def phase_to_bit_oracle(oracle_circuit):
    n = sum(oracle_circuit.regs)            ◁── Gets the number of
    q = QuantumRegister(n)                      qubits used for the
    a = QuantumRegister(1)                      phase oracle
    qc = QuantumCircuit(q, a)
    qc.h(a[0])
```

```
qc.c_append(oracle_circuit, a[0], q)
qc.h(a[0])

return qc
```
◁ **Applies the phase oracle circuit controlled on the ancilla qubit**

For example, let's create the phase oracle circuit for $n = 3$ qubits and good outcomes 1, 3, and 5:

```
n = 3
items = [1, 3, 5]
oracle_circuit = phase_oracle_match(n, items)
```

This phase oracle circuit is illustrated in figure 5.13. The bit oracle circuit created using this phase oracle circuit is shown in figure 5.14.

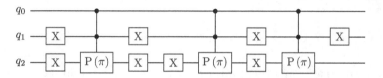

Figure 5.13 Circuit diagram of the phase oracle O_P for $n = 3$ qubits and good outcomes 1, 3, and 5

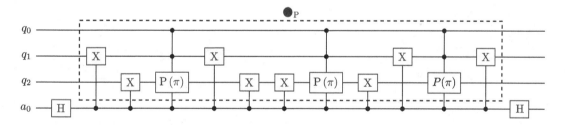

Figure 5.14 Circuit diagram of the bit oracle created using the phase oracle O_P for $n = 3$ qubits and good outcomes 1, 3, and 5 in figure 5.13

In figure 5.14, each gate in the phase oracle circuit O_P is applied with the ancilla qubit as an additional control qubit. Remember, we can use the c_append method of our QuantumCircuit class to apply a circuit to another circuit with an additional control qubit.

As we did in the first section, let's use the generate_state function to generate a random state with $n = 3$ qubits. This time, we will add an ancilla qubit:

```
state = generate_state(n, seed=777) + [0 for _ in range(2**n)]
```

> **Initializing any state**
>
> In this chapter, we will add the `initialize` method to the `QuantumCircuit` class, which allows us to set the state in a `QuantumCircuit` class instance:
>
> ```
> def initialize(self, state):
>     self.state = state
> ```

Now, let's create a circuit with the random state above as the prepared state and then append the converted oracle to the circuit instance:

```
q = QuantumRegister(n)
a = QuantumRegister(1)

qc = QuantumCircuit(q, a)
qc.initialize(state.copy())

qc.append(phase_to_bit_oracle(oracle_circuit), QuantumRegister(n+1))
```

Figure 5.15 illustrates applying this converted oracle to the random state. In the second state table in the figure, we can see that the applied circuit acted as a bit oracle.

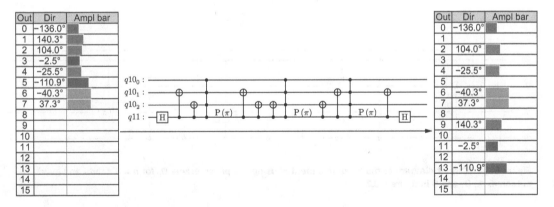

Figure 5.15 The state tables before and after applying the bit oracle in figure 5.14 to a random $n = 3$ qubit state

5.3.2 Converting a bit oracle to a phase oracle

If we have the bit oracle circuit for a set of good outcomes and n qubits, we can create a circuit that will apply the phase oracle. The circuit diagram in figure 5.16 illustrates the circuit to create a phase oracle using a bit oracle circuit O_B.

5.3 Converting between phase and bit quantum oracles

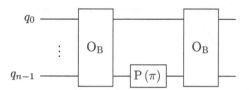

Figure 5.16 Circuit diagram of a phase oracle using the corresponding bit oracle O_B

We can use the following function to create a circuit that will act as a phase oracle, where the parameter `oracle_circuit` is a bit oracle:

```
def bit_to_phase_oracle(oracle_circuit):
    n = sum(oracle_circuit.regs)
    q = QuantumRegister(n)
    qc = QuantumCircuit(q)
    qc.append(oracle_circuit, q)
    qc.p(pi, q[len(q)-1])
    qc.append(oracle_circuit, q)

    return qc
```

Let's create the bit oracle circuit for our example problem where $n = 3$ qubits and the good outcomes are 1, 3, and 5:

```
n = 3
items = [1, 3, 5]
oracle_circuit = bit_oracle_match(n, items)
```

Remember, this circuit will include an ancilla qubit.

The bit oracle circuit is illustrated in figure 5.17. The phase oracle circuit created using the bit oracle circuit in figure 5.17 is shown in figure 5.18.

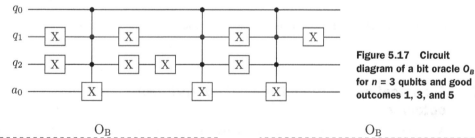

Figure 5.17 Circuit diagram of a bit oracle O_B for $n = 3$ qubits and good outcomes 1, 3, and 5

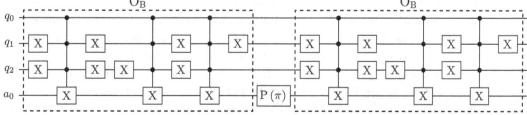

Figure 5.18 Circuit diagram of a phase oracle created using a bit oracle O_B for $n = 3$ qubits and good outcomes 1, 3, and 5 in figure 5.17

Let's implement the same example using a phase oracle created from a bit oracle:

```
n = 3
items = [1, 3, 5]
oracle_circuit = bit_oracle_match(n, items)

state = generate_state(n, seed=777) + [0 for _ in range(2**n)]

q = QuantumRegister(n)
a = QuantumRegister(1)
qc = QuantumCircuit(q, a)

qc.initialize(state.copy())

qc.append(bit_to_phase_oracle(oracle_circuit), QuantumRegister(n+1))
```

Figure 5.19 visualizes this example. We can see that the applied circuit acts as a phase oracle, and the amplitudes corresponding to the good outcomes are rotated by 180°.

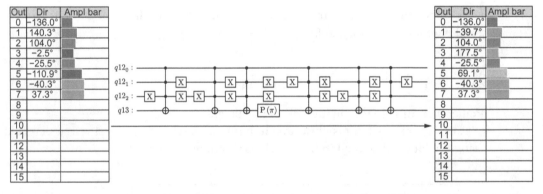

Figure 5.19 The state tables before and after applying the phase oracle in figure 5.18 to a random n = 3 qubit state

5.4 Fibonacci numbers and the golden ratio with good outcomes

As we will see in the next chapter, we use oracles to increase the probability of good outcomes and decrease the probability of bad outcomes. In this section, we will look at an outcome selection example related to Fibonacci numbers and the golden ratio, where we make the bad outcomes impossible (probability 0).

We know that a quantum computation on $n > 0$ qubits has 2^n outcomes. Let's define the good outcomes as those whose binary representation does not contain two consecutive 1s. We will call this set G_n, and we denote its size by $|G_n|$. If $n = 1$, then $|G_1| = 2$ because binary strings with one digit do not contain consecutive 1s. If $n = 2$, then $|G_2| = 3$ because only one out of the four possible binary strings has two consecutive 1s (11).

5.4 Fibonacci numbers and the golden ratio with good outcomes

For $n > 2$, the number of good outcomes is

$$|G_n| = |G_{n-1}| + |G_{n-2}|$$

To understand this, we will consider the following two cases:

1. If the first digit of a binary string in G_n is 0, the binary string made up from its last $n-1$ digits needs to be in G_{n-1}.
2. If the first digit of a binary string in G_n is 1, the digit after it must be 0, and the binary string made up from its last $n-2$ digits needs to be in G_{n-2}.

> **Example**
>
> For $n = 3$, the set of good outcomes is
>
> $$G_3 = \{000, 001, 010, 100, 101\}$$
>
> There are three binary strings in the set of good outcomes G_3 with the first digit 0: 000, 001, and 010. The binary string made up of the last $n - 1 = 2$ digits in each of these binary strings (00, 01, 10) is in the set
>
> $$G_{n-1} = G_2 = \{00, 01, 10\}$$
>
> There are two binary strings in G_3 with the first digit 1: 100 and 101. The binary string made up of the last ($n - 2 = 1$) digit is in the set
>
> $$G_{n-2} = G_1 = \{0, 1\}$$

> **Exercise 5.3**
>
> Show that the two properties described in the previous example are true for the set of good outcomes G_4.

You may recognize this pattern of a sequence of numbers where each number is the sum of the two before it. It matches the *Fibonacci sequence*.

> **Fibonacci numbers**
>
> We can compute the nth number in the Fibonacci sequence (denoted by F_n) using the following recursive Python function:
>
> ```
> def recursive_fib(n):
>     assert n >= 0
> ```

> **(continued)**
> ```
> if n <= 1:
>     return n
> else:
>     return recursive_fib(n - 1) + recursive_fib(n - 2)
> ```
>
> We can use the recursive function to create a list of the first 10 Fibonacci numbers:
>
> ```
> [recursive_fib(n) for n in range(10)]
> ```
>
> The output is
>
> ```
> [0, 1, 1, 2, 3, 5, 8, 13, 21, 34]
> ```
>
> As the Fibonacci numbers get larger, the ratio between consecutive numbers approaches *the golden ratio*. The golden ratio is the irrational number
>
> $$\frac{1 + \sqrt{5}}{2}$$
>
> and is denoted by φ.

For n qubits, the number of good outcomes—outcomes without consecutive 1s—is the Fibonacci number F_{n+2} ($|G_n| = F_{n+2}$). We can create a circuit that identifies the good outcomes and makes the bad outcomes impossible. The function `fib_circuit` creates this circuit for a given number of qubits $n > 0$:

```
from math import asin

def fib_circuit(n):
    theta = 2*asin((sqrt(5) - 1)/2)

    q = QuantumRegister(n)
    qc = QuantumCircuit(q)

    for i in range(n):
        qc.ry(theta, q[i])

    for i in range(n - 1):
        qc.cry(-theta, q[i], q[i + 1])

    return qc
```

Let's create the circuit for one qubit:

```
qc = fib_circuit(1)
```

5.4 Fibonacci numbers and the golden ratio with good outcomes

In the state prepared by this circuit, shown in figure 5.20, we can see that both outcomes are identified as good outcomes ($|G_1| = F_3 = 2$).

Outcome	Binary	Amplitude	Amplitude bar	Probability
0	0	0.79		0.62
1	1	0.62		0.38

Figure 5.20 A single-qubit state with good outcomes G_1

If $n = 2$, there are $|G_2| = F_4 = 3$ good outcomes. Figure 5.21 shows the state created with $n = 2$ qubits.

Outcome	Binary	Amplitude	Amplitude bar	Probability
0	00	0.62		0.38
1	01	0.62		0.38
2	10	0.49		0.24
3	11	−0.00		0.00

Figure 5.21 A two-qubit state with good outcomes G_2

For a given number of qubits n, we can see that

- There are F_{n+1} good outcomes with the first binary digit 0 (top half of the state table), and the amplitudes corresponding to these outcomes are all equal.
- There are F_n good outcomes with the first binary digit 1 (bottom half of the state table), and the amplitudes corresponding to these outcomes are all equal.

The ratio of the probabilities of a good outcome that starts with 1 and a good outcome that starts with 0 is the golden ratio.

In figure 5.21, there are $F_{n+1} = 2$ good outcomes with the first digit 0 in their binary form and $F_n = 1$ good outcome with the first digit 1 in their binary form. We can check that the ratio of the probability of a good outcome that starts with 0 and that of a good outcome that starts with 1 is the golden ratio:

```
from util import is_close

qc = fib_circuit(2)
state = qc.run()

assert is_close(abs(state[0])**2/abs(state[2])**2, (1+sqrt(5))/2)
assert is_close(abs(state[1])**2/abs(state[2])**2, (1+sqrt(5))/2)
```

Checks that the ratio between the probability of outcome 00 and outcome 10 is the golden ratio

Checks that the ratio between the probability of outcome 01 and outcome 10 is the golden ratio

Figure 5.22 shows the state created with $n = 3$ qubits. In this state table, there are $|G_3| = F_5 = 5$ good outcomes.

Outcome	Binary	Amplitude	Amplitude bar	Probability
0	000	0.49		0.24
1	001	0.49		0.24
2	010	0.49		0.24
3	011	−0.00		0.00
4	100	0.38		0.15
5	101	0.38		0.15
6	110	0.00		0.00
7	111	−0.00		0.00

Figure 5.22 A three-qubit state with good outcomes G_3

There are $F_{n+1} = 3$ good outcomes with the first digit 0 in their binary form and $F_n = 2$ good outcomes with the first digit 1 in their binary form.

Exercise 5.4
There are only two distinct nonzero probabilities for all outcomes. Check that their ratio is the golden ratio.

Summary

- To solve problems that search for specific outcomes or estimate the probability of specific outcomes, we need mechanisms to identify outcomes of interest.
- The quantum circuits used to identify certain outcomes that we refer to as "good" outcomes are called oracles.
- Phase oracles rotate the amplitudes of the good outcomes by 180 degrees.
- Bit oracles entangle outcomes with an additional qubit so that the good ones are associated with its measurement of 1 and the bad ones with its measurement of 0.
- We can convert from a bit oracle to a phase oracle and vice versa.

Quantum search and probability estimation

This chapter covers
- Amplifying magnitudes of desired outcomes with Grover operators
- Searching for desired outcomes of quantum computations with measurement

In this chapter, we will see how quantum measurement can help us with our second main pattern of quantum computations: searching for specific outcomes. Specifically, we will learn about *Grover's algorithm* and related methods, such as *amplitude amplification*. Grover's algorithm can offer quadratic speed up (with respect to the number of queries) over classical approaches for certain problems. Therefore, the methods introduced in this chapter have broad applications, such as search, optimization, and machine learning. To start, we will dive into one of the most common and consequential computational challenges: unstructured search.

Suppose we have an unstructured database with N items, and we want to find one specific item in the list. To perform this search classically, we can use a query function that checks whether an item meets the desired search criteria. We will have to decide the order in which to perform the queries and check one item at a time. Best-case scenario, we happen to find the right item on the first try! Worst-case scenario, we have to check all N items, and the correct one is the last one we check. In a classical solution, we might need to perform anywhere from 1 to N checks or queries. For a large enough N, we know that the best classical algorithms find the right item with a high probability within $N/2$ checks.

If we use a quantum solution to this problem, each time we perform the equivalent quantum query or evaluation of the search criteria, we increase the probability of finding the right item on measurement. To find one specific item in an unordered list of N items, we will have a very high probability of finding the item after applying approximately $\sqrt{N}$ queries. In figure 6.1, we compare the number of steps (queries) needed to have a high probability of finding the one desired item in an unordered list of N items using classical search methods versus Grover's algorithm.

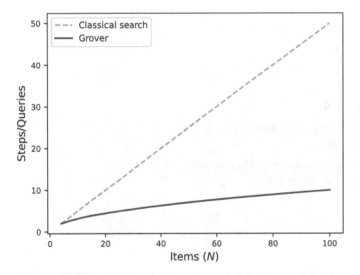

Figure 6.1 The number of steps (queries) needed to find one item in an unordered list of *n* items with a high probability

In chapter 5, we learned about quantum oracles. In this chapter, we will learn about another procedure, called *inversion* or *inversion by the mean*. These two concepts are used to implement Grover's algorithm, as shown in figure 6.2.

6.1 Amplitude amplification: Intuition and classical implementation

Assume we want to find one or more items in an unordered list of N items. We can represent each of the items as an outcome of a state with at least $\lceil \log_2 N \rceil$ qubits. To find the desired items, we need to increase the probability of measuring their corresponding outcomes. To do this, we will use a method typically called *amplitude amplification*, more accurately referred to as *magnitude amplification*.

6.1 Amplitude amplification: Intuition and classical implementation

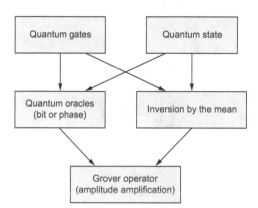

Figure 6.2 A dependency diagram of concepts introduced in this chapter

To apply the amplitude amplification algorithm, we need to apply the following two steps:

1. Prepare an initial state using a circuit (operator) A.
2. Construct an operator G, and apply it j times, for an integer $j > 0$ whose choice will be discussed in this chapter.

The operator G is called a *Grover iterate*, or *Grover operator*. The construction of the operator consists of a quantum oracle and the *inversion* operator.

Figure 6.3 illustrates this method with a circuit diagram. As we have done in previous chapters, we will simulate these steps using classical implementations and then introduce the corresponding quantum circuits.

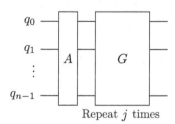

Figure 6.3 Circuit diagram of the magnitude (amplitude) amplification method where operator A prepares a state and operator G is the Grover iterate

6.1.1 Finding good outcomes with oracles

Assume we want to find one special item in a list of $N = 8$ items, but we do not know where the item is. We can represent each of the items as an outcome of a quantum state with $n = 3$ qubits. Any randomly selected outcome has the same probability of being the good outcome. We represent this with equal amplitudes for each outcome:

```
from math import sqrt

n = 3
state = [1/sqrt(2**n) for _ in range(2**n)]
```

This state is illustrated in figure 6.4.

Outcome	Binary	Amplitude	Direction	Magnitude	Amplitude bar
0	000	0.35	0.0°	0.35	
1	001	0.35	0.0°	0.35	
2	010	0.35	0.0°	0.35	
3	011	0.35	0.0°	0.35	
4	100	0.35	0.0°	0.35	
5	101	0.35	0.0°	0.35	
6	110	0.35	0.0°	0.35	
7	111	0.35	0.0°	0.35	

Figure 6.4 A three-qubit state where all amplitudes have equal, real values

In chapter 5, we learned how a quantum oracle identifies, or "tags," specific outcomes. We call the tagged outcomes *good* outcomes and all the other outcomes *bad* outcomes. We covered two types of oracles:

- Phase oracles, which rotate the amplitudes of the good outcomes by 180°
- Bit oracles, which entangle the good outcomes with another qubit that is measured 1

Let's look at an example of the classical implementation of a phase oracle from chapter 5. The `predicate` function identifies good outcome 3 as the only good outcome:

```
predicate = lambda k: True if k == 3 else False
```

We can use this predicate for the classical implementation of a phase oracle and apply it to the state shown in figure 6.4:

```
def oracle(state, predicate):
    for item in range(len(state)):
        if predicate(item):
            state[item] *= -1

oracle(state, predicate)
```

The resulting state is shown in figure 6.5.

In this chapter, we will learn how to manipulate the amplitudes of outcomes tagged by oracles, increasing the probability of measuring those outcomes. In the context of an unstructured search for a single item in a list, this method allows us to increase the probability of measuring the outcome that represents the item we are looking for as long as it is tagged by an oracle.

6.1 Amplitude amplification: Intuition and classical implementation

Outcome	Binary	Amplitude	Direction	Magnitude	Amplitude bar
0	000	0.35	0.0°	0.35	
1	001	0.35	0.0°	0.35	
2	010	0.35	0.0°	0.35	
3	011	−0.35	180.0°	0.35	
4	100	0.35	0.0°	0.35	
5	101	0.35	0.0°	0.35	
6	110	0.35	0.0°	0.35	
7	111	0.35	0.0°	0.35	

Figure 6.5 A three-qubit state after a phase oracle for good outcome 3 is applied to the state in figure 6.4

NOTE In the examples in this chapter, the outcomes we are searching for—the good outcomes—are classically known for the sake of understanding. In many problems, the good outcomes are not known before we run a quantum computation. The true power of Grover's algorithm will become apparent in the coming chapters when we look at problems with multiple registers of qubits.

6.1.2 Computing similarity with inner products

Inner products are used in many problems where we need to measure the similarity between vectors. In particular, the projection of one vector onto another can be calculated using an inner product, as shown in figure 6.6.

$v = v_{\parallel} + v_{\perp}, \|u\| = 1$

$v_{\parallel} = \langle v, u \rangle$

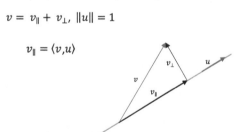

Figure 6.6 The projection of a two-dimensional vector onto another as an inner product

You may be familiar with the SUMPRODUCT operation in Excel or the weighted sums used in combining inputs with weights in neural networks. These are examples of inner products, sometimes called *dot products* in these contexts.

Let's use a simple example to break down the main idea behind computing inner products. Imagine that we have a shopping list of items. For example, say we bought four apples, two oranges, two peaches, and three bananas. Let's assume that one apple costs $1.20, one orange costs $1.50, one peach costs $2.00, and one banana costs $0.70. We can express these quantities and prices as lists:

```
quantities = [4, 2, 2, 3]
prices = [1.2, 1.5, 2, 0.7]
```

To calculate the total price for the list of items, we multiply the quantity of each item by its price and add the results together:

```
print(sum([quantities[k] * prices[k] for k in range(len(quantities))]))
```

The printed sum is

```
13.9
```

In this example, we have a quantity list (vector) and a price list (vector). The printed sum is the inner product of the two vectors. The inner product of two vectors v_1 and v_2 is typically denoted by $\langle v_1, v_2 \rangle$.

The inner product of two complex vectors is defined as the sum of the products of each element in the first vector and the conjugate of the corresponding element in the second vector. The two vectors must have the same number of elements.

The following Python code computes the inner product of two state vectors, `state1` and `state2`:

```
sum(state1[k]*state2[k].conjugate() for k in range(len(state1)))
```

The `numpy` package provides a function called `vdot` (vector dot product) for this functionality. However, to avoid additional code dependencies, we can use the `inner` function defined as follows.

Listing 6.1 Computing the inner product of two state vectors

```
def inner(v1, v2):
    assert(len(v1) == len(v2))
    return sum(z1*z2.conjugate() for z1, z2 in zip(v1, v2))
```

For two vectors v_1 and v_2, we will use the notation $\langle v_1, v_2 \rangle$ to denote their inner product, just as for the dot product. This is the most common definition in mathematical literature, but it is also possible to conjugate the first vector instead of the second, which is equivalent to switching the order of the vectors in the inner product.

Exercise 6.1
What is the inner product of *i, i* and *−i, i*?

The inner product of two quantum states of the same length is a complex number with a magnitude of at most 1. The magnitude is 1 when the states are identical, meaning the inner product of a quantum state with itself is 1. This is because when you multiply a complex number with its conjugate, you get its squared magnitude. And when you sum up the squared magnitudes of the amplitudes in a quantum state, you get 1.

6.1.3 The inversion operator

With the good outcome(s) tagged by a quantum oracle, we use a procedure that is often called *inversion by the mean* to increase the magnitude of the good outcome(s). We will simply call this operator *inversion*.

> **NOTE** The name *inversion by the mean* applies to the original context of the Grover algorithm, where the initial state consists of amplitudes with equal magnitudes (equal superposition).

Geometrically, the inversion operator reflects, or mirrors, a state vector v into another state vector u. We will typically denote this operator by M_u, or simply by M when the state vector u is clear from the context.

To understand what it does, let's look at a classical equivalent implementation using the function defined in listing 6.1. The function takes two parameters: a state before (`original`) and after (`current`) the amplitudes corresponding to the good outcomes have been multiplied by –1. It uses the `inner` function defined in listing 6.1 to compute their similarity.

Listing 6.2 Classical implementation of the inversion operator

```
def inversion(original, current):
    proj = inner(original, current)
    for k in range(len(current)):
        current[k] = 2*proj*original[k] - current[k]
```

The inner product between the `original` state vector and the `current` state is a complex number that reflects the similarity between the two states. Its magnitude is at most 1.

Let's understand the effect of the inversion transformation with a visual example. We will look at complex numbers as points in a plane (endpoints of vectors starting at the origin). Figure 6.7 illustrates example amplitudes of an outcome k in the states `original` and `current`.

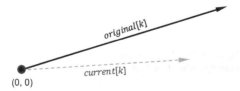

Figure 6.7 Vector visualization of the amplitudes of an outcome k in the states `original` and `current`

To find the new amplitude of outcome *k*, we do the following:

1. Multiply the original amplitude of outcome *k* by the inner product between the entire `original` and `current` state vectors. The result is a single complex number (point in the plane).
2. Update the current amplitude of outcome *k* to be its inversion (reflection) with respect to the complex number (or vector) in the previous step.

This step is illustrated in figure 6.8.

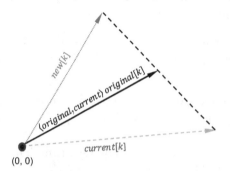

Figure 6.8 The value new [*k*] is the inversion of current [*k*] around the point ⟨original,current⟩original[*k*].

The power of the inversion operator comes when it is applied one or more times after an oracle is applied. The effect increases or decreases the magnitudes of the good states (as tagged by the oracle). Let's look at an example using vector visualizations.

THE EFFECT OF THE INVERSION OPERATOR ON THE AMPLITUDES OF BAD OUTCOMES

The amplitudes of the bad outcomes are not changed when an oracle is applied. In figure 6.9, we show the amplitudes of a bad outcome *k* before and after an oracle is applied.

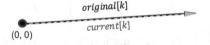

Figure 6.9 The amplitude of a bad outcome *k* before (original[*k*]) and after (current[*k*]) an oracle is applied

The effect of the inversion transformation on the amplitudes of bad outcomes is to decrease the magnitude of the current amplitude. Figure 6.10 illustrates this transformation.

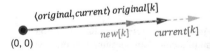

Figure 6.10 The inversion of the amplitude corresponding to a bad outcome *k*

6.1 Amplitude amplification: Intuition and classical implementation

THE EFFECT OF THE INVERSION OPERATOR ON THE AMPLITUDES OF GOOD OUTCOMES

The oracle multiplies the amplitudes of good outcomes by −1. This flips the amplitude in the opposite direction, as shown in figure 6.11. The inversion transformation increases the magnitude of the amplitude of the good outcome k, as shown in figure 6.12.

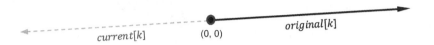

Figure 6.11 The amplitude of a good outcome k before (original[k]) and after (current[k]) an oracle is applied

Figure 6.12 The inversion of the amplitude corresponding to a good outcome k

Let's look at a code example. We'll use the three-qubit state in figure 6.5, obtained by applying an oracle that tags the outcome 3 to a state where the amplitudes are in equal superposition:

```
n = 3
state = [1/sqrt(2**n) for _ in range(2**n)]
s = state.copy()                          ⟵  Copies the original
                                              state to use for the
oracle(state, predicate)                      inversion
```

Now we can apply the inversion operator that reflects the current state into the original state (the state before the oracle was applied):

```
inversion(s, state)      ⟵  The parameter s is the initial state
                             before the oracle was applied.
```

We will denote this inversion operator as M_s, where s is the state before the oracle is applied. The resulting state table is shown in figure 6.13.

Let's look at another example, with a random $n = 3$ qubit state and good outcome 5:

```
from util import generate_state

n = 3
state = generate_state(n)

s = state.copy()

predicate = lambda k: True if k == 5 else False
oracle(state, predicate)
```

Outcome	Binary	Amplitude	Direction	Magnitude	Amplitude bar
0	000	0.18	0.0°	0.18	
1	001	0.18	0.0°	0.18	
2	010	0.18	0.0°	0.18	
3	011	0.88	0.0°	0.88	
4	100	0.18	0.0°	0.18	
5	101	0.18	0.0°	0.18	
6	110	0.18	0.0°	0.18	
7	111	0.18	0.0°	0.18	

Figure 6.13 The three-qubit state in figure 6.5 after applying the inversion operator M_s

Figure 6.14 illustrates the application of this oracle to a random state. We can see that the amplitude for the good outcome 5 is multiplied by –1, and the rest of the amplitudes remain unchanged.

Out	Bin	Ampl	Dir	Mag	Ampl bar
0	000	−0.19 − 0.13i	−144.1°	0.23	
1	001	0.21 + 0.03i	7.0°	0.21	
2	010	0.27 + 0.28i	45.6°	0.39	
3	011	0.49 + 0.11i	12.5°	0.50	
4	100	−0.20 + 0.02i	175.0°	0.20	
5	101	0.32 + 0.09i	15.1°	0.33	
6	110	−0.17 − 0.34i	−116.4°	0.38	
7	111	0.32 + 0.32i	45.0°	0.45	

$\xrightarrow{O}$

Out	Bin	Ampl	Dir	Mag	Ampl bar
0	000	−0.19 − 0.13i	−144.1°	0.23	
1	001	0.21 + 0.03i	7.0°	0.21	
2	010	0.27 + 0.28i	45.6°	0.39	
3	011	0.49 + 0.11i	12.5°	0.50	
4	100	−0.20 + 0.02i	175.0°	0.20	
5	101	−0.32 − 0.09i	−164.9°	0.33	
6	110	−0.17 − 0.34i	−116.4°	0.38	
7	111	0.32 + 0.32i	45.0°	0.45	

Figure 6.14 A random $n = 3$ qubit state before and after an oracle for good outcomes 5 is applied

Next, we perform the inversion:

```
inversion(s, state)
```

Figure 6.15 illustrates the state before and after this step. We can see that the magnitude of the amplitude of the good outcome increases, and the rest decrease.

Out	Bin	Ampl	Dir	Mag	Ampl bar
0	000	−0.19 − 0.13i	−144.1°	0.23	
1	001	0.21 + 0.03i	7.0°	0.21	
2	010	0.27 + 0.28i	45.6°	0.39	
3	011	0.49 + 0.11i	12.5°	0.50	
4	100	−0.20 + 0.02i	175.0°	0.20	
5	101	−0.32 − 0.09i	−164.9°	0.33	
6	110	−0.17 − 0.34i	−116.4°	0.38	
7	111	0.32 + 0.32i	45.0°	0.45	

$\xrightarrow{M}$

Out	Bin	Ampl	Dir	Mag	Ampl bar
0	000	−0.10 − 0.07i	−144.1°	0.13	
1	001	0.11 + 0.01i	7.0°	0.12	
2	010	0.15 + 0.15i	45.6°	0.22	
3	011	0.27 + 0.06i	12.5°	0.28	
4	100	−0.11 + 0.01i	175.0°	0.11	
5	101	0.82 + 0.22i	15.1°	0.85	
6	110	−0.10 − 0.19i	−116.4°	0.21	
7	111	0.18 + 0.18i	45.0°	0.25	

Figure 6.15 Applying the inversion operator to a random $n = 3$ qubit state with good outcome 5

Visualizing inversion by the mean

In general, the quantity

$$\langle \text{original}, \text{current}\rangle \text{original}[k]$$

is different for each outcome k. However, in the specific case that the original state vector is the equal superposition obtained by applying a Hadamard gate to each qubit in the state, this quantity is the average, or mean, of the amplitudes in the current state. Hence the name *inversion by the mean*.

For example, let's create an $n = 3$ qubit state in equal superposition and apply an oracle for good outcome 3:

```
n = 3
state = [1/sqrt(2**n) for _ in range(2**n)]

s = state.copy()

predicate = lambda k: True if k == 3 else False
oracle(state, predicate)
```

We can check that the mean of the amplitudes is equal to the quantity defined previously for bad outcomes k:

```
from util import is_close

amplitude_mean = sum(state)/2**n

proj = inner(s, state)
for k in range(len(state)):
    if k != 3:
        assert is_close(proj*state[k], amplitude_mean)
```

We visualize the amplitudes of the state after the oracle is applied with a vertical bar graph that shows negative amplitudes. The dashed line is the mean of the amplitudes.

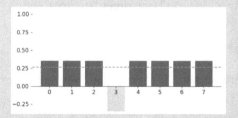

The amplitudes of a three-qubit state prepared with amplitudes in equal superposition after applying an oracle for good outcome 3

Now we can simulate the inversion by the mean with the following Python code:

```
for k in range(len(state)):
    state[k] = 2*amplitude_mean-state[k]
```

The resulting state is the same as the state in figure 6.13.

6.1.4 Putting it together: The Grover iterate

The combination of an oracle *O* and the inversion operator *M* corresponding to an initial state is called a *Grover operator* or *Grover iterate*. The term *iterate* comes from the fact that it is applied multiple times, iteratively.

If the initial state (which contains the magnitudes we want to amplify) is prepared by a circuit *A*, then the magnitude amplification procedure consists of *A* followed by a number of applications of *G*. This can be expressed as $G^j A$ for an integer $j > 0$. More precisely, the diagram in figure 6.16 reflects the fact that the Grover iterate consists of the application of a given oracle *O*, followed by the inversion operator *M* corresponding to the state prepared by operator *A*.

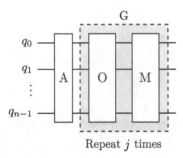

Figure 6.16 Circuit diagram of the magnitude amplification procedure $G^j A$, where g consists of an oracle O and the inversion operator M

Let's look closer at what happens each time we apply the operator *G*. Assume the initial combined measurement probability of good outcomes is

$$\sin^2(\theta)$$

for some angle θ. Note that any real number between 0 and 1 can be expressed in this form.

After $j \geq 0$ applications of the Grover iterate (oracle followed by inversion), the combined measurement probability of the good outcomes becomes

$$\sin^2((2j + 1)\theta)$$

The inner product of the state after operator *A* is applied and the state after *j* applications of the Grover iterate is

$$\cos(2j\theta)$$

In summary, the state tables in figure 6.17 show the combined probabilities of the good outcomes and bad outcomes before and after *j* applications of the Grover iterate. Using this knowledge, we can add assertions to the classical implementation of the Grover iterate to check the amplitudes of the state, as in the following listing.

6.1 Amplitude amplification: Intuition and classical implementation

Outcomes	Combined probability
bad	$\cos^2(\theta)$
good	$\sin^2(\theta)$

$\xrightarrow{G^j}$

Outcomes	Combined probability
bad	$\cos^2((2j+1)\theta)$
good	$\sin^2((2j+1)\theta)$

Figure 6.17 The combined measurement probabilities of good and bad outcomes before and after *j* applications of the Grover iterate

Listing 6.3 Classical implementation of the Grover iterate

```
from math import cos

def classical_grover(state, predicate, iterations):
    s = state.copy()
    items = [k for k in range(len(state)) if predicate(k)]

    p = sum([abs(s[k])**2 for k in items])
    theta = asin(sqrt(p))
    assert is_close(inner(s, state), 1)

    for it in range(1, iterations + 1):
        oracle(state, predicate)
        inversion(s, state)
        assert is_close(inner(s, state), cos(2 * it * theta))

        p = sum([abs(state[k])**2 for k in items])
        assert is_close(p, sin((2 * it + 1)*theta)**2)
```

Uses the probability of measuring a good outcome to define an angle theta

The inner product of the state after operator A is applied and the state after j applications of the Grover iterate is cos(2jθ).

Finds the new probability of measuring a good outcome

Checks that the probability of good outcomes is sin2((2j+1)θ)

In the case that the operator *A* prepares a state with a uniform distribution, the magnitudes of good outcomes are given by the following function, where the parameter n is the number of qubits, L is the number of good outcomes, and j is the number of iterations:

```
from math import sin, asin

def target_amplitude_uniform(n, l, j):
    theta = asin(sqrt(1/2**n))
    return sin((2*j+1)*theta)/sqrt(l)
```

Let's apply one iteration of the Grover operator to our example state, where $n = 3$ and outcome 3 is the good outcome:

```
n = 3
items = [3]
predicate = lambda i: True if i in items else False

state = [1/sqrt(2**n) for _ in range(2**n)]
```

```
classical_grover(state, predicate, iterations = 1)

assert is_close(state[items[0]], target_amplitude_uniform(3, 1, 1))
```

This is the same process we performed in the previous section, and the resulting state table is shown in figure 6.18.

Outcome	Binary	Amplitude	Direction	Magnitude	Amplitude bar	Probability
0	000	0.18	0.0°	0.18		0.03
1	001	0.18	0.0°	0.18		0.03
2	010	0.18	0.0°	0.18		0.03
3	011	0.88	0.0°	0.88		0.78
4	100	0.18	0.0°	0.18		0.03
5	101	0.18	0.0°	0.18		0.03
6	110	0.18	0.0°	0.18		0.03
7	111	0.18	0.0°	0.18		0.03

Figure 6.18 A three-qubit state with good outcome 3 after applying operator A and one Grover iteration

Let's apply another iteration:

```
n = 3
items = [3]
predicate = lambda i: True if i in items else False

state = [1/sqrt(2**n) for _ in range(2**n)]

classical_grover(state, predicate, iterations = 2)

assert is_close(state[items[0]], target_amplitude_uniform(3, 1, 2))
```

In the resulting state, shown in figure 6.19, the magnitude of the amplitude of the good outcome is increased even more.

Let's try three iterations:

```
n = 3
items = [3]
predicate = lambda i: True if i in items else False

state = [1/sqrt(2**n) for _ in range(2**n)]

classical_grover(state, predicate, iterations = 3)

assert is_close(state[items[0]], target_amplitude_uniform(3, 1, 3))
```

6.1 Amplitude amplification: Intuition and classical implementation

Outcome	Binary	Amplitude	Direction	Magnitude	Amplitude bar	Probability
0	000	−0.09	180.0°	0.09		0.01
1	001	−0.09	180.0°	0.09		0.01
2	010	−0.09	180.0°	0.09		0.01
3	011	0.97	0.0°	0.97		0.95
4	100	−0.09	180.0°	0.09		0.01
5	101	−0.09	180.0°	0.09		0.01
6	110	−0.09	180.0°	0.09		0.01
7	111	−0.09	180.0°	0.09		0.01

Figure 6.19 A three-qubit state with good outcome 3 after applying operator A and two Grover iterations

If we measure the resulting state, shown in figure 6.20, the probability of getting the good outcome, although still higher than the probabilities of the bad outcomes, is smaller than the probability of the good outcome in the state prepared with two iterations. That is, applying three iterations is not as good as applying two iterations.

Outcome	Binary	Amplitude	Direction	Magnitude	Amplitude bar	Probability
0	000	−0.31	180.0°	0.31		0.10
1	001	−0.31	180.0°	0.31		0.10
2	010	−0.31	180.0°	0.31		0.10
3	011	0.57	0.0°	0.57		0.33
4	100	−0.31	180.0°	0.31		0.10
5	101	−0.31	180.0°	0.31		0.10
6	110	−0.31	180.0°	0.31		0.10
7	111	−0.31	180.0°	0.31		0.10

Figure 6.20 A three-qubit state with good outcome 3 after applying operator A and three Grover iterations

How many iterations?
Given a state with n qubits prepared in equal superposition, the amplitude(s) corresponding to L good outcome(s) after j iterations is

$$\frac{\sin((2j+1)\theta)}{\sqrt{L}}$$

(continued)

where the angle $\theta = \arcsin\left(\sqrt{\dfrac{L}{2^n}}\right)$ satisfies the property $\sin^2(\theta) = \dfrac{L}{2^n}$.

The following graph shows the amplitude corresponding to a single good outcome in a state with $n = 3$ qubits as the number of iterations j increases: the largest amplitude is after two iterations.

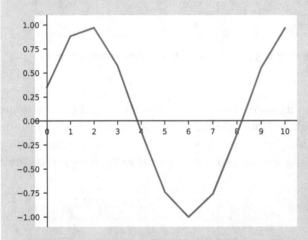

The amplitude of a single good outcome (in a state with $n = 3$ qubits) as a function of the number of Grover iterations performed

The next graph shows the amplitudes corresponding to the case when we have two good outcomes in a state with $n = 3$ qubits as the number of iterations j increases: the largest amplitude is after one iteration.

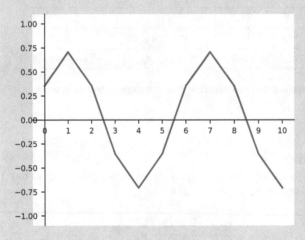

The amplitudes of the two good outcomes (in a state with $n = 3$ qubits) as a function of the number of Grover iterations performed

6.1 Amplitude amplification: Intuition and classical implementation

> Due to the periodicity of the sine function, the magnitude of the good outcomes(s) repeats as more iterations are applied. Given a state with n qubits, $N = 2^n$ amplitudes, and the number of good outcomes L, the optimal number of Grover iterations to perform is
>
> $$\left\lfloor \frac{\pi}{4} \sqrt{\frac{N}{L}} \right\rfloor$$

Using the number of good outcomes, `L = len(items)`, and the total number of outcomes, `2**n`, we can find the optimal number of iterations with

```
from math import floor, pi

num_iterations = int(floor(pi/4*sqrt(2**n/len(items))))
```

> **NOTE** In the function `classical_grover` we iterate through a range from 1 to the number of iterations plus 1 (`range(1, num_iterations + 1)`).

Let's look at another example, this time using a random two-qubit state and good outcome 1:

```
n = 2
items = [1]
predicate = lambda i: True if i in items else False

num_iterations = 3

state = generate_state(n)
for it in range(1, num_iterations + 1):
    s = state.copy()
    classical_grover(s, predicate, iterations = it)
```

This example is illustrated using unit color wheels in figure 6.21. The first wheel shows the random two-qubit state, and each subsequent wheel shows an increasing number of Grover iterations, from one to three.

Figure 6.21 A random two-qubit state with good outcome 1; and the state after one, two, and three Grover iterations

Exercise 6.2
Using the code introduced in this section, create a random state with $n = 4$ qubits, and apply the classical magnitude amplification procedure for good outcomes 3 and 10.

6.1.5 A classical but quantum-friendly implementation of the inversion operator

The quantum circuit implementation of the inversion operator is not as intuitive as the classical implementation. In this section, we will look at a different implementation of the operator that is easy to translate into a quantum version.

When the starting state is prepared with a circuit (operator) A, we can express its corresponding inversion operator M as AM_0A^{-1}, where M_0 is the inversion in the initial state. The circuit diagram of the magnitude amplification circuit using this operator for the inversion is shown in figure 6.22.

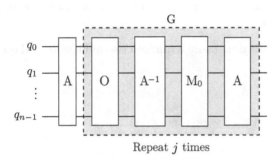

Figure 6.22 Circuit diagram for the magnitude amplification procedure G^jA, where the operator g consists of an oracle O and the inversion operator $M = AM_0A^{-1}$

The structure of this circuit ensures that the amplitude of the 0 outcome is always real before M_0 is applied. The operator M_0 simply multiplies all amplitudes by –1 except the amplitude of 0.

In the previous implementation, we inverted the amplitude corresponding to an outcome k around the complex number

$$\langle \text{original}, \text{state}\rangle \, \text{original}[k]$$

where original is the state prepared by the given operator A. In this implementation, we will invert around the point

$$\langle \text{default}, \text{state}\rangle \, \text{default}[k]$$

where original is a default n-qubit state. Remember that in the default state, only the amplitude corresponding to outcome 0 is 1, and the rest are 0, so

$$\langle \text{default}, \text{state}\rangle \, \text{default}[k] = \text{state}[k] \, \text{default}[k]$$

6.1 Amplitude amplification: Intuition and classical implementation

For the amplitude corresponding to the outcome 0 (state [0]) we will invert around itself, leaving it unchanged; for all other outcomes, we will invert around 0. Inverting around 0 is the same as multiplying the amplitude by –1.

In this section, we will use a randomly generated operator A. To create such an operator for n qubits, we will use the function `random_transformation` defined in the chapter code. For simplicity, this function returns a random transformation and its inverse. Let's create a random transformation (and its inverse) for $n = 3$ qubits:

```
from util import random_transformation

n = 3
f = random_transformation(n)
A = f[0]                            The first returned value is the random
A_inverse = f[1]                    transformation, and the second is the inverse.
```

Let's look at the state prepared by this random operator. We do this by initializing a state and then applying the random transformation:

```
from sim_core import init_state

state = init_state(n)
A(state)
```

The state created is shown in figure 6.23. Now we can use the following, which performs the operation AM_0A^{-1}.

Outcome	Binary	Amplitude	Direction	Magnitude	Amplitude bar	Probability
0	000	0.09 + 0.40i	77.8°	0.41		0.17
1	001	0.17 + 0.23i	53.2°	0.29		0.08
2	010	–0.43 – 0.05i	–174.0°	0.43		0.19
3	011	–0.20 – 0.03i	–170.6°	0.20		0.04
4	100	0.44 + 0.17i	20.5°	0.47		0.22
5	101	0.17 – 0.22i	–51.8°	0.27		0.08
6	110	0.10 – 0.39i	–76.2°	0.40		0.16
7	111	–0.11 – 0.22i	–116.9°	0.24		0.06

Figure 6.23 A three-qubit state after applying a random operator A

Listing 6.4 Function to perform the inversion operation

```
from math import log2

def inversion_0_transformation(f, state):
    n = int(log2(len(state)))
```

```
transform = f[0]
inverse_transform = f[1]

inverse_transform(state)          ←── Applies the inverse
assert is_close(state[0].imag, 0)      of operator A
for k in range(1, len(state)):
    state[k] = -state[k]          ←── Applies the operator M₀
transform(state)                  ←── Applies the operator A
```

Let's use the same operator A we used to create the state in figure 6.23, and apply an oracle for the good outcome 3:

```
predicate = lambda k: True if k == 3 else False
oracle(state, predicate)
```

Now we can apply the inversion operation to the state:

```
inversion_0_transformation(f, state)
```

Figure 6.24 shows the state tables after each operation is applied to the state. When M_0 is applied, all the amplitudes are multiplied by −1 except the amplitude corresponding to outcome 0. In the last state table, the magnitude of the amplitude of the good outcome is amplified, and all the other magnitudes have decreased. Next, we will see that the new implementation of the inversion operator in this section can be translated into a quantum circuit implementation.

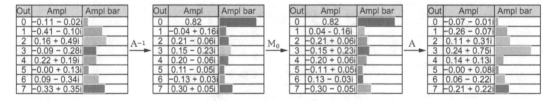

Figure 6.24 Application of the operator $M = AM_0A^{-1}$ to a three-qubit state prepared with a random operator A, followed by the application of an oracle O for the good outcome 3

6.2 Magnitude amplification: Quantum circuit implementation

The quantum implementation of the magnitude amplification procedure mirrors the classical one we introduced in the previous section. In this section, we will use our Python simulator to build the quantum circuit illustrated in figure 6.25.

The efficiency of a Grover operator implementation depends on the efficiency of the oracle implementation, which is required as a starting point. Changing amplitudes by itself does not provide an advantage. As we will see, we need quantum measurement to get an advantage in solving search problems with a quantum approach.

6.2 Magnitude amplification: Quantum circuit implementation

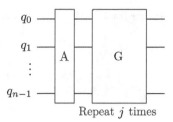

Figure 6.25 Circuit diagram of magnitude (amplitude) amplification

6.2.1 Quantum oracle

The quantum oracle circuit O tags the good outcomes. Using a list of good outcomes items, we can use the `phase_oracle_match` function from chapter 5 to create a circuit that multiplies the amplitudes corresponding to the good outcomes by -1.

Listing 6.5 Function to create a phase oracle circuit

```
from sim_circuit import *

def is_bit_not_set(m, k):
    return not (m & (1 << k))

def phase_oracle_match(n, items):
    q = QuantumRegister(n)
    qc = QuantumCircuit(q)

    for m in items:
        for i in range(n):
            if is_bit_not_set(m, i):
                qc.x(q[i])

        qc.mcp(pi, [q[i] for i in range(len(q) - 1)], q[len(q) - 1])

        for i in range(n):
            if is_bit_not_set(m, i):
                qc.x(q[i])
    return qc
```

6.2.2 The inversion operator

Next, we will create a quantum circuit that performs the inversion transformation denoted by M. Remember, given a state-preparation operator A, we can express its corresponding inversion operator M as $M = AM_0A^{-1}$. The classical implementation of the operator M_0 reflects the formal mathematical theory of Grover operators. In the quantum implementation, we use the operator $-M_0$ instead of M_0 because it is much more efficient to implement with quantum gates. This operator effectively multiplies the amplitude corresponding outcome 0 by -1, leaving all the other amplitudes unchanged. Using $-M_0$ instead of M_0 does not affect the outcome probabilities after applying any number of Grover iterations. Going forward, we will use the notation M_0

154 CHAPTER 6 *Quantum search and probability estimation*

for the negative of the M_0 operator we used in the previous sections. This way, all the formulas will stay the same.

The following function creates the circuit M_0 for n qubits.

Listing 6.6 Function to create a circuit for n qubits that multiplies outcome 0 by –1

```
def inversion_0_circuit(n):
    q = QuantumRegister(n)
    qc = QuantumCircuit(q)
    
    for i in range(n):
        qc.x(q[i])
    
    qc.mcp(pi, [q[i] for i in range(n - 1)], q[n - 1])
    
    for i in range(n):
        qc.x(q[i])
    
    return qc
```

The circuit diagram in figure 6.26 shows the operator M_0 for three qubits. For example, when applied to a random state, as shown in figure 6.27, the amplitude of outcome 0 is multiplied by –1.

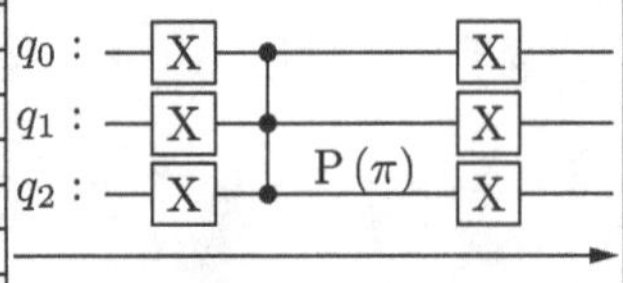

Figure 6.26 Circuit M_0 for three qubits

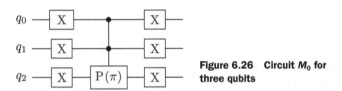

Figure 6.27 Applying operator M_0 to a random three-qubit state

When the operator A consists of a Hadamard gate applied to each qubit, we can create the circuit M with the function defined in listing 6.7. The parameter `A` is the circuit A for n qubits.

> **NOTE** The `inverse` method of a circuit returns its inverse. The implementation applies the inverses of each gate in the circuit's transformation list in reverse order.

Listing 6.7 Function to create the inversion circuit

```
def inversion_circuit(A):
    n = sum(A.regs)
    q = QuantumRegister(n)
    qc = QuantumCircuit(q)

    qc.append(A.inverse(), q)

    qc.append(inversion_0_circuit(n), q)

    qc.append(A, q)

    return qc
```

6.2.3 Grover iterate

Using the general form of the Grover iterate $G = AM_0A^{-1}O$, we can define the function `grover_iterate_circuit`, which creates the Grover iterate circuit. The function takes two parameters: the oracle (O) for n qubits and the operator (A) that is used to prepare the initial state.

Listing 6.8 Function to create the Grover iterate circuit

```
def grover_iterate_circuit(A, O):
    n = sum(O.regs)
    q = QuantumRegister(n)
    qc = QuantumCircuit(q)

    qc.append(O, q)

    qc.append(inversion_circuit(A), q)

    return qc
```

6.2.4 Putting it all together: Grover's algorithm

We can use the functions introduced in this section to build the quantum circuit for magnitude amplification (or Grover's algorithm). The function in listing 6.9 creates the circuit in figure 6.28, where the parameters A and O are the n-qubit circuits A and O, respectively. The `iterations` parameter determines how many times the Grover iterate is applied, which is constructed using `grover_iterate_circuit` (defined in listing 6.8).

Listing 6.9 Function to create the magnitude amplification circuit

```
def grover_circuit(A, O, iterations):
    n = sum(A.regs)
    q = QuantumRegister(n)
    qc = QuantumCircuit(q)
```

```
qc.append(A, q)

for i in range(1, iterations + 1):
    qc.append(grover_iterate_circuit(A, O), q)
    qc.report(f'iteration_{i}')

return qc
```

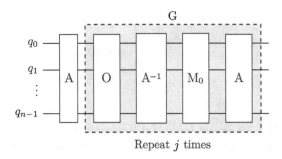

Figure 6.28 Circuit diagram of the magnitude amplification procedure G^jA, where the operator g consists of an oracle O and the inversion operator $M = AM_0A^{-1}$

NOTE We can use the `report()` method of the circuit to create a snapshot report containing the transformations applied since the last report, and the states before and after applying those transformations. We can use such reports to visualize the encoding process, as you will see in the chapter code.

Suppose we have a list of $N = 8$ items, represented as the outcomes of a quantum computation with $n = 3$ qubits, and an oracle tagging three good outcomes. We can use the `uniform` function from chapter 4 to create a circuit A that prepares a state with equal magnitudes:

```
def uniform(n):
    q = QuantumRegister(n)
    qc = QuantumCircuit(q)

    for i in range(len(q)):
        qc.h(q[i])

    return qc
```

With `uniform` as our operator A, $n = 3$ qubits, and good outcomes 1, 3, and 7, we can define the following circuit:

```
n = 3
items = [1, 3, 7]
num_iterations = int(floor(pi/4*sqrt(2**n/len(items))))

qc = grover_circuit(uniform(n), phase_oracle_match(n, items), num_iterations)
```

This circuit is illustrated in figure 6.29. Note that the optimal number of iterations in this example is one, so the Grover iterate does not repeat.

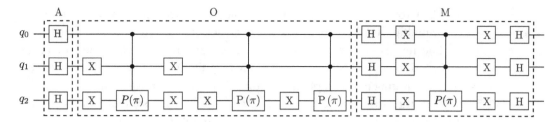

Figure 6.29 The quantum circuit for three qubits and good outcomes 1, 3, and 7

We can check the amplitudes at each step using the reports generated with the following code:

```
for i in range(1, num_iterations + 1):
    for m in items:
        assert is_close(
            qc.reports[f'iteration_{i}'][2][m],
            (-1)**i * target_amplitude_uniform(n, len(items), i)
        )
```

> **Exercise 6.3**
> Create a magnitude amplification circuit for *n* = 3 qubits and single good outcome 5 using the circuit returned by the function `prepare_binomial` from chapter 4 as the initial state-preparation operator (with `theta = 4*pi/7`):
>
> ```
> def prepare_binomial(n, theta):
>     q = QuantumRegister(n)
>     qc = QuantumCircuit(q)
> 
>     for i in range(len(q)):
>         qc.ry(theta, q[i])
> 
>     return qc
> ```

Summary

- Grover's algorithm can offer a quadratic speedup over classical algorithms for unstructured database searches, requiring only approximately $\sqrt{N}$ queries compared to $N/2$ queries classically to have a high probability of finding a specific item.
- The inner product of two state vectors measures their similarity.
- The magnitude (amplitude) amplification method is used to increase the probability of measuring one or more good outcomes. This procedure can be expressed as $G^j A$ for an integer $j > 0$, where A is an operator that prepares a starting state and G is the Grover iterate.

- The Grover operator G consists of a quantum oracle that tags desired outcomes by multiplying their amplitudes by -1, followed by an inversion operator.
- The inversion operator increases the magnitude of amplitudes for tagged (good) outcomes while decreasing the magnitude of untagged (bad) outcomes.
* The quantum-circuit implementation of Grover's algorithm uses the general form of the Grover iterate $G = AM_0 A^{-1} O$, where A is the state preparation operator, O is the oracle, and M_0 is the inversion operator.

The quantum Fourier transform

This chapter covers
- Periodic signals and periodic quantum states
- Converting directions into magnitudes
- Introducing the quantum Fourier transform and its inverse

The *quantum Fourier transform* (QFT) is an essential operation in quantum computing. The QFT is a crucial building block in numerous quantum algorithms, including some you may have already heard of, like Shor's algorithm and quantum phase estimation. As a quantum computing developer, you need to understand the details of the QFT and the role it plays in other quantum algorithms. In this chapter, we will look closely at the structure and functionality of the QFT (see figure 7.1). Primarily, we will see how the QFT allows us to translate information encoded in amplitude directions (phases) into amplitude magnitudes. We will also see how the QFT can be performed efficiently on a quantum computer by taking advantage of quantum parallelism and interference. The efficiency of the QFT makes it a key tool in developing quantum solutions that perform better than their classical counterparts.

CHAPTER 7 The quantum Fourier transform

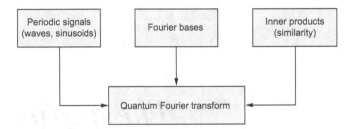

Figure 7.1 A dependency diagram of concepts introduced in this chapter

To illustrate its significance, we will begin by looking at its classical counterpart: the *discrete Fourier transform* (DFT). You may be familiar with Fourier transforms if you studied computer graphics, digital signal processing, or sound engineering. Even if the term is new to you, chances are you've encountered technologies that rely on Fourier transforms, such as digital recordings of songs.

The first machine that could record sound and play it back was the phonograph, invented by Thomas Edison in 1877. A phonograph uses records with grooves of varying depth and width, which reflect the audio waveform. To play a song, a stylus is dragged over the record, creating electrical signals that can be amplified into audible sound waves. The phonograph uses *analog encoding*, where the information is represented with continuous signals (the electrical signals produced by the grooves).

To save songs or other audio as digital files, we convert the sound waves into numbers and store them in a special way. To listen to these saved songs, we need to convert the numbers back into sound waves. The DFT is a tool that helps us find the different frequencies in a sound wave and represent them as numbers. We can also use the inverse version of this tool to re-create a sound wave from these numbers. This mechanism is used by some audio encoding algorithms. Let's examine frequencies and sound waves in more detail.

7.1 Periodic patterns in sound waves and quantum states

Every day, we come across various repeating patterns in the world around us, some of which occur naturally and others designed by humans. Patterns that repeat at regular intervals, such as seasons or ocean tides, are *periodic*. The sound wave created by a musical note, for example, exhibits a repeating pattern as it travels through the air. This wave is a specific type of *periodic signal*. When we encounter these periodic patterns, we often consider whether they are repeating over time (like a clock ticking regularly) or over space (like a series of evenly spaced objects).

> **NOTE** A *signal* can be any pattern or data that changes over time or space, including sound, images, numerical data, and more. In a mathematical sense, a signal is a function that represents how a quantity changes with respect to an independent variable, such as time.

7.1.1 Periodic patterns in sound waves

Most of the sounds we hear in our daily lives are a mix of different individual sound waves. These mixed sound waves are called *composite sound waves*.

> **Singing glasses**
>
> We can make a sound with a glass by tapping it or running a wet finger around its rim. The size and shape of a glass determine its *resonant frequency*, which is the frequency of the sound wave it produces. The *frequency* of a sound wave is the number of repetitions (or cycles) completed in one unit of time. Generally, larger glasses have lower resonant frequencies, and smaller glasses have higher ones. If we run a wet finger around the edge of a glass, record it, and play the same sound back at a high volume, the glass will start vibrating or even break (if the volume is high enough).
>
> You may have heard about using glasses of different shapes and sizes as a musical instrument, which is called a glass harmonica. People can make music with a glass harmonica by vibrating the glasses with the desired frequencies. If they use three glasses to play a note in a song, the sound we hear is a mix of all the notes from those glasses. In other words, the sound wave we hear is a composition of the frequencies of each glass.
>
>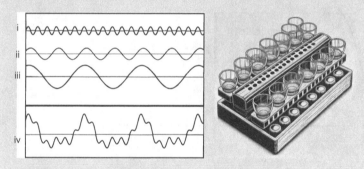
>
> **A glass harmonica and the composition of waves**

Composite sound waves can be broken down into simpler *sinusoidal waves*, or *sinusoids*. A sinusoid can be defined using a sine or cosine function. The sine function defined on the interval $[-2\pi, 2\pi]$ is illustrated in figure 7.2.

Sinusoidal waves have a *frequency, amplitude,* and *phase*. The frequency of a sinusoidal wave tells us how many cycles are completed within a given interval of time (for example, 2π). The wave in figure 7.2, $\sin(x)$ for $-2\pi \leq x \leq 2\pi$, completes one cycle every 2π interval, and therefore it has a frequency of 1. One cycle of the wave is highlighted in figure 7.3. The amplitude of a sinusoidal wave is the peak height of the wave. We can see that the sine wave in figure 7.3 has an amplitude of 1. The sinusoidal wave can be shifted horizontally. This shift is called the phase of the wave. The phase of our simple sine wave is 0, as shown in figure 7.3.

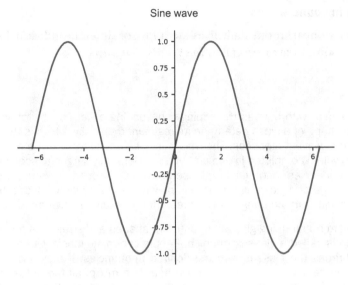

Figure 7.2 A simple sinusoidal wave, sin (x) for $-2\pi \leq x \leq 2\pi$

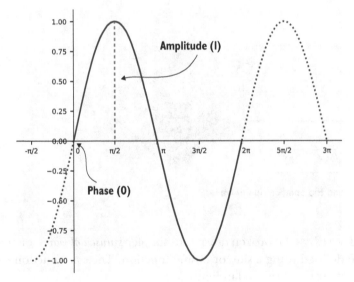

Figure 7.3 The sinusoidal wave sin(x) for real values x has amplitude 1, phase 0, and frequency 1.

A sinusoid can also be defined in terms of the cos function. Cosine and sine waves have the same shape, but they are shifted by $\pi/2$ radians, as illustrated in 7.4.

In its most general form, a sinusoid can be expressed as $A \cos(2\pi f t + \varphi)$, where

- t is time.
- A is the amplitude (height of the wave).
- φ is the phase (in radians when $t = 0$).
- f is the frequency.

7.1 Periodic patterns in sound waves and quantum states

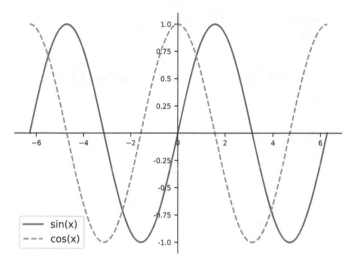

Figure 7.4 The sine and cosine waves plotted together

NOTE As is often the case in science and technology, the meaning of a term may vary depending on the context or area it's used in. The amplitude of a wave as defined here is different from the amplitude corresponding to an outcome in a quantum state.

In the glass harmonica example, each glass generates a sound with a standard frequency. When multiple glasses are used at the same time, a more complex sound results. Complex sound waves can be decomposed into sinusoids with standard frequencies. These frequencies can then be stored digitally and recombined later to replay the original sound. This is where Fourier transforms come into play. Let's consider a simple example of this process.

We start with a (continuous) sinusoidal wave defined by $\frac{1}{\sqrt{8}} \cos\left(2\pi \cdot 1.7 \frac{t}{N}\right)$ as a function of time $0 \leq t < N$ for a given positive integer n. To turn the continuous wave into a discrete signal, we will take n samples at the equally spaced points in time {0, 1, ..., $N-1$}. For example, for $N = 8$, we can define discrete samples of the signal using the following Python code:

```
from math import sqrt, pi, cos

N = 8
frequency = 1.7
samples = [1/sqrt(8)*cos(2 * pi * frequency * (t / N)) for t in range(N)]
```

Now we can visualize the wave and the eight values we computed previously:

```
import numpy as np
import matplotlib.pyplot as plt
```

```
x = np.linspace(0, N, 50)
wave = [1/sqrt(8)*cos(2 * pi * frequency * (t/N)) for t in x]
plt.plot(x, wave, label='signal', color='red')
plt.scatter(range(N), samples)
plt.show()
```

The resulting graph is shown in figure 7.5. As expected, we see 1.7 cycles of the wave in the eight time intervals.

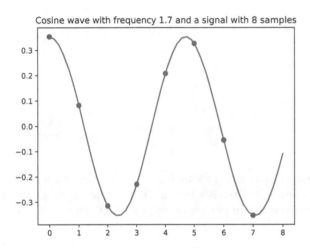

Figure 7.5 Visualization of the signal with the eight discrete values

> **NOTE** Sound waves are typically modeled as real-valued signals, meaning they have values that are real numbers.

7.1.2 Periodic patterns in quantum states

Now let's look at how we can represent periodic patterns in quantum states. We cannot directly translate the classical implementation that uses a single sinusoid. It would conflict with the rule that the squared magnitudes of the complex numbers that form a quantum state must add up to 1. However, we can use two sinusoids, either separately or combined into a *complex sinusoid*.

Figure 7.6 illustrates a complex sinusoid with the cosine and sine parts as projections on the real and imaginary planes, respectively.

Consider the complex sinusoid

$$\frac{1}{\sqrt{N}}(\cos(k\theta) + i\sin(k\theta))$$

where n is the interval of time we are working with, $0 \le k < N$, and the angle θ depends on the frequency of the signal.

> **NOTE** Recall that the relationship between a given angle θ and a given frequency v is $\theta/(2\pi) = v/N$.

7.1 Periodic patterns in sound waves and quantum states

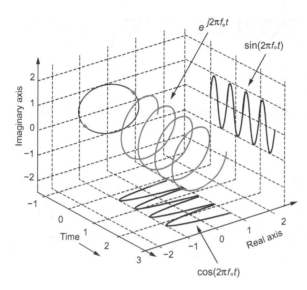

Figure 7.6 Projections of the sine and cosine parts of a complex sinusoid

We can create a quantum state with amplitudes that are discrete samples of this complex signal with a given theta (for example, $\pi/3$) using the following code:

```
from util import cis
from math import sin

theta = pi/3
state = [sqrt(1/N) * cis(k*theta) for k in range(N)]
```

> **The cis shortcut function**
> Remember, we can use the shortcut function `cis` defined as
>
> ```
> def cis(theta):
>     return cos(theta) + 1j*sin(theta)
> ```

We call this a *geometric sequence* or complex sinusoid state. Figure 7.7 shows the state table for this state.

Outcome	Amplitude
k	$\frac{1}{\sqrt{2^n}}\operatorname{cis}(k\theta)$

Figure 7.7 The geometric sequence state for an angle θ. The direction of the amplitude corresponding to outcome k is $k\theta$.

Let's define a reusable function `geom` that creates a geometric sequence defined by an angle `theta` and is a valid n-qubit quantum state.

Listing 7.1 Function for creating a geometric sequence state

```
def geom(n, theta):
    N = 2**n
    return [sqrt(1/N) * cis(k*theta) for k in range(N)]
```

Let's use it to create a three-qubit quantum state that is a geometric sequence with $\theta = \pi/3$:

```
state = geom(3, pi/3)
```

As we can see in the definition of the function geom, each amplitude will have a magnitude of $\frac{1}{\sqrt{N}}$; in this example, $\frac{1}{\sqrt{8}}$. The amplitude at an index $0 \leq k < 8$ will have a direction of $k\pi/3$. We can print the direction (phase) of each of the amplitudes in the example state defined previously:

```
from math import atan2

for k in range(len(state)):
    print("phase of amplitude ", k, ":", round(atan2(state[k].imag,
       state[k].real), 5))
```

Due to the periodicity of cosine and sine, the phases start repeating at outcome 6:

```
phase of amplitude  0 : 0.0
phase of amplitude  1 : 1.0472
phase of amplitude  2 : 2.0944
phase of amplitude  3 : 3.14159
phase of amplitude  4 : -2.0944
phase of amplitude  5 : -1.0472
phase of amplitude  6 : -0.0
phase of amplitude  7 : 1.0472
```

Using the unit color wheel, we can visualize the frequency of the sequence as the number of rotations around the wheel as we step through the sequence. As we know, a full rotation around the unit circle covers 2π radians (or $360°$). In this example, there are eight steps, each spanning one-sixth of a full rotation. In total, we will have $1 + 1/3$ rotations around the circle (see figure 7.8). Therefore, the frequency is $4/3$.

Figure 7.8 Unit color wheel representation of the geometric sequence state for $\theta = \pi/3$

7.1 Periodic patterns in sound waves and quantum states

Let's create a three-qubit quantum state, which is a geometric sequence with $\theta = \pi/6$:

```
state = geom(3, pi/6)
```

Each amplitude in this state will have the same magnitude of $\frac{1}{\sqrt{8}}$ and a phase of $k\pi/6$, where $0 \leq k < 8$, as shown in figure 7.9.

Figure 7.9 Unit color wheel for the geometric sequence state for $\theta = \pi/6$

We know that each of the eight angle steps is $\theta = \pi/6$, adding up to $4/3\,\pi$, which represents $2/3$ of 2π (a full cycle). Therefore, the frequency is $2/3$.

We can prepare an n-qubit geometric sequence state for a given value v using the geometric_sequence_circuit function. Remember the relationship between v and θ: $\theta = v\,2\pi/N$.

Listing 7.2 Creating the circuit for encoding a geometric sequence state

```
from sim_circuit import *

def geometric_sequence_circuit(n, v):
    theta = v*2*pi/N

    q = QuantumRegister(n)
    qc = QuantumCircuit(q)

    for j in range(n):
        qc.h(q[j])

    for j in range(n):
        qc.p(2 ** j * theta, q[j])

    return qc
```

If we use this function to encode the geometric sequence for the frequency $v = 1.7$, we get the state shown in figure 7.10:

```
n = 3
v = 1.7
qc = geometric_sequence_circuit(n, v)
state = qc.run()
```

Outcome	Binary	Amplitude	Direction	Magnitude	Amplitude bar	Probability
0	000	0.354	0.0°	0.354		0.125
1	001	0.083 + 0.344i	76.5°	0.354		0.125
2	010	−0.315 + 0.161i	153.0°	0.354		0.125
3	011	−0.230 − 0.269i	−130.5°	0.354		0.125
4	100	0.208 − 0.286i	−54.0°	0.354		0.125
5	101	0.327 + 0.135i	22.5°	0.354		0.125
6	110	−0.055 + 0.349i	99.0°	0.354		0.125
7	111	−0.352 + 0.028i	175.5°	0.354		0.125

Figure 7.10 **The three-qubit geometric sequence state for v = 1.7**

In this state, all the amplitudes match those of the example signal, $\frac{1}{\sqrt{8}}$, and the directions reflect the expected frequency of 1.7. We can check this using the following code:

```
from util import all_close

theta = v*2*pi/2**n
assert all_close(state, [sqrt(1/2**n) * cis(k*theta) for k in range(2**n)])
```

This type of encoding is simpler than using real sinusoids, and we will study it in more detail. Now we will look at a special type of periodic pattern that is essential to Fourier transforms.

7.1.3 Roots of unity and their geometric sequences

A *root of unity* is a complex number ω that is 1 when raised to a specific positive integer power n, ($\omega^N = 1$). Then the following powers of ω are also roots of unity: ω^0, ω^1, ω^2, ..., ω^{N-1}. Graphically, they represent equally spaced points on the unit circle, the vertices of a regular n-sided polygon (see figure 7.11).

For a given integer n, we typically denote the root of unity with the smallest non-zero phase (direction) as

$$\omega_N = \cos\left(\frac{2\pi}{N}\right) + i \sin\left(\frac{2\pi}{N}\right) = \text{cis}\left(\frac{2\pi}{N}\right)$$

For example, let's check that $\omega_N^N = 1$ for $N = 8$:

```
N = 8
omega = cis(2*pi/N)
print(abs(omega**N))
```

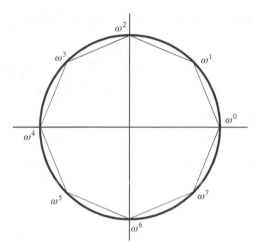

Figure 7.11 Roots of unity ω^0, ω^1, ω^2, ..., ω^{N-1} where $N = 8$ on the unit circle

The printed output is

```
1.0
```

In code, we can express the power sequence corresponding to ω^N as

```
omega = cis(2*pi/N)
sequence = [omega**k for k in range(N)]
```

We can also use the `cis` function to do the same:

```
N = 8
sequence_cis = [cis(l*2*pi/N) for l in range(N)]

assert all_close(sequence, sequence_cis)
```

> **Exercise 7.1**
> Make the previous sequence into a valid quantum state.

7.2 Converting from phase to magnitude encoding with the Hadamard gate

If we have a signal encoded in a periodic quantum state, the angle of the geometric sequence state contains information about the frequency of the signal. The QFT allows us to convert that information encoded in the angle of the geometric sequence state into magnitudes.

For example, let's represent the frequency 1/3 in a single-qubit state. To do this, we will prepare a single-qubit geometric sequence state with the angle $\theta = \pi/3$:

```
state = geom(1, pi/3)
```

The circuit to encode this state and the resulting state table are illustrated in figure 7.12.

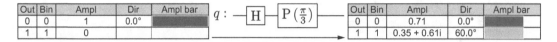

Figure 7.12 Phase encoding for a single qubit with $\theta = \pi/3$

In the resulting state, the encoded angle is represented in the phase of the amplitude corresponding to outcome 1.

> **Exercise 7.2**
> Show that the encoded angle is represented in the phase of the amplitude corresponding to outcome 1.

However, the amplitudes of the resulting state have equal magnitudes and therefore equal probabilities for each outcome. If we run this circuit on a quantum computer, we will not be able to infer the frequency of the signal represented by the state.

To learn about the encoded signal, we convert the information encoded in the phase of the geometric sequence state into magnitudes. If we apply an additional Hadamard gate, the magnitudes of both amplitudes will change. Let's look at the following implementation:

```
q = QuantumRegister(1)
qc = QuantumCircuit(q)

theta = pi/3
qc.h(q[0])
qc.p(theta, q[0])
qc.h(q[0])

state = qc.run()
```

Figure 7.13 shows the state before and after applying the last Hadamard gate.

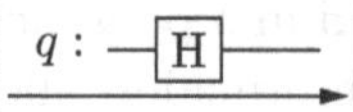

Figure 7.13 Converting difference in phase ($\theta = \pi/3$) to difference in magnitudes

In this state, the encoded angle is translated into the magnitudes of the amplitudes. The amplitudes of the resulting state have magnitudes $\cos \theta/2$ and $\sin \theta/2$:

```
from util import is_close

theta = pi/3
assert is_close(abs(state[0]), cos(theta/2))
assert is_close(abs(state[1]), sin(theta/2))
```

The probability of outcome 0 is $\cos^2 \theta/2$, and the probability of outcome 1 is $\sin^2 \theta/2$. If we run this circuit on a quantum computer, we will be able to use the frequency of outcomes to infer the encoded angle.

This pattern of applying a Hadamard gate to a single qubit to retrieve information encoded in the phases of a quantum state is the simplest example of a QFT. This pattern is shown in figure 7.14.

Outcome	Amplitude
0	$\frac{1}{\sqrt{2}}$
1	$\frac{1}{\sqrt{2}}\text{cis}(\theta)$

$\xrightarrow{H}$

Outcome	Amplitude
0	$\cos(\frac{\theta}{2})\text{cis}(\frac{\theta}{2})$
1	$\sin(\frac{\theta}{2})\text{cis}(\frac{\theta-\pi}{2})$

Figure 7.14 Conversion from phase to magnitude encoding in a single-qubit state with a Hadamard gate

7.3 From classical to quantum Fourier transforms

Now that we understand some concepts crucial to Fourier transforms, like roots of unity, we can dive into more details. In this section, we will review the implementation of classical Fourier transforms before discussing the quantum counterparts.

7.3.1 The classical (discrete) Fourier transform

The DFT takes discrete signals (e.g., samples from a continuous signal, like a sound wave) and computes the frequency components of the signal. The DFT essentially calculates the contribution of each frequency component to an approximation of the continuous signal by measuring the similarity, or correlation, between the signal and a set of sinusoidal basis functions of different frequencies. The DFT decomposes the input signal into multiple frequency bins and determines the magnitude and phase of each frequency component.

When we perform the DFT on a discrete signal $\{x_0, ..., x_{N-1}\}$ of length $N > 1$, we will get a sequence of complex numbers $\{y_0, ..., y_{N-1}\}$, where each entry is the inner product of the given sequence and the corresponding *Fourier basis*. For $0 \leq l < N$, the lth Fourier basis is

$$F_l = \begin{bmatrix} \omega_N^0 \\ \omega_N^l \\ \omega_N^{2l} \\ \vdots \\ \omega_N^{(N-1)l} \end{bmatrix}$$

where $\omega_N = \cos(2\pi/N) + i\sin(2\pi/N)$. Note that depending on the implementation, each basis may be multiplied by a common factor $1/N$ or $\frac{1}{\sqrt{N}}$. We will see that the QFT uses a constant of $\frac{1}{\sqrt{N}}$.

For example, for $N = 4$, and with the notation $\omega = \omega_4$, the Fourier bases for indices $0 \leq l < 4$ are

$$F_0 = \begin{bmatrix} \omega^0 \\ \omega^0 \\ \omega^0 \\ \omega^0 \end{bmatrix}, F_1 = \begin{bmatrix} \omega^0 \\ \omega^1 \\ \omega^2 \\ \omega^3 \end{bmatrix}, F_2 = \begin{bmatrix} \omega^0 \\ \omega^2 \\ \omega^4 \\ \omega^6 \end{bmatrix}, F_3 = \begin{bmatrix} \omega^0 \\ \omega^3 \\ \omega^6 \\ \omega^9 \end{bmatrix}$$

Note that $\omega^0 = 1$.

We can represent each Fourier basis in Python code with a list:

```
N = 4
omega = cis(2*pi/N)

F_0 = [omega**(0*k) for k in range(N)]
F_1 = [omega**(1*k) for k in range(N)]
F_2 = [omega**(2*k) for k in range(N)]
F_3 = [omega**(3*k) for k in range(N)]
```

If we inspect the first basis, we see that all its components are equal to 1:

```
print(F_0)
[(1+0j), (1+0j), (1+0j), (1+0j)]
```

Alternatively, we can use the following code to find the four Fourier bases:

```
N = 4

F_0 = [cis(k*0*2*pi/N) for k in range(N)]
F_1 = [cis(k*1*2*pi/N) for k in range(N)]
F_2 = [cis(k*2*2*pi/N) for k in range(N)]
F_3 = [cis(k*3*2*pi/N) for k in range(N)]
```

Let's return to our earlier example of samples from a sinusoidal wave:

```
N = 8
frequency = 1.7
samples = [1/sqrt(N)*cos(2 * pi * frequency * (i / N)) for i in range(N)]
```

To get the first item of the DFT of this signal, we need to compute the inner product between the discrete signal and the corresponding Fourier basis (F_0). We will use the inner function from chapter 6:

7.3 From classical to quantum Fourier transforms

```
def inner(v1, v2):
    assert(len(v1) == len(v2))
    return sum(z1*z2.conjugate() for z1, z2 in zip(v1, v2))
```

Now we can get the first item:

```
F_0 = [cis(k*0*2*pi/N) for k in range(N)]
similarity = inner(samples, F_0)

print(round(similarity.real, 5) + 1j*round(similarity.imag, 5))
```

The printed output is

```
(0.01814+0j)
```

We can compute the entire sequence with a list comprehension:

```
dft = [inner(samples, [cis(k*l*2*pi/N) for k in range(N)]) for l in range(8)]

for x in dft:
    print(round(x.real, 5) + 1j*round(x.imag, 5))
```

The resulting sequence is

```
(0.01814+0j)
(-0.11374+0.34545j)
(0.93169-0.99125j)
(0.40522-0.17397j)
(0.36394+0j)
(0.40522+0.17397j)
(0.93169+0.99125j)
(-0.11374-0.34545j)
```

We can use the `fft` package in `numpy` to check that these results match. Note that the *fast Fourier transform* (FFT) is a high-performance classical algorithm for computing the DFT:

```
f = np.fft.fft(samples)

for x in f:
    print(round(x.real, 5) + 1j*round(x.imag, 5))
```

The resulting sequence is

```
(0.01814+0j)
(-0.11374+0.34545j)
(0.93169-0.99125j)
(0.40522-0.17397j)
(0.36394+0j)
(0.40522+0.17397j)
(0.93169+0.99125j)
(-0.11374-0.34545j)
```

NOTE In mathematical notation, the DFT of a sequence $\{x_0, ..., x_{N-1}\}$ is the sequence $\{y_0, ..., y_{N-1}\}$ defined by $y_k = \sum_{l=0}^{N-1} x_l e^{-lki\frac{2\pi}{N}}$, for each $0 \leq k < N$. The inverse DFT has a positive instead of a negative sign in the exponents: $y_k = \sum_{l=0}^{N-1} x_l e^{lki\frac{2\pi}{N}}$.

7.3.2 Introducing the QFT and IQFT

Before going into the quantum circuits for the QFT and the inverse QFT (IQFT), we will use simpler classical code to understand how they work. The QFT performs the same computation, up to a constant, as the inverse DFT on a state vector. Given a sequence $\{x_0, ..., x_{N-1}\}$ of complex numbers of length n, its Fourier transform (direct or inverse) is a sequence $\{y_0, ..., y_{N-1}\}$ of the same length, where each entry is the sum of the entries in the given sequence rotated by specific angles (counterclockwise for direct, clockwise for inverse).

NOTE In mathematical (ket) notation, the QFT acts on a state $|x\rangle$ and maps it to the state $|y\rangle$ defined by $y_k = \frac{1}{\sqrt{N}} \sum_{l=0}^{N-1} x_l e^{lki\frac{2\pi}{N}}$, for each $0 \leq k < N$. The IQFT has a negative instead of a positive sign in the exponents: $y_k = \frac{1}{\sqrt{N}} \sum_{l=0}^{N-1} x_l e^{-lki\frac{2\pi}{N}}$.

SIMULATING THE IQFT WITH CLASSICAL CODE

We will start with the IQFT because it uses counterclockwise rotations like the DFT to decompose signals into frequencies. The result of the IQFT is a state where each amplitude is the sum of the original amplitudes rotated by certain angles. Remember from chapter 3 that rotations of complex numbers act as multiplication. To simulate the effect of the IQFT on a quantum state with n qubits, we compute the inner product of the state vector and each corresponding Fourier basis state.

The general-form state table for a Fourier basis F_l is shown in figure 7.15. Note the use of the $\frac{1}{\sqrt{N}}$ constant as the magnitude of each entry in all Fourier bases, making the bases valid quantum states. As you can see, a Fourier basis state is the geometric sequence state with frequency l.

Outcome	Amplitude
k	$\frac{1}{\sqrt{N}}\text{cis}(kl\frac{2\pi}{N})$

Figure 7.15 Fourier bases n-qubit quantum state where $N = 2^n$, $0 \leq k < N$, and $0 \leq l < N$

In code, we can use the following function to create a Fourier basis state in Python.

7.3 From classical to quantum Fourier transforms

Listing 7.3 Computing the Fourier basis for a given N and l

```
def fourier_basis(N, l):
    return [1/sqrt(N) * cis(k*l*2*pi/N) for k in range(N)]
```

We will use this `fourier_basis` function to compute the IQFT of a list representing a quantum state. The following function simulates the IQFT using simple classical code, so we call it `icft`.

Listing 7.4 Classical implementation of the IQFT

```
def icft(state):
    N = len(state)
    s = [state[k] for k in range(N)]

    for k in range(N):
        state[k] = inner(s, fourier_basis(N, k))
```

The IQFT of a quantum state is another quantum state, as shown in figure 7.16, where each entry is the inner product between the given state and the Fourier basis corresponding to the entry index.

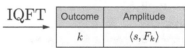

Figure 7.16 The general form of the amplitudes of a quantum state before and after applying the IQFT

Exercise 7.3

In the gate-based implementation of the IQFT, the rotations are applied incrementally with controlled phase rotations. To make it easier to understand the effect of the nested `for` loops in the quantum implementation, here is a classical equivalent of its effect. This function is analogous to the FFT:

```
from math import log2

def bin_digit(k, j):
    return 1 if k & (1 << j) else 0

def cfft(state):
    n = int(log2(len(state)))
    for j in range(n)[::-1]:
        for k in range(len(state)):
            if bin_digit(k, j) == 0:
                state[k] = 1/sqrt(2)*(state[k] + state[k+2**
                state[k+2**j] = state[k] - sqrt(2)*state[k+2**j]
            else:
                state[k] *= cis(-pi * (k%2**j)*2**-j)
```

Computes the sum and difference of the amplitude pair

Verify that this function gives the same output as the FFT (with a constant $\frac{1}{\sqrt{N}}$ and bit reversal).

SIMULATING THE QFT WITH CLASSICAL CODE

To simulate the QFT, we perform the same computation as the IQFT with negative angles (the conjugates of each Fourier basis). If we perform a QFT on a quantum state, the amplitudes will change, as shown in figure 7.17. This is the same as rotating each amplitude in the state vector clockwise by multiples of the same angle and then adding up the results.

Outcome	Amplitude
k	s_k

$\xrightarrow{\text{QFT}}$

Outcome	Amplitude
k	$\langle s, F_{-k} \rangle$

Figure 7.17 The general form of a quantum state before and after applying the QFT

NOTE The conjugate $\bar{F}_k$ of F_k is the same as F_{-k} if we allow negative values for k.

We can use the following function to classically simulate the application of the QFT to a list representing a quantum state.

Listing 7.5 Classical implementation of the QFT

```
def cft(state):
    N = len(state)
    s = [state[k] for k in range(N)]

    for k in range(N):
        state[k] = inner(s, fourier_basis(N, -k))
```

The single-qubit QFT and IQFT are the Hadamard gate

As we know, a Hadamard gate replaces a pair of amplitudes with their sum and difference multiplied by the square root of 2. For a single-qubit state with amplitudes z_0 and z_1, the new amplitudes will be $\frac{1}{\sqrt{2}}(z_0 + z_1)$ and $\frac{1}{\sqrt{2}}(z_0 - z_1)$.

The Fourier bases for a single qubit are

$$F_0 = \begin{bmatrix} \frac{1}{\sqrt{2}}\omega^0 \\ \frac{1}{\sqrt{2}}\omega^0 \end{bmatrix}, F_1 = \begin{bmatrix} \frac{1}{\sqrt{2}}\omega^0 \\ \frac{1}{\sqrt{2}}\omega^1 \end{bmatrix}$$

where $\omega = \cos(\pi) + i \sin(\pi) = -1$.

Therefore,

$$F_0 = \bar{F}_0 = \begin{bmatrix} \frac{1}{\sqrt{2}} \\ \frac{1}{\sqrt{2}} \end{bmatrix}, F_1 = \bar{F}_1 = \begin{bmatrix} \frac{1}{\sqrt{2}} \\ -\frac{1}{\sqrt{2}} \end{bmatrix}$$

7.3 From classical to quantum Fourier transforms

> Taking the inner product of the state vector $\begin{bmatrix} z_0 \\ z_1 \end{bmatrix}$ with F_0 and F_1 leads to the same result as applying the Hadamard gate to it.

In figures 7.18 and 7.19, we show the result of applying a QFT to three-qubit states with a single nonzero amplitude, called *computational bases*. The resulting states can be thought of as signals whose frequency is the index of the nonzero amplitude. For example, when the nonzero amplitude is at index 2, the state after applying the

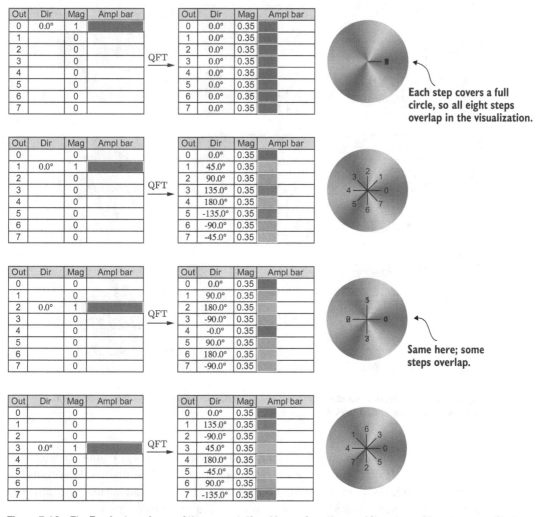

Figure 7.18 The Fourier transforms of the computational bases for a three-qubit system with nonzero amplitudes 0, 1, 2, and 3

QFT covers two full trips around the circle with $N = 8$ steps. They are also geometric sequence states.

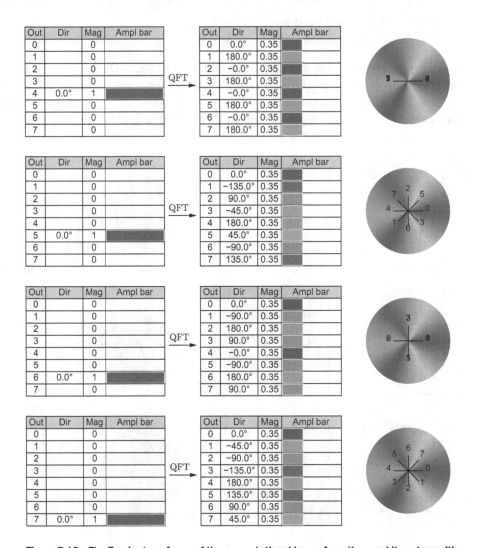

Figure 7.19 The Fourier transforms of the computational bases for a three-qubit system with nonzero amplitudes 4, 5, 6, and 7

When given a frequency encoded in a quantum register, the QFT builds a signal with that frequency. If the frequency is encoded as one of the computational bases, its Fourier transform is the corresponding Fourier basis. The inverse Fourier transform does the opposite: given a signal, it creates a representation of its frequency.

7.4 Quantum circuits for the QFT and IQFT

The quantum-gate-based implementations of the Fourier transform and its inverse mirror the efficient classical implementations of the FFT. On a quantum computer, we can take advantage of quantum parallelism and interference and perform a QFT with a small number of instructions. As a result, the QFT is exponentially faster than the FFT. The number of operations (basic quantum gates) needed for the QFT grows quadratically with the number of qubits (binary digits). The number of operations (additions and subtractions) needed for the FFT grows exponentially with the number of binary digits (see figure 7.20).

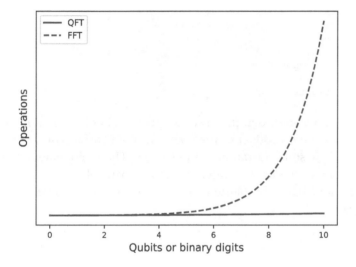

Figure 7.20 A relative comparison of the operations required to compute the QFT and the FFT for a growing number of qubits or binary digits

Listing 7.6 contains the implementations of the QFT and IQFT circuits from our simulator.

Listing 7.6 Quantum circuits for the QFT and IQFT

```
def qft(qc, targets, swap=True):
    for j in range(len(targets))[::-1]:
        qc.h(targets[j])
        for k in range(j)[::-1]:
            qc.cp(pi * 2.0 ** (k - j), targets[j], targets[k])

    if swap:
        qc.mswap(targets)


def iqft(qc, targets, swap=True):
    for j in range(len(targets))[::-1]:
        qc.h(targets[j])
        for k in range(j)[::-1]:
            qc.cp(-pi * 2 ** (k - j), targets[j], targets[k])
```

```
        if swap:
            qc.mswap(targets)

class QFT(QuantumCircuit):
    def __init__(self, m, reversed=False, swap=True):
        super().__init__(QuantumRegister(m))
        targets = range(m)
        if reversed:
            targets = targets[::-1]

        qft(self, targets, swap)


class IQFT(QuantumCircuit):
    def __init__(self, m, reversed=False, swap=True):
        super().__init__(QuantumRegister(m))
        targets = range(m)
        if reversed:
            targets = targets[::-1]

        iqft(self, targets, swap)
```

We will not give a rigorous proof that the previous quantum implementation matches the result of taking the inner product of the state with the Fourier bases, but we can verify its correctness by testing on random input states. These implementations are designed to take advantage of quantum interference and parallelism.

To add the QFT and IQFT to quantum circuits, we will use the methods of the `QuantumCircuit` class.

Listing 7.7 Methods to append QFT and IQFT to a circuit instance

```
def append_qft(self, reg, reversed=False, swap=True):
    self.append(QFT(len(reg), reversed, swap), reg)

def append_iqft(self, reg, reversed=False, swap=True):
    self.append(IQFT(len(reg), reversed, swap), reg)
```

> **Deep dive: Efficient classical implementation**
>
> The following is a much more efficient version of the classical implementation of the IQFT shown in the previous section. For each of the $n > 0$ digits, we traverse the whole list (of 2^n elements) to compute the new values. Therefore, the number of operations is proportional to $n\, 2^n$:
>
> ```
> def classical_inverse_fourier(state, step, targets):
>     n = len(targets)
>     sq2 = sqrt(2)
>     sq2i = 1/sqrt(2)
>     for j in range(n)[::-1]:
>         dist = 2**j
>         rot = cis(-pi/dist)
> ```

```
                rots = [1 for _ in range(dist)]
                r = 1
                for m in range(dist):
                    rots[m] = r
                    r = r*rot

                for l in range(2**(n-j-1)):
                    i = 0
                    for k in range(2*l*dist, (2*l+1)*dist):
                        state[k] = sq2i*(state[k] + state[k+dist])
                        state[k+dist] = (state[k] - sq2*state[k+dist])*rots[i]
                        i += 1
```

Figure 7.21 shows the circuit for performing a QFT on a four-qubit system. The controlled phase gates rotate amplitudes with 1 in both target and control, so the roles of target and control qubits are interchangeable. Note that in some cases the swapping is not needed, or the list of qubits to which the Fourier transforms are applied is reversed.

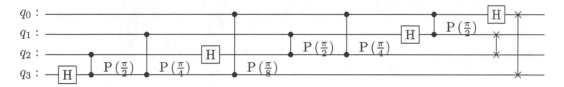

Figure 7.21 Circuit diagram of the QFT on a four-qubit system

Figure 7.22 shows the circuit diagram for performing an IQFT on a four-qubit system. Note that the only difference between the inverse circuit and the circuit in figure 7.21 is the rotation by negative angles.

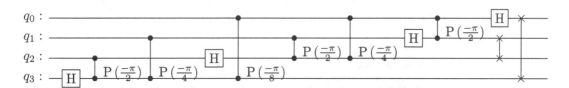

Figure 7.22 Circuit diagram of the IQFT on a four-qubit system

7.4.1 Understanding the effect of the IQFT on a geometric sequence state

Let's look at how the IQFT works on one of the Fourier bases, such as F_{13}, with a four-qubit state. We show the steps that recover the frequency of the periodic signal represented by F_{13}: basically, its index in the state vector, which is 13, or 1101 in binary representation.

Each step (outer for loop) in the IQFT will reveal one binary digit of the frequency, starting from the right. This is essentially the same as the *successive division* method, reviewed next, and is also akin to a binary search.

> **Successive division**
>
> Here is how the successive division method works. We start by dividing a given decimal number (13) by 2 and record the quotient and remainder. Because 13 = 6·2 + 1, the quotient is 6, and the remainder is 1. The remainder (1) is the first binary digit of the given number (starting from the right).
>
> Python has a built-in function called divmod that gives the quotient and remainder of a division. If we use it, we get the expected results:
>
> ```
> divmod(13, 2)
> (6, 1)
> ```
>
> Then we continue the process by applying divmod to the quotients:
>
> ```
> divmod(6, 2)
> (3, 0)
> ```
>
> The second binary digit from the right is 0:
>
> ```
> divmod(3, 2)
> (1, 1)
> ```
>
> The third binary digit from the right is 1:
>
> ```
> divmod(1, 2)
> (0, 1)
> ```
>
> The fourth binary digit from the right is 1, and we are done. The binary representation of 13 is 1101.

Let's now look at the quantum gate-based implementation of IQFT:

1 Apply the Hadamard gate (H) to the last qubit, and subtract the contribution of the last digit in terms of phase shifts (figure 7.23). This reveals the last digit of the encoded integer (1) by making all outcomes ending with 0 impossible.
2 Apply the Hadamard gate to the third qubit, and subtract its contribution to the phase shifts (figure 7.24). This way, we recover the third digit of the encoded integer. Only the amplitudes corresponding to outcomes that have the correct digits in the fourth and third positions are nonzero.

7.4 Quantum circuits for the QFT and IQFT

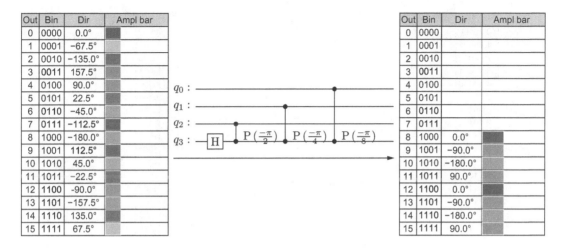

Figure 7.23 The first step of the IQFT on a four-qubit state, where a Hadamard gate is applied to the qubit in position 3, followed by three controlled phase rotations

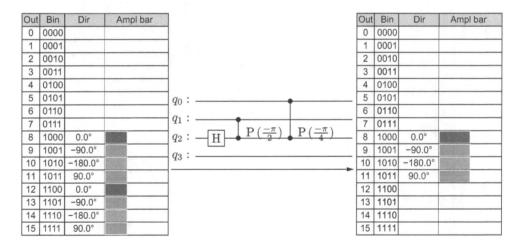

Figure 7.24 The second step of the IQFT on a four-qubit state, where a Hadamard gate is applied to the qubit in position 2, followed by two controlled phase rotations

3. Do the same for the second qubit (figure 7.25).
4. Apply the Hadamard gate to the first qubit to recover the first digit and therefore the integer value that was encoded (figure 7.26).
5. Swap the qubits, arriving at the computational basis corresponding to 13, or 1101 in binary format.

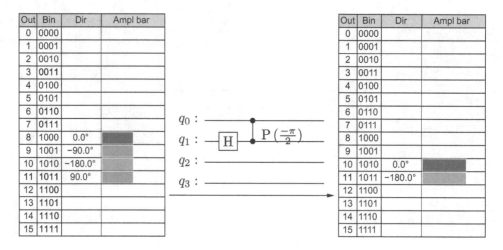

Figure 7.25 The third step of the IQFT on a four-qubit state, where a Hadamard gate is applied to the qubit in position 1, followed by one controlled phase rotation

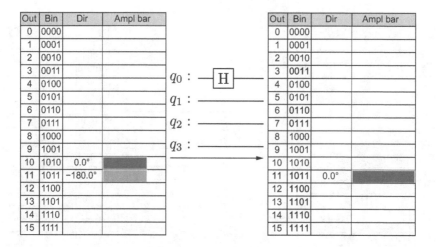

Figure 7.26 The fourth step of the IQFT on a four-qubit state, where a Hadamard gate is applied to the qubit in position 0

Summary

- The QFT is essential in many quantum algorithms. It can convert information stored in the phase of a quantum state to magnitudes.
- We can represent periodic patterns in quantum states by creating a quantum state with amplitudes that are discrete samples of a complex signal. The frequency of the encoded signal is reflected in the phases of the amplitudes.

Summary

- The discrete Fourier transform (DFT) takes discrete signals and computes their frequency components by measuring the similarity, or correlation, between the signal and a set of sinusoidal basis functions of different frequencies (Fourier bases).
- The quantum Fourier transform (QFT) performs the same mathematical operation as the inverse DFT. The implementation of the QFT uses quantum parallelism and interference so that the number of operations (gates) needed grows quadratically with the number of qubits (binary digits). The number of operations needed for the most efficient classical implementation grows exponentially with the number of binary digits.
- The inverse QFT (IQFT) can be used to recover frequency information from geometric sequence states.

Using the quantum Fourier transform

This chapter covers
- Introducing the discrete sinc distribution and phased discrete sinc quantum states
- Using the IQFT to find the encoded frequency of periodic quantum states
- Using the QFT to encode some trigonometric distributions in quantum states

Now that we understand what happens when the quantum Fourier transform (QFT) and inverse QFT (IQFT) are applied to a quantum state, let's look at how we can use them. We will look at examples of two of the most common uses of the QFT: converting difference in phase to difference in magnitude and efficiently preparing some useful quantum states.

In the previous chapter, we saw how to encode a certain frequency into a quantum state in the form of a geometric sequence state. The encoded frequency is reflected in directions of the amplitudes of a geometric sequence state. In this chapter, we will use the IQFT to convert difference in phase to difference in magnitude. The magnitudes after applying the IQFT to a geometric sequence state match the values of the *discrete sinc* function. We will go deeper into understanding the significance of this pattern in both wave diffraction (single-slit experiment) and quantum states.

Encoding a periodic quantum state and decoding its frequency can be seen as encoding a number (the frequency of the complex sinusoidal signal represented in the state). In particular, this encoding allows for efficient manipulation of numbers (e.g., quantum arithmetic, polynomial encoding) that will be used in applications such as optimization.

Next, we will use the QFT to prepare some useful quantum states efficiently. We will see how we can borrow tools from digital signal processing to encode useful trigonometric distributions. Figure 8.1 illustrates the relationships between the concepts covered in this chapter.

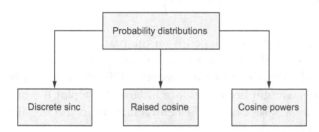

Figure 8.1 A dependency diagram of concepts covered in this chapter

8.1 The single-slit experiment: Wave diffraction

The *single-slit* experiment is a fundamental physics experiment where a particle source, typically a light source, is directed through a narrow slit onto a wall. The experiment demonstrates a foundational principle of quantum mechanics that has a profound impact on our understanding of the behavior of particles at the quantum level and has numerous practical applications in science and technology. The pattern we observe in the single-slit experiment also appears in several quantum computing algorithms.

The setup for the single-slit experiment consists of a light source (a beam of photons), a barrier with a thin slit, and a screen or detector placed behind the slit. The light source is usually a laser beam, and the slit is typically less than 0.1 mm wide. The screen can be white paper or a wall coated with a fluorescent material to make the light easier to observe.

As the laser beam sends photons through the slit, a pattern emerges of alternating dark and light bands. This phenomenon is known as *diffraction*, and it occurs because light behaves like a wave and spreads out when it passes through a narrow opening. The *diffraction pattern* consists of the central bright spot, known as the *central maximum*, surrounded by a series of alternating bright and dark areas, known as the diffraction *maxima* and *minima*, respectively. An example of a diffraction pattern on a screen is shown in figure 8.2.

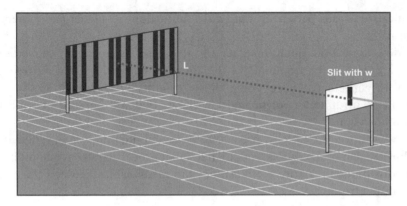

Figure 8.2 The diffraction pattern on a screen resulting from a single-slit experiment

The spacing of the light and dark areas depends on the particle wavelength and the width of the slit, with narrower slits or longer wavelengths producing wider spacing between the maxima. As the slit becomes narrower, the diffraction pattern becomes sharper, and the central maximum becomes more intense. If we plot the diffraction intensity, as shown in figure 8.3, we can see the central maximum and the diffraction maxima and minima on either side.

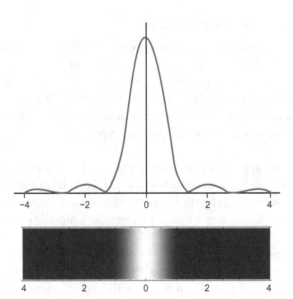

Figure 8.3 An example plot of diffraction intensity based on a diffraction pattern where the *x* axis is the distance from the slit

The diffraction pattern created by the single-slit experiment can be used to determine the wavelength of the laser beam. Similarly, in this chapter, we will show how to use the analogous pattern in a quantum state to determine the frequency of the encoded periodic signal.

8.1.1 Introducing the discrete sinc function

The distribution created when plotting the diffraction pattern in the single-slit experiment, as shown in figure 8.3, appears frequently in the field of digital signal processing. The function that defines this distribution is called the *sinc* function (pronounced "sink"). The sinc function is expressed as

$$\operatorname{sinc}(x) = \begin{cases} 1 & \text{if } x = 0 \\ \frac{\sin(x)}{x} & \text{otherwise} \end{cases}$$

where x is a real number.

> **Product form of the sinc function**
> The sinc function can also be written as an infinite product:
>
> $$\operatorname{sinc}(x) = \prod_{j=1}^{\infty} \cos\left(\frac{x}{2^j}\right)$$

We will use a function we call the *discrete sinc*, or sincd_n function, for a positive integer n defined by

$$\operatorname{sincd}_n(x) = \prod_{j=1}^{n} \cos\left(\frac{x}{2^j}\right) = \frac{\operatorname{sinc}(x)}{\operatorname{sinc}(\frac{x}{2^n})}$$

where x is a real number.

The discrete sinc function is the discrete version of the sinc function pattern. For example, in figure 8.4, we plot sincd_3 for $-8 \leq x \leq 8$.

8.2 Encoding a periodic signal using discrete sinc quantum states

In chapter 7, we learned how to encode a (complex) geometric sequence as a periodic quantum state. In summary, for n qubits and a frequency $0 \leq v < 2^n$, we encode the geometric sequence $\frac{1}{\sqrt{2^n}} \operatorname{cis}(k\theta)$ for $0 \leq k < 2^n$, where $\theta = v\frac{2\pi}{2^n}$. The general form of a geometric sequence state is shown in figure 8.5. This geometric sequence is called a complex sinusoid in digital signal processing.

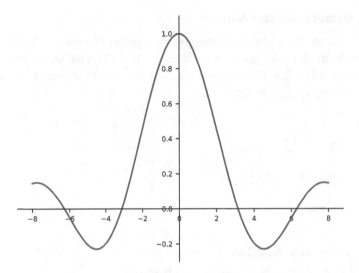

Figure 8.4 Plot of $sincd_3$ for $-8 \leq x \leq 8$

NOTE Throughout the book, we will interchangeably use either an angle or its corresponding value mapped to a relevant numerical range. In this case, θ and v are related by the formula $\theta/(2\pi) = v/2^n$.

Outcome	Amplitude
k	$\frac{1}{\sqrt{2^n}} \mathrm{cis}(k\theta)$

Figure 8.5 An *n*-qubit geometric sequence state for an angle θ, where $0 \leq k < 2^n$

In the previous chapter, we introduced the quantum circuit to encode a geometric sequence state. We define the same circuit in the following listing with an angle parameter theta (in radians).

Listing 8.1 Creating a circuit for encoding a geometric sequence state

```
from sim_circuit import QuantumRegister, QuantumCircuit

def geometric_sequence_circuit(n, theta):

    N = 2**n

    q = QuantumRegister(n)
    qc = QuantumCircuit(q)

    for j in range(n):
        qc.h(q[j])

    for j in range(n):
        qc.p(2 ** j * theta, q[j])

    return qc
```

Iterates through all n qubits

8.2 Encoding a periodic signal using discrete sinc quantum states

Let's break down the construction of this circuit. The goal is to create a state where all the amplitudes have the same magnitude, $\frac{1}{\sqrt{2^n}}$, and the amplitude of the outcome with index $0 \leq k < 2^n$ has direction $k\theta$. To create this state, we apply a Hadamard gate and a phase gate to each qubit in the circuit. For each target qubit, j, the angle parameter of the phase gate is $2^j\theta$.

For example, let's look at the circuit for encoding a geometric sequence state with $n = 3$ qubits and $\theta = \pi/3$:

1. A Hadamard gate is applied to each of the three qubits (figure 8.6).

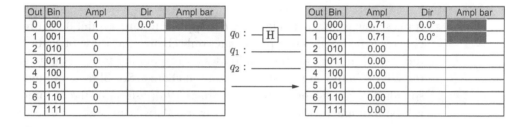

Figure 8.6 The state tables of a three-qubit state after applying a Hadamard gate to each qubit, starting with the default state

a. The first Hadamard gate is applied to the initial state, so the amplitudes corresponding to outcomes 0 and 1 become $\frac{1}{\sqrt{2}}$, and the rest of the amplitudes remain 0.

b When the second Hadamard gate is applied to target qubit 1, there are only two pairs with a nonzero amplitude. All the amplitudes corresponding to outcomes in these pairs (outcomes 0 and 2 and outcomes 1 and 3) become the previous value of the 0 side of the pair multiplied by $\frac{1}{\sqrt{2}}$.

c Similarly, when the third Hadamard gate is applied to target qubit 2, all the amplitudes become the previous value of the 0 side of the pair multiplied by $\frac{1}{\sqrt{2}}$. Therefore, the amplitudes of the state after applying a Hadamard gate to each qubit are all $\frac{1}{\sqrt{8}}$.

2 A phase gate with the angle $2^0\theta = \theta$ is applied to target qubit 0 (figure 8.7). In chapter 3, we learned that phase gates only change the 1 side of a pair of amplitudes. This means only the amplitudes corresponding to binary outcomes with the value 1 in the target qubit position will change. So, all the amplitudes corresponding to an outcome with binary digit 1 in position 0 (the rightmost digit) will be multiplied by $\text{cis}(\theta)$ (rotated by θ). As we can see in the second state table in figure 8.7, the amplitudes of the 1 side of each pair become $\frac{1}{\sqrt{8}}\text{cis}(\theta)$.

Out	Bin	Ampl	Dir	Ampl bar
0	000	0.35	0.0°	
1	001	0.35	0.0°	
2	010	0.35	0.0°	
3	011	0.35	0.0°	
4	100	0.35	0.0°	
5	101	0.35	0.0°	
6	110	0.35	0.0°	
7	111	0.35	0.0°	

Out	Bin	Ampl	Dir	Ampl bar
0	000	0.35	0.0°	
1	001	0.18 + 0.31i	60.0°	
2	010	0.35	0.0°	
3	011	0.18 + 0.31i	60.0°	
4	100	0.35	0.0°	
5	101	0.18 + 0.31i	60.0°	
6	110	0.35	0.0°	
7	111	0.18 + 0.31i	60.0°	

Figure 8.7 The state tables before and after applying a phase gate to target qubit 0 with angle $\theta = \pi/3$

3 A phase gate with the angle $2^1\theta = 2\theta$ is applied to target qubit 1 (figure 8.8). Only the amplitudes corresponding to outcomes with binary digit 1 in position 1 (the middle digit) change. The amplitudes corresponding to outcomes with digit 1 in the target qubit position are multiplied by $\text{cis}(2\theta)$. The directions of these amplitudes are rotated by 2θ or 120°, which we can clearly see when comparing the state tables.

4 A phase gate with the angle $2^2\theta = 4\theta$ is applied to target qubit 2 (figure 8.9). The amplitudes corresponding to binary outcomes with the digit 1 in the target qubit position (the rightmost digit) are multiplied by $\text{cis}(4\theta)$.

8.2 Encoding a periodic signal using discrete sinc quantum states

Out	Bin	Ampl	Dir	Ampl bar
0	000	0.35	0.0°	
1	001	0.18 + 0.31i	60.0°	
2	010	0.35	0.0°	
3	011	0.18 + 0.31i	60.0°	
4	100	0.35	0.0°	
5	101	0.18 + 0.31i	60.0°	
6	110	0.35	0.0°	
7	111	0.18 + 0.31i	60.0°	

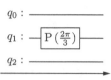

Out	Bin	Ampl	Dir	Ampl bar
0	000	0.35	0.0°	
1	001	0.18 + 0.31i	60.0°	
2	010	−0.18 + 0.31i	120.0°	
3	011	−0.35	180.0°	
4	100	0.35	0.0°	
5	101	0.18 + 0.31i	60.0°	
6	110	−0.18 + 0.31i	120.0°	
7	111	−0.35	180.0°	

Figure 8.8 The state tables before and after applying a phase gate to target qubit 1 with angle 2 $\theta = 2\pi/3$

Out	Bin	Ampl	Dir	Ampl bar
0	000	0.35	0.0°	
1	001	0.18 + 0.31i	60.0°	
2	010	−0.18 + 0.31i	120.0°	
3	011	−0.35	180.0°	
4	100	0.35	0.0°	
5	101	0.18 + 0.31i	60.0°	
6	110	−0.18 + 0.31i	120.0°	
7	111	−0.35	180.0°	

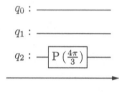

Out	Bin	Ampl	Dir	Ampl bar
0	000	0.35	0.0°	
1	001	0.18 + 0.31i	60.0°	
2	010	−0.18 + 0.31i	120.0°	
3	011	−0.35	180.0°	
4	100	−0.18 − 0.31i	−120.0°	
5	101	0.18 − 0.31i	−60.0°	
6	110	0.35	−0.0°	
7	111	0.18 + 0.31i	60.0°	

Figure 8.9 The state tables before and after applying a phase gate to target qubit 2 with angle 4 $\theta = 4\pi/3$

It is helpful to visualize the resulting state with a tree diagram: see figure 8.10. In this diagram, the amplitude of each outcome is the product of the complex numbers on the edges of the path to it from the root of the tree. The direction of each amplitude is the sum of the rotation angles on the edges of the path.

When we encode a geometric sequence state with n qubits and an angle θ, each qubit $0 \leq j < n$ contributes a phase shift of $2^j \theta$ through a phase gate applied to target qubit j. Interference will ensure that the amplitude of the outcome with index k has direction $k\theta$ for each $0 \leq k < 2^n$. The Hadamard gates make all amplitudes have the same magnitude, $\frac{1}{\sqrt{2^n}}$. The result is a product state that can be built recursively, qubit by qubit. Figure 8.11 shows the contribution to the amplitudes when applying a Hadamard gate and phase gate to target qubit 0, target qubits $0 < k < n-1$, and target qubit $n-1$.

> **Deep dive: Ket notation**
>
> We can use Ket notation to express a three-qubit geometric sequence state with angle θ:
>
> $$\left(\frac{1}{\sqrt{2}}|0\rangle + e^{i4\theta}|1\rangle\right) \otimes \left(\frac{1}{\sqrt{2}}|0\rangle + e^{i2\theta}|1\rangle\right) \otimes \left(\frac{1}{\sqrt{2}}|0\rangle + e^{i\theta}|1\rangle\right)$$
>
> We can express an n-qubit geometric sequence state as
>
> $$\left(\frac{1}{\sqrt{2}}|0\rangle + e^{i2^{n-1}\theta}|1\rangle\right) \otimes \cdots \otimes \left(\frac{1}{\sqrt{2}}|0\rangle + e^{i2^0\theta}|1\rangle\right)$$

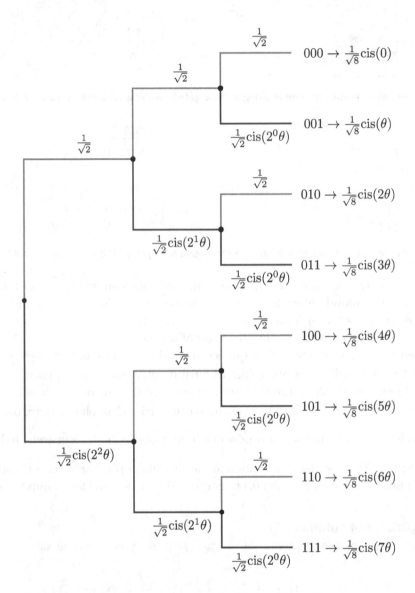

Figure 8.10 A tree diagram representation of the encoding pattern for a geometric sequence state with $n = 3$ qubits and an angle $\pi/3$

8.2 Encoding a periodic signal using discrete sinc quantum states

Target qubit 0	
Outcome	Amplitude
0	$\frac{1}{\sqrt{2}}$
1	$\frac{1}{\sqrt{2}}\operatorname{cis}(2^0\theta)$

Target qubits $0 < k < n-1$	
Outcome	Amplitude
0	$\frac{1}{\sqrt{2}}$
1	$\frac{1}{\sqrt{2}}\operatorname{cis}(2^k\theta)$

Target qubit $n-1$	
Outcome	Amplitude
0	$\frac{1}{\sqrt{2}}$
1	$\frac{1}{\sqrt{2}}\operatorname{cis}(2^{n-1}\theta)$

Figure 8.11 In a geometric sequence state with n qubits and an angle θ, the amplitude corresponding to each outcome $0 < k < 2^n$ is the product of the factor for the target qubit digit in the binary form of the outcomes.

> **Exercise 8.1**
>
> The circuit to encode a geometric sequence state applies a Hadamard gate to each qubit and then a phase gate to each qubit. Instead, we can apply a Hadamard gate and a phase gate to each qubit in a single for-loop.
>
> ```
> def geometric_sequence_circuit_single_loop(n, theta):
>
>     N = 2**n
>
>     q = QuantumRegister(n)
>     qc = QuantumCircuit(q)
>
>     for j in range(n):
>         qc.h(q[j])
>         qc.p(2 ** j * theta, q[j])
>
>     return qc
> ```
>
> Create a quantum state using this function, and then check that it is a geometric sequence state.

8.2.1 Phase-to-magnitude frequency encoding with the IQFT

Now let's look again at the effect of applying the IQFT to a geometric sequence state. We will switch to using the frequency v directly instead of its corresponding angle $\theta = v\, 2\pi/2^n$. The code for the circuit that combines the encoding of a geometric sequence with frequency v and the application of IQFT is shown next.

Listing 8.2 Creating the circuit for encoding a frequency in a quantum state

```
from math import pi

def encode_frequency(n, v):
    q = QuantumRegister(n)
    qc = QuantumCircuit(q)

    for j in range(n):
        qc.h(q[j])
```

```
for j in range(n):
    qc.p(2 * pi / 2 ** (n - j) * v, q[j])

qc.report('geometric_sequence')

qc.append_iqft(q)

qc.report('iqft')

return qc
```

The phase gate angle is $2^j\theta$; we use the equivalent angle $2^j\theta = v\, 2\pi/2^{n-j}$.

NOTE As we have done in previous chapters, we can use the report() method of the circuit to create a snapshot report containing the transformations applied since the last report and the states before and after applying those transformations. We can use such reports to visualize the encoding process.

ENCODING AN INTEGER AS A FREQUENCY

Let's look at the encoding of frequency $v = 4$ in a three-qubit state ($n = 3$). Figure 8.12 shows the encoding of the corresponding geometric sequence.

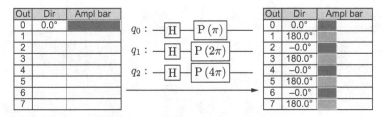

Figure 8.12 The encoding of a geometric sequence state with $n = 3$ qubits and angle $\theta = 4\dfrac{2\pi}{2^n} = \pi$, starting with the default state

Now we apply the IQFT to the state, as shown in figure 8.13. After applying the IQFT, we get a state where the magnitudes of the amplitudes reflect the frequency of the geometric sequence. In this example, the encoded frequency is an integer, so the magnitude of the amplitude corresponding to outcome 4 is 1, and all the other amplitudes are 0.

ENCODING A NON-INTEGER AS A FREQUENCY

If we encode a non-integer frequency, such as $v = 4.7$, in a three-qubit state ($n = 3$), the pattern is different. Figure 8.14 shows the state table after encoding the geometric sequence state, and figure 8.15 shows the state table after applying the IQFT.

To help understand this result, let's visualize the amplitudes of the resulting state with a color wheel, as shown in figure 8.16. In the resulting state, the directions are $\pi/8$ radians or 22.5 degrees apart, increasing from the first (amplitude 0) to the floor (the rounded-down integer value) of the encoded frequency (in this example, 4) and decreasing (in reverse order) from the first toward the ceiling (the rounded-up integer

8.2 Encoding a periodic signal using discrete sinc quantum states

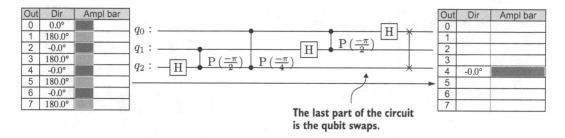

Figure 8.13 The state tables before and after applying the IQFT to the geometric sequence state with $n = 3$ qubits and angle $\theta = 4\frac{2\pi}{2^n} = \pi$

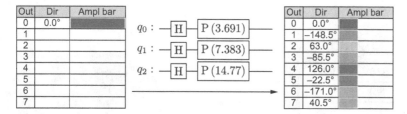

Figure 8.14 The encoding of a geometric sequence state with $n = 3$ qubits and an angle $\theta = 4.7\frac{2\pi}{2^n}$, starting with the default state

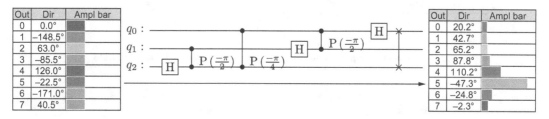

Figure 8.15 The state tables before and after applying the IQFT to the geometric sequence state with $n = 3$ qubits and an angle $\theta = 4.7\frac{2\pi}{2^n}$

value) of the encoded frequency (in this example, 5). We can see in figure 8.16 that the magnitude of the amplitude corresponding to outcome 5 is the largest because it is the closest integer to the encoded frequency. The magnitude corresponding to outcome 4 is the second largest because it is the next-closest integer.

The magnitudes reflect an approximation of the frequency of the periodic state in terms of integer frequencies. Figure 8.17 shows the state table and vector representation of the amplitudes of a three-qubit state with the frequency $v = 4.3$.

Outcome	Direction	Magnitude	Amplitude bar
0	20.2°	0.11	
1	42.8°	0.10	
2	65.2°	0.12	
3	87.8°	0.16	
4	110.3°	0.37	
5	−47.2°	0.86	
6	−24.7°	0.21	
7	−2.2°	0.13	

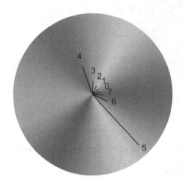

Figure 8.16 The amplitude pattern for the encoding of $v = 4.7$ in a three-qubit state

Outcome	Direction	Magnitude	Amplitude bar
0	−42.8°	0.10	
1	−20.3°	0.11	
2	2.2°	0.13	
3	24.7°	0.21	
4	47.2°	0.86	
5	−110.3°	0.37	
6	−87.8°	0.16	
7	−65.2°	0.12	

Figure 8.17 The amplitude pattern for the encoding of $v = 4.3$ in a three-qubit state

> **Exercise 8.2**
> Justify that using the circuit in listing 8.2 to encode a frequency $0 \leq v < 2$ in a single-qubit state is the same as the phase-to-magnitude method we saw in chapter 7. The phase is $\theta = v\pi$.

8.2.2 Some useful numerical forms of the frequency encoding pattern

The amplitudes of a quantum state after encoding a frequency value v form a pattern we will see in many applications throughout this book. This pattern shows up in one of the most important quantum computing algorithms: quantum phase estimation, which we will discuss in the next chapter.

At the beginning of this chapter, we talked about the sinc and discrete sinc (sincd_n) functions. We can express the sincd_n function for a real number x as

8.2 Encoding a periodic signal using discrete sinc quantum states

$$\text{sincd}_n(x) = \prod_{j=1}^{n} \cos\left(\frac{x}{2^j}\right) = \begin{cases} 1 & \text{if } x = 0 \\ \frac{1}{2^n} \frac{\sin(x)}{\sin(\frac{x}{2^n})} & \text{otherwise} \end{cases}$$

If we have a quantum state with n qubits and an encoded frequency v, after applying the IQFT, the magnitudes of the amplitude corresponding to each outcome $0 \le k < 2^n$ will be

$$|\text{sincd}_n((v-k)\pi)| = \left|\prod_{m=0}^{n-1} \cos\left((v-k)\frac{\pi}{2^{m+1}}\right)\right| = \frac{1}{2^n} \left|\frac{\sin((v-k)\pi)}{\sin\left((v-k)\frac{\pi}{2^n}\right)}\right|$$

The magnitudes match the discrete sinc function. As we saw in the examples, if the encoded value is a non-integer, the amplitudes also have a phase. So, we will call the resulting state a *phased discrete sinc state*.

For example, let's create the three-qubit state shown in figure 8.17:

```
n = 3
v = 4.3
qc = encode_frequency(n, v)
state = qc.run()
```

Let's check that the magnitudes of the state match the outputs of the function $|\text{sincd}_n((v-k)\pi)|$ for $0 < k \le 2^n$, where $n = 3$ and $v = 4.3$. We will use the following prod function to compute each product of cosines:

```
def prod(iterable):
    p = 1
    for n in iterable:
        p *= n
    return p
```

We can use the following assert statement to check the magnitudes of the example state:

```
from math import cos
from util import all_close

N = 2**n
assert all_close([abs(state[k]) for k in range(N)], [
    abs(prod(cos((v - k) * pi / 2 ** (m + 1)) for m in range(n))) for k in
    range(N)])
```

We can create a phased discrete sinc state using the following function:

```
from util import cis

def phased_sincd(n, v):
    N = 2 ** n
```

```
return [prod(
    cos((v - k) * pi / 2 ** (j + 1)) * cis((v - k) * pi / 2 ** (j + 1))
    for j in range(n)) for k in range(2 ** n)]
```

Let's double-check that the outcome of this function for n = 3 and v = 4.3 matches the example state created using the `encode_frequency` function:

```
assert all_close(state, phased_sincd(3, 4.3))
```

The general form of a phased discrete sinc state using the same form as in the `phased_sincd` function is shown in figure 8.18.

Outcome	Amplitude	Magnitude
k	$\prod_{m=0}^{n-1}\left(\operatorname{cis}((v-k)\frac{\pi}{2^{m+1}})\cos((v-k)\frac{\pi}{2^{m+1}})\right)$	$\prod_{m=0}^{n-1}\lvert\cos((v-k)\frac{\pi}{2^{m+1}})\rvert$

Figure 8.18 The general form of a phased discrete sinc state with *n* qubits, where 0 ≤ *k* < 2ⁿ, and an encoded frequency *v*, where 0 ≤ *v* < 2ⁿ

We can express the phased discrete sinc state in other useful forms. We do this because these formulas help with frequency estimation, as we will see later in the book.

In figure 8.18, the amplitudes of a phased discrete sinc are expressed as a product. We know that the product of complex numbers is effectively rotation. Therefore, the product of complex numbers

$$\prod_{m=0}^{n-1} \operatorname{cis}\left((v-k)\frac{\pi}{2^{m+1}}\right)$$

can also be expressed as

$$\operatorname{cis}\left(\sum_{m=0}^{n-1}(v-k)\frac{\pi}{2^{m+1}}\right) = \operatorname{cis}\left((N-1)(v-k)\frac{\pi}{N}\right)$$

where $N = 2^n$.

We can use this `cis` expression, combined with the product of cosines, to create a phased discrete sinc quantum state with the following Python code:

```
def phased_sincd_combined_cis(n, v):
    N = 2 ** n
    return [prod(cos((v - k) * pi / 2 ** (m + 1)) for m in range(n)) * cis(
        (N - 1) / N * (v - k) * pi) for k in range(2 ** n)]
```

8.2 Encoding a periodic signal using discrete sinc quantum states

Let's check that this form also creates the phased discrete sinc state with n = 3 and v = 4.3:

```
assert all_close(state, phased_sincd_combined_cis(3, 4.3))
```

The general form of a phased discrete sinc state using the form in the `phased_sincd_combined_cis` function is shown in figure 8.19.

Outcome	Amplitude	Magnitude
k	$\operatorname{cis}\left((N-1)(v-k)\frac{\pi}{N}\right) \prod_{m=0}^{n-1} \cos\left((v-k)\frac{\pi}{2^{m+1}}\right)$	$\prod_{m=0}^{n-1} \left\|\cos\left((v-k)\frac{\pi}{2^{m+1}}\right)\right\|$

Figure 8.19 The general form of a phased discrete sinc state with *n* qubits, where $0 \leq k < 2^n$, and an encoded frequency *v*, where $0 \leq v < 2^n$

Exercise 8.3
Write code that uses random states to verify the following alternative expression for the amplitudes of a periodic *n*-qubit quantum state, with $N = 2^n$.

Outcome	Amplitude
k	$\operatorname{cis}\left((N-1)(v-k)\frac{\pi}{N}\right) \cdot \frac{2}{N} \cdot \sum_{m=0}^{N/2} \cos\left((2m+1)(v-k)\frac{\pi}{N}\right)$

If v is a non-integer, the set of directions of the amplitudes is determined by the decimal part of the value, $v - \lfloor v \rfloor$, but the order will differ based on $\lfloor v \rfloor$. The general form of the state, which shows the differences in direction using the decimal part of the encoded value, is shown in figure 8.20.

Outcome	Amplitude	Direction	Magnitude
$k < v$	$\operatorname{cis}\left((N-1)(v-k)\frac{\pi}{N}\right) \frac{1}{N} \frac{\sin(v-k)\pi}{\sin(v-k)\frac{\pi}{N}}$	$\left(-\frac{v-k}{N} + v - \lfloor v \rfloor\right)180°$	$\frac{1}{N}\left\|\frac{\sin(v-k)\pi}{\sin(v-k)\frac{\pi}{N}}\right\|$
$k = v$	1	0°	1
$k > v$	$\operatorname{cis}\left((N-1)(v-k)\frac{\pi}{N}\right) \frac{1}{N} \frac{\sin(v-k)\pi}{\sin(v-k)\frac{\pi}{N}}$	$\left(-\frac{v-k}{N} + v - \lfloor v \rfloor - 1\right)180°$	$\frac{1}{N}\left\|\frac{\sin(v-k)\pi}{\sin(v-k)\frac{\pi}{N}}\right\|$

Figure 8.20 The general form of a phased discrete sinc quantum state with *n* qubits, where $0 \leq k < 2^n$, and an encoded frequency *v*, where $0 \leq v < 2^n$

Exercise 8.4

Verify that the amplitudes of a phased discrete state can be expressed recursively, as shown in the following tree for a three-qubit state:

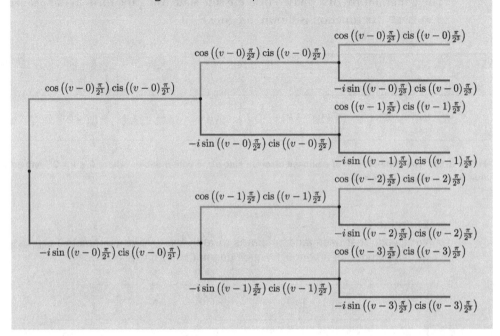

NOTE For n qubits and any real number v, not necessarily in the interval 0, 2^n, we can encode the geometric sequence for the angle $v\, 2\pi/2^n$. This way, all values that differ by a multiple of 2^n are mapped to the same geometric sequence state because adding any number of full rotations to a direction does not change it. For example, for $n = 3$ qubits, encoding $v = 4.7$ and $v = 12.7$ creates the same state.

8.2.3 Reversed qubit implementation of phased discrete sinc quantum states

We can use an alternative implementation for encoding a phased discrete sinc quantum state that avoids the qubit swapping step in the IQFT. First we will build a geometric sequence state with amplitudes corresponding to outcomes in the reverse order as in the previous implementation. For example, if $n = 3$, the amplitude that corresponded to the outcome 1 ('001') in the previous implementation will now be the amplitude corresponding to the outcome 4 ('100'). The amplitude values in the normal index sequence [0, 1, 2, 3, 4, 5, 6, 7] will be reordered as [0, 4, 2, 6, 1, 5, 3, 7].

In the alternative implementation, we apply phase gates to the target qubits with the reverse order of angles to create a geometric sequence state with qubits in

8.2 Encoding a periodic signal using discrete sinc quantum states

a reversed order. The quantum circuit implementation is shown in the following listing.

Listing 8.3 Creating the circuit for the reversed geometric sequence state

```
def geom_alt(n, v):
    q = QuantumRegister(n)
    qc = QuantumCircuit(q)

    for j in range(n):
        qc.h(q[j])

    for j in range(n):
        qc.p(pi * 2 ** -j * v, q[j])

    return qc
```

> The phase gate angle is $2^{n-1-j}\theta$ ($n-1-j$ is the reversed qubit index). We use the equivalent angle $2^{n-1-j}\theta = 2^n/2^{j+1}\theta = 2^n/2^{j+1} v\,2\pi/2^n = v\pi/2j$.

Let's use this method to create a phased discrete sinc state with $n = 3$ qubits and $v = 4$. The state before and after preparing the geometric sequence using the alternative method is shown in figure 8.21. We can see that the angles in the circuit in figure 8.21 are in the reverse order of the angles in the circuit used for the previous method in figure 8.12.

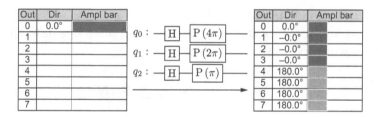

Figure 8.21 Encoding a geometric sequence state using the reverse index order with $n = 3$ qubits and an angle $\theta = 4\dfrac{2\pi}{2^n} = \pi$

Now we will apply the IQFT to the qubits in reversed order without swapping at the end. The complete circuit is shown next.

Listing 8.4 Creating the frequency encoding circuit with reversed qubit order

```
def encode_frequency_q_alt(n, v):
    q = QuantumRegister(n)
    qc = QuantumCircuit(q)

    for j in range(n):
        qc.h(q[j])
        qc.p(pi * 2 ** -j * v, q[j])

    qc.report('signal')
```

```
qc.append_iqft(q, reversed=True, swap=False)

qc.report('iqft')

return qc
```
◁— Applies the IQFT to qubits in reverse order and skips the qubit swapping in the IQFT

Figure 8.22 shows the state tables and circuit for applying the IQFT to the qubits in reversed order and without swapping. The resulting state is the same as with the original method.

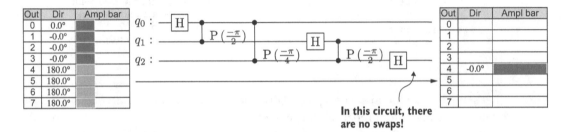

In this circuit, there are no swaps!

Figure 8.22 The state tables before and after applying the IQFT (without swaps)

Next, let's look at the example with $n = 3$ qubits and $v = 4.7$ using the alternative method. The geometric sequence state has the same amplitudes in a different order than in the previous method, as shown in figure 8.23.

Figure 8.23 The encoding of a geometric sequence state using the reverse index order with $n = 3$ qubits and angle $\theta = 4.7 \dfrac{2\pi}{2^n}$

Next, we apply the IQFT to the qubits in reversed order and without swapping at the end, as shown in figure 8.24. Once again, the resulting state is the same as the state created using the original method. The only difference is that we got to skip the swaps in the IQFT, making the circuit more efficient.

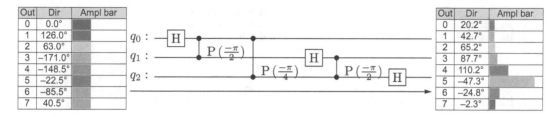

Figure 8.24 The state tables before and after applying the IQFT (without swaps)

8.3 Discrete sinc as a sequence of coin flips

In chapter 4, we looked at encoding a binomial distribution in a quantum state. As a reminder, the binomial distribution is a probability distribution that models the number of successes in a fixed number of sequential and independent trials. Each trial results in one of two possible outcomes, commonly called success and failure, or 0 and 1. The binomial distribution can be used to describe a series of coin tosses.

We can also model the discrete sinc distribution as a sequence of coin tosses. If the total number of tosses is n, the bias of the coin tossed at trial $0 \leq m < n$ depends on the previous toss results. If the decimal representation of the binary number formed with the results of the first $m-1$ flips is k, with $0 \leq k < 2^m$, the probability of getting 0 or 1 in the mth flip is $\cos^2\left((v-k)\frac{\pi}{2^{m+1}}\right)$ or $\sin^2\left((v-k)\frac{\pi}{2^{m+1}}\right)$, respectively.

Let's look at an example for $n = 3$ tosses and a value $v = 4.7$. For the first step (or toss), $m = 0$:

- The probability of getting 0 is $\cos^2\left(4.7\frac{\pi}{2}\right)$.
- The probability of getting 1 $\sin^2\left(4.7\frac{\pi}{2}\right)$.

For the second toss ($m = 1$),

- If the first toss was 0 ($k = 0$),
  - The probability of getting 0 is $\cos^2\left(4.7\frac{\pi}{4}\right)$.
  - The probability of getting 1 is $\sin^2\left(4.7\frac{\pi}{4}\right)$.
- If the first toss was 1 ($k = 1$),
  - The probability of getting 0 is $\cos^2\left(3.7\frac{\pi}{4}\right)$.
  - The probability of getting 1 is $\sin^2\left(3.7\frac{\pi}{4}\right)$.

206   CHAPTER 8   *Using the quantum Fourier transform*

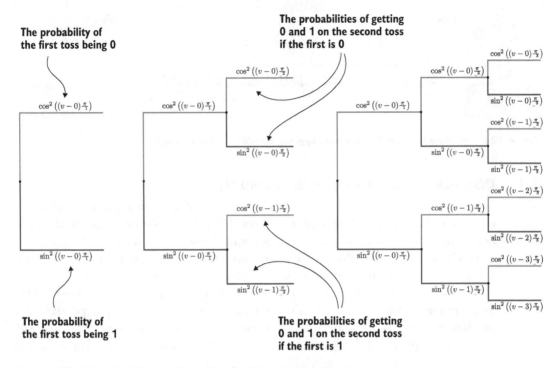

Figure 8.25   The probability of getting a 0 or 1 with each of the three tosses

The probabilities for each toss are shown in figure 8.25. The following function validates these probabilities:

```
from util import is_close
from math import sin

def discrete_sinc_by_digit(n , v):

    probs = [_ for _ in range(2**n)]
    for l in range(2**n):
        s = bin(l)[2:].zfill(n)
        assert(len(s) == n)
        p = 1
        k = 0
        for m in range(n):
            if s[m] == '0':
                p *= cos((v - k)*pi/2**(m+1))**2
            else:
                p *= sin((v - k)*pi/2**(m+1))**2
                k += 2**m

        probs[k] = p

    return probs
```

Iterates through all the possible sequences (binary strings) of outcomes for n trials

Iterates through each digit in the possible sequence (binary string) of outcomes

8.3 Discrete sinc as a sequence of coin flips

```
n = 3
v = 4.7

probs = discrete_sinc_by_digit(n, v)
for k in range(len(probs)):
    assert is_close(probs[k], prod(cos((v-k)*pi/2**(j+1)) for j in range(n))**2)
```
> Asserts that the probability of the sequence of outcomes matches the probabilities shown in the tree

We can also compute the probability for each possible sequence of outcomes with the following recursive function:

```
def recursive_discrete_sinc(n, v):
    if n == 1:
        return [cos(v*pi/2)**2, sin(v*pi/2)**2]

    p = recursive_discrete_sinc(n-1, v)

    return [p[k] * cos((v - k) * pi / 2 ** n) ** 2 for k in
            range(2 ** (n - 1))] + [p[k] * sin((v - k) * pi / 2 ** n) ** 2
                                    for k in range(2 ** (n - 1))]
```

We can also model a sequence of n coin tosses with probabilities defined by n and the frequency v several times and examine the frequency we observe each possible sequence. The function can be used to simulate a given number (count) of n coin tosses:

```
import numpy as np

def discrete_sinc_coin_flips(n, v, count=10000):
    samples = []
    for _ in range(count):
        k = 0
        for m in range(n):
            flip = np.random.binomial(1, sin((v-k)*pi/2**(m+1))**2)
            k += flip*2**m

        samples.append(k)

    return samples
```

Figure 8.26 illustrates the samples returned from `discrete_sinc_coin_flips` for $v = 4.7$ for $n = 1$, $n = 2$, and $n = 3$. Note that if v is a real value that is not in the interval $0 \leq v < 2^n$, the encoded frequency will be $v \bmod 2^n$. This is why for $n = 1$ and $n = 2$, the actual encoded frequency is 0.7. The histograms show the frequency of each outcome (in decimal form) in the 10,000 samples. The line plot shows the discrete sinc probability distribution for the same values n and v. We can see that the results closely match the discrete sinc probability distribution.

Figure 8.27 shows the same visualization for $v = 4.5$. The magnitudes corresponding to outcomes 4 and 5 are equal.

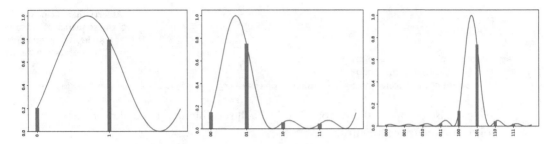

Figure 8.26 Frequency of outcomes and discrete sinc probability distribution for v = 4.7 and n = 1, n = 2, and n = 3. Note that for n = 1 and n = 2, the actual encoded frequency is 0.7.

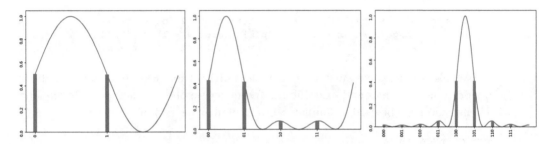

Figure 8.27 Frequency of outcomes and discrete sinc probability distribution for v = 4.5 and n = 1, n = 2, and n = 3. Note that for n = 1 and n = 2, the actual encoded frequency is 0.5

8.4 Encoding trigonometric distributions in a quantum state

As we have discussed, random sampling from probability distributions is one of the most promising near-term applications for quantum computing. We have already looked at a couple of examples where we encode a certain probability distribution, such as the uniform distribution, in a quantum state for sampling. Generally, we prepare a quantum state with n qubits, where the probabilities of the outcomes represent the probabilities of the distribution. We only encode discrete probabilities in a quantum state, so we can only approximate a continuous distribution with a discretized version.

The uniform distribution is straightforward to encode; we simply apply a Hadamard gate to each qubit. Many other distributions that appear in other problems are more complex to encode in a quantum state. Preparing quantum states that reflect specific distributions, often referred to as *state preparation*, is very important in quantum computing. State preparation is an area that is actively researched today.

Bell-shaped distributions, such as the normal distribution, are important in computations for many applications, including statistics, financial modeling, and machine learning. Encoding a discretized normal distribution in a quantum state is notoriously difficult. In some problem contexts, an approximation for the normal distribution is satisfactory. The examples in this section show how we can use the QFT to efficiently encode approximations for the normal distribution in a quantum state.

> **The normal distribution**
>
> The normal distribution, often referred to as the Gaussian distribution, is a fundamental probability distribution in statistics. It was named the normal distribution because it occurs frequently in everyday situations, such as the heights in a large adult population and the birth weights of newborns.
>
> The normal distribution has several distinctive features:
>
> - It has a symmetric bell-shaped curve.
> - The mean and median are equal.
> - About 68% of the data falls within one standard deviation of the mean, about 95% falls within two standard deviations of the mean, and about 99.7% falls within three standard deviations of the mean.

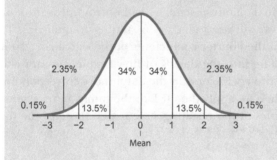

Figure 8.28 The standard deviations of the normal distribution

8.4.1 Raised cosine

In 1961, Raab and Green introduced the idea of using the *raised cosine* distribution as an approximation for the normal distribution.[1] This can only be used in cases where the long tails of the normal distribution can be ignored.

The following probability density function defines the raised cosine distribution

$$p(x) = \frac{1}{2s}\left(1 + \cos\frac{x-\mu}{s}\pi\right) = \frac{1}{s}\cos^2\left(\frac{x-\mu}{2s}\pi\right)$$

---

[1] David H. Raab and Edward H. Green. A cosine approximation to the normal distribution. *Psychometrika*, 26(4): 447–450, 1961.

210 CHAPTER 8 *Using the quantum Fourier transform*

The raised cosine probability density function is shown in figure 8.29 where μ is a real number and *s* is a positive number for $\mu - s \leq x \leq \mu + s$ and 0 for *x* outside of this range.

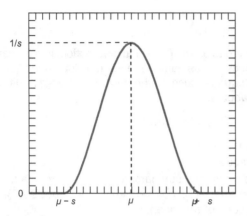

Figure 8.29 The raised cosine probability density function

To encode the raised cosine in a quantum state, we will borrow ideas from digital signal processing. Specifically, we will use well-chosen starting frequencies. These frequencies can be derived from the Fourier coefficients of the signal corresponding to the specific state. Without going into the details of how frequencies are chosen, for the raised cosine, we encode two coefficients in the amplitudes corresponding to outcome 0 and outcome 2^{n-1}. Then we apply the QFT to the qubits in reverse order and without swaps. The probabilities of the resulting state match those of the discretized raised cosine distribution for $s = 2^{n-1}$:

$$p(x) = \frac{1}{2^{n-1}} \cos^2\left(\frac{x-\mu}{2^n}\pi\right)$$

where $0 \leq x \leq 2^n$.

The simplest example is the raised cosine where $\mu = s = 2^{n-1}$. In this case, we can simplify the probability density function:

$$\frac{1}{2^{n-1}} \cos^2\left(\frac{x - 2^{n-1}}{2^n}\pi\right) = \frac{1}{2^{n-1}} \sin^2\left(\frac{x}{2^n} - \frac{1}{2}\right)\pi$$

where $0 \leq x \leq 2^n$.

TIP Remember that $\cos\left(\frac{\pi}{2} - \theta\right) = \pm \sin\theta$.

Let's look at an example where $n = 3$ and therefore $\mu = s = 2^{n-1} = 4$. First we encode the starting frequencies in the amplitudes of the state (figure 8.30).

8.4 Encoding trigonometric distributions in a quantum state

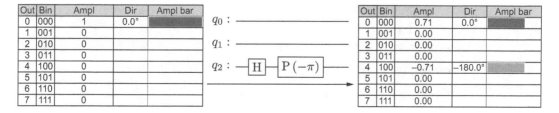

Figure 8.30 Encoding the starting frequencies for the raised cosine in the amplitudes of a three-qubit quantum state

Next we apply the QFT to the qubits in reverse order and without swaps (figure 8.31). The probabilities of the resulting state reflect the raised cosine distribution for $\mu = s = 2^{n-1}$, as shown in the resulting state table in figure 8.32.

Figure 8.31 Applying the QFT to the qubits in a three-qubit state in reverse order (without swaps)

Outcome	Amplitude	Probability
$k = 0$	$\frac{1}{\sqrt{2}}$	$\frac{1}{2}$
$0 < k < 2^{n-1}$	0	0
$k = 2^{n-1}$	$-\frac{1}{\sqrt{2}}$	$\frac{1}{2}$
$2^{n-1} < k < 2^n$	0	0

$\xrightarrow{\text{QFT}}$

Outcome	Amplitude	Probability
k	$\frac{1}{\sqrt{2^{n-1}}} \sin(\frac{k}{2^n}\pi)\text{cis}(\frac{k}{2^n} - \frac{1}{2})\pi$	$\frac{1}{2^{n-1}} \sin^2(\frac{k}{2^n}\pi)$

Figure 8.32 The general state tables for encoding the raised cosine probability density function for $\mu = s = 2^{n-1}$ in a quantum state

For a general value μ, the resulting state will have amplitudes and probabilities as shown in the state tables in figure 8.33. To create the state with these encoded frequencies, we can use the same gates as for the previous example, but the angle of the phase rotation will be determined by μ. The function for creating the circuit to encode the raised cosine in a quantum state with n qubits is shown in the following listing.

Outcome	Amplitude	Probability
$k = 0$	$\frac{1}{\sqrt{2}}$	$\frac{1}{2}$
$0 < k < 2^{n-1}$	0	0
$k = 2^{n-1}$	$-\frac{1}{\sqrt{2}}\text{cis}(\pi - \mu\frac{2\pi}{2^n})$	$\frac{1}{2}$
$2^{n-1} < k < 2^n$	0	0

$\xrightarrow{\text{QFT}}$

Outcome	Amplitude	Probability
k	$\frac{1}{\sqrt{2^{n-1}}}\cos((k-\mu)\frac{\pi}{2^n})\text{cis}(k-\mu)\frac{\pi}{2^n}$	$\frac{1}{2^{n-1}}\cos^2(k-\mu)\frac{\pi}{2^n}$

Figure 8.33 The general state tables for encoding the raised cosine probability density function in a quantum state

Listing 8.5 Creating the circuit for encoding the raised cosine distribution

```
def raised_cosine(n, mu):
    N = 2 ** n
    assert (0 <= mu < 2 ** n)

    q = QuantumRegister(n)
    qc = QuantumCircuit(q)

    qc.h(q[n - 1])
    qc.p(-pi * mu / N * 2, q[n - 1])

    qc.report('fourier_coefficients')

    qc.append_qft(q, reversed=True, swap=False)

    qc.report('qft')

    return qc
```

For example, let's use this function to encode the raised cosine distribution in the probabilities of a three-qubit state with μ = 3.25:

```
qc = raised_cosine(3, 3.25)
state = qc.run()
```

We can use the following code to check that the amplitudes of the state match the expected amplitudes (as shown in figure 8.33):

```
from math import sqrt

N = 8
mu = 3.25
a = [sqrt(2/N) * cos((k - mu)*pi/N) * cis((k-mu)*pi/N) for k in range(N)]
assert all_close(state, a)
```

We can also check that the probabilities align with the raised cosine distribution for $s = 2^{n-2} = N/2$:

```
s = N / 2
p = [1 / (2 * s) * (1 + cos((x - mu) / s * pi)) for x in range(N)]
p1 = [1 / s * cos((x - mu) / (2 * s) * pi) ** 2 for x in range(N)]
```

8.4 *Encoding trigonometric distributions in a quantum state* 213

```
probs = [2/N*(cos((k - mu)*pi/N))**2 for k in range(N)]

assert all_close(p, probs)
assert all_close(p1, probs)
```

Figure 8.34 shows examples of encoding the raised cosine distribution in a three-qubit quantum state with μ = 3.25, μ = 3.5, and μ = 3.75.

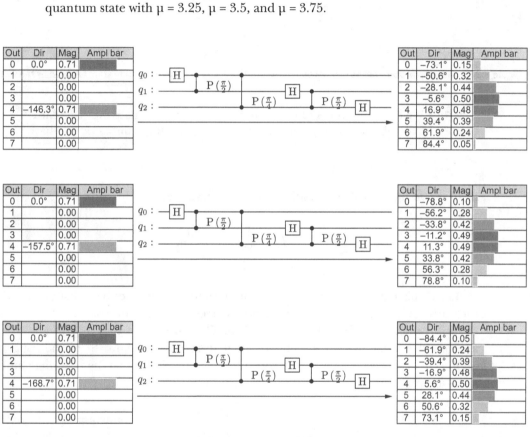

Figure 8.34 Examples of encoding the raised cosine probability density function in a three-qubit quantum state with varying μ values

8.4.2 *Other trigonometric functions*

We can use the same method to encode the raised cosine distribution and other trigonometric functions in a quantum state. For example, we can use well-chosen starting frequencies for the function $\sin^4$ to encode an even closer approximation of the normal distribution. The state tables in figure 8.35 show the starting frequencies encoded in the amplitudes of the state and the probabilities after applying the QFT.

214 CHAPTER 8 *Using the quantum Fourier transform*

Outcome	Amplitude	Probability
$k = 0$	$\sqrt{\frac{2}{3}}$	$\frac{2}{3}$
$0 < k < 2^{n-1}$	0	0
$k = 2^{n-1}$	$-\frac{1}{\sqrt{6}}$	$\frac{1}{6}$
$2^{n-1} < k < 2^n - 1$	0	0
$k = 2^n - 1$	$-\frac{1}{\sqrt{6}}$	$\frac{1}{6}$

$\xrightarrow{\text{QFT}}$

Outcome	Amplitude	Probability
k	$\frac{1}{\sqrt{3 \cdot 2^{n-3}}} \sin^2\left(\frac{k}{2^n}\pi\right)$	$\frac{1}{3 \cdot 2^{n-3}} \sin^4\left(\frac{k}{2^n}\pi\right)$

Figure 8.35 The general state tables for encoding three starting frequencies in a quantum state followed by the QFT

NOTE We can use powers of cosine functions to approximate the (standard) normal distribution if we consider that for any real number x, we have

$$\lim_{m \to \infty} \cos^m\left(\frac{x}{\sqrt{m}}\right) = e^{-\frac{x^2}{2}}.$$

As shown in figure 8.35, the resulting state will have the probability distribution

$$p(k) = \frac{8}{3N} \sin^4\left(k\frac{\pi}{N}\right)$$

for $0 \leq k < N$.

Let's look at an example using a quantum state with three qubits. First we encode the starting frequencies into the amplitudes corresponding to outcomes 0, 4, and 7, as shown in the first state table in figure 8.35. The three-qubit state before and after applying the circuit that encodes the coefficients is shown in figure 8.36. The last gate on the circuit diagram represents a controlled X gate. Notice that the resulting amplitudes are real.

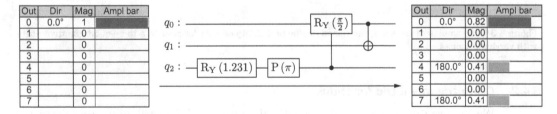

Figure 8.36 Encoding three starting frequencies in the amplitudes of a three-qubit quantum state

Next we apply the QFT to the qubits in reverse order and without swaps, as shown in figure 8.37. The probabilities of the resulting state have the desired probability distribution.

8.4 Encoding trigonometric distributions in a quantum state

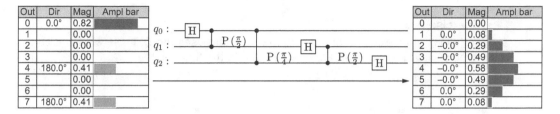

Figure 8.37 Applying the QFT to the qubits in a three-qubit quantum state in reverse order (without swaps)

For a given number of qubits (n), the function `sin_4` creates the circuit for encoding the desired probability distribution.

Listing 8.6 Creating the circuit for encoding the $\sin^4$ probability distribution

```
from math import acos

def sin_4(n):
    theta = acos(sqrt(2 / 3))
    q = QuantumRegister(n)
    qc = QuantumCircuit(q)

    qc.ry(2 * theta, q[n - 1])
    qc.p(pi, q[n - 1])
    qc.cry(pi / 2, q[n - 1], q[0])

    for i in range(1, n - 1):
        qc.cx(q[0], q[i])

    qc.report('frequencies')

    qc.append_qft(q, reversed=True, swap=False)

    qc.report('qft')

    return qc
```

Let's create the same three-qubit state as shown in figure 8.37 with this function:

```
n = 3
N = 2 ** n
qc = sin_4(n)
state = qc.run()
```

We can check that the probabilities of the resulting state reflect the encoded probability distribution using the following code:

```
s = [sqrt(8 / (3 * N)) * (sin(k * pi / N)) ** 2 for k in range(N)]
assert all_close(state, s)
p = [8 / 3 / N * (sin(k * pi / N)) ** 4 for k in range(N)]
assert all_close([abs(state[k])**2 for k in range(N)], p)
```

⟵ Alternatively, we can use `8/3/N*(cos((k - N/2)*pi/N))**4`.

Exercise 8.5
Let's look at an example of a quantum circuit that uses the QFT. We will initialize a three-qubit state and apply an $R_Y(-\pi/2)$ gate to the first qubit:

```
n = 3
theta = -pi/2
q = QuantumRegister(n)
qc = QuantumCircuit(q)
qc.ry(theta, q[0])
qc.report('state')
```

The resulting state can be expressed with the following list comprehension:

```
N = 8
s = [cos(k*pi/2 - theta/2) if k in [0, 1] else 0 for k in range(N)]
assert all_close(qc.reports['state'][2], s)
```

Now let's perform the QFT on all the qubits in the system:

```
qc.qft(q)
qc.report('qft')
```

Find a list comprehension expression of the state after applying the QFT (like the previous one) that will satisfy the following `assert` statement:

```
assert all_close(qc.reports['qft'][2], s)
```

Exercise 8.6
Verify that for a given integer n, the following circuit encodes a quantum state (shown in the figure) with the following properties:

- The probability of the 0 outcome is 1/2.
- The probability of an odd outcome $0 < k < 2^n$ is $\dfrac{\sqrt{2}}{2^n} \dfrac{1}{\sin^2(k\frac{\pi}{2^n})}$.
- The probability of the other outcomes, which are all even, is 0:

```
def one_over_sine(n):
    q = QuantumRegister(n)
    qc = QuantumCircuit(q)

    for i in range(1, n):
        qc.h(i)

    qc.x(0)
    qc.append_iqft(q, reversed=True, swap=False)

    return qc
```

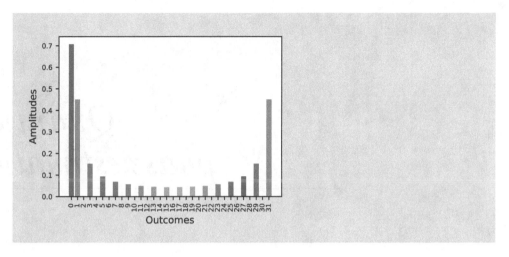

Summary

- The discrete sinc function comes from the sinc function, which is very important in the field of digital signal processing. For example, the sinc function distribution is seen in single-slit experiments.
- The discrete sinc function also appears in quantum computing: specifically, when the IQFT is applied to a geometric sequence state. The magnitudes of the amplitudes of the resulting state match the discrete sinc function. We call a state with this pattern a phased discrete sinc state.
- We can use a phased discrete sinc state to estimate an encoded frequency value, v. If v is an integer, the magnitude of the amplitude corresponding to that integer will be 1, and the rest will be 0. If v is a non-integer, the outcomes corresponding to the two closest integers will have the two largest magnitudes.
- The QFT can be used to efficiently encode certain probability distributions in quantum states. Efficient encoding of probability distributions through QFT operations provides a foundation for quantum algorithms in optimization, machine learning, and statistical applications.
- To encode a trigonometric function like the raised cosine or $\sin^4$ in a quantum state, we encode well-chosen starting frequencies derived from the Fourier coefficients of the function into the phase of the quantum state and then apply the QFT. Trigonometric distributions can be used as close approximations of the normal distribution, which is especially difficult to encode in a quantum state.

Quantum phase estimation

This chapter covers
- Estimating the frequency of a periodic quantum state
- Eigenstates and eigenvalues
- Estimating the angle of rotation of a quantum circuit
- Quantum amplitude estimation and applications (quantum counting)

Now that we have learned about the QFT, we can implement one of the most useful quantum algorithms: quantum phase estimation (QPE). QPE is sometimes called the "Swiss army knife" of quantum computing. Many quantum algorithms use it as a building block. In particular, QPE plays an important role in Shor's algorithm, a quantum computing algorithm that provides an exponential speedup over known classical algorithms for factoring integers, threatening to break the most common encryption methods used today, which involve factors of very large numbers.

Figure 9.1 shows the concepts introduced in this chapter. First we will review periodic quantum states and how to estimate the frequency of a period quantum state with measurement. Then we will learn about QPE. Finally, we will introduce another essential algorithm, *quantum amplitude estimation*, and look at example applications, specifically quantum counting.

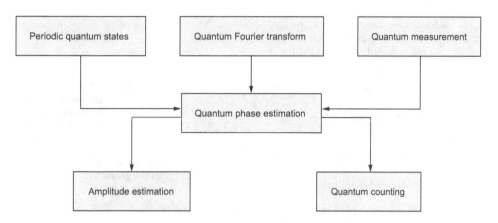

Figure 9.1 A dependency diagram of concepts covered in this chapter

9.1 Estimating the frequency of a periodic quantum state

In chapter 8, we looked at how to encode a value as a frequency of a periodic quantum state. First we prepared a geometric sequence state, where the encoded frequency value is reflected in the difference between the phases of the amplitudes of the state. Then we applied the inverse quantum Fourier transform (IQFT) to the geometric sequence state, which converts the difference in phases to differences in magnitudes (phase-to-magnitude conversion). Figure 9.2 shows the circuit diagram for encoding a frequency value in a quantum state.

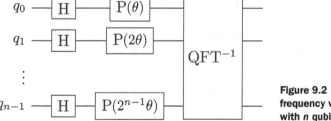

Figure 9.2 The circuit for encoding a frequency value v in a quantum state with n qubits, where $\theta = v\, 2\pi/2^n$

The following creates the circuit to encode a value (frequency) v in a quantum state with n qubits.

Listing 9.1 Creating the circuit that encodes a frequency in a quantum state

```
from sim_circuit import QuantumRegister, QuantumCircuit
from math import pi

def encode_frequency(n, v):
    q = QuantumRegister(n)
    qc = QuantumCircuit(q)

    for j in range(n):
        qc.h(q[j])

    for j in range(n):
        qc.p(2 * pi / 2 ** (n - j) * v, q[j])

    qc.report('geometric_sequence')

    qc.append_iqft(q)

    qc.report('iqft')

    return qc
```

> The phase gate angle is $2j\ \theta$. We use the equivalent angle $2^j \theta = v\ 2\pi/2^{n-j}$.

> This report will show us the geometric sequence state.

Recall that we call the state created by this function a *phased discrete sinc state*. In chapter 8, we covered several useful forms to express the amplitudes of such a state. We capture one of these forms in a utility function called `phased_sincd`, which will be used in many examples.

Listing 9.2 Generating a phased discrete sinc state

```
from util import cis, prod

def phased_sincd(n, v):
    N = 2 ** n
    return [prod(
        cos((v - k) * pi / 2 ** (j + 1)) * cis((v - k) * pi / 2 ** (j + 1))
        for j in range(n)) for k in range(2 ** n)]
```

Let's consider two examples. We will create two circuits with $n = 3$ qubits and frequencies $v = 3$ and $v = 3.8$ using the following function calls:

```
n = 3

qc1 = encode_frequency(n, 3)

qc2 = encode_frequency(n, 3.8)
```

Recall that when we run a circuit on a quantum computer, the only information we can extract from the quantum state is a measurement outcome. We can run the circuit several times to create a distribution of outcomes that reflects the probabilities of the encoded state.

Next, let's simulate measurements of each of these circuits. To simulate measurement counts, we will use the measure method of the QuantumCircuit class, where the shots parameter is the number of measurements to simulate. Each run, or shot, results in one measurement outcome. We can simulate the repeated execution of a circuit, followed by measurement, by adjusting the shots parameter.

Let's simulate 10 runs of this circuit:

```
result = qc1.measure(shots = 10)
```

If we print the results, we see that all the measurement outcomes were 3:

```
print(result['counts'])
```

```
{3: 10}
```

We can plot the frequency of outcomes (the number of times each outcome occurred divided by the total) as a bar graph, as shown in figure 9.3. As we saw in chapter 6, when the encoded value is an integer in the resulting state, the outcome corresponding to the encoded value will have an amplitude of 1, and the rest of the amplitudes will be zero. Therefore, all the measurement results are 011 (decimal value 3).

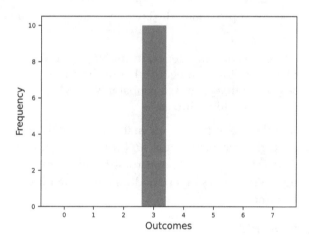

Figure 9.3 Measurement outcome frequencies from 10 shots of a phased discrete sinc state with $n = 3$ qubits and the encoded frequency value $v = 3$

NOTE The measure method uses the random Python package to simulate measurement, so each time we run the previous code snippet, we get slightly different counts!

Next, let's simulate 10 runs of the second example circuit (v = 3.8):

```
result = qc2.measure(shots = 10)
```

Figure 9.4 illustrates the resulting measurement counts with a bar chart. Note that each time we run the code snippet, we typically get a different outcome based on the underlying probability distribution.

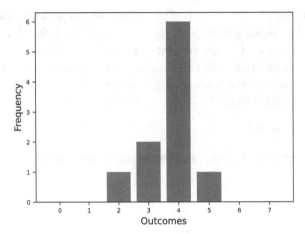

Figure 9.4 Measurement outcome frequencies from 10 shots of a phased discrete sinc state with $n = 3$ qubits and the encoded frequency value $v = 3.8$

The simplest way to get an estimation of the frequency value is to approximate it with the most frequent measurement outcome. In the first example, shown in figure 9.3, the most frequent outcome (and the only outcome) is 011 (3 in decimal form). We know that the encoded value is 3, so this estimation method gives us an exact result. In the second example, shown in figure 9.4, the most frequent outcome is 100 (4 in decimal form). Using this method, we approximate the encoded value 3.8 by the integer estimate 4.

> **NOTE** When the encoded value is not an integer, it can be proven that with one measurement, we will get the closest integer with a probability of at least $4/\pi^2 \approx 40\%$. It can also be proven that there is a probability of at least $8/\pi^2 \approx 81\%$ that we will get one of the two closest integers.

An estimate for the frequency value v also gives an estimate for the angle parameter θ, given the relationship between the two parameters: $\theta/(2\pi) = v/2^n$. In essence, the goal of the QPE algorithm is to estimate an unknown rotation angle for an operator. We can do that by estimating the frequency of a periodic state created with the given circuit through repeated measurement.

9.1.1 Getting better angle estimates with more qubits

For the remainder of the chapter, we will look at estimating (rotation) angles through corresponding frequencies. When we create a periodic state for a given angle θ, we have a choice of how many qubits to use. As we will see, the more qubits we use, the better the precision for estimating the angle will be.

We can think of the possible outcomes as tick markers on a ruler. If the frequency value is an integer, the probability of one of the ticks will be 1, and the rest will be 0. If we have $n = 3$ qubits, we can imagine that we have a ruler with eight ticks, like the one in figure 9.5. Using more qubits adds more ticks (possible outcomes) to our ruler, as shown in figure 9.6. If the frequency value v is not an integer, its true value is in between the ticks.

9.1 Estimating the frequency of a periodic quantum state

Figure 9.5 Using n = 3 qubits is like using a ruler with eight ticks.

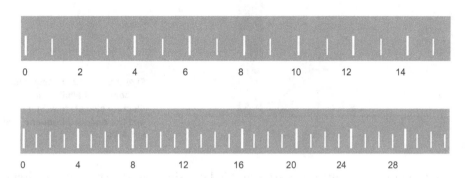

Figure 9.6 Using one more qubit (n = 4) doubles the number of ticks on the ruler. Using n = 5 qubits doubles the number of ticks again.

NOTE If v is a real value that is not in the interval $0 \leq v < 2^n$, the estimate we get will be $v \bmod 2^n$. This is because values of v that differ by 2^n correspond to the same angle when creating the geometric sequence state. For example, if $n = 3$, for the value $v = 3.8$ the angle parameter is $\theta = 3.8\pi/4$, and for the value $v = 11.8$ the angle parameter is $\theta = 11.8\pi/4$, which is equivalent to $3.8\pi/4$ (the two angles differ by 2π, the length of a full unit circle). We can think of this as wrapping the ruler.

Remember that the relationship between the frequency and angle parameters is $\theta/(2\pi) = v/2^n$. When the number of qubits needs to be explicit, we will use the notation v_n. When we use more qubits for the same angle parameter θ, the encoded value is multiplied by a power of 2: $v_n = 2^{n-m} v_m$ for $n > m$.

Let's use the angle parameter $\theta = 3.74$. If we encode the corresponding frequency with three qubits, the true value of the frequency encoded is $v_3 = \theta 2^3/(2\pi) = 4.76$. If we use five qubits, the encoded frequency value is $v_5 = \theta 2^5/(2\pi) = 19.05$. The estimates for v_3 and v_5 both give us approximations for θ.

First let's create a circuit with $n = 3$ and $v_3 = 4.76$:

```
qc = encode_frequency(3, 4.76)
```

Figure 9.7 shows a histogram visualization of the measurement outcome probabilities of the resulting state. We can see that outcome 5 has the highest probability, followed by outcome 4, and the rest are more or less improbable.

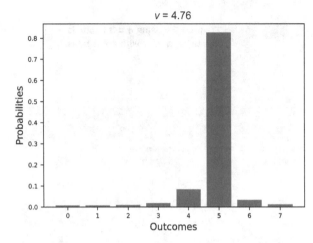

Figure 9.7 The measurement outcome probabilities for a phased discrete sinc state with n = 3 qubits and the encoded frequency value v = 4.76

The two most likely outcomes are 4 and 5. Let's simulate 100 shots of this circuit:

```
result = qc.measure(shots = 100)
print(result['counts'])
```

The printed counts are

{5: 79, 4: 12, 6: 3, 7: 3, 3: 2, 2: 1}

As expected, the most frequent outcome is 5. The corresponding estimate of the parameter θ is 5 $(2\pi)/2^3$ = 3.93.

> **NOTE** We can obtain estimates with better precision if we use more measurements. The number of necessary measurements for a desired precision can be calculated using exact formulas, which we will not cover in this book.

Next, let's create a circuit with $n = 5$ and $v_5 = 19.05$:

```
qc = encode_frequency(5, 19.05)
```

A histogram of the measurement outcome probabilities is shown in figure 9.8.

Let's simulate 100 runs of this circuit:

```
result = qc.measure(shots = 100)
print(result['counts'])
```

The printed counts are

{19: 98, 22: 1, 20: 1}

The most frequent outcome is 19, so the corresponding estimate for θ is 3.73 ($\theta = 19\ 2\pi/2^5$). This is a pretty good estimate for the encoded angle parameter $\theta = 3.74$.

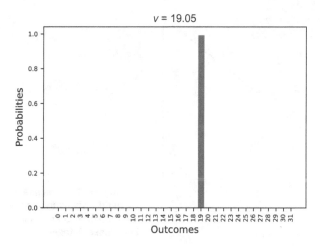

Figure 9.8 The measurement outcome probabilities for a phased discrete sinc state with $n = 5$ qubits and the encoded frequency value $v = 19.05$

9.1.2 Reading between the ticks: Getting better estimates with interpolation

Approximating an encoded frequency with the most likely outcome is like using the closest tick mark on a measuring tape in real-life tasks. If we want more precise measurements, we can use a measuring tape with finer-grained tick marks. In reality, before getting a new tape, we often approximate the fraction that falls between the two ticks that are closest to the real value being measured. Intuitively, we assign weights to the two enclosing ticks that are proportional to how close they are to the measured value. This process is called *linear interpolation*, and the human mind is adept at this type of linear approximation.

It is possible to perform a similar process of estimation in the context of frequency encoding. Let's denote by p_a and p_b the probabilities of the outcomes that fall above and below the true value v of a frequency that is not an integer. The values of the probabilities can be calculated using any of the expressions for the phased discrete sinc state.

The equivalent of what we do in real life with a measuring tape is to approximate the decimal part of the frequency with

$$\frac{p_a}{p_a + p_b}$$

A plot of the results of this approximation against the real decimal value for numbers between two integers is shown in figure 9.9. We can see that this approximation method can add more precision to the standard estimation with integers, even though it approximates a line by a wave.

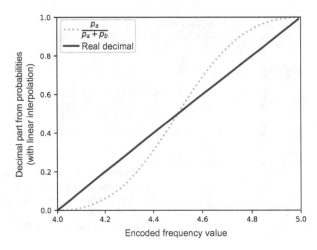

Figure 9.9 Real decimal value versus the approximation from the ratio of frequencies of the two closest integers

Can we do better than that if we use magnitudes (square roots of probabilities) instead of probabilities in the interpolation? To use approximations of the magnitudes instead of probabilities, we use the formula

$$\frac{\sqrt{p_a}}{\sqrt{p_a} + \sqrt{p_b}}$$

This formula gives a very good approximation for the decimal part of the real value of a frequency, as shown in figure 9.10.

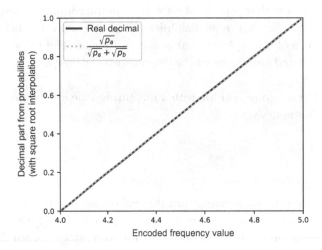

Figure 9.10 Real decimal value versus the approximation from the ratio of the approximate magnitudes of the two closest integers

Exact formula for estimating the decimal part of the frequency

For N outcomes, the exact formula for the decimal part of a frequency is

$$\frac{N}{\pi} \arctan \frac{\sqrt{p_a} \sin \frac{\pi}{N}}{\sqrt{p_a} \cos \frac{\pi}{N} + \sqrt{p_b}}$$

The simpler approximation we used

$$\frac{\sqrt{p_a}}{\sqrt{p_a} + \sqrt{p_b}}$$

is derived from this exact formula. The approximation becomes more precise as N increases.

In practice, other techniques, like the maximum likelihood estimation (MLE), can also be used to approximate the decimal part of a frequency. The appeal of our approximation is that it uses only the two most likely outcomes. This is possible because of the special properties of phased discrete sinc states.

Let's apply this method by revisiting the circuit for $n = 3$ and $v_3 = 4.76$, where the simulated measurement results were

{5: 79, 4: 12, 6: 3, 7: 3, 3: 2, 2: 1}

In the pseudo-random samples, the two most frequent outcomes were 4 and 5. So, we estimate the integer part of the encoded value with 4. We can compute our estimate of the decimal part of the encoded value with the following Python code:

```
from math import sqrt

p_4 = result['counts'][4]/sum(result['counts'].values())
p_5 = result['counts'][5]/sum(result['counts'].values())

decimal_estimate = sqrt(p_5)/(sqrt(p_4)+ sqrt(p_5))
```

Finds the proportion of outcomes with the value 4

Finds the proportion of outcomes with the value 5

In this example, we get 0.7195580800495327. If we round to two decimal points and add the integer part of the estimate, we get $v \approx 4.72$. Our goal is to get an estimate for the true value of $\theta = 3.74$. Using this method, we find an estimate of $\theta = v\, 2\pi/2^3 \approx 3.71$. With the same measurement information, this method gives us a much better estimate than 3.93, which we got using the closest integer approximation for the associated frequency.

> **Exercise 9.1**
> Using the angle parameter $\theta = 12.85$ and $n = 4$ qubits, use both methods (integer and ratio of magnitudes) to get an estimate for θ using 100 shots.

Next we will apply frequency estimation to the scenario in which a circuit acts as a rotation on a quantum register.

9.2 Quantum circuits as rotations with eigenstates and eigenvalues

It is very common in the sciences to learn something about a system from its effects on other systems or the environment. Attributes that are invisible or hidden become measurable. The QPE algorithm falls into this category. Given a quantum circuit that acts as a rotation on a quantum register, we can use it to create a periodic quantum state in a second register whose frequency reflects the unknown rotation angle for the circuit. Then we can estimate the frequency of the periodic state and, subsequently, the rotation angle.

To understand the details of the QPE algorithm, we need to first discuss the concepts of *eigenvectors* and *eigenvalues* in the context of quantum transformations represented by quantum circuits. A quantum state vector is called an eigenvector (or *eigenstate*) of a circuit transformation U if all its amplitudes are multiplied by a corresponding eigenvalue (a complex number that must have a magnitude of 1) as a result of the circuit application. This is the same as rotating all amplitudes in the state by the phase of the eigenvalue.

Figure 9.11 shows the algebraic form of the effect of a quantum circuit, denoted by U, when applied to one of its eigenstates: all amplitudes are multiplied by the corresponding eigenvalue, $\mathrm{cis}(\theta)$. Note that a circuit can have multiple eigenstates.

Outcome	Amplitude
k	s_k

$\xrightarrow{U}$

Outcome	Amplitude
k	$\mathrm{cis}(\theta) s_k$

Figure 9.11 The effect of a quantum circuit U when applied to one of its eigenstates

Let's look at the single-qubit circuit in figure 9.12, which consists of one R_Y gate with an angle parameter of 2θ. The function `ry_circuit` takes an angle parameter `theta` and creates this circuit:

```
def ry_circuit(theta):
    q = QuantumRegister(1)
    qc = QuantumCircuit(q)
    qc.ry(2*theta, q[0])

    return qc
```

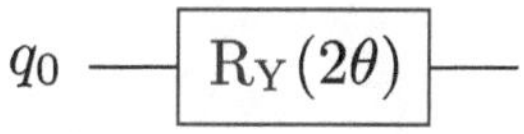

9.2 Quantum circuits as rotations with eigenstates and eigenvalues

q_0 — $R_Y(2\theta)$ —

Figure 9.12 A single-qubit circuit transformation $U = R_Y(2\theta)$

It turns out that the state $\left[\frac{i}{\sqrt{2}}, \frac{1}{\sqrt{2}}\right]$ is an eigenstate for the R_Y gate for any value of the angle parameter. Let's verify that applying $R_Y(2\theta)$ to this state rotates both its amplitudes by θ, meaning the eigenvalue for this eigenstate is $\text{cis}(\theta)$.

First we need a circuit that prepares the single-qubit state $\left[\frac{i}{\sqrt{2}}, \frac{1}{\sqrt{2}}\right]$. The circuit returned by the function `ry_eigen_circuit` does just that:

```
def ry_eigen_circuit():
    q = QuantumRegister(1)
    qc = QuantumCircuit(q)

    qc.x(q[0])
    qc.rx(-pi/2, q[0])

    return qc
```

The state table for a single-qubit state after applying this circuit is shown in figure 9.13. We can check that the state prepared by the circuit matches $\left[\frac{i}{\sqrt{2}}, \frac{1}{\sqrt{2}}\right]$ using the following code:

```
from util import all_close

qc = ry_eigen_circuit()
state = qc.run()

assert all_close(state, [1j/sqrt(2), 1/sqrt(2)])
```

Out	Bin	Ampl	Dir	Ampl bar
0	0	1	0.0°	
1	1	0		

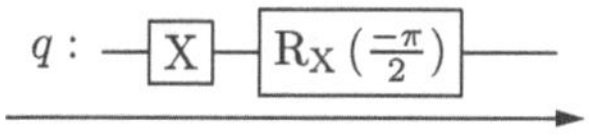

$q:$ —X— $R_X\left(\frac{-\pi}{2}\right)$ —

Out	Bin	Ampl	Dir	Ampl bar
0	0	0.00 + 0.71i	90.0°	
1	1	0.71	0.0°	

Figure 9.13 A single-qubit state in its default state and after applying the circuit $R_X(-\pi/2)X$

Now let's apply the $R_Y(\pi/3)$ gate to the eigenstate:

```
q = QuantumRegister(1)
qc = QuantumCircuit(q)

qc.x(q[0])
qc.rx(-pi/2, q[0])
```

```
theta = pi/6

qc.ry(2*theta, q[0])

state = qc.run()
```

The resulting state table after applying this circuit is shown in figure 9.14.

Out	Bin	Ampl	Dir	Ampl bar
0	0	0.00 + 0.71i	90.0°	
1	1	0.71	0.0°	

Out	Bin	Ampl	Dir	Ampl bar
0	0	–0.35 + 0.61i	120.0°	
1	1	0.61 + 0.35i	30.0°	

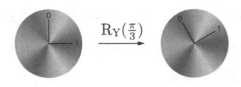

Figure 9.14 The state tables before and after applying the circuit $R_Y(\pi/3)$

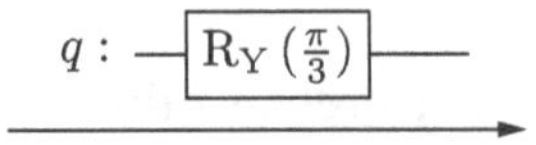

We can visualize the effect of the circuit on the state $\left[\frac{i}{\sqrt{2}}, \frac{1}{\sqrt{2}}\right]$ using the color wheel visualization in figure 9.15. The lengths (magnitudes) of the amplitudes do not change, but both amplitudes are rotated by the same angle, and they stay perpendicular.

Figure 9.15 The color wheel visualization of the amplitudes of a single-qubit state before and after the circuit $R_Y(\pi/3)$ is applied

We can apply the circuit to the eigenstate multiple times, and the magnitudes of the amplitudes will not change, but the amplitudes will be rotated by the same angle every time:

```
q = QuantumRegister(1)
qc = QuantumCircuit(q)

qc.x(q[0])
qc.rx(-pi/2, q[0])

theta = pi/6

qc.ry(2*theta, q[0])
qc.ry(2*theta, q[0])

state = qc.run()
```

Applies the circuit twice

The resulting state table is shown in figure 9.16.

In this example, the state created by the circuit created by `ry_eigen_circuit` is an eigenstate of the circuit (transformation) in figure 9.12, and the complex number cis(θ) is the corresponding eigenvalue. The eigenvalue is the complex number whose

9.2 Quantum circuits as rotations with eigenstates and eigenvalues

Outcome	Binary	Amplitude	Direction	Magnitude	Amplitude bar	Probability
0	0	−0.61 + 0.35i	150.0°	0.71		0.50
1	1	0.35 + 0.61i	60.0°	0.71		0.50

Figure 9.16 The state table after applying the circuit $R_Y(\pi/3)$ twice

direction is the angle the amplitudes are rotated by when the second circuit is applied: in this example, $\pi/3$.

Eigenstates and eigenvalues with Ket notation
If we have a complex number λ and a nonzero vector $|\psi\rangle$ that satisfies the equation

$$U|\psi\rangle = \lambda|\psi\rangle$$

then we say that λ is an eigenvalue of the eigenvector $|\psi\rangle$.

Exercise 9.2
We can describe the eigenstate in this example as

$$|\psi\rangle = \begin{bmatrix} \frac{i}{\sqrt{2}} \\ \frac{1}{\sqrt{2}} \end{bmatrix}$$

The operator is a R_Y gate with angle parameter 2θ. The two-by-two matrix form of an R_Y gate is

$$\begin{bmatrix} \cos\theta & -\sin\theta \\ \sin\theta & \cos\theta \end{bmatrix}$$

We can express the application of the operator to the eigenstate as

$$R_Y(2\theta)|\psi\rangle$$

Show that the complex number cis(θ) is the eigenvalue of the eigenstate $|\psi\rangle$.

Exercise 9.3
Let's look at the phase gate in the context of eigenstates and eigenvalues. The circuit will be

$$q_0 — \boxed{P(\theta)} —$$

(continued)

An eigenstate of the circuit can be created by applying an X gate to a single qubit in its initial state. The following Python code creates this state:

```
q = QuantumRegister(1)
qc = QuantumCircuit(q)
qc.x(q[0])

state = qc.run()
```

Apply the circuit to the state created previously using various values for θ. Check that each time the circuit is applied, the amplitudes of the state are multiplied by cis(θ).

9.3 The quantum phase estimation algorithm

We will use the fact that a quantum circuit rotates all the amplitudes of one of its eigenstates by the phase of the corresponding eigenvalue to build a periodic quantum state. To do this, we will use a pattern similar to the geometric sequence encoding pattern. Given an m-qubit circuit U, where $m > 1$, we will implement the following steps:

0. Start with an n-qubit register, called the *estimation* register, which will be measured to obtain the desired phase estimate, and an m-qubit register, called the *target* register, which will be used to encode an eigenstate of the circuit U.
1. Prepare an eigenstate of the circuit U in the m-qubit target register. Let's denote the rotation angle by θ, corresponding to the eigenvalue cis(θ).
2. Apply a Hadamard gate to each qubit in the n-qubit estimation register.
3. For each integer $0 \leq k < n$, apply (each gate in) the circuit U to the target register, controlled on the qubit k of the estimation register, 2^k times.
4. (Optional) Apply the inverse of the circuit that prepared the eigenstate of U to the target register.
5. Apply the IQFT to the estimation register.
6. Estimate the frequency value $v = \theta 2^n / (2\pi)$ as the most frequent measurement of the estimation register or using any other method we have discussed. This will give an estimate of θ.

These steps are captured in the circuit diagram in figure 9.17. It is a relatively complex circuit, but we will look at a step-by-step example to make it easier to understand.

Let's look at a visual representation of the process for the single-qubit ($m = 1$) circuit $U = R_Y(2\theta)$, where $\theta = 4.7 \, (2\pi)/2^n$ for $n = 3$. The eigenvalue of U is cis(θ). Our goal is to get an estimate for θ using the measurement outcome of the estimation register.

Our step 0 is to create two registers: one with m qubits that will be used to encode the eigenstate (the target register) and one with n qubits that we will use to obtain the

9.3 The quantum phase estimation algorithm

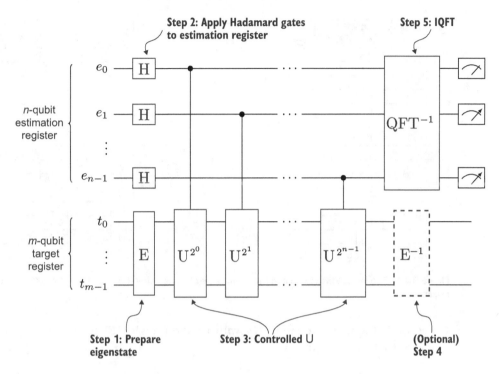

Figure 9.17 The QPE algorithm where *U* is an *m*-qubit circuit and *E* prepares an eigenstate of the circuit

estimate (the estimation register). In this example, we only need one qubit for our target register, and we will use $n = 3$ qubits for our estimation register:

```
n = 3
q = QuantumRegister(n)
a = QuantumRegister(1)
qc = QuantumCircuit(q, a)
```

Step 1 is to prepare an eigenstate of the circuit *U* in the target register:

```
qc.x(a[0])
qc.rx(-pi/2, a[0])
```

If we were to run this part of the circuit, the state tables before and after are shown in figure 9.18.

Next we apply Hadamard gates to each of the qubits in the estimation register. Then, for each qubit *k* in the estimation register, we apply the circuit *U* to the target register 2^k times, controlled on qubit *k*. To perform this step (step 2), we can write two `for` loops. The first applies a Hadamard gate to each qubit, and the second is a nested

234   CHAPTER 9   Quantum phase estimation

Out	Dir	Mag	Ampl bar
0	0.0°	1	▰▰▰▰
1		0	
2		0	
3		0	
4		0	
5		0	
6		0	
7		0	
8		0	
9		0	
10		0	
11		0	
12		0	
13		0	
14		0	
15		0	

$q0_0$: ———————
$q0_1$: ———————
$q0_2$: ———————
$q1$: —[X]—[$R_X(\frac{-\pi}{2})$]—

Out	Dir	Mag	Ampl bar
0	90.0°	0.71	▰▰
1		0.00	
2		0.00	
3		0.00	
4		0.00	
5		0.00	
6		0.00	
7		0.00	
8	0.0°	0.71	▰▰
9		0.00	
10		0.00	
11		0.00	
12		0.00	
13		0.00	
14		0.00	
15		0.00	

Figure 9.18   The initial state table and the state table after applying the circuit $R_X(-\pi/2)X$ to the target register

for loop that applies the circuit U (with rotation angle 2θ) to the target register k times for each control qubit k:

```
for i in range(n):
    qc.h(q[i])

theta = 4.7*2*pi/2**n

for i in range(n):
    for _ in range(2**i):
        qc.cry(2*theta, q[i], a[0])
```
⟵ The total rotation angle is $2^i\theta$.

This step is illustrated in figure 9.19. The resulting state is a superposition of geometric sequence states that reflect the angle θ. If we perform the (optional) step to reverse

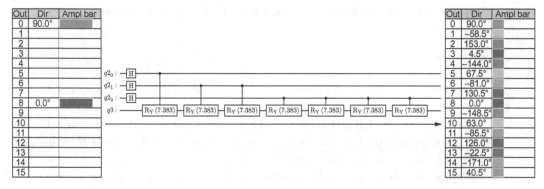

Figure 9.19   The state table where an eigenstate is prepared in the target register, the circuit that applies Hadamard gates to each qubit in the estimation register, followed by controlled applications of the circuit $R_Y(2\theta)$

9.3 The quantum phase estimation algorithm

the eigenstate preparation in the target register, we will get a single geometric sequence state in the estimation register.

Remember from chapter 3 that the inverse of an $R_X(\theta)$ rotation is $R_X(-\theta)$ and that the X gate is its own inverse. We can apply the inverse of the circuit that prepares the eigenstate with the following code:

```
qc.rx(pi/2, a[0])
qc.x(a[0])
```

This step is illustrated in figure 9.20. We can see a single geometric sequence state in the estimation register.

Out	Dir	Mag	Ampl bar
0	90.0°	0.25	
1	−58.5°	0.25	
2	153.0°	0.25	
3	4.5°	0.25	
4	−144.0°	0.25	
5	67.5°	0.25	
6	−81.0°	0.25	
7	130.5°	0.25	
8	0.0°	0.25	
9	−148.5°	0.25	
10	63.0°	0.25	
11	−85.5°	0.25	
12	126.0°	0.25	
13	−22.5°	0.25	
14	−171.0°	0.25	
15	40.5°	0.25	

Out	Dir	Mag	Ampl bar
0	0.0°	0.35	
1	−148.5°	0.35	
2	63.0°	0.35	
3	−85.5°	0.35	
4	126.0°	0.35	
5	−22.5°	0.35	
6	−171.0°	0.35	
7	40.5°	0.35	
8		0.00	
9		0.00	
10		0.00	
11		0.00	
12		0.00	
13		0.00	
14		0.00	
15		0.00	

Figure 9.20 The state table of geometric sequence states in superposition, the inverse of the circuit that prepared the eigenstate, and the resulting geometric sequence state in the estimation register

Finally, we apply an IQFT to the estimation register. We can do this with the following code:

```
qc.append_iqft(q)
```

If step 4 *was not* performed, we get a superposition of phased discrete sinc states, as shown in figure 9.21. If step 4 *was* performed, we get a single-phased discrete sinc state in the estimation register, as shown in figure 9.22.

If we perform repeated measurements of the resulting state(s) in figure 9.21 or 9.22, we can perform the last step: estimating the frequency value and the corresponding

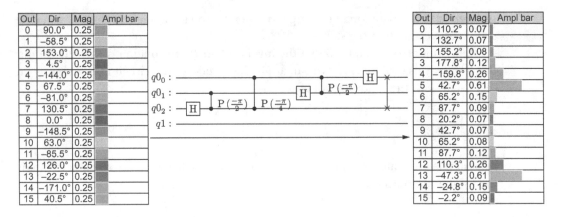

Figure 9.21 The state table of geometric sequence states in superposition, the IQFT applied to the estimation register, and the state table of the superposition of phased discrete sinc states

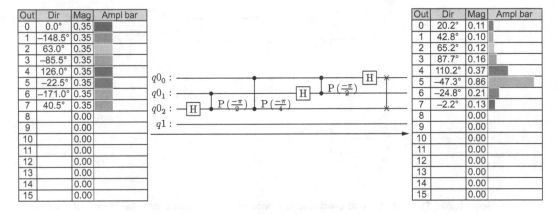

Figure 9.22 The state table of geometric state in the estimation register, the IQFT applied to the estimation register, and the state table of the resulting phased discrete sinc state

angle of the eigenvalue. We can check that the estimation register in figure 9.22 is the phased discrete sinc state we expect with the following Python code:

```
from util import all_close
from math import cos

state = qc.run()

n = 3
theta = 4.7*2*pi/2**n
s = phased_sincd(n, theta/(2*pi)*2**n)
assert all_close(state[:2**n], s)
```

> **Exercise 9.4**
> Use the state created in figure 9.22 to get an estimate for the true angle parameter θ.

Next we will add some additional methods to our quantum circuit simulator so that we can easily build the phase estimation circuit.

9.4 Circuit-level implementation of the quantum phase estimation algorithm

To perform the phase estimation algorithm, we need to build the phase estimation circuit shown in figure 9.23. We can use the `phase_estimation_circuit` function to do so, where n is the number of qubits in the estimation register, circuit is the circuit whose rotation angle we want to find, and the optional parameter `eigen_circuit` prepares an eigenvector of the circuit.

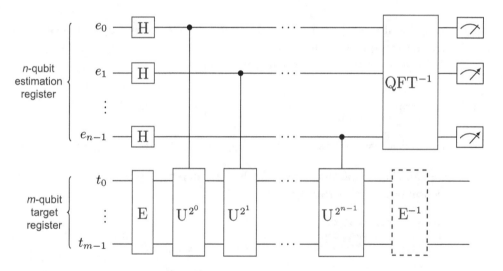

Figure 9.23 The phase estimation algorithm where *U* is an *m*-qubit circuit and *E* prepares an eigenstate of the circuit

Listing 9.3 Function for creating the phase estimation circuit

```
def phase_estimation_circuit(n, circuit, eigen_circuit=None):
    q = QuantumRegister(n)
    a = QuantumRegister(sum(circuit.regs))
    qc = QuantumCircuit(q, a)
```

The target register is last.

Step 0: the size of the target register is the same as the number of qubits in the circuit parameter.

```
        if eigen_circuit is not None:              ◄─┐  Step 1: If a circuit that prepares an
            qc.append(eigen_circuit, a)              │  eigenstate is passed to the function,
            qc.report('eigenstate')                  │  we apply it to the target register.

        for i in range(n):                         ◄─┐  Step 2
            qc.h(q[i])

        for i in range(n):                         ◄──  Step 3
            for _ in range(2**i):
                qc.c_append(circuit, q[i], a)

        qc.report('geometric_sequence_superposition')

        if eigen_circuit is not None:              ◄──  Optional step 4
            qc.append(eigen_circuit.inverse(), a)
            qc.report('geometric_sequence')

        qc.append_iqft(q)                          ◄──  Step 5
        qc.report('estimate')

        return qc
```

Note that if the `eigen_circuit` parameter is `None`, we end up with a superposition of geometric sequence states.

Let's create the circuit for the previous example:

```
n = 3
N = 2**n
theta = 4.7*2*pi/N

qc = phase_estimation_circuit(n, ry_circuit(2*theta), ry_eigen_circuit())
```

We can check that this circuit matches the step-by-step results we got in the previous section using the following code:

```
eig = qc.reports['eigenstate'][2]
assert all_close(eig, [1j/sqrt(2) if k == 0 else 0 for k in range(N)] +
    [1/sqrt(2) if k == 0 else 0 for k in range(N)])

geom = qc.reports['geometric_sequence'][2]
g = [1/sqrt(N)*cis(k*theta) for k in range(N)]
assert all_close(geom[:N], g)

estimate = qc.reports['estimate'][2]
s = phased_sincd(n, theta/(2*pi)*N)
assert all_close(estimate, s + [0 for _ in range(N)])
```

9.5 An alternative implementation of the phase estimation circuit without qubit swaps

We can create a phase estimation circuit that does not require the qubit swaps in the IQFT and therefore is more efficient. In the alternative implementation, the controlled

9.5 An alternative implementation of the phase estimation circuit without qubit swaps

applications of the circuit are applied to the target qubits in reverse order with decreasing multiples of θ. In the previous implementation, the circuit was applied to each target qubit $0 \leq k < n$ in the n-qubit estimation register 2^k times. This means the total rotation angle applied to target qubit k was $2^k\theta$. In the alternative version, the circuit is applied 2^{n-1-k} times to each target qubit k, so the total rotation angle applied to target qubit k is $2^{n-1-k}\theta$. This reorders the amplitudes of the periodic quantum state.

> **NOTE** The amplitudes of the periodic quantum state created using the alternative implementation correspond to qubits in reversed order. For example, using an estimation register with $n = 3$ qubits, the amplitude corresponding to outcome 001 in the previous implementation would now be the amplitude corresponding to outcome 100.

If we apply the IQFT to qubits in reversed order and without swapping qubits at the end, we get the same phased discrete sinc (or superposition of phased discrete sinc states) as in the previous version. The function in listing 9.4 includes a parameter swap. If swap = True (the default value), the function returns a circuit using the previous implementation (with swaps). If swap = False, the function returns a circuit using the alternative implementation (without swaps).

Listing 9.4 Alternative implementation for creating the QPE circuit

```
def phase_estimation_circuit(n, circuit, eigen_circuit=None, swap=True):
    q = QuantumRegister(n)
    a = QuantumRegister(sum(circuit.regs))
    qc = QuantumCircuit(q, a)

    if eigen_circuit is not None:
        qc.append(eigen_circuit, a)
        qc.report('eigenstate')

    for i in range(n):
        qc.h(q[i])

    for i in range(n):
        if swap:
            for _ in range(2**i):
                qc.c_append(circuit, q[i], a)
        else:
            for _ in range(2**i):
                qc.c_append(circuit, q[n-1-i], a)         ◁── Reverses the target qubit order

    qc.report('geometric_sequence_superposition')

    if eigen_circuit is not None:
        qc.append(eigen_circuit.inverse(), a)

    qc.report('geometric_sequence')

    qc.append_iqft(q, False if swap else True, swap)     ◁── Applies an IQFT to the estimation register with qubits in reverse order and without swaps
    qc.report('estimate')

    return qc
```

240   CHAPTER 9   *Quantum phase estimation*

The following Python code creates a circuit for the same problem as in the previous section using the alternative implementation:

```
n = 3
N = 2**n
theta = 4.7*2*pi/N
swap = False

qc = phase_estimation_circuit(n, ry_circuit(2*theta), ry_eigen_circuit(), swap)
```

Let's look at the geometric sequence state created using this circuit in figure 9.24. We can check that the amplitudes of the geometric sequence state in figure 9.24 match the geometric sequence state created using the first method with the following code:

```
from util import reverse_index_state

geom = qc.reports['geometric_sequence'][2]
g = [1/sqrt(N)*cis(k*theta) for k in range(N)]
assert all_close(geom[:N], g if swap else reverse_index_state(g))
```

> The periodic state created has amplitudes in reversed order. We can use the utility function reverse_index_state to reorder the amplitudes.

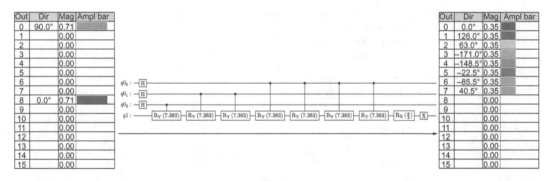

Figure 9.24 The state table where an eigenstate is prepared in the target register and the state table of the geometric sequence state with amplitudes in reversed order (previous amplitudes [0, 1, 2, 3, 4, 5, 6, 7] map to amplitudes [0, 4, 2, 6, 1, 5, 3])

Next we apply the IQFT to the qubits in reverse order and without swaps, as shown in figure 9.25. We end up with the same phased discrete sinc state as the one created using the first implementation. Let's check that with the following code:

```
estimate = qc.reports['estimate'][2]
s = phased_sincd(n, theta/(2*pi)*N)
assert all_close(estimate, s + [0 for _ in range(N)])
```

9.5 An alternative implementation of the phase estimation circuit without qubit swaps

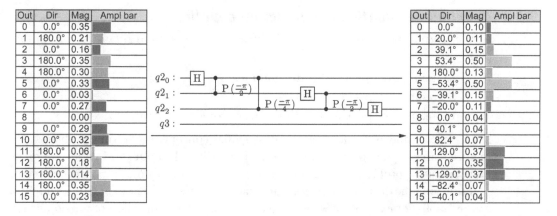

Figure 9.25 The state table of the geometric sequence state with qubits in reverse order, the circuit for applying the IQFT to the estimation register in reverse order and without qubit swaps, and the resulting state table for the phased discrete sinc state

The function `test_ry_phase_estimation` checks that the amplitudes of the state match the expected values for 10 pseudo random values of θ:

```
from random import uniform

def test_ry_phase_estimation():
    n = 3
    N = 2**n

    random_thetas = [uniform(-pi, pi) for _ in range(10)]

    for theta in random_thetas:
        for swap in [True, False]:
            qc = phase_estimation_circuit(n, ry_circuit(theta),
 ry_eigen_circuit(), swap)

            eig = qc.reports['eigenstate'][2]
            assert all_close(eig, [1j/sqrt(2) if k == 0 else 0 for k in
 range(N)] +
                            [1/sqrt(2) if k == 0 else 0 for k in range(N)])

            geom = qc.reports['geometric_sequence'][2]
            g = [1/sqrt(N)*cis(k*theta/2) for k in range(N)]
            assert all_close(geom[:N], g if swap else reverse_index_state(g))

            estimate = qc.reports['estimate'][2]
            s = phased_sincd(n, theta/2/(2*pi)*N)
            assert all_close(estimate[:N], s)
```

We can use either implementation to create the phase estimation circuit. The resulting state is used to estimate the angle of the circuit's eigenvalue.

9.6 Amplitude estimation and quantum counting

At the beginning of this book, we discussed three common quantum computing patterns:

- Sampling from probability distributions
- Searching for specific outcomes
- Estimating the probability of specific outcomes

In chapters 5 and 6, we learned about essential concepts for solving problems that require searching for specific outcomes. Now we will look at our third pattern of quantum computing problems: estimating the probability of one or more specific outcomes.

Estimating the distribution of good and bad outcomes is similar to polling a sample of a population. For example, if we want to understand what proportion of the population prefers each of the candidates in an upcoming election, instead of asking every member of the population, we can use a smaller sample to estimate the real distribution. The statistics methods used for estimating the real distribution by sampling from it also apply to estimating the probability of good and bad outcomes of quantum computations.

It is helpful to use a visual representation of the random samples from a large set of outcomes, like the one in figure 9.26. Imagine that the large set is represented by marbles in a bin: the dark marbles correspond to good outcomes, and the light marbles correspond to bad outcomes. For n qubits, the number of outcomes (all marbles in the bin) is 2^n. The number of outcomes can be very large. For example, if we have $n = 42$ qubits, the number of outcomes is over a trillion. Instead of using all the outcomes, we can use a much smaller sample to estimate the real distribution (proportion) of dark and light marbles. It is intuitive that the larger the sample is, the smaller the margin of error will be.

Figure 9.26 Representation of random samples taken from a large bin of marbles. The dark marbles correspond to good outcomes, and the light marbles correspond to bad outcomes.

> **How many samples do we need to get a good estimate of the real distribution?**
> According to the *Hoeffding Inequality*, the probability that the proportion of dark marbles in a sample deviates from the real proportion by a certain amount $\varepsilon > 0$ is less than $2e^{-2\varepsilon^2 M}$, where M is the number of samples. Note that only the sample size, M, affects this bound, not the total number of marbles.
>
> It is remarkable that such a bound exists. If more information about the real distribution is known, the number of samples to achieve the desired margin error can be reduced. For example, if the probability of choosing a dark marble is close to 1, then a much smaller number of samples will suffice to estimate it.

9.6.1 Amplitude estimation

Given a quantum state, we can estimate the probability of a set of good outcomes by repeatedly measuring the quantum state. However, this may require a very large number of measurements. *Amplitude estimation* is an algorithm that can drastically reduce the number of measurements needed to obtain a very good estimation for the number or the probability of the set of good outcomes, but at the expense of adding more qubits and performing a more complex quantum computation.

Given an *m*-qubit circuit A, where $m > 1$, and an *m*-qubit oracle circuit O, we will implement the following steps:

0. Start with an *n*-qubit register (the estimation register), which will be measured to obtain the desired estimate, and an *m*-qubit register (the target register), which will be used to apply the circuit A.
1. Apply circuit A to the target register and a Hadamard gate to each qubit in the *n*-qubit estimation register.
2. Build the Grover iterate $G = MO = AM_0 A^{-1} O$. Then, for each integer $0 \leq k < n$, apply (each gate in) the circuit G to the target register, controlled on the qubit k of the estimation register, 2^k times.
3. Apply the IQFT to the estimation register.
4. Measure the estimation register (we will actually measure both registers and group the results that have the same estimation register value).

These steps are captured in the circuit diagram in figure 9.27.

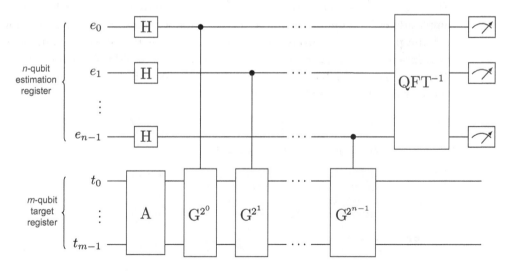

Figure 9.27 The amplitude estimation diagram where A is an m-qubit circuit and G is a Grover operator constructed using an m-qubit oracle circuit

You may recognize that the structure of the circuit diagram in figure 9.27 is similar to that of the QPE diagram in figure 9.23.

To estimate the probability of good outcomes or their count, we repeat the computation in the algorithm several times and take the most frequent estimation register value $0 \leq v < 2^n$ obtained through measurements. Using this result, we can do the following:

- Estimate the probability of good outcomes as

$$\sin^2\left(\pi \frac{v}{2^n}\right)$$

- Estimate the number of good outcomes (assuming all outcomes have equal probability) as the closest integer to

$$2^m \sin^2\left(\pi \frac{v}{2^n}\right)$$

> **NOTE** As usual, we will not go into mathematical proofs of the results related to various algorithms, but in essence, the Grover operator G acts as a rotation, which allows us to use any known methods for estimating the rotation angle by building a geometric sequence and applying an IQFT. For a given oracle that tags L good outcomes, the corresponding Grover operator rotates the initial state by an angle 2θ, with $\sin^2 \theta = L/2^n$, where $n > 0$ is the number of qubits. Therefore, an estimate for θ gives us an estimation for L.

The `amplitude_estimation_circuit` function, defined in listing 9.5, creates the amplitude estimation circuit where n is the number of qubits in the estimation register, the parameter A represents a circuit A, and O is the oracle circuit. We use the `grover_iterate_circuit` function from chapter 6 to build the Grover iterate circuit. The swap parameter has the default value True. We will look at examples where we can set this parameter to False to create a more efficient circuit.

> Listing 9.5 Function to create the amplitude estimation circuit

```
from algo import grover_iterate_circuit

def amplitude_estimation_circuit(n, A, O, swap=True):
    c = QuantumRegister(n)
    q = QuantumRegister(sum(A.regs))
    qc = QuantumCircuit(c, q)

    for i in range(n):
        qc.h(c[i])

    qc.append(A, q)

    for i in range(n):
        for _ in range(2**i):
```

9.6 Amplitude estimation and quantum counting

```
        if swap:
            qc.c_append(grover_iterate_circuit(A, O), c[i], q)
        else:
            qc.c_append(grover_iterate_circuit(A, O), c[n-1-i], q)

    qc.iqft(c if swap else c[::-1], swap)

    return qc
```

> We use the method c_append to apply a circuit to a register with a control qubit in a different register

> **Why we can apply QPE to Grover iterates**
> In amplitude estimation, we want to find the eigenvalues of the Grover operator G built from a state-preparation operator A and an oracle O. The eigenvalues of G are all 1 or −1 except two (nontrivial) eigenvalues that are conjugate (phases that are opposite each other). The nontrivial eigenstates allocate equal total probability to good and bad outcomes. If 2θ is the phase of one of them, the probability of good outcomes is $\sin^2 \theta$.

9.6.2 Estimating the number of good outcomes with quantum counting

Let's look at an example problem where we want to know the number of outcomes tagged by an oracle. We call this *quantum counting*. We can use amplitude estimation to solve this problem.

We will use the function in listing 9.5 to create an amplitude estimation circuit. Let's start with two registers of qubits: a three-qubit target register and a five-qubit estimation register. We also define an oracle using the phase_oracle_match function introduced in chapter 5 that tags good outcomes 0, 1, and 2. The initial state in the target register is an equal superposition state prepared by applying a Hadamard gate to each qubit in the register. To prepare this state, we will use the uniform function that we have used in previous chapters. We will choose to avoid qubit swaps in the inverse quantum Fourier transform (swap = False):

```
from algo import uniform, phase_oracle_match

n = 5
m = 3
items = [0, 1, 2]

qc = amplitude_estimation_circuit(
    n,
    prepare_uniform(m),
    phase_oracle_match(m, items),
    False
)
```

Let's create a histogram to visualize the measurement outcome probabilities of the estimation register:

```
state = qc.run()

probs = [0 for _ in range(2**n)]
for k in range(2**m):
    for j in range(2**n):
        probs[j] += abs(state[k*2**n + j])**2

plot_bars(list_to_dict(probs, False), '', 'Outcomes', 'Probability')
```

The resulting histogram is shown in figure 9.28. You may notice that the probabilities are symmetrical with respect to the outcome $N/2$. We can use only the second half of the probabilities:

```
probs_half = [2*probs[k] for k in range(len(probs)//2 + 1, len(probs))]
probs_half = [1 - sum(probs_half)] + probs_half         ◁──┐ Sets the probability
                                                           of outcome 0 to be
plot_bars(list_to_dict(probs_half, False), '', '', '')     the remainder
```

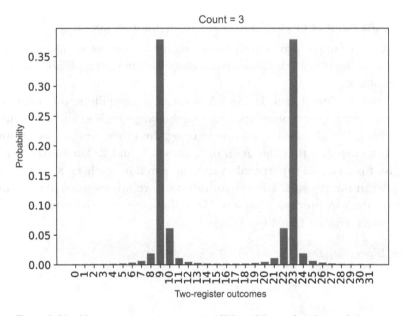

Figure 9.28 Measurement outcome probabilities of the estimation register

The histogram of the probabilities of the second half of the estimation register outcomes is shown in figure 9.29. As discussed, we can use the results to estimate the number of good outcomes as the closest integer to

$$2^m \sin^2\left(\pi \frac{v}{2^n}\right)$$

9.6 Amplitude estimation and quantum counting

where v is the most frequent outcome of the estimation register.

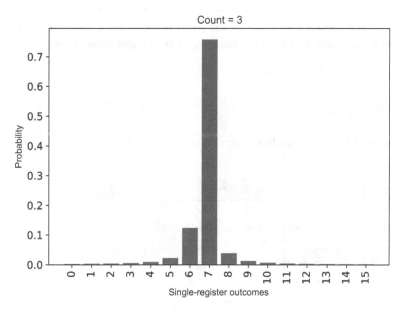

Figure 9.29 Measurement probabilities of the second half of the estimation register outcomes

In code, we can set v to be the outcome with the highest probability:

```
import numpy as np
from math import sin

v = np.argmax(probs[int(len(probs)/2):])
print('v:', v)
count = int(2**m*sin(7*pi/2**n)**2)
print('count:', count)

assert(count == len(items))
```

In this example, we know the count should be equal to the number of good outcomes.

In this example, the printed output is

```
v: 7
count: 3
```

9.6.3 Estimating the probability of good outcomes with amplitude estimation

Instead of the number of good outcomes, suppose we want to know the combined probability of those outcomes. We can use the amplitude estimation algorithm to approximate the probability of one or more outcomes.

The initial state in the target register can be prepared with a quantum circuit (operator). We will use the `random_circuit` function to generate random quantum circuits in the same way we generated random transformations in chapter 6. The complete definition of the function can be found in the chapter code. For example, let's use the `random_circuit` function to create an example operator A for m = 3 qubits:

```
from util import random_circuit

m = 3
C = random_circuit(m)
```

The state created with this random circuit is shown in figure 9.30.

Outcome	Binary	Amplitude	Direction	Magnitude	Amplitude bar	Probability
0	000	−0.32 − 0.05i	−171.0°	0.32		0.10
1	001	−0.26 + 0.14i	151.1°	0.30		0.09
2	010	0.67 + 0.25i	20.4°	0.71		0.51
3	011	0.03 − 0.07i	−69.0°	0.08		0.01
4	100	−0.28 - 0.18i	−147.0°	0.33		0.11
5	101	−0.04 − 0.03i	−139.9°	0.05		0.00
6	110	0.14 − 0.03i	−13.5°	0.14		0.02
7	111	0.16 + 0.37i	65.7°	0.40		0.16

Figure 9.30 **A three-qubit state prepared with a randomly generated circuit**

Let's set the good outcomes 0 and 1:

```
items = [0, 1]
```

We can find the probability of measuring one of the good outcomes with the following function:

```
def good_probs(qc, items):
    state = qc.run()
    return sum([abs(state[k])**2 for k in items])
```

Let's find the probability of getting one of the good outcomes from the state in figure 9.30:

```
q = QuantumRegister(m)
qc = QuantumCircuit(q)
qc.append(C, q)

prob_g = good_probs(qc, items)
```

In this example, `prob_g` is 0.1897666121194554.

Using the circuit defined previously as the operator A, let's apply the amplitude estimation algorithm with $n = 8$ target qubits. This time, let's use the swaps in the IQFT (`swap = True`):

```
n = 8

qc = amplitude_estimation_circuit(n, C, phase_oracle_match(m, items),
    swap=True)

state = qc.run()
```

Once again, we create a list of the probabilities of estimation register outcomes:

```
probs = [0 for _ in range(2**n)]
for k in range(2**m):
    for j in range(2**n):
        probs[j] += abs(state[k*2**n + j])**2
```

We can use the most frequent measurement outcome v to estimate the probability of good outcomes as

$$\sin^2\left(\pi \frac{v}{2^n}\right)$$

We will define v as the estimation register outcome with the highest probability and compute our estimate using the following Python code:

```
v = np.argmax(probs[int(len(probs)/2):])
print('v =', v)
estimate = round(sin(v*pi/2**n)**2, 4)
print('estimate ~', estimate)

assert(abs(prob_g - estimate) < 0.01)
```

In this example, the printed output is

```
v = 37
estimate ~ 0.1924
```

This is a reasonably good estimate of the expected probability of getting one of the good outcomes.

Summary

- The quantum phase estimation (QPE) algorithm serves as a fundamental building block for many quantum algorithms, including Shor's algorithm.
- If we have measurement results from a phased discrete sinc state with n qubits and an unknown encoded frequency value v, we can get an estimate for the true

value of v and the corresponding angle parameter $\theta = v\, 2\pi/2^n$. In this chapter, we learned two methods for getting an estimate: using the most frequent integer outcome and using the relation between the approximate magnitudes of the two most frequent consecutive integer outcomes.

- A quantum state vector is called an eigenvector (or eigenstate) of a circuit transformation U if all its amplitudes are multiplied by a corresponding eigenvalue (a complex number of length 1) as a result of the circuit application.
- Given an m-qubit circuit U (where $m > 1$), we can implement the phase estimation circuit to create a phased discrete sinc state in the estimation register. We can use the state created to get an estimate for the phase of eigenvalue corresponding to the eigenstate using the methods covered in this chapter or more advanced methods (such as Maximum Likelihood Estimation).
- The amplitude estimation algorithm extends QPE to estimate the number of good outcomes, called quantum counting, or estimate the probability of good outcomes. This algorithm can drastically reduce the number of measurements needed to obtain a very good estimate for the number or the probability of the set of good outcomes but at the expense of adding more qubits and performing a more complex quantum computation.

Part 3

Quantum solutions: Optimization and beyond

Many of today's most challenging computational problems are optimization problems—from portfolio management to supply chain logistics. This final part of the book shows how quantum computing can tackle these problems by combining the fundamental building blocks you've learned into sophisticated quantum optimization techniques.

The journey begins in chapter 10 with an essential pattern: encoding classical functions into quantum states. Chapter 11 introduces Grover adaptive search and guides you through implementing your own quantum optimizer. Chapter 12 concludes by opening windows to advanced quantum computing topics, showing you where your quantum computing journey can take you next.

Encoding functions in quantum states

This chapter covers

- Representing integer key–value pairs in quantum states
- Extending frequency (value) encoding to (polynomial) function encoding
- Using Grover's algorithm to search for function values

In classical computing, we can use several data structures to represent pairs, such as attributes and corresponding values or the inputs and outputs of a function. One such data structure is a dictionary, where unique keys are mapped to specific values. In this chapter, we will learn how to represent such integer key–value pairs in a quantum state. We will use two qubit registers: one to represent keys and one to represent values. We will entangle the registers so that if a measurement is performed, the outcome will contain a key paired with its corresponding value.

NOTE You can think of integer key–value pairs as a *quantum dictionary*.

We will use the frequency-value-encoding method introduced in chapter 8 to encode integer-valued functions by entangling inputs in one register with outputs in another. We encode a value in a single quantum register by creating a geometric sequence state where the encoded value is reflected in the (progression of the) phases of the state's amplitudes and then applying the inverse quantum Fourier transform (IQFT).

Figure 10.1 shows the concepts discussed in this chapter. We will learn how to encode various functions, including the weight and value functions in the knapsack example problem discussed in chapter 2. Then we will look at other problems that use this encoding method, such as searching for function values with Grover's algorithm.

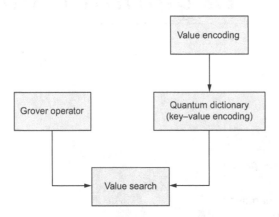

Figure 10.1 A dependency diagram of concepts covered in this chapter

10.1 Encoding function inputs and outputs

In this section, we will encode the integer inputs and outputs of a function in a quantum state. We will use two registers, which we will call the *key* and *value* registers. The key register encodes function inputs, and the value register encodes the corresponding outputs.

Let's denote the number of qubits in the key register with n and the number of qubits in the value register with m. This allows for encoding functions with 2^n integer inputs and 2^m integer outputs. If a measurement is performed, the key part of the outcome represents an input value of the encoded function, and the value part of the outcome represents the corresponding output value.

For example, we can encode a function f with the set {0, ..., 7} as inputs and with values in the set {0, ..., 7} in a quantum state with $n = 3$ key qubits and $m = 3$ value qubits. Figure 10.2 shows an example measurement outcome representing the input–output pair (2, 4). Note that the registers are shown in an intuitive order, but when we

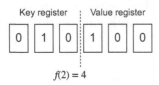

Figure 10.2 An example measurement outcome of a quantum state with $n = 3$ key qubits and $m = 3$ value qubits and an encoded function f representing the input–output pair (2, 4)

10.1 Encoding function inputs and outputs

implement this method in the next section, the value-register qubits will be the leftmost qubits.

> **Exercise 10.1**
> What measurement outcomes (using $n = 3$ key qubits and $m = 3$ value qubits) would represent the input–output pair (0, 1)?

10.1.1 Encoding a simple function

To start, let's encode key–value pairs where the value is the sum of the binary digits in the key (for example, the sum of the binary digits in the key 011 is 2). If we use a key register with $n = 3$ qubits, the sum of the binary digits of an integer k, with $0 \leq k < 2^n$, is given by the expression

$$s(k) = k_2 + k_1 + k_0$$

where k_0, k_1, and k_2 are 0 or 1 (the binary digits of k).

We know that the outputs of this function will be integers between 0 and 3, so we'll need two qubits for the value register ($m = 2$). The key–value pairs we will encode are shown in table 10.1.

Table 10.1 The inputs and outputs and the corresponding key and value register binary outcomes

Input (k)	Key register	Output (s(k))	Value register
0	000	0	00
1	001	1	01
2	010	1	01
3	011	2	10
4	100	1	01
5	101	2	10
6	110	2	10
7	111	3	11

First we create a circuit with two registers:

```
from sim_circuit import QuantumRegister, QuantumCircuit

n_key = 3
n_value = 2
```

```
key = QuantumRegister(n_key)
value = QuantumRegister(n_value)
qc = QuantumCircuit(key, value)
```

We start with an equal superposition in both registers:

```
for i in range(n_key):
    qc.h(key[i])
```
Puts the key register in equal superposition

```
for i in range(n_value):
    qc.h(value[i])
```
Puts the value register in equal superposition

As mentioned, we will use the value encoding pattern we learned in chapter 6 to create a geometric sequence state where the step-angle parameter θ is calculated from the given value v using the formula $\theta = v\, 2\pi/2^n$. For example, if $n = 3$ and $v = 2$, the (step) angle parameter is $\theta = v\, 2\pi/2^n = \pi/2$.

> **NOTE** Remember, in a geometric sequence state, the phase of the kth amplitude is $k\theta$.

To encode key–value pairs where the value is the sum of the binary digits in the key, we can use the binary decomposition of integers.

> **Binary decomposition of integers**
>
> An integer k with $0 \leq k < 2^n$ can be represented as a binary string with n digits. We can generate the positions of the digits that are 1 using the following code:
>
> ```
> def one_digits(n, k):
>     for i in range(n):
>         if k & (1 << i):
>             yield i
> ```
>
> For example, the binary form of $k = 4$ with $n = 3$ digits is 100, so the function `one_digits` will yield position 2:
>
> ```
> n = 3
> k = 4
>
> for i in one_digits(n, k):
>     print(i)
> ```
>
> ```
> 2
> ```
>
> As we know, the decimal form of an integer k, where $0 \leq k < 2^n$, is the sum of powers of 2 corresponding to these positions. The value $k = 4$ is decomposed into powers of 2 as follows:
>
> ```
> sum([2**i for i in one_digits(n,k)])
> ```

We can use this sum representation of k to obtain a sum representation of $k\theta$ for a given angle θ. For example, if $n = 3$ and $\theta = \pi/4$, the multiple 4θ can be expressed as

```
sum([2**i * theta for i in one_digits(n,k)])
```

The following code snippet verifies that the decomposition is correct:

```
from math import pi
from util import is_close

theta = pi/4
assert is_close(4*theta, sum([2**i * theta for i in one_digits(n, k)]))
```

We use a sequence of controlled phase rotations to create geometric quantum states. Each 1 digit in the key register part of the outcome contributes a value of 1, which corresponds to an angle of $\theta = 2\pi/2^n$. For each 1 digit in the key register part of the outcome, each qubit i in the value register (for $0 \leq i < m$) contributes an angle of $2^i \theta = \pi/2^{n-1-i}$:

```
for j in range(n_key):
    for i in range(n_value):
        qc.cp(pi / 2 ** (n_key-1-i), key[j], value[i])
```

After this step, the amplitudes of the outcomes with the same key form a geometric sequence that reflects the (frequency) value corresponding to the key. Figure 10.3 shows a modified state table where the amplitudes are grouped by key register outcomes: the phases of the amplitudes increase by the step angle that corresponds to the value we want to encode in the value register.

Exercise 10.2
Check that the amplitudes of the outcomes having 7 as a key match the geometric sequence for $\theta = 3\pi/4$.

Finally, we apply the IQFT to the value register:

```
qc.iqft(value, swap=True)
```

Remember from chapter 8 that when we prepare a geometric sequence with qubits in reverse order, we can skip the swaps in the IQFT. We will apply controlled phase rotations with the same angles as before to the qubits in reverse order (qubit i becomes qubit $n - i - 1$):

```
for j in range(n_key):
    for i in range(n_value):
        qc.cp(pi / 2**i, key[j], value[i])

qc.iqft(value[::-1], swap=False)
```

258   CHAPTER 10   *Encoding functions in quantum states*

Key	Binary	Value	Binary	Magnitude	Direction	Amplitude Bar	
0	000	0	00	0.1768	0.00°	▇	$s(0) = 0$
0	000	1	01	0.1768	0.00°	▇	
0	000	2	10	0.1768	0.00°	▇	$v = 0, \theta = 0$
0	000	3	11	0.1768	0.00°	▇	
1	001	0	00	0.1768	0.00°	▇	$s(1) = 1$
1	001	1	01	0.1768	45.00°	▇	
1	001	2	10	0.1768	90.00°	▇	$v = 1, \theta = \dfrac{\pi}{4}$
1	001	3	11	0.1768	135.00°	▇	
2	010	0	00	0.1768	0.00°	▇	$s(2) = 1$
2	010	1	01	0.1768	45.00°	▇	
2	010	2	10	0.1768	90.00°	▇	$v = 1, \theta = \dfrac{\pi}{4}$
2	010	3	11	0.1768	135.00°	▇	
3	011	0	00	0.1768	0.00°	▇	$s(3) = 2$
3	011	1	01	0.1768	90.00°	▇	
3	011	2	10	0.1768	180.00°	▇	$v = 2, \theta = \dfrac{\pi}{2}$
3	011	3	11	0.1768	-90.00°	▇	
4	100	0	00	0.1768	0.00°	▇	$s(4) = 1$
4	100	1	01	0.1768	45.00°	▇	
4	100	2	10	0.1768	90.00°	▇	$v = 1, \theta = \dfrac{\pi}{4}$
4	100	3	11	0.1768	135.00°	▇	
5	101	0	00	0.1768	0.00°	▇	$s(5) = 2$
5	101	1	01	0.1768	90.00°	▇	
5	101	2	10	0.1768	180.00°	▇	$v = 2, \theta = \dfrac{\pi}{2}$
5	101	3	11	0.1768	-90.00°	▇	
6	110	0	00	0.1768	0.00°	▇	$s(6) = 2$
6	110	1	01	0.1768	90.00°	▇	
6	110	2	10	0.1768	180.00°	▇	$v = 2, \theta = \dfrac{\pi}{2}$
6	110	3	11	0.1768	-90.00°	▇	
7	111	0	00	0.1768	0.00°	▇	$s(7) = 3$
7	111	1	01	0.1768	135.00°	▇	
7	111	2	10	0.1768	-90.00°	▇	$v = 3, \theta = \dfrac{3\pi}{4}$
7	111	3	11	0.1768	45.00°	▇	

Figure 10.3 A quantum state where the value register encodes a geometric sequence for each key. The angle parameter of a geometric sequence reflects the value corresponding to its key.

In this chapter, we will use a utility function `grid_state` to visualize a quantum state as a grid. This representation uses only the amplitude bar column of a state table and reorganizes it into a two-dimensional table where each column represents an input and each row represents an output. For each input (column), the encoding of a function will have a single row with a nonzero amplitude:

```
from util import grid_state

grid_state(qc.run(), n_key, neg=False, show_probs=False)
```

> **NOTE** We can use the `grid_state` function parameter `show_probs` to include the numeric probability next to the amplitude bar. We can also use the

parameter neg if we are working with negative values, as we will see in the next section.

The resulting grid visualization is shown in figure 10.4. If we measure the illustrated state, we will get a measurement outcome where the key register and the value register represent a key–value pair.

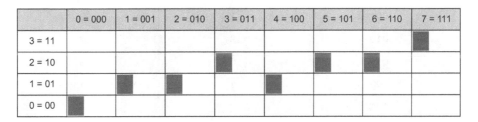

Figure 10.4 Grid visualization of the encoded function inputs (columns) and outputs (rows)

TIP The binary outcome will have the value register followed by the key register due to the order of the registers when we create the circuit.

10.1.2 Encoding the knapsack problem

In chapter 2, we looked at an example of a common binary optimization problem: the knapsack problem. In this example, we have three items with the values and weights shown in table 10.2. We use three registers to encode each of the possible selections and the weight and value of each selection (see figure 10.5).

Table 10.2 The items, weights, and values for the example knapsack problem

Item label	Value	Weight
0	2 ($2,000)	3
1	3 ($3,000)	2
2	1 ($1,000)	1

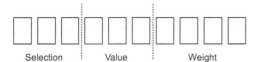

Figure 10.5 Three registers encoding an item selection, its total value, and its total weight for solving the knapsack problem

NOTE You can think of these three registers as a dictionary with two values for each key.

To represent the possible selections, we use a register with three qubits, one for each item. If an item is included in the selection, the corresponding qubit has a value of 1.

Otherwise it has a value of 0. Table 10.3 shows the value and weight of each possible combination of items.

Table 10.3 Each possible selection of items and the corresponding value and weight

Selection	Value	Weight
000	0	0
001	2	3
010	3	2
011	5	5
100	1	1
101	3	4
110	4	3
111	6	6

We can express the value and weight of each selection using linear functions of binary variables:

$$v(k_0, k_1, k_2) = 2k_0 + 3k_1 + k_2$$
$$w(k_0, k_1, k_2) = 3k_0 + 2k_1 + k_2$$

where k_0, k_1, and k_2 are binary variables indicating whether an item is included in the knapsack.

> **A quick review of linear functions of binary variables**
> A linear function of binary variables is a mathematical expression of the form
>
> $$f(x_0, x_1, \ldots, x_{n-1}) = c + c_0 x_0 + c_1 x_1 + \cdots + c_{n-1} x_{n-1} = c + \sum_{k=0}^{n-1} c_k x_k$$
>
> where $x_0, \ldots, x_{n-1}$ are either 0 or 1 and $c, c_0, \ldots, c_{n-1}$ are constant real numbers.

Let's encode the value for each possible selection. First we create a circuit with just the selection and value registers, and we put both in equal superposition:

```
n_key = 3
n_value = 3
```

10.1 Encoding function inputs and outputs

```
key = QuantumRegister(n_key)
value = QuantumRegister(n_value)
qc = QuantumCircuit(key, value)

for i in range(n_key):
    qc.h(key[i])

for i in range(n_value):
    qc.h(value[i])
```

We can represent the linear function

$$v(k_0, k_1, k_2) = 2k_0 + 3k_1 + k_2$$

with a list of tuples where the first element is the coefficient and the second element is a list of the variables in the term (i.e., the qubit indices corresponding to the binary variable):

```
terms = [(2, [0]), (3, [1]), (1, [2])]
```

We can use the following `for` loop to apply the controlled phase rotations:

```
for (coeff, vars) in terms:
    for i in range(n_value):
        qc.cp(pi * 2 ** -i * coeff, key[vars[0]], value[i])
```

Next we apply the IQFT to the value register:

```
qc.iqft(value[::-1], swap=False)
```

The resulting grid state visualization is shown in figure 10.6. We can see that only outcomes that correspond to item selections (columns) and their values (rows) are possible.

	0 = 000	1 = 001	2 = 010	3 = 011	4 = 100	5 = 101	6 = 110	7 = 111
7 = 111								
6 = 110								■
5 = 101				■				
4 = 100						■		
3 = 011			■			■		
2 = 010		■						
1 = 001					■			
0 = 000	■							

Figure 10.6 The value (rows) of each possible knapsack selection (columns)

Next we will encode the weight function. We will start with only three qubits for the weight register. Later, we will need to use four qubits for the weight register when we adjust the weight function to help us search for specific outcomes.

The weight function can be represented with the following list of tuples:

```
terms = [(3, [0]), (2, [1]), (1, [2])]
```

We can encode this function using the following Python code:

```
n_key = 3
n_weight = 3

key = QuantumRegister(n_key)
weight = QuantumRegister(n_weight)
qc = QuantumCircuit(key, weight)

for i in range(n_key):
    qc.h(key[i])

for i in range(n_weight):
    qc.h(weight[i])

for (coeff, vars) in terms:
    for i in range(n_weight):
        qc.cp(pi * 2 ** -i * coeff, key[vars[0]], weight[i])

qc.iqft(weight[::-1], swap=False)
```

The resulting grid state visualization is shown in figure 10.7.

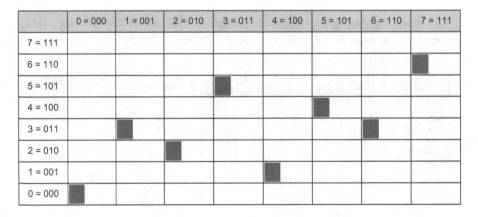

Figure 10.7 The weight (rows) of each possible knapsack selection (columns)

10.1.3 Encoding polynomials of binary variables

What if the function we want to encode is not a linear function? For example, what if we want to encode the function $f(k) = k^2 + 2$ (where $0 \leq k < 2^n$)? To do this, we will need to represent polynomial functions of an integer variable as functions of binary variables, a *polynomial of binary variables*.

We can write an integer k as a sum of powers of 2:

$$k = \sum_{j=0}^{n-1} 2^j k_j$$

where k_j is 0 or 1. Using this equation, if $n = 2$, then an integer k can be expressed with

$$k = 2k_1 + k_0$$

Exercise 10.3
Write the expression of an integer $k > 0$ as a function of $n = 3$ binary variables.

Using the previous expression of an integer k for $n = 2$, we can also write k^2 as

$$k^2 = (2k_1 + k_0)(2k_1 + k_0) = 4k_1^2 + 4k_1 k_0 + k_0^2 = 4k_1 + 4k_1 k_0 + k_0$$

because the square of a binary digit is itself. Now we can express the function $f(k) = k^2 + 2$ for $n = 2$ as the polynomial of binary variables:

$$p(k_0, k_1) = 4k_1 + 4k_1 k_0 + k_0 + 2$$

Example inputs and outputs of a polynomial of binary variables
Let's check the inputs and outputs using the polynomial of binary variables defined previously:

$$p(0, 0) = 4 \times 0 + 4 \times 0 \times 0 + 0 + 2 = 2$$
$$p(1, 0) = 4 \times 0 + 4 \times 0 \times 1 + 1 + 2 = 3$$
$$p(0, 1) = 4 \times 1 + 4 \times 1 \times 0 + 0 + 2 = 6$$
$$p(1, 1) = 4 \times 1 + 4 \times 1 \times 1 + 1 + 2 = 11$$

Each term of the polynomial is called a *monomial*.

As in the previous example, we will use a list of tuples to represent the terms of the polynomial we want to encode. Each term, or monomial, is expressed as a tuple where the first element is the coefficient and the second element is a list of the binary variables (qubits). To include a constant, we include a tuple with an empty list as the second element:

```
terms = [(4, [1]), (4, [1, 0]), (1, [0]), (2, [])]
```

To encode each term, we need to account for the number of variables for each coefficient as well as any constants. The function `encode_term` defined in the following listing applies the phase rotations according to the number of coefficients in the term.

Listing 10.1 Creating the circuit that encodes a given term

```
def encode_term(coeff, vars, circuit, key, value):
    for i in range(len(value)):
        if len(vars) > 1:
            circuit.mcp(pi * 2 ** -i * coeff, [key[j] for j in vars],
    value[i])
        elif len(vars) > 0:
            circuit.cp(pi * 2 ** -i * coeff, key[vars[0]], value[i])
        else:
            circuit.p(pi * 2 ** -i * coeff, value[i])
```

The coefficient of a term only contributes to the total output when all its variables are 1. Therefore, the phase rotations are controlled on all the variables with a multi-control phase gate (`mcp`). The constant is added to every output, so there is no control for the phase gate applied for a constant term.

Now we can use the `build_polynomial_circuit` function defined next to encode any polynomial expressed as a list of tuples (`terms`), using a key register with `key_size` qubits and a value register with `value_size` qubits.

Listing 10.2 Creating the circuit for encoding a polynomial in a quantum state

```
def build_polynomial_circuit(key_size, value_size, terms):
    key = QuantumRegister(key_size)
    value = QuantumRegister(value_size)
    circuit = QuantumCircuit(key, value)

    for i in range(len(key)):
        circuit.h(key[i])

    for i in range(len(value)):
        circuit.h(value[i])

    for (coeff, vars) in terms:
        encode_term(coeff, vars, circuit, key, value)

    circuit.iqft(value[::-1], swap=False)

    return circuit
```

10.1 Encoding function inputs and outputs

Next we encode our polynomial of binary variables. We will need $m = 4$ value qubits to encode the outputs:

```
n_key = 2
n_value = 4

qc = build_polynomial_circuit(n_key, n_value, terms)
```

The resulting grid visualization is shown in figure 10.8.

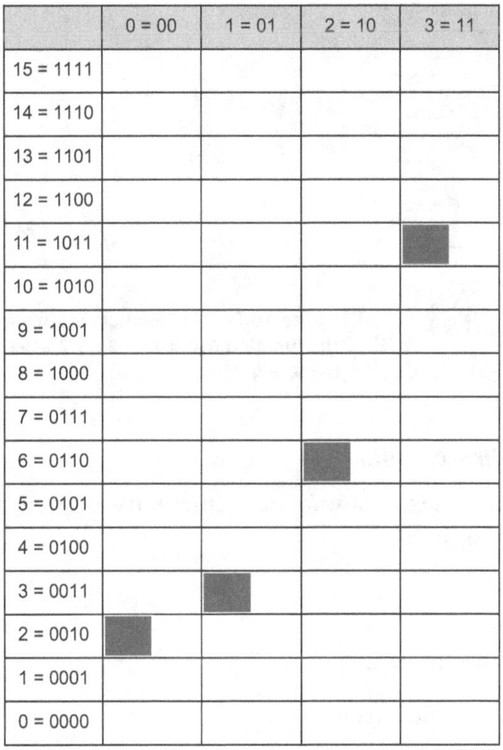

	0 = 00	1 = 01	2 = 10	3 = 11
15 = 1111				
14 = 1110				
13 = 1101				
12 = 1100				
11 = 1011				■
10 = 1010				
9 = 1001				
8 = 1000				
7 = 0111				
6 = 0110			■	
5 = 0101				
4 = 0100				
3 = 0011		■		
2 = 0010	■			
1 = 0001				
0 = 0000				

Figure 10.8 The quantum state encoding the function $f(k) = k^2 + 2$, where $0 \leq k < 4$

Let's look at another example. This time, let's consider the function $f(k) = k^2 - 5k + 7$ with integer inputs {0, 1, 2, 3}. To represent all the inputs, we need $n = 2$ qubits. When we expand k as a binary expression, this function becomes a polynomial of binary variables:

$$p(k_0, k_1) = -6k_1 + 4k_1k_0 - 4k_0 + 7$$

The following list is a specification of this polynomial:

```
terms = [(-6, [1]), (4, [1, 0]), (-4, [0]), (7, [])]
```

We can encode this polynomial using $n = 2$ key qubits and $m = 3$ value qubits:

```
n_key = 2
n_value = 3

qc = build_polynomial_circuit(n_key, n_value, terms)
```

The resulting grid visualization is shown in figure 10.9.

	0 = 00	1 = 01	2 = 10	3 = 11
7 = 111	■			
6 = 110				
5 = 101				
4 = 100				
3 = 011		■		
2 = 010				
1 = 001			■	■
0 = 000				

Figure 10.9 The quantum state encoding the function $f(k) = k^2 - 5k + 7$ where $0 \leq k < 4$

10.1.4 Complexity of polynomial-encoding circuits

Let's do a quick analysis of the complexity of encoding functions in quantum states using this method. Assume the following:

- We have an n-qubit key register.
- We have an m-qubit value register.
- The polynomial has t terms (monomials).

The circuit that encodes the term coefficients uses

- $n + m$ Hadamard gates
- mt controlled phase gates

Then we apply the IQFT to the value register using

- m Hadamard gates
- $m(m-1)/2$ controlled phase gates

The total number of gates applied is

$$n + (t+2)m + \frac{m(m-1)}{2}$$

We can check that this is the total number of gates using the following `assert` statement:

```
qc = build_polynomial_circuit(n, m, terms)
t = len(terms)
assert len(qc.transformations) == n + (t + 2)*m + m*(m - 1 )/2
```

For a quadratic polynomial (used in many optimization problems), the number of terms is at most $n(n+1)/2 + 1$ (one constant term, n single-variable terms, and $n(n-1)/2$ two-variable terms). This means the number of terms for encoding a quadratic polynomial of binary variables is a low-degree polynomial in the number of qubits.

The number of control qubits is also an important factor in complexity analysis. Each term (monomial) of a polynomial of binary variables requires a multicontrolled phase gate. The number of control qubits is the number of binary variables in the term. If we limit the number of variables in a term to two, we end up with a quadratic polynomial, which is often enough to encode difficult optimization problems.

10.1.5 Representing negative values

We can map the 2^m binary strings of length $m > 0$ to any range of integers of length 2^m. By default, we work with the range $[0, 2^m - 1]$ of integers. Two's Complement representation allows us to map the binary strings that start with 0 to the range $[0, 2^{m-1} -1]$ and those that start with 1 to the range $[-2^{m-1}, -1]$. If you need a refresher on Two's Complement, you can refer to appendix A.1.

For example, to encode the function $f(k) = k^2 - 3$ for integer inputs $\{0, 1, 2, 3\}$, we express the function as a polynomial of binary variables:

$$p(k_0, k_1) = 4k_1 + 4k_1 k_0 + k_0 - 3$$

where k_0 and k_1 are the binary digits of an input.

To do this, all we have to do is add a constant term to the list:

```
terms = [(4, [1]), (4, [1, 0]), (1, [0]), (-3, [])]
```

The lowest output is –3, and the highest output is 0. To encode negative values, we will use Two's Complement:

```
n_key = 2
n_value = 4

qc = build_polynomial_circuit(n_key, n_value, terms)
```

To visualize the resulting state, we can set the third parameter of the `grid_state` function to `neg = True`:

```
grid_state(qc.run(), n_key, neg = True, show_probs = False)
```

We get the state shown in figure 10.10. The input 0 maps to the output –3, which we represent using Two's Complement as 1101. We can see that the shape stays the same but is shifted.

	0 = 00	1 = 01	2 = 10	3 = 11
7 = 0111				
6 = 0110				■
5 = 0101				
4 = 0100				
3 = 0011				
2 = 0010				
1 = 0001			■	
0 = 0000				
–1 = 1111				
–2 = 1110		■		
–3 = 1101	■			
–4 = 1100				
–5 = 1011				
–6 = 1010				
–7 = 1001				
–8 = 1000				

Figure 10.10 The quantum state encoding the function $f(k) = k^2 - 3$ for $0 \leq k < 4$

10.2 Searching for function values

After a function is encoded in a quantum state, all the input–output pairs have equal measurement probability. If we are interested in specific outcomes, we can use Grover's algorithm to amplify the probability of measuring those outcomes. For example, we can search for pairs where the output is negative or within a given range.

We can use simple oracles that match binary digits. These oracles are straightforward to implement and extremely useful. Figure 10.11 shows the range of values (highlighted) specified by various oracles. In the first table, we use an oracle that matches 1 in the first digit of the value register to find values in the upper half of the range of outcomes. In the second table, we use the same oracle that matches 1 in the first digit to find all the pairs with negative output using Two's Complement. We can use this oracle to search for positive or negative outputs of an encoded function. In the third table, we use an oracle that matches 1 in the first digit and 0 in the second digit to find the lower half of the range of negative values.

10.2 Searching for function values

Value
7 = 111
6 = 110
5 = 101
4 = 100
3 = 011
2 = 010
1 = 001
0 = 000

Value
3 = 011
2 = 010
1 = 001
0 = 000
−1 = 111
−2 = 110
−3 = 101
−4 = 100

Value
3 = 011
2 = 010
1 = 001
0 = 000
−1 = 111
−2 = 110
−3 = 101
−4 = 100

Figure 10.11 (Left) Values identified by an oracle that matches 1 in the first digit. (Center) Values (using Two's Complement) identified by an oracle that matches 1 in the first digit. (Right) Values (using Two's Complement) identified by an oracle that matches 1 in the first digit and 0 in the second digit.

The following two Python functions create oracles that match 1 or 0 in the position `tag_bit`:

```
def oracle_match_1(bits, tag_bit):
    q = QuantumRegister(bits)
    qc = QuantumCircuit(q)

    qc.p(pi, tag_bit)

    return qc

def oracle_match_0(bits, tag_bit):
    q = QuantumRegister(bits)
    qc = QuantumCircuit(q)

    qc.x(q[tag_bit])
    qc.p(pi, tag_bit)
    qc.x(q[tag_bit])

    return qc
```

We can use these oracles to construct Grover operators. For example, say we want to find input values of the function $f(k) = k + 1$ where the output value is 4 or greater.

> **Exercise 10.4**
> Write the function $f(k) = k + 1$ as a polynomial of $n = 2$ binary variables (where $0 \leq k < 2^n$).

First, let's encode the function $f(k) = k + 1$ with $n = 2$ key qubits:

```
n_key = 2
n_value = 3

terms = [(2, [1]), (1, [0]), (1, [])]

prepare = build_polynomial_circuit(n_key, n_value, terms)
```

270   CHAPTER 10   *Encoding functions in quantum states*

The state after encoding the function with given coefficients is shown in figure 10.12. The output values that meet our criteria are highlighted.

	0 = 00	1 = 01	2 = 10	3 = 11
7 = 111				
6 = 110				
5 = 101				
4 = 100				■
3 = 011			■	
2 = 010		■		
1 = 001	■			
0 = 000				

Figure 10.12 The quantum state encoding the function $f(k) = k + 1$ for $0 \leq k < 4$. The values that meet our search criteria are highlighted.

Now we can create an oracle that matches 1 in the first digit of the value register and use it to create a Grover operator using the `grover_circuit` function from chapter 6:

```
from algo import grover_circuit

prepare = build_polynomial_circuit(n_key, n_value, terms)
oracle = oracle_match_1(n_key + n_value, n_key + n_value - 1)

qc = grover_circuit(prepare, oracle, 1)
```

The state after applying one iteration of this Grover operator is shown in figure 10.13. The only key–value pair that meets our criteria has a magnitude of 1. If we measure this state, we will find our desired input–output pair.

	0 = 00	1 = 01	2 = 10	3 = 11
7 = 111				
6 = 110				
5 = 101				
4 = 100				■
3 = 011				
2 = 010				
1 = 001				
0 = 000				

Figure 10.13 The result of applying a Grover iteration to the quantum state encoding the function $f(k) = k + 1$, for $0 \leq k < 4$, with an oracle that tags outcomes with 1 as the first digit in the value register

10.2 Searching for function values

Let's look at searching for negative values. For example, let's encode the function $f(k) = k^2 - 5$ for $n = 2$ and search for outputs less than -4:

```
n_key = 2
n_value = 4

terms = [(4, [1]), (4, [1, 0]), (1, [0]), (-5, [])]

prepare = build_polynomial_circuit(n_key, n_value, terms)
```

The resulting state table is in figure 10.14. The desired output values are highlighted.

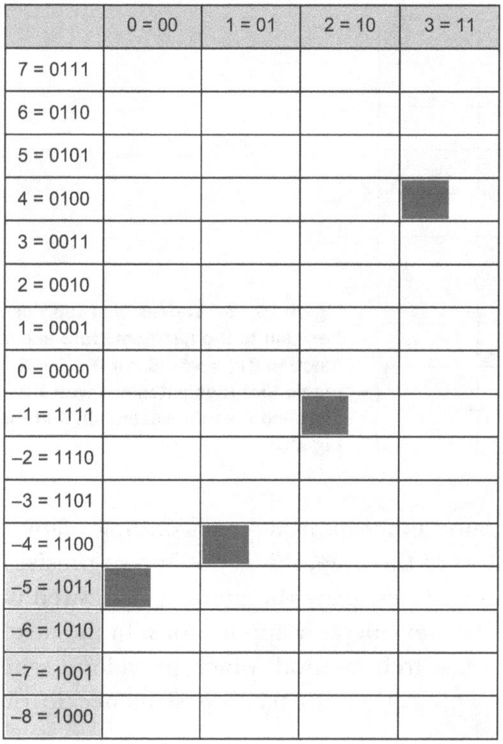

Figure 10.14 The quantum state encoding the function $f(k) = k^2 - 5$ for $0 \leq k < 4$. The values that meet the search criteria are highlighted.

Next we need to define an oracle that matches 1 in the first digit and 0 in the second digit of the value register. We will use this oracle in our Grover operator:

```
q = QuantumRegister(n_key + n_value)
oracle = QuantumCircuit(q)

oracle.x(q[n_key + n_value - 2])
oracle.cp(pi, n_key + n_value - 2, n_key + n_value - 1)
oracle.x(q[n_key + n_value - 2])

qc = grover_circuit(prepare, oracle, 1)
```

The resulting state table is shown in figure 10.15.

	0 = 00	1 = 01	2 = 10	3 = 11
7 = 0111				
6 = 0110				
5 = 0101				
4 = 0100				
3 = 0011				
2 = 0010				
1 = 0001				
0 = 0000				
−1 = 1111				
−2 = 1110				
−3 = 1101				
−4 = 1100				
−5 = 1011	▓			
−6 = 1010				
−7 = 1001				
−8 = 1000				

Figure 10.15 The result of applying a Grover iteration to the quantum state encoding the function $f(k) = k^2 - 5$, for $0 \leq k < 4$, with an oracle that tags outcomes with 1 as the first digit and 0 as the second digit in the value register

The ideal number of Grover operator applications depends on how many outcomes are specified by a given oracle. Most of the time, this is not known precisely beforehand. We can use quantum counting to estimate the number of desired outcomes, or we can try random numbers of Grover operator applications. In the next chapter, we will look at the Grover adaptive search method, which provides a schedule for the number of Grover operator applications to try in a sequence to obtain the desired outcome.

10.3 Finding zeros of polynomial functions

Algorithms that find the inputs where the value of a function is 0 have numerous applications across various fields. In financial engineering, investment portfolios are optimized by finding where the derivative of a profit or cost function is 0. In statistics and machine learning, they are used to find parameters that minimize the error (difference between predicted and actual outcomes). These algorithms are also applied in cryptography schemes. In practice, the search space (input–output pairs of a function) can be extremely large. We will look at a simple example to understand how we can implement a quantum solution to these types of problems.

10.3 Finding zeros of polynomial functions

Let's again consider a quadratic polynomial

$$p(k) = k^2 - 4$$

for $0 \leq k < 8$.

We can encode this function in a quantum state with the following code:

```
n_key = 2
n_value = 4

terms = [(4, [1]), (4, [1, 0]), (1, [0]), (-4, [])]

qc = build_polynomial_circuit(n_key, n_value, terms)
```

The grid state table in figure 10.16 is also a visual representation of the graph of the function (a parabola). The row corresponding to the 0 value is highlighted.

	0 = 00	1 = 01	2 = 10	3 = 11
7 = 0111				
6 = 0110				
5 = 0101				■
4 = 0100				
3 = 0011				
2 = 0010				
1 = 0001				
0 = 0000			■	
−1 = 1111				
−2 = 1110				
−3 = 1101		■		
−4 = 1100	■			
−5 = 1011				
−6 = 1010				
−7 = 1001				
−8 = 1000				

Figure 10.16 The quantum state encoding the function $f(k) = k^2 - 4$, where $0 \leq k < 4$. The value register corresponding to outcome 0 is highlighted.

Next we can use the following Python function to create an oracle that specifies outcomes with all 0 digits in the value register:

```
def oracle_match_0_multi(bits, tag_bits):
    q = QuantumRegister(bits)
    qc = QuantumCircuit(q)

    for t in tag_bits:
        qc.x(q[t])

    qc.mcp(pi, [q[t] for t in tag_bits[:-1]], q[len(q) - 1])

    for t in tag_bits:
        qc.x(q[t])

    return qc
```

We create the oracle by passing each of the value-register qubits as `tag_bits`:

```
prepare = build_polynomial_circuit(n_key, n_value, terms)

oracle = oracle_match_0_multi(
    n_key + n_value,
    [n_key + i for i in range(n_value)]
)

qc = grover_circuit(prepare, oracle, 1)
```

The resulting state is shown in figure 10.17.

	0 = 00	1 = 01	2 = 10	3 = 11
7 = 0111				
6 = 0110				
5 = 0101				
4 = 0100				
3 = 0011				
2 = 0010				
1 = 0001				
0 = 0000			▓	
−1 = 1111				
−2 = 1110				
−3 = 1101				
−4 = 1100				
−5 = 1011				
−6 = 1010				
−7 = 1001				
−8 = 1000				

Figure 10.17 The result of applying a Grover iteration to the quantum state encoding the function $f(k) = k^2 - 4$, for $0 \leq k < 4$, with an oracle that tags outcomes with 0 in the value register

We can use this method to efficiently find the 0s of our encoded function. As mentioned, in the next chapter we will learn how to search for minimum values.

Summary

- Integer key–value pairs, such as input–output pairs of a function, can be represented in a quantum state using two registers: a key register for inputs and a value register for outputs. The registers are entangled so that if a measurement is performed, the outcome will contain a key paired with its corresponding value.
- We can encode any polynomial function of an integer variable by representing it as a function of binary variables, a polynomial of binary variables. The terms of polynomials of binary variables are represented as a list of tuples in the implementation.
- The method is implemented with the following steps:
  - Create two registers with enough qubits to represent the inputs and outputs. Negative values are represented using Two's Complement.
  - Put the key register and value register in equal superposition.
  - Phase rotations are applied to the value register and controlled on the key register. This creates a state where the amplitudes of the outcomes with the same key form a geometric sequence that reflects the value corresponding to the key.
  - Apply the IQFT to the value register.
- After a function is encoded in a quantum state, all the input–output pairs have equal measurement probability.
- To find specific outcomes, such as inputs where the function is 0 or inputs where the output is negative, we can use Grover's algorithm.

Search-based quantum optimization

This chapter covers

- Searching for desired outcomes with Grover adaptive search
- Finding the maxima or minima of a polynomial function using a Grover optimizer
- A solution for the knapsack problem

Grover's algorithm can offer a quadratic speed increase (in the number of queries) over classical approaches for certain optimization problems. We have discussed using Grover operators in several contexts, including search, quantum counting, and amplitude estimation.

> **NOTE** Remember, to implement Grover's algorithm for a given operator A that prepares the quantum state to be searched and a quantum oracle O, we build the Grover operator G. Then we can use the operator G^jA to increase the probability of the outcomes tagged by the oracle, with a well-chosen integer $j > 0$.

In this chapter, we introduce a method called *Grover adaptive search* (GAS) that uses Grover's algorithm to solve optimization problems where the number of good outcomes is not known. We will use GAS to build a *Grover optimizer*, a *hybrid algorithm* that dynamically adjusts the number of iterations and the parameters of the circuit that prepares the state to be searched to efficiently find optimal solutions. Then we will use the Grover optimizer method to find a solution to the knapsack problem. The concepts introduced in this chapter are outlined in figure 11.1.

> **NOTE** A *hybrid algorithm* combines classical and quantum computational techniques to solve problems. Outcomes of the quantum computation are processed classically before the quantum computation is adjusted and repeated.

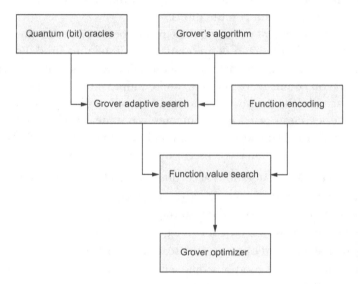

Figure 11.1 A dependency diagram of concepts covered in this chapter

11.1 Finding desired outcomes with Grover adaptive search

We learned how to increase the probability of measuring one or more desired outcomes of a quantum computation through the application of a number of Grover iterations. Repeatedly applying the Grover operator can increase the probability of measuring a desired outcome to 0.5 or higher.

In chapter 10, we used Grover's algorithm to search for desired function values. In these example problems, the operator A encoded input–output pairs of a function in a quantum state, and we applied a fixed, small number of Grover iterations.

The ideal number of the Grover iterations depends on the number of desired outcomes. However, in many contexts, the number of desired outcomes is not known. We can use the amplitude-estimation algorithm to count the good outcomes (using quantum counting), as discussed in chapter 9. However, amplitude estimation is a computationally expensive algorithm, especially for the currently available quantum hardware.

As in the Grover search algorithm, assume that we are given a circuit, A, that prepares a quantum state and a quantum oracle, O, that tags the desired outcomes, and we want to build the corresponding Grover operator G. Instead of using the ideal number of iterations, the *Grover adaptive search* method uses a schedule to try various numbers of iterations. We can use several methods to choose the number of iterations, including these:

- Randomly choosing from a range whose size increases exponentially[1]
- Using a fixed pattern (e.g., [0, 0, 0, 1, 1, 0, 1, 1, 2, 1, 2, 3, 1, 4, 5, 1, 6, 2, 7, 9, 11, 13, 16, 5, 20, 24, 28, 34, 2, 41, 49, 4, 60])[2]

These schedules offer theoretical efficiency guarantees that we will not cover here. Some schedules assume single-shot computations.

Note that zero iterations means not using the Grover operator but directly performing a measurement in the hope that a desired outcome will be measured. For ease of understanding, this chapter's implementations will use a simple version of a fixed schedule with just two iteration counts (zero and one) and multiple-shot computations.

In addition to a schedule for applying iterations, we need to define a stopping condition for ending the search in case a good outcome is not measured during the process (e.g., the number of failures to measure a good outcome). The GAS algorithm for finding a desired (good) outcome consists of the following steps:

1. Choose a number $r \geq 0$ of iterations according to the chosen schedule.
2. Prepare an initial quantum state using the circuit A, apply r iterations of the Grover operator G, and measure the resulting state.
3. Check whether the measured outcome is a good outcome.
    a. If the outcome is a good outcome, the search is complete.
    b. If the outcome is not a good outcome, check the stopping condition, which indicates whether it's worth continuing the search. If the condition is satisfied, give up on the search, inferring that there is no desired outcome. If the stopping condition is not satisfied, go back to step 1, choose the next value for r according to the chosen schedule, and repeat the steps.

This is a hybrid algorithm. Only step 2 involves a quantum computation; the rest are classical processing steps. Figure 11.2 outlines the steps of the GAS algorithm.

Let's look at the example of searching for nonnegative outputs of the function $f(k) = \_k^2 - 5$ defined for $k = 0, 1, 2, 3$. The function table showing inputs and outputs is shown in table 11.1.

---

[1] Boyer, Michel, et al. Tight bounds on quantum searching. *Fortschritte der Physik: Progress of Physics* 46(4–5): 493–505, 1998.
[2] Baritompa, William, et al. Grover's quantum algorithm applied to global optimization. *SIAM Journal on Optimization* 15(4): 1170–1184, 2005.

11.1 Finding desired outcomes with Grover adaptive search

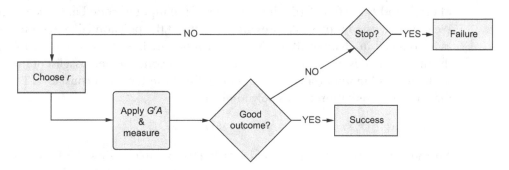

Figure 11.2 A flow diagram of Grover adaptive search

Table 11.1 Function table for the function $f(k) = k^2 - 5$ with $0 \leq k < 4$

k	$f(k) = k^2 - 5$
0	−5
1	−4
2	−1
3	4

We will represent this function as a polynomial of binary variables that can be encoded in a quantum state. Remember, we can write an integer k as a sum of powers of 2

$$k = \sum_{j=0}^{n-1} 2^j k_j$$

where, again, k_j (for $0 \leq j < n$) is the jth binary digit of k (starting from the right).

For $n = 2$, this expression becomes

$$k = \sum_{j=0}^{1} 2^j k_j = 2k_1 + k_0$$

and we can express k^2 as

$$k^2 = (2k_1 + k_0)(2k_1 + k_0) = 4k_1^2 + 4k_1 k_0 + k_0^2 = 4k_1 + 4k_1 k_0 + k_0$$

because the square of a binary digit is itself. To express the function $f(k) = k^2 - 5$ as a polynomial of $n = 2$ binary variables, we add the constant −5 to the previous expression of k^2:

$$p(k_0, k_1) = 4k_1 + 4k_1 k_0 + k_0 - 5$$

where k_0 and k_1 are 0 or 1 (the binary digits of the input encoded in the key register). We will use a list of tuples to represent the terms of the polynomial we want to encode, as introduced in chapter 10. Each term, or monomial, is expressed as a tuple where the first element is the term's coefficient and the second element is a list of the indices of the term's binary variables (or an empty list if the term is a constant). Therefore, the term representation of this polynomial is

```
terms = [(4, [1]), (4, [1, 0]), (1, [0]), (-5, [])]
```

Now we can encode our polynomial of binary variables using the function `build_polynomial_circuit` from chapter 10. We will use $n = 4$ value qubits to encode the outputs:

```
from sim_circuit import *
from algo import build_polynomial_circuit

n_key = 2
n_value = 4

qc = build_polynomial_circuit(n_key, n_value, terms)
```

Because some outputs of the function are negative, we will use the Two's Complement interpretation for the value register. Four qubits allow for the representation of integers between –8 and 7.

Remember from chapter 10 that we can set the third parameter of the `grid_state` function to `neg = True` to visualize negative values:

```
from util import grid_state

grid_state(qc.run(), n_key, neg = True, show_probs = False)
```

The resulting grid visualization is shown in figure 11.3.

We can now perform a measurement without applying the Grover operator. When the proportion of desired outcomes relative to the total number of outcomes is small, this measurement will likely not succeed in yielding a desired outcome. However, when we do not know the number of desired outcomes, it is a good idea to perform one or more measurements without any applications of the Grover operator.

To search for nonnegative outputs of a function, we use an oracle that matches outcomes that have 0 as the first digit in the value register. In the grid state visualizations, these outcomes will be in the top half of the grid representation of the quantum state. We can use the `oracle_match_0` function from chapter 10 to create this oracle. Remember that `oracle_match_0` takes the parameter `bits`, the total number of qubits in the circuit, and `tag_bit`, the position of the tag bit:

```
from algo import oracle_match_0

oracle = oracle_match_0(n_key + n_value, n_key + n_value - 1)
```

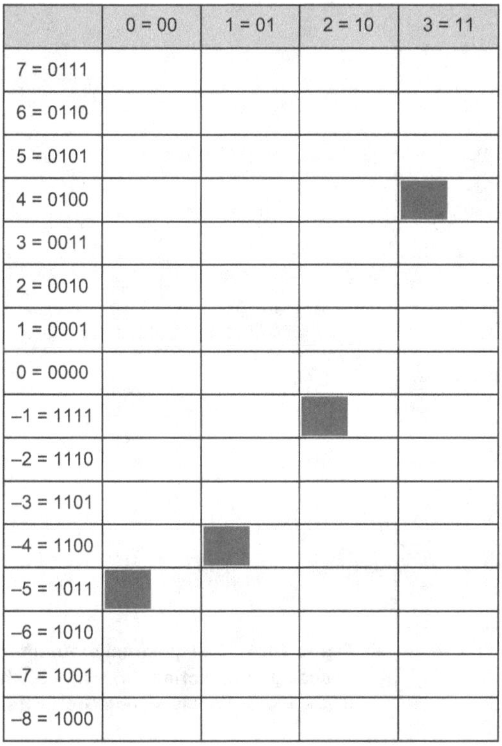

11.1 Finding desired outcomes with Grover adaptive search

	0 = 00	1 = 01	2 = 10	3 = 11
7 = 0111				
6 = 0110				
5 = 0101				
4 = 0100				■
3 = 0011				
2 = 0010				
1 = 0001				
0 = 0000				
−1 = 1111			■	
−2 = 1110				
−3 = 1101				
−4 = 1100		■		
−5 = 1011	■			
−6 = 1010				
−7 = 1001				
−8 = 1000				

Figure 11.3 The quantum state encoding the function $f(k) = k^2 - 5$ with $0 \leq k < 4$

Let's use this oracle to build the Grover operator (using the `grover_circuit` function from chapter 6) and apply one iteration:

```
from algo import grover_circuit

prepare = build_polynomial_circuit(n_key, n_value, terms)

qc = grover_circuit(prepare, oracle, 1)
```

The state after applying one iteration of this Grover operator is shown in figure 11.4. It has only one nonzero amplitude, and that amplitude corresponds to a nonnegative output value. Any measurement will successfully yield this nonnegative function value.

If we apply two iterations, we get a state with all outputs having equal probability, as shown in figure 11.5:

```
qc = grover_circuit(prepare, oracle, 2)
```

We will now use GAS to build a Grover optimizer that efficiently searches for optimal outcomes by further adapting computation parameters at each step.

	0 = 00	1 = 01	2 = 10	3 = 11
7 = 0111				
6 = 0110				
5 = 0101				
4 = 0100				▓
3 = 0011				
2 = 0010				
1 = 0001				
0 = 0000				
−1 = 1111				
−2 = 1110				
−3 = 1101				
−4 = 1100				
−5 = 1011				
−6 = 1010				
−7 = 1001				
−8 = 1000				

Figure 11.4 The quantum state after encoding the function $f(k) = k^2 - 5$ with $0 \leq k < 4$ and applying one Grover iteration

	0 = 00	1 = 01	2 = 10	3 = 11
7 = 0111				
6 = 0110				
5 = 0101				
4 = 0100				▓
3 = 0011				
2 = 0010				
1 = 0001				
0 = 0000				
−1 = 1111			▓	
−2 = 1110				
−3 = 1101				
−4 = 1100		▓		
−5 = 1011	▓			
−6 = 1010				
−7 = 1001				
−8 = 1000				

Figure 11.5 The quantum state encoding the function $f(k) = k^2 - 5$ with $0 \leq k < 4$ after applying two Grover iterations

11.2 Finding optimal outcomes with the Grover optimizer

We will use the function-encoding method introduced in chapter 10 to incrementally encode adjusted versions of a given function to search for lower and lower (or higher and higher) function values. This method, which we refer to as a *Grover optimizer*, allows us to efficiently find the global minimum or maximum of a given function.

As illustrated in the flow diagram in figure 11.6, we start with an operator A that prepares the quantum state to be searched and a Grover operator G that is applied according to a chosen schedule. We use the result of each search to update the parameters and configuration of the circuit A.

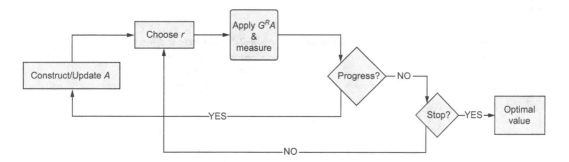

Figure 11.6 A flow chart of the Grover optimizer

Let's walk through the steps of an example problem using the Grover optimizer method. In this example, we want to find the maximum of the function

$$f(k) = -(k-3)^2 + 3$$

where $0 \leq k < 8$. The graph of this function has the shape of an upside-down parabola.

In this example, the circuit A that prepares the quantum state will be the function-encoding circuit for a given function f, which we will denote by A_f. As illustrated in the flow diagram in figure 11.6, if we get a good outcome, we update the encoded function f for the next iteration so the oracle will tag outcomes that will yield a better result than the one we just found.

We will perform successive searches to arrive at the maximum value. At each step, we will decrease the number of search candidates by adjusting the function encoded in the quantum state.

Let's start with the first step, as shown in figure 11.7: constructing the circuit A_f that encodes the function f. The inputs and outputs of the function are shown in table 11.2.

We will use $n = 3$ qubits for the key register to represent integer inputs $0 \leq k < 8$ and $m = 6$ qubits for the value register to represent the outputs using Two's Complement:

```
n_key = 3
n_value = 6
```

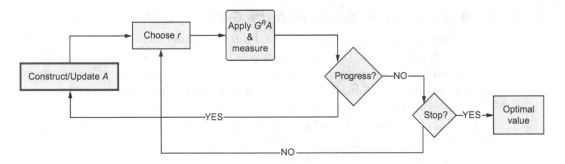

Figure 11.7 Construct or update the circuit A. These parameters are updated based on the results of the previous search.

Table 11.2 Function table for the function $f(k) = -(k-3)^2 + 3$, where $0 \le k < 8$

k	$f(k) = -(k-3)^2 + 3$
0	−6
1	−1
2	2
3	3
4	2
5	−1
6	−6
7	−13

We will express the function as a polynomial of binary variables. First we can rewrite the function as

$$f(k) = -k^2 + 6k - 6$$

We can use the expansion of k for $n = 3$ as a sum of powers of 2 to express k^2 as a polynomial of binary variables

$$\begin{aligned} k^2 &= (4k_2 + 2k_1 + k_0)^2 \\ &= (4k_2 + 2k_1 + k_0)(4k_2 + 2k_1 + k_0) \\ &= 16k_2 + 4k_1 + k_0 + 16k_2k_1 + 8k_2k_0 + 4k_1k_0 \end{aligned}$$

where k_0, k_1, and k_2 are the binary digits of k. To represent the term $-k^2$, we use the expression of k^2 and multiply it by -1:

$$-k^2 = -16k_2 - 4k_1 - k_0 - 16k_2k_1 - 8k_2k_0 - 4k_1k_0$$

To represent the term $6k$, we use the expression of k as a polynomial of binary variables and multiply it by 6:

$$6k = 24k_2 + 12k_1 + 6k_0$$

We combine these terms and add the constant -6 to arrive at the representation of the function f as the polynomial of binary variables:

$$p(k_0, k_1, k_2) = 8k_2 + 8k_1 + 5k_0 - 16k_2k_1 - 8k_2k_0 - 4k_1k_0 - 6$$

The list of tuples for the terms of binary variables is as follows:

```
terms = [(8, [2]), (8, [1]), (5, [0]), (-16, [1, 2]), (-8, [0, 2]), (-4, [0, 1]),
    (-6, [])]
```

We can check that these terms are correct using the `poly` function defined in the chapter code. This function takes the parameters `n_key` (the number of qubits in the key register), the list of `terms`, and an optional `print` parameter. We can assert that each output of the polynomial of binary variables is equal to the output of the function using the following code:

```
from util import poly

p = poly(n_key, terms, False)
f = lambda k: -(k - 3)**2 + 3

for k in range(len(p)):
    assert(p[k] == f(k))
```

> **Representing any function as a polynomial of binary variables**
>
> When the number of inputs is large, it is helpful to use Python list comprehensions to create the list of tuples corresponding to the terms of the binary polynomial to be encoded. We can write an integer k as a sum of powers of 2
>
> $$k = \sum_{j=0}^{n-1} 2^j k_j$$
>
> where k_j (for $0 \leq j < n$) is the jth binary digit of k and therefore is either 0 or 1. Using this formula, we can express a term ck, where c is a constant, with this Python list comprehension
>
> ```
> [(c*2**j, [j]) for j in range(n_key)]
> ```
>
> where `n_key` is the number of binary digits for representing function inputs.

> **(continued)**
> Similarly, we can express k^2 as
>
> $$k^2 = \left(\sum_{j=0}^{n-1} 2^j k_j\right)^2 = \sum_{j=0}^{n-1} (2^j k_j)^2 + 2\sum_{j<l} 2^j k_j 2^l k_l$$
>
> $$= \sum_{j=0}^{n-1} 2^{2j} k_j + \sum_{0 \le j < l < n} 2^{j+l+1} k_j k_l$$
>
> where we again use the fact that $k_j^2 = k_j$ for $0 \le j < n$.
>
> We can express a term ck^2, where c is a constant, with this Python list comprehension:
>
> ```
> [(c*2**(2*j), [j]) for j in range(n_key)] + [(c*2**(j+l+1), [j, l]) for
>     j in range(n_key) for l in range(n_key) if j < l]
> ```

Let's create the circuit that encodes the function f in a quantum state using the variables defined previously:

```
qc = build_polynomial_circuit(n_key, n_value, terms)
```

The resulting state is illustrated as a grid in figure 11.8.

> **NOTE** Throughout the rest of the chapter, we will use a compact version of the grid state visualization like the one in figure 11.8.

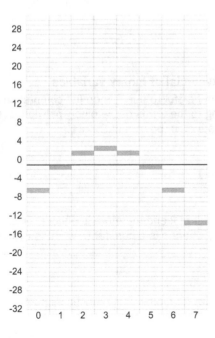

Figure 11.8 The grid state representation of the quantum state encoding the function $f(k) = -(k-3)^2 + 3$

We will use a Python dictionary, `flow_state`, to keep track of the flow state while progressing through the steps. The items in the dictionary include the following:

- `last_good_outcome_results`—The best result so far, typically the outcome and the corresponding value. In this example, we start with `(None, -1)` because we are searching for the maximum value.
- `failure_count`—Count of the number of search steps performed where no progress was made. We can use this variable in the stop condition.
- `circuit_params`—A dictionary with the parameters used to build the circuit A. These parameters may be changed from step to step. In this example, the dictionary contains the two-qubit registers (key and value) and the terms representing the function to be encoded in the state.
- `initial_circuit_params`—A copy of the dictionary with the initial circuit parameters:

```
import copy

circuit_params = {'n_key': n_key, 'n_value': n_value, 'terms': terms}
flow_state = {
    'last_good_outcome_results': (None, -1),
    'failure_count': 0,
    'circuit_params': circuit_params,
    'initial_circuit_params': copy.deepcopy(circuit_params)
}
```

We also need to define a stop condition. In this example, we will use the number of failures (`failure_count`):

```
stopping_condition = lambda flow_state: flow_state['failure_count'] > 7
```

Next we need to choose the number of Grover iterations $r \geq 0$ to perform at each step according to the selected schedule (figure 11.9). In this example, we will use the schedule [0, 1] for applying the Grover operator.

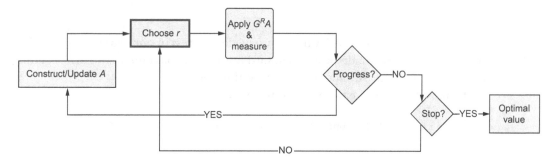

Figure 11.9 Choose the number of iterations $r \geq 0$ to be performed at each step according to the selected schedule.

CHAPTER 11 *Search-based quantum optimization*

Now we will build the Grover operator circuit, apply the appropriate number of iterations according to the schedule, and measure the state (see figure 11.10). We build a Grover operator circuit using the circuit that prepares the quantum state to be searched for optimal values, and an oracle.

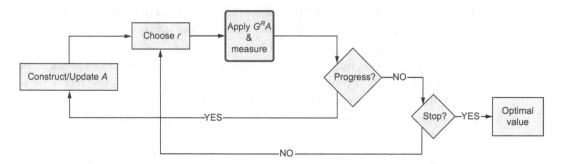

Figure 11.10 Apply the Grover operator G'A, where *r* is the number of iterations according to the chosen schedule.

The maximum value of the function that has at least one nonnegative value has to be nonnegative. To search for nonnegative values, we use an oracle that tags the outcomes with 0 in the first digit of the value register:

```
prepare = build_polynomial_circuit(n_key, n_value, terms)

oracle = oracle_match_0(n_key + n_value, n_key + n_value - 1)
```

Let's start with $r = 0$, meaning no Grover iterations are applied. We will simulate 100 measurements of this circuit:

```
qc = grover_circuit(prepare, oracle, 0)

shots = 100
result = qc.measure(shots = shots)
```

We can use the results to check whether we made progress in our search (figure 11.11). To check whether we made progress toward finding the maximum, we start by getting the most-frequent measurement outcome at this step.

The most frequent measurement outcome is

```
outcome = max(result['counts'].items(), key = lambda k: k[1])[0]
```

11.2 Finding optimal outcomes with the Grover optimizer

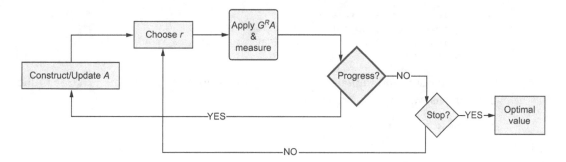

Figure 11.11 Check whether the result of this search is better than the result in the previous step (or the default value).

We can use the following function to get the input–output pair that this outcome corresponds to:

```
from util import padded_bin

def process_outcome(outcome, state):
    binary_string = padded_bin(n_key + n_value, outcome)
    k = int(binary_string[n_value:], 2)
    v = int(binary_string[:n_value], 2)

    if v >= 2**(n_value - 1):
        v = v - 2**n_value

    v -= (
        state['circuit_params']['terms'][0][0] -
        state['initial_circuit_params']['terms'][0][0]
    )

    assert(v == p[k])
    return (k, v)
```

Note that we have an equal likelihood of getting any of the encoded input–output pairs at this step because we did not apply a Grover operator:

```
outcome_results = process_outcome(outcome, flow_state)
print(outcome_results)
```

In this particular run, the output shows this input–output pair:

```
(5, -1)
```

Keep in mind that you may get a different result each time you run the code.

We will use the `progress` function to check whether the outcome is better than the previous result:

```
def progress(results, state):
    if state['last_good_outcome_results'][1]:
        return results[1] > state['last_good_outcome_results'][1]
    return True
```

We set the last found value to be –1 for the first step. In this case, the `progress` function returns `False`:

```
progress(outcome_results, flow_state)
```

```
False
```

So we increase the `failure_count` variable as we failed to make progress:

```
flow_state['failure_count'] += 1
```

Now we check whether the stop condition is satisfied (figure 11.12):

```
stopping_condition(flow_state)
```

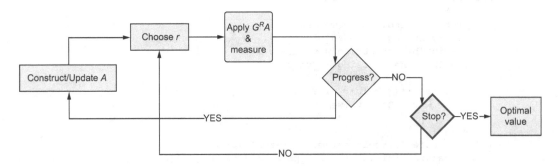

Figure 11.12 If progress was not made, check the stop condition.

The stop condition is not satisfied, so we will perform one Grover iteration ($r = 1$):

```
qc = grover_circuit(prepare, oracle, 1)
```

The state at this step is shown in figure 11.13.
Let's take 100 simulated measurements of this circuit:

```
shots = 100
result = qc.measure(shots = shots)
```

Now we will check whether this outcome is higher than our previous best value (figure 11.14). Again, we look at the input–output pair that the most frequent outcome corresponds to:

```
outcome = max(result['counts'].items(), key = lambda k: k[1])[0]
```

```
outcome_results = process_outcome(outcome, state)
```

11.2 Finding optimal outcomes with the Grover optimizer

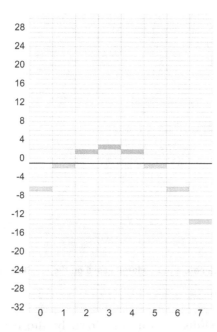

Figure 11.13 The grid state representation of the quantum state encoding the function $f(k) = -(k-3)^2 + 3$ and applying one Grover iteration

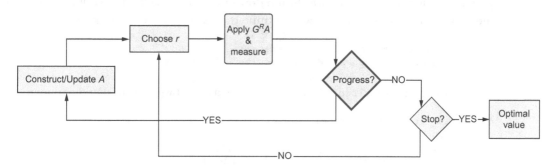

Figure 11.14 Check whether the result of this search is better than the result in the previous step (or the default value).

In this example, we get the input–output pair (3,3). This is a higher value than the previous best value, so the progress function returns True:

```
progress(outcome_results, flow_state)
```

As shown in the flow diagram in figure 11.15, if there is progress, we update the parameters of the encoded function and reconstruct the circuit to prepare the state. We will use the update_circuit_params function to update the parameters of the circuit A:

```
def update_circuit_params(outcome_results, flow_state):
    circuit_params = flow_state['circuit_params']
    k, v = outcome_results
```

```
t = circuit_params['terms']
t[0] = (t[0][0] - v - 1, [])
print('\n-----------------------')
print('New free term:', t[0][0])
```

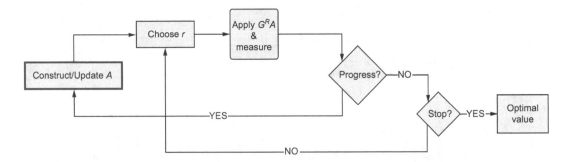

Figure 11.15 Construct or update the circuit A. These parameters are updated based on the results of the previous search.

The `update_circuit_params` function shifts the outputs down by the new value plus 1. In this case, all values are shifted down by 4 (because 3 + 1 = 4). We do this so the new value becomes −1, and we continue the search for nonnegative values:

```
if progress(outcome_results, flow_state):
    update_circuit_params(outcome_results, flow_state)
```

We will use the `build_circuit` function to create a circuit with the updated parameters:

```
def build_circuit(flow_state):
    return build_polynomial_circuit(
        flow_state['circuit_params']['n_key'],
        flow_state['circuit_params']['n_value'],
        flow_state['circuit_params']['terms']
    )
```

Next we encode the updated function and repeat the iteration schedule, starting with no Grover iterations:

```
prepare = build_circuit(flow_state)

oracle = oracle_match_0(n_key + n_value, n_key + n_value - 1)

qc = grover_circuit(prepare, oracle, 0)
```

The state at this step is shown in figure 11.16. Let's simulate 100 measurements of this state:

```
shots = 100
result = qc.measure(shots = shots)
```

11.2 Finding optimal outcomes with the Grover optimizer

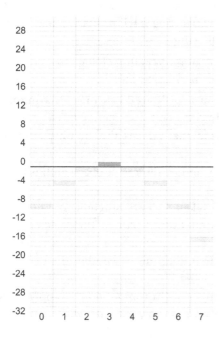

Figure 11.16 The grid state representation of the quantum state encoding the function $f(k) = -(k-3)^2 + 3$ shifted by -4

Now let's check whether we made progress toward finding the maximum:

```
outcome = max(result['counts'].items(), key = lambda k: k[1])[0]
outcome_results = process_outcome(outcome, state)

if progress(outcome_results, state):
    update_circuit_params(outcome_results, state['circuit_params'])
```

The progress function returns False, and we increase the failure count:

```
flow_state['failure_count'] += 1
```

The steps continue until the failure count triggers the stop condition (figure 11.17). In this small example, by examining the values in the function table, we know that 3 is the maximum value.

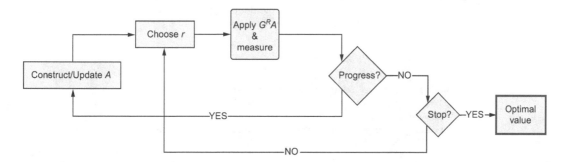

Figure 11.17 Once the stop condition is met, the optimal value is returned.

The `grover_optimizer` function defined in listing 11.1 performs these steps for a given problem. The function takes the following parameters:

- `circuit_params`—A dictionary with parameters that change from step to step
- `build_circuit`—A function that creates the circuit A
- `oracle`—A circuit for the oracle that tags desired outcomes (having nonnegative integers in the value and weight registers)
- `update_circuit_params`—A function that adjusts the circuit parameters and configuration
- `progress`—A function that checks whether the result of a search is better than the previous best result
- `process_outcome`—A function that takes a binary outcome and decomposes it into meaningful parts (e.g., the input–output pair or the selection, its value, and its weight)
- `stopping_condition`—A function that determines whether the process should stop
- `schedule`—A sequence with the number of Grover iterations to apply at each step
- `starting_result`—The starting input–output pair to which results will be compared

Listing 11.1 Function to implement the Grover optimizer

```
def grover_optimizer(
    circuit_params,
    build_circuit,
    oracle,
    update_circuit_params,
    progress,
    process_outcome,
    stopping_condition=lambda flow_state: flow_state['failure_count'] > 7,
    schedule=[0, 1],
    starting_result=(None, -1)
):
    flow_state = {
        'last_good_outcome_results': starting_result,
        'failure_count': 0,
        'initial_circuit_params': copy.deepcopy(circuit_params),
        'circuit_params': circuit_params
    }

    shots = 100

    def update(outcome_results, flow_state):
        flow_state['last_good_outcome_results'] = outcome_results
        flow_state['failure_count'] = 0
        update_circuit_params(outcome_results, flow_state)

    done = False
    counter = 0
```

11.2 Finding optimal outcomes with the Grover optimizer

```
while not done:
    counter += 1
    for r in schedule:
        print('\niteration', r)
        function = build_circuit(flow_state)
        qc = grover_circuit(function, oracle, r)

        result = qc.measure(shots=shots)
        flow_state['last_run_result'] = result

        outcome = max(
            result['counts'].items(),
            key=lambda k: k[1]
        )[0]

        outcome_results = process_outcome(outcome, flow_state)

        if progress(outcome_results, flow_state):
            print('progress', outcome_results)
            update(outcome_results, flow_state)
            break
        else:
            flow_state['failure_count'] += 1
            print('failure', outcome_results)

            if stopping_condition(flow_state):
                print(
                    '\nSTOPPING WITH OUTCOME RESULTS',
                    flow_state['last_good_outcome_results']
                )
                done = True
                break

return flow_state['last_good_outcome_results']
```

Let's use this function to solve our example problem:

```
n_key = 3
n_value = 6

terms = [
    (8, [2]),
    (8, [1]),
    (5, [0]),
    (-16, [1, 2]),
    (-8, [0, 2]),
    (-4, [0, 1]),
    (-6, [])
]

grover_optimizer(
    {
        'n_key': n_key,
        'n_value': n_value,
```

```
        'terms': terms
    },
    build_circuit,
    oracle,
    update_circuit_params,
    progress,
    process_outcome
)
```

The printed output is shown next. Unlike in the previous example, progress is made in the first step. Seven more steps are performed without progress before the stop condition is met and the optimal result is returned:

```
iteration 0
progress (2, 2)

-----------------------
New free term: -9

iteration 0
failure (1, -1)

iteration 1
progress (3, 3)

-----------------------
New free term: -13

iteration 0
failure (5, -1)

iteration 1
failure (2, 2)

iteration 0
failure (1, -1)

iteration 1
failure (6, -6)

iteration 0
failure (5, -1)

iteration 1
failure (3, 3)

iteration 0
failure (3, 3)

iteration 1
failure (4, 2)

STOPPING WITH OUTCOME RESULTS (3, 3)
```

> **Exercise 11.1**
> Use the `grover_optimizer` function defined in listing 11.1 to find the minimum of the function $f(k) = -(k-3)^2 + 3$, where $0 \leq k < 8$.

11.3 Solving the knapsack problem with a Grover optimizer

We will use the example knapsack problem that we looked at in chapters 2 and 10. As a quick reminder, in our example problem, we have three items with the values and weights shown in table 11.3, and a maximum weight capacity of 4.

Table 11.3 The items, weights, and values for the example knapsack problem

Item label	Value	Weight
0	2 ($2,000)	3
1	3 ($3,000)	2
2	1 ($1,000)	1

We can express the value and weight of each selection using linear functions of binary variables

$$v(k_0, k_1, k_2) = 2k_0 + 3k_1 + k_2$$
$$w(k_0, k_1, k_2) = 3k_0 + 2k_1 + k_2$$

where k_0, k_1, and k_2 are binary variables indicating whether an item is included in the knapsack.

In chapter 10, we showed how to encode item selections, their values, and their weights. Now we have all the building blocks we need to use the Grover optimizer method to solve the knapsack problem. Let's look at the components of the Grover optimizer used for this problem.

11.3.1 Preparing the state

We use three registers to encode each of the possible selections and the weight and value of each selection (figure 11.18). Let's define the size of each register:

```
n_key = 3
n_value = 3
n_weight = 4
```

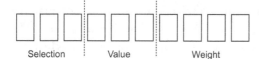

Figure 11.18 Three registers encoding an item selection, its total value, and its total weight for solving the knapsack problem

We can use a list of tuples to represent these value and weight functions:

```
v = [(2, [0]), (3, [1]), (1, [2])]

w = [(3, [0]), (2, [1]), (1, [2])]
```

The `build_knapsack_circuit` function creates a circuit with three registers (with the given sizes n_key, n_value, and n_weight) and encodes the given value and weight functions (v and w, respectively):

```
from algo import encode_term

def build_knapsack_circuit(n_key, n_value, n_weight, v, w):
    key = QuantumRegister(n_key)
    value = QuantumRegister(n_value)
    weight = QuantumRegister(n_weight)
    circuit = QuantumCircuit(key, value, weight)

    for i in range(len(key)):
        circuit.h(key[i])

    for i in range(len(value)):
        circuit.h(value[i])

    for i in range(len(weight)):
        circuit.h(weight[i])

    for (term, vars) in v:                                  ◁── Encodes the
        encode_term(term, vars, circuit, key, value)             value function

    circuit.iqft(value[::-1], swap=False)

    for (term, vars) in w:                                  ◁── Encodes the
        encode_term(term, vars, circuit, key, weight)            weight function

    circuit.iqft(weight[::-1], swap=False)

    return circuit
```

Let's create the starting circuit:

```
qc = build_knapsack_circuit(n_key, n_value, n_weight, v, w)
```

The resulting state is shown in figure 11.19. The outcomes corresponding to each possible selection have equal probability (and all other outcomes have a probability of 0).

11.3.2 Encoding constraints

To encode the constraint that the weight of a selection is less than or equal to 4, we will adjust the encoded weight function to $w' = 4 - w$ so that the integer encoded in the weight register will be nonnegative for selections that meet the weight requirement

11.3 Solving the knapsack problem with a Grover optimizer

Selection	Value	Weight	Direction	Magnitude	Amplitude bar	Probability
000	0	0	−0.00°	0.35		0.12
001	2	3	0.00°	0.35		0.12
010	3	2	−0.00°	0.35		0.12
011	5	5	0.00°	0.35		0.12
100	1	1	0.00°	0.35		0.12
101	3	4	−0.00°	0.35		0.12
110	4	3	−0.00°	0.35		0.12
111	6	6	0.00°	0.35		0.12

Figure 11.19 A quantum state after encoding the values and weights of each possible selection

($w' \geq 0$). This way, our oracle will tag selections with a total weight of 4 or less. We adjust the terms using the following code:

```
w = [(3, [0]), (2, [1]), (1, [2])]
max_weight = 4

w_adjusted = [(max_weight, [])] + [(-item[0], item[1]) for item in w]
```

Similarly, we adjust the encoded value function. We can see that the most valuable item has a value of 3, and its weight is less than the allowed capacity. This information helps us restrict the search to selections that have a combined value of at least 3. We will shift the values down by 3 by adjusting the value function ($v' = v - 3$) so that the integer encoded in the value register for the desired selections will be nonnegative ($v' \geq 0$). We adjust the terms using the following code:

```
values = [2, 3, 1]
v = [(2, [0]), (3, [1]), (1, [2])]

v_adjusted = [(-max(values), [])] + v
```

> **NOTE** The number of qubits in the key register is the number of items. Because we know the maximum weight of desired selections, we can choose the size of the weight register to accommodate this weight. How do we choose the number of qubits for the value register? If the register is not large enough, the integer encoded in the register will be the remainder of the division of the value by 2^n, where n is the number of qubits in the register. Fortunately, we can detect if the register is not large enough, and we can increase the number of qubits. For the small example in this chapter, we use registers that are large enough to accommodate all integers that will be encoded at all steps of the algorithm. In general, we might need to adjust the number of qubits used to represent the adjusted weights and values.

11.3.3 Defining the parameters of the Grover optimizer

We will use the `grover_optimizer` function defined in the previous section to implement the solution to this problem. To do that, we need to define the arguments that will be passed to it.

Using the adjusted value and weight encoding, we can use an efficient oracle that tags outcomes that have 0 as the first digit in both the value and weight registers. We can use the function `oracle_match_0_multi` defined in chapter 10 to create this oracle:

```
from algo import oracle_match_0_multi

oracle = oracle_match_0_multi(
    n_key + n_value + n_weight,
    [
        n_key + n_value - 1,
        n_key + n_value + n_weight - 1
    ]
)
```

We will use the `build_circuit` function to create the circuit to encode the selections and their corresponding values and weights:

```
def build_circuit(flow_state):
    return build_knapsack_circuit(
        flow_state['circuit_params']['n_key'],
        flow_state['circuit_params']['n_value'],
        flow_state['circuit_params']['n_weight'],
        flow_state['circuit_params']['v'],
        flow_state['circuit_params']['w']
    )
```

To interpret the measurement outcome at each step, we will use the `process_outcome` function, which takes the binary outcome and returns the selection that the outcome corresponds to and the weight and value of the selection:

```
def process_outcome(outcome, flow_state):
    n = (
        flow_state['circuit_params']['n_key'] +
        flow_state['circuit_params']['n_value'] +
        flow_state['circuit_params']['n_weight']
    )
    outcome_selection = padded_bin(n, outcome)[-n_key:]
    outcome_value = get_selection_value(outcome_selection, v)
    outcome_weight = get_selection_weight(outcome_selection, w)
    return outcome_selection, outcome_value, outcome_weight
```

To check whether there is progress, we will use this function:

```
def progress(results, flow_state):
    outcome_selection, outcome_value, outcome_weight = results
    min_value = flow_state['circuit_params']['min_value']
    return (outcome_value >= min_value) and (outcome_weight <= max_weight)
```

11.3 Solving the knapsack problem with a Grover optimizer

The `update_circuit_params` function shifts the value function to search for selections with values higher than the current best selection at a given step, and the `action_on_progress` function prints useful information about each step (the complete definition can be found in the book's code repository):

```
def update_circuit_params(outcome_results, flow_state):
    circuit_params = flow_state['circuit_params']
    outcome_selection, outcome_value, outcome_weight = outcome_results
    v = circuit_params['v']

    v[0] = (-outcome_value - 1, [])

    circuit_params['min_value'] = outcome_value + 1
    action_on_progress(flow_state)
```

Now we are ready to use the `grover_optimizer` function. Note that in the second parameter, we include the minimum value to look for:

```
grover_optimizer(
    {
        'n_key': n_key,
        'n_value': n_value,
        'n_weight': n_weight,
        'v': v_adjusted,
        'w': w_adjusted,
        'min_value': min_value
    },
    build_circuit,
    oracle,
    update_circuit_params,
    progress,
    process_outcome,
    stopping_condition=lambda flow_state: flow_state['failure_count'] > 3
)
```

The implementation starts by looking for selections with a maximum weight of 4 and a minimum value of 3 (`min_value`). When we don't apply any iteration of the Grover operator, we have an equal likelihood of measuring each of the possible selections. In this particular run, we get '000':

```
iteration 0
failure ('000', 0, 0)
```

Next, one Grover iteration is applied (according to the schedule). The state prepared at this step is shown in figure 11.20.

In this particular run, we get the selection register outcome '010'. The value of this selection is 3, and the weight is 2:

```
iteration 1
progress ('010', 3, 2)
```

Selection	Value	Weight	Direction	Magnitude	Amplitude bar	Probability
000	0	0	–0.00°	0.18		0.03
001	2	3	0.00°	0.18		0.03
010	3	2	180.00°	0.53		0.28
011	5	5	0.00°	0.18		0.03
100	1	1	–0.00°	0.18		0.03
101	3	4	180.00°	0.53		0.28
110	4	3	180.00°	0.53		0.28
111	6	6	0.00°	0.18		0.03

Figure 11.20 The selection register outcome probabilities after looking for selections with a maximum weight of 4 and a minimum value of 3

After this step, we try increasing the minimum value to see if we can find a solution with a higher value than the best solution at this step. We increase the minimum value from 3 to 4 and update the parameters of the circuit that prepares the state to be searched. Now we apply Grover iterations according to the schedule and analyze the results (figure 11.21):

```
Looking for values >=  {4}

iteration 0
failure ('010', 3, 2)

iteration 1
progress ('110', 4, 3)
```

Selection	Value	Weight	Direction	Magnitude	Amplitude bar	Probability
000	0	0	180.00°	0.18		0.03
001	2	3	–180.00°	0.18		0.03
010	3	2	180.00°	0.18		0.03
011	5	5	–180.00°	0.18		0.03
100	1	1	–180.00°	0.18		0.03
101	3	4	–180.00°	0.18		0.03
110	4	3	180.00°	0.88		0.78
111	6	6	–180.00°	0.18		0.03

Figure 11.21 The selection register outcome probabilities after looking for selections with a maximum weight of 4 and a minimum value of 4

We continue to perform more steps until the stop condition is satisfied:

```
Looking for values >=  {5}

iteration 0
failure ('111', 6, 6)

iteration 1
failure ('000', 0, 0)

iteration 0
failure ('010', 3, 2)

iteration 1
failure ('000', 0, 0)

STOPPING WITH OUTCOME RESULTS ('110', 4, 3)
('110', 4, 3)
```

> **Exercise 11.2**
> Pass a different schedule to `grover_optimizer` to solve the knapsack problem, such as the schedule mentioned previously: [0, 0, 0, 1, 1, 0, 1, 1, 2, 1, 2, 3, 1, 4, 5, 1, 6, 2, 7, 9, 11, 13, 16, 5, 20, 24, 28, 34, 2, 41, 49, 4, 60].[a]
>
> [a] Baritompa, William, et al. Grover's quantum algorithm applied to global optimization. *SIAM Journal on Optimization*, 15(4): 1170–1184, 2005.

Note that we can use a hybrid approach, where a value found with classical methods can be used as the starting point for the Grover optimizer to find a better value.

Summary

- Grover adaptive search can be used to solve optimization problems when the number of good outcomes is unknown:
    - It uses schedules to determine how many Grover iterations to try at each step, such as random sequences or fixed patterns.
    - It requires a stop condition, which can be based on the number of consecutive failures to find better solutions.
    - It can be used to build a Grover optimizer: a hybrid algorithm that dynamically adjusts the number of iterations and the parameters of the circuit that prepares the state to be searched to efficiently find optimal solutions.
- When searching for maximum or minimum values of a function using the Grover optimizer, the parameters of the encoded function are updated after each successful measurement to restrict the search space to better solutions.
- The key to an efficient Grover optimizer is using an efficient underlying oracle. For example, we can search for negative or nonnegative integers with oracles using the Two's Complement interpretation.

Conclusions and outlook

This chapter covers
- Reviewing essential quantum computing concepts introduced throughout the book
- The importance of the butterfly computing pattern
- Running experiments on real quantum computers
- An overview of additional quantum solutions, including optimization problems and Shor's algorithm

This book is designed to be a foundational resource for quantum computing developers. With the knowledge you gained throughout the book, you are better equipped to design and implement quantum solutions.

In this chapter, we will review (and expand on) important concepts introduced in the book. We will also briefly discuss some areas that are beyond the scope of this book but are important to be aware of, such as encoding and optimizing polynomials with noninteger coefficients and factorization using Shor's algorithm.

12.1 Quantum concepts in review

Quantum computing can be used to solve specific problems in areas like truly random sampling, optimization, and machine learning. Quantum approaches can speed up or improve the quality of certain classical solutions, and quantum computing applications will likely be specialized computations used in conjunction with classical computing. To become a successful adopter of quantum computing solutions, a strong understanding of what quantum computers can and cannot do is necessary.

12.1.1 Quantum readiness

Both quantum hardware and quantum software are essential to unlock the full potential of quantum computing. Even before large-scale quantum hardware becomes available, we can proactively identify and analyze technical and business problems that could benefit from a quantum approach. This strategy allows us to build a robust foundation for future quantum applications and become "quantum ready."

The evolution of neural networks serves as an analogue for the progress of quantum computing. In the early days of neural networks, research was primarily theoretical due to the limited computational power that was available. Later advancements in computer hardware enabled large-scale implementation, and those who were prepared benefited greatly. Even though some aspects of deep learning are not fully understood theoretically, they have still been successfully applied to real-world problems. Quantum computing is showing promise in specific areas, such as optimization, and it will be beneficial to be quantum ready when quantum hardware is widely accessible.

12.1.2 Quantum advantage and its limitations

Throughout the book, we have discussed quantum parallelism and measurement as the superpowers of quantum computing. Quantum parallelism can be thought of as instant multiplication of matrices that have a specific structure. This structure imposes limitations on the types of problems that can benefit from quantum parallelism. Quantum solutions need to align with this structure.

In chapter 7, we saw how quantum parallelism makes quantum Fourier transforms (QFTs) more efficient than their classical counterpart. Additionally, we saw how quantum parallelism facilitates the efficient encoding of geometric sequence states, where each qubit contributes a rotation, and rotations interfere to create the final result.

Quantum measurement enables efficient sampling from the probability distributions defined by quantum states. The way we interpret measurement counts depends on the problem to be solved. For example, in Grover's algorithm, we amplify the magnitudes of desired outcomes and therefore their probability of being measured so that we can find the desired outcomes upon measurement.

In chapter 1, we discussed three main patterns for quantum computations:

- *Sampling from probability distributions*—Throughout the book, we implemented useful distributions (binomial, raised cosine, normal approximation) for truly random sampling.
- *Searching for specific outcomes*—We learned how to implement a quantum search and looked at several examples, including the knapsack problem and finding the minima or maxima of a given function.
- *Estimating the probability of specific outcomes*—We did this in chapter 9 using quantum amplitude estimation.

12.2 Building quantum software and running on real quantum computers

This book is meant to provide you with the necessary knowledge to understand and adopt various quantum computing tools. We provide tools to seamlessly convert the simulator code to Qiskit to run on quantum hardware. The building blocks of our simulator can easily be translated into other languages; for example, a JavaScript version of our quantum simulator is included in the book's repository.

12.2.1 The importance of a fast, flexible quantum simulator

The core concepts of quantum computing are relatively easy to represent with classical code, as we have shown in this book. It only takes a couple hundred lines of code to create a functioning quantum computing simulator. This is similar to how students of deep learning start by implementing neural networks from scratch, which is one of the best ways to learn. However, quantum computing simulators are used for more than learning purposes. To experiment with existing algorithms and create new ones, it is essential to have a flexible simulator.

Simulating quantum circuits classically is computationally expensive. Often, quantum computations are simulated with large matrix operations. In some cases, we want to take shortcuts to cut down on the computational complexity of simulating specific quantum operations.

For example, a (phase) oracle multiplies the amplitudes of desired outcomes by –1. This is straightforward to implement in a simulator without using quantum gates. Additionally, the quantum Fourier transform can be implemented in a simulator using the fast Fourier transform (FFT) instead of quantum gates.

12.2.2 Source-level compatibility between Hume and Qiskit

Throughout the book, we have built a quantum computing simulator called Hume. The complete implementation of Hume can be found in the src/hume directory in the book's companion repository.

The syntax for writing quantum circuits using Hume closely matches that of Qiskit. This is intentional, as Qiskit is among the most popular quantum computing SDKs. Our implementation is simpler than Qiskit's for ease of understanding and is designed for better performance.

12.2 Building quantum software and running on real quantum computers

We made some choices that differ from Qiskit's design. For example, we added methods for the QFT and inverse QFT (IQFT) in the QuantumCircuit class. Additionally, we use the method c_append to append a circuit to a register with controlled transformations. To achieve source-level compatibility between Hume and Qiskit, we enhanced Qiskit's QuantumCircuit class with the same functionality using the following code, which you can find in the hume/qiskit/__init__.py file in the book's companion repository:

```python
from collections import Counter
from random import choices

from qiskit import QuantumCircuit
from qiskit.circuit.add_control import add_control
from qiskit.circuit.library import QFT
from qiskit.quantum_info import Statevector


def run(self):
    return Statevector(self).data

def c_append(self, U, c, q):
    cU = add_control(U.to_instruction(), 1, '', 0)
    self.append(cU, [c] + [qb for qb in q])


def qft(self, targets, swap=True):
    qft = QFT(
        num_qubits=len(targets),
        do_swaps=swap,
        inverse=False
    )
    self.append(qft, qargs=targets)


def iqft(self, targets, swap=True):
    iqft = QFT(num_qubits=len(targets), do_swaps=swap, inverse=True)
    self.append(iqft, qargs=targets if swap else targets[::-1])


def measure(self, shots=0):
    state = self.run()
    samples = choices(
        range(len(state)),
        [abs(state[k]) ** 2 for k in range(len(state))],
        k=shots)
    counts = {}
    for (k, v) in Counter(samples).items():
        counts[k] = v
    return {'state vector': state, 'counts': counts}

setattr(QuantumCircuit, 'run', run)
setattr(QuantumCircuit, 'c_append', c_append)
```

```
setattr(QuantumCircuit, 'qft', qft)
setattr(QuantumCircuit, 'iqft', iqft)
setattr(QuantumCircuit, 'measure', measure)
```

Now we can run the same code using Hume or Qiskit. You can find an example of doing this in the chapter code notebook.

SWITCHING BETWEEN HUME AND QISKIT

We rely on a configuration file to switch between Hume or Qiskit. This configuration file can be found in src/config.py. The default is to use Hume as the simulator:

```
SIMULATOR = 'hume'
# SIMULATOR = 'qiskit'
```

In hume/__init__.py, we conditionally import the desired `QuantumRegister` and `QuantumCircuit` implementations from the Hume source code or from Qiskit, according to the chosen simulator:

```
from config import SIMULATOR

if SIMULATOR == 'qiskit':
    from qiskit import QuantumRegister, QuantumCircuit
elif SIMULATOR == 'hume':
    from hume.simulator.circuit import QuantumCircuit, QuantumRegister
```

The following code will run using both Hume and Qiskit, with a simple configuration change:

```
from hume import QuantumRegister, QuantumCircuit

q = QuantumRegister(3)
qc = QuantumCircuit(q)

qc.h(q[0])
qc.h(q[1])
qc.mcx([q[0], q[1]], q[2])

state = qc.run()
```

12.2.3 Running on real quantum hardware

We also created tools to seamlessly convert Hume circuits to Qiskit circuits without having to change the configuration from Hume to Qiskit. This makes it simple to run examples from the book on IBM quantum backends, both simulators and real quantum computers. For example, to convert a Hume circuit to a Qiskit circuit, we use the hume_to_qiskit function:

```
qiskit_circuit = hume_to_qiskit(hume_circuit)
```

12.2 Building quantum software and running on real quantum computers

The function returns a Qiskit `QuantumCircuit` instance. We also include a function to run a circuit using Qiskit's state vector simulator. These tools allow you to run code written in Hume on real quantum hardware.

AN EXAMPLE OF RUNNING ON A REAL QUANTUM COMPUTER

At the time of publication of this book, anyone can create an account with IBM Quantum and run experiments on real quantum hardware via the IBM Quantum Platform Open Plan.

> **NOTE** Qiskit and the associated IBM Quantum products are continuously evolving; the offerings used in this example may have changed or may no longer be available in the future. Please refer to the book's repository for updates.

We have included a notebook in the book's repository with instructions for running the code from the book on IBM's quantum computers. The notebook uses the Qiskit Runtime Sampler Primitive, so in addition to Qiskit, we need to install the `qiskit-ibm-runtime` package and import the following:

```
from qiskit_ibm_runtime import QiskitRuntimeService, Sampler
from qiskit.compiler import transpile
from qiskit.visualization import plot_histogram
```

First, insert your IBM Quantum API key and authenticate to the service. Note that this uses the default instance for Open Plan users. If you are using a different plan (i.e., pay-as-you-go), you can change your instance using the `instance` parameter:

```
QiskitRuntimeService.save_account(
    channel="ibm_quantum",
    token="<MY_IBM_QUANTUM_TOKEN>",
    instance="ibm-q/open/main",
    overwrite=True
)
```

Now initialize the service:

```
service = QiskitRuntimeService()
```

You can view the systems available with the following code:

```
service.backends()
```

Let's build a small example circuit using Hume:

```
from hume.simulator.circuit import QuantumRegister, QuantumCircuit

q = QuantumRegister(3)
qc = QuantumCircuit(q)
```

```
qc.h(q[0])
qc.h(q[1])
qc.mcx([q[0], q[1]], q[2])
```

We use Hume's Qiskit utility function `hume_to_qiskit` to convert the Hume circuit instance to a Qiskit circuit instance:

```
from hume.qiskit.util import hume_to_qiskit

qc_qiskit = hume_to_qiskit(qc.regs, qc.transformations)
```

We must add measurement to the circuit. We can use the `measure_all` method to measure all the qubits in the circuit:

```
qc_qiskit.measure_all()
```

We can also visualize the circuit using Qiskit's `draw()` method:

```
qc_qiskit.draw()
```

The output is shown in figure 12.1.

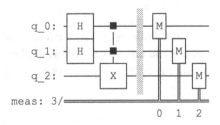

Figure 12.1 Circuit diagram created using Qiskit's `draw()` method

Now we will choose a backend on which to run our experiment. In this example, we use the least busy backend:

```
backend = service.least_busy(operational=True, simulator=False)
print(backend.name)
```

When this example was run, the least busy backend was

```
ibm_sherbrooke
```

Let's create a `sampler` object:

```
sampler = Sampler(backend=backend)
```

Next we do a basic transpilation (no optimization):

```
qc_transpiled = transpile(qc_qiskit, backend)
```

Finally, we submit a job to the chosen backend. In this example, we chose to run 1,000 shots:

```
job = sampler.run(qc_transpiled, shots = 1000)
```

Let's look at the results:

```
result = job.result()
```

We will use Qiskit's built-in visualization function `plot_histogram` to visualize the results. We plot the distribution of results, or "quasi-probabilities":

```
quasi_probs = result.quasi_dists

plot_histogram(quasi_probs, figsize=(9,5))
```

The histogram created when this example was run is shown in figure 12.2.

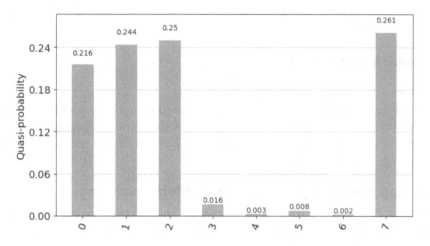

Figure 12.2 Histogram of the quasi-probability distribution

12.2.4 Quantum assistant

Practice and repetition are essential to learning. To make this process as intuitive and quick as possible, we have created several tools for you to use that complement the material in this book. One such tool is a voice-controlled AI assistant that uses the code implemented in the book. This assistant can help perform several tasks, including circuit building. It can also demonstrate solutions implemented in the book.

> **NOTE** The example below is captured at the time this book was completed. AI tools are rapidly evolving, and the assistant will likely be updated, but the simulator will stay the same.

Let's ask it to solve the example knapsack problem. We start by saying that we want to solve a knapsack problem with three items, and we specify the weights and values of those items, as you can see in the recognized command in figure 12.3. The output from the assistant is the optimal selection (figure 12.4).

```
🎤 Press Enter for voice command 🎤
Listening for 6 seconds...
Recognizing......

💡 Recognized command:
Solve the knapsack problem for 3 items with values 2, 3, 1, weights 3, 2, 1 and maximum weight 4.
```

Figure 12.3 Asking the assistant to solve the example knapsack problem

```
🔊 Assistant:
The optimal selection includes items 1 and 2. The combined weight is 3, and the combined value is 4.
```

Figure 12.4 The output is the optimal solution.

We can also ask it to show all the steps it performed to solve the problem. It will show state table visualizations, along with more details about the computation. We encourage you to explore the assistant's capabilities on your own and use them in whatever way best supports your learning.

12.3 Revisiting quantum gates and the butterfly pattern

A quantum computation consists of elementary instructions (single-qubit gates) that are applied to specific qubits in a specific order. It is essential to understand how single-qubit gates transform a quantum state.

A single-qubit gate recombines pairs of amplitudes determined by the target and control qubits according to the specific gate formula. That specific gate formula is defined by a two-by-two (unitary) matrix. Controlled transformations have one or more control qubits in addition to a target qubit, which reduce the numbers of pairs that are recombined.

The recombination of amplitudes can be represented with butterfly diagrams, which also happen to be used to visualize the steps of the classical FFT algorithm (see figure 12.5). Quantum parallelism allows any number of these pair-wise operations to be performed simultaneously.

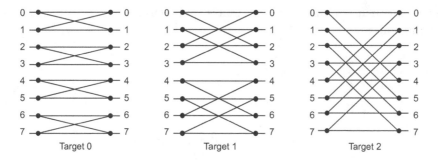

Figure 12.5 Butterfly diagrams for a three-qubit system and targets 0, 1, and 2

12.3.1 Another look at single-qubit gates and the butterfly pattern

Given a quantum system with $n \geq 1$ qubits and a target qubit t, where $1 \leq t \leq n$, and a single-qubit gate represented by a two-by-two (unitary) matrix

$$U = \begin{bmatrix} a & b \\ c & d \end{bmatrix}$$

the effect of the gate on the state of the quantum system can be described as follows. First we identify the pairs of amplitudes to be recombined based on the target qubit. In the following code, we create a two-row matrix with the amplitudes of each pair:

```
import numpy as np

def get_two_row_matrix_from_state(state, t):
    stride = 2**t

    chunks = np.array_split(state, int(len(state)/stride))
    evens = np.concatenate(chunks[0::2])
    odds = np.concatenate(chunks[1::2])

    return np.stack((evens, odds))
```

If we denote this matrix by A_t, the effect of the gate represented by U can be described by

$$UA_t$$

Then we can use the following function to assemble the quantum state from the matrix:

```
def get_state_from_two_row_matrix(matrix_state, t):
    chunk_size = int(matrix_state.shape[1] / 2**t)

    chunks_0 = np.array_split(matrix_state[0], chunk_size)
    chunks_1 = np.array_split(matrix_state[1], chunk_size)
    return np.hstack((chunks_0, chunks_1)).flatten()
```

For a unitary matrix U of size 2^m-by-2^m that is applied to $m > 0$ target qubits, the conversion functions are

```python
def get_matrix_state(state, t, m):
    n = int(np.log2(len(state)))
    o_dim = 2**(n-m)
    u_dim = 2**m
    stride = 2**t

    matrix_state = np.zeros((u_dim, o_dim), dtype=complex)

    for remainder in range(stride):
        for idx in range(u_dim):
            matrix_state[idx, remainder::stride] = state[
                remainder + idx * stride::u_dim*stride
            ]

    return matrix_state

def get_state_from_matrix(matrix_state, t, m):
    n = int(np.log2(matrix_state.shape[0] * matrix_state.shape[1]))

    u_dim = 2**m
    stride = 2**t

    state = np.zeros(2**n, dtype=complex)

    for remainder in range(stride):
        for idx in range(u_dim):
            state[idx * stride + remainder::u_dim*stride] = matrix_state[
                idx,
                remainder::stride
            ]

    return state
```

Let's use these functions to simulate applying a unitary transformation (represented by a four-by-four unitary matrix) of a state a randomly generated state with $n = 3$ qubits:

```python
from hume.utils.common import generate_state, print_state_table
from hume.utils.matrix import rvs

n = 3
t = 1
m = 2

state = generate_state(n)

U = rvs(2**m)

matrix = get_matrix_state(state.copy(), t, m)
s1 = get_state_from_matrix(U@matrix, t, m)
```

12.4 Quantum states as an image

Now let's apply the same transformation to the same state using our QuantumCircuit class:

```
from hume.simulator.circuit import QuantumRegister
from hume.simulator.circuit import QuantumCircuit

q = QuantumRegister(3)
qc = QuantumCircuit(q)
qc.initialize(state.copy())
qc.unitary(U, t)

s2 = qc.run()
```

Finally, we can check that the resulting states are equivalent:

```
assert all_close(s1, s2)
```

12.4 Quantum states as an image

Throughout the book, we illustrated amplitudes using colored bars or pixels. The direction (phase) of a complex number determines the hue of the color, and the magnitude determines the length of the bar or the intensity of the pixel.

If a circuit consists of two registers of qubits as in the function-encoding case, the quantum state resulting from running the circuit can be visualized as a table or a grid state (like those in chapters 10 and 11). Similarly, we can visualize any quantum state as an array of pixels like those in figure 12.6. Each pixel corresponds to an outcome, and the color of the pixel is determined by the amplitude corresponding to that outcome.

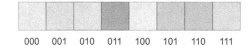

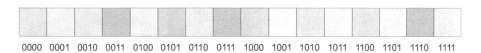

Figure 12.6 A three-qubit quantum state (top) and a four-qubit quantum state (bottom) illustrated as arrays of pixels

We can rearrange the one-dimensional array as a two-dimensional one by splitting it into multiple rows. This is similar to the grid state used to visualize more than one register of qubits. We partition the qubits into a prefix and a suffix. Figure 12.7 shows two-dimensional versions of the previous three-qubit and four-qubit states.

316 CHAPTER 12 *Conclusions and outlook*

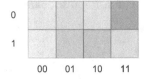

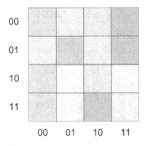

Figure 12.7 A three-qubit quantum state (top) and a four-qubit quantum state (bottom) illustrated as two-dimensional arrays of pixels

The effect of applying a gate to a state represented as an image is the recombination of pairs of columns (if the target qubit is in the prefix) or rows (if the target qubit is in the suffix). We illustrate examples of transformations on a seven-qubit quantum state divided into a three-qubit suffix and a four-qubit prefix in figure 12.8. For simplicity,

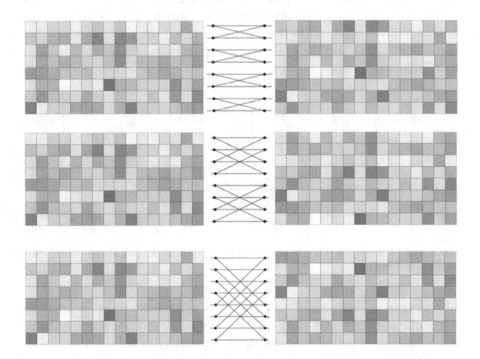

Figure 12.8 Visualizations of quantum transformations on different target qubits

we use the X gate applied to each target qubit in the suffix; this is simple to visualize because it has the effect of swapping the rows.

Here is how we can formulate the four essential quantum properties of a qubit system using the image representation:

- *Quantum state*—A quantum state is visualized as an (intensity-normalized) image with dimensions that are powers of 2.
- *System composition*—Adding a qubit doubles the number of columns or rows (we can choose the prefix and suffix in such a way that the image is closer to a square).
- *State evolution*—A quantum state can be changed by using a 2×2 gate to recombine columns or rows, depending on the target qubit. The recombination follows complex number addition and multiplication translated to colors.
- *Quantum measurement*—Measuring the state reveals the coordinates of a pixel and nothing else. The probability of a pixel being measured is the square of its intensity.

12.4.1 Visualizing quantum state evolution

Custom visualizations are easier to create when you have full control over your simulator. For example, we can implement a version of running a quantum circuit that yields all the quantum transformations applied to the initial quantum state and the evolution of the state after each transformation. We use the run_and_yield method of our QuantumCircuit class:

```
def run_and_yield(self):
    yield None, self.state
    for tr in self.transformations:
        self.apply_transformation(tr)
        yield tr, self.state
    self.transformations = []
```

We can use this method to visualize quantum state evolution. For example, we can use the following code to visualize each step of a quantum computation using pixel grid visualizations, shown in figure 12.9:

```
transformations = qc.run_and_yield()
for idx, (tr, state) in enumerate(transformations):
    # save the state as an image
```

We can also capture a quantum state evolution as a video. We have included such a video in the companion repository; the screenshots shown in figure 12.9 are reminiscent of the changes of 0s and 1s from the movie *The Matrix*. The state of a quantum system may be thought of as a "quantum matrix," where complex numbers (represented as color pixels here) change with every quantum instruction. The 0s and 1s are only the result of quantum measurement.

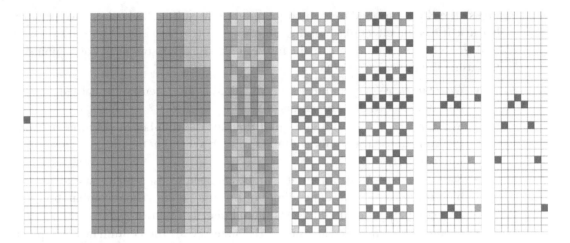

Figure 12.9 Pixel grid visualizations of selected intermediate steps of a simulated quantum computation

12.5 Combinatorial optimization problems

We learned how to encode polynomials of binary variables and optimize them according to constraints encoded in registers. The formal name of this technique is *constrained polynomial binary optimization* (CPBO). In particular, we can solve problems that fall under the category of *quadratic unconstrained binary optimization* (QUBO). The optimization function in such problems is quadratic, meaning each term contains at most two binary variables. The general form of such a function is

$$\sum_{j=0}^{n-1} c_j x_j + \sum_{0 \leq j < l < n} c_{jl} x_j x_l$$

where $n > 0$ is the number of binary variables and c_j and c_{jl} are real numbers, for $0 \leq j < n$ and $0 \leq j < l < n$.

We have only looked at one optimization method, Grover optimizer, but there are other methods you can study after reading this book. The quantum approximate optimization algorithm (QAOA) is a physics-inspired hybrid algorithm that is currently popular in the quantum computing community. It requires understanding concepts like the Hamiltonian of a system, which we will not discuss here. QAOA circuits require fewer gates than Grover optimizer circuits, but more classical processing is needed between successive quantum runs.

12.5.1 Encoding polynomials with noninteger coefficients

Even though we have been using polynomial functions with integer coefficients in our optimization examples, the polynomial encoding method can handle noninteger coefficients. Instead of a single value, each input will have a corresponding discrete-sinc

12.5 Combinatorial optimization problems

distribution encoding its corresponding output. Let's look at the concrete example of the function

$$f(k) = 0.4k^2 - 2.3$$

defined for $0 \leq k < 4$. The corresponding function table is shown in table 12.1.

Table 12.1 The function table for the function $f(k) = 0.4k^2 - 2.3$ with $0 \leq k < 4$

k	$f(k) = 0.4k^2 - 2.3$
0	−2.3
1	−1.9
2	−0.7
3	1.3

The quantum state encoding its inputs and outputs is illustrated in figure 12.10. The principles we learned in chapter 11 can also be applied to optimizing polynomials of binary variables with noninteger coefficients.

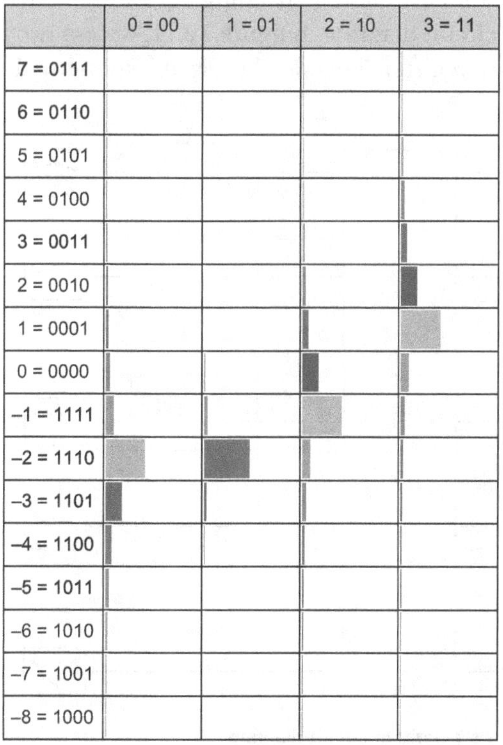

Figure 12.10 Quantum state encoding the function $f(k) = 0.4k^2 - 2.3$ for $0 \leq k < 4$

12.5.2 Shor's factorization algorithm

Shor's algorithm challenges the security of RSA encryption, which is a widely used method for securely transmitting data over the internet. Developed by the mathematician Peter Shor in 1994, this algorithm efficiently solves the problem of integer factorization—a task that is extremely difficult for classical computers. Specifically, RSA encryption relies on the computational difficulty of factoring a large integer that is the product of two prime numbers. The security of RSA is based on the premise that although multiplying two large primes is easy, reversing the process (i.e., determining the original prime factors) is computationally infeasible for classical computers. However, Shor's algorithm can perform this factorization exponentially faster than the best-known classical algorithms.

Shor's algorithm has a structure similar to the one we used to encode and search for values of polynomial functions. In Shor's algorithm, we encode an exponential function of the form

$$f(k) = a^k \mod N$$

where a is a chosen integer and N is the number to be factored.

Shor's algorithm works by finding the period of the encoded function. This is similar to how we encoded periodic signals (complex sinusoids) before applying the IQFT to find the encoded frequency value. The structure of the circuit used by Shor's algorithm is very similar to the polynomial function-encoding algorithm introduced in chapter 10. As you can see in the circuit diagram in figure 12.11, we use two registers, apply Hadamard gates to the first register, encode the given exponential function

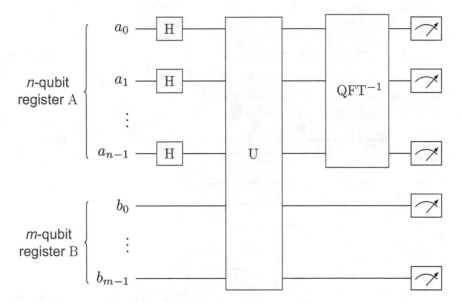

Figure 12.11 High-level view of the Shor's algorithm circuit diagram

using both registers (operator *U* in the circuit diagram), and then apply the IQFT to the first register.

Summary

- The book's code repository contains tools to seamlessly convert Hume circuits to Qiskit circuits. This makes it easy to run code from the book using IBM quantum backends, both simulators and real quantum computers.
- At the most basic level, the state of a qubit system changes according to a butterfly pattern, a pattern that occurs in several other classical computing contexts.
- Large unitary matrices are useful for theoretical research, but for practical quantum computing, developers need to understand elementary quantum gates.
- The state of a qubit system can be thought of as an image whose pixels change by recombining rows or columns of the image.
- There is a lot more to be learned about quantum computing. This book has laid the foundation for you to continue your learning journey into more advanced topics.

appendix A
Math refresher

This appendix contains a quick review of binary strings and complex numbers.

A.1 Diving deeper into binary strings

The only information we can get from a quantum computation is the measurement outcome. We represent this outcome as a binary string. Therefore, to interpret the results of a quantum computation, we need to be able to interpret binary strings.

Typically, the information processed by a classical computer uses a binary system, so you may already be familiar with interpretations of binary strings. Of course, present-day programmers rarely need to interact with binary code. In contrast, in the current stage of quantum computing, we have to be able to think in terms of binary representations of variables to implement quantum programs. In the following sections, we will review a few relevant features of binary strings.

A.1.1 Converting between binary and decimal values

Most of the time, we work with integers in their decimal (base 10) form. The decimal form of an integer is a sequence of digits, where each digit is one of 10 possible values (0 through 9). The position of each digit then tells us which power of 10 the value represents. As we move from right to left, the power of 10 increases. For example, in a three-digit positive integer, the leftmost digit represents how many hundreds (10^2) are in the integer, the middle digit how many tens (10^1), and the rightmost is how many ones (10^0), as shown in figure A.1.

In general, we take each digit, multiply its value by its corresponding power, and add it to a total. In the decimal form of 104, we add 1 hundred, 0 tens, and 4 ones. Therefore, a 0 digit represents a lack of that power. If we represent the integer 8 in

A.1 Diving deeper into binary strings

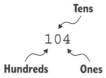

Figure A.1 The number 104 written in decimal (base 10) form

its decimal form with three digits, it is 008: we have no hundreds or tens to contribute to the total, which means their digits are simply 0.

Similarly, the binary (base 2) form of an integer is expressed using two digits: 0 and 1. Each digit shows whether the corresponding power of 2 is present, again increasing in power from right to left.

To convert a binary string to its decimal form, we consider each digit from the right to the left. Each digit represents a power of 2, starting from 2^0 for the rightmost digit and increasing with each digit to the left. If we move one digit to the left, we find the value corresponding to 2^1, and so on. In the general case, we multiply the value of each digit by its power and add this to the running total for the final decimal value. Because binary strings are made up of only 0s and 1s, this is simple: we either add a power of 2 or we don't. Figure A.2 shows an example of finding the decimal value from the binary form of 104.

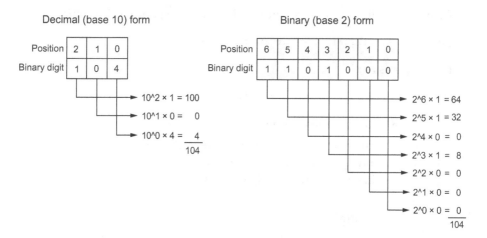

Figure A.2 Example of representing the same number in decimal form and binary form

A given number of digits can represent a limited range of integers in binary form. Figure A.3 shows the decimal values of binary strings of lengths one, two, and three.

Two binary digits can represent the (base 10) integers 0 to 3 in binary form. The following Python code produces the binary form of these integers:

```
[bin(k)[2:].zfill(2) for k in range(2**2)]
```

Figure A.3 The decimal value of binary strings of length one, two, and three

One-qubit outcomes

Binary form	Decimal form
0	0
1	1

Two-qubit outcomes

Binary form	Decimal form
00	0
01	1
10	2
11	3

Three-qubit outcomes

Binary form	Decimal form
000	0
001	1
010	2
011	3
100	4
101	5
110	6
111	7

The output is

```
['00', '01', '10', '11']
```

Three binary digits can represent the (base 10) integers 0 to 7 in binary form:

```
[bin(k)[2:].zfill(3) for k in range(2**3)]
```

The output is

```
['000', '001', '010', '011', '100', '101', '110', '111']
```

A.1.2 Adding a digit to a binary string

We know that there are 2^n binary strings of length n. That means if we add one more digit, we will end up with double the number of possible strings. Each time we add a digit to the string, we can use another power of 2, as shown in figure A.4.

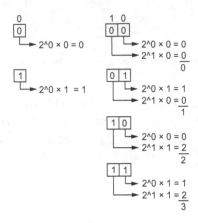

Figure A.4 Adding a digit to the binary string means two times as many values can be represented.

A.1 Diving deeper into binary strings

Similarly, because we have four strings of length 2, we will have eight strings of length 3. Four of them begin with 0, and the other four begin with 1, as shown in figure A.5.

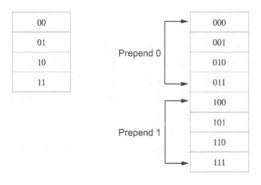

Figure A.5 Building three-digit binary strings by prepending 0 and 1 to the two-digit strings

A.1.3 Visualizing binary strings with binary trees

Binary trees are another way to represent a series of binary choices. Figure A.6 shows the binary trees corresponding to strings of one, two, and three digits. Each level, or step, gives us the option to go up (adding digit 0) or down (adding digit 1). When we choose a sequence of up or down moves as a path in the tree, it is equivalent to building a binary string. Adding a step is the same as adding a digit to the binary string.

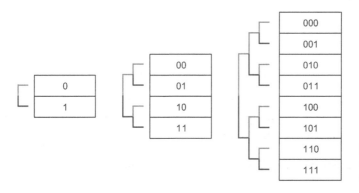

Figure A.6 Binary tree view of binary strings of lengths one, two, and three

A.1.4 Joining and splitting binary strings with prefixes and suffixes

We can create a new binary string by joining (concatenating) two binary strings. The length of the new string will be the sum of the lengths of the two strings. We can also do this with their corresponding binary trees: we add a copy of the second binary tree to each leaf of the first, producing a new binary tree with a total number of levels equal to the sum of the two original binary trees. The number of leaves of the new tree is equal to the product of the number of leaves of the two trees.

We can also split a binary string into two parts: a prefix and a suffix. In a binary tree, this corresponds to dividing the path from the root to a leaf into two sections at a certain level.

A.1.5 *Encoding negative integers*

Now we know how to represent nonnegative integers in binary form. However, depending on the problem, we will need to represent negative numbers. To do this, we will take the set of possible binary strings of a given length and divide it in two. The first half will represent nonnegative integers, and the second half will represent negative integers.

Let's use an example to understand how this works. Assume we have three binary digits. We know that there are 2^3 possible binary strings of length 3. So, we can represent the following range of eight nonnegative integers:

```
n = 3
decimal_range = [k for k in range(2**n)]
print(decimal_range)
```

The output is

```
[0, 1, 2, 3, 4, 5, 6, 7]
```

We can represent the same range in binary form:

```
binary_range = [bin(k)[2:].zfill(3) for k in range(2**n)]
print(binary_range)
```

The output is

```
['000', '001', '010', '011', '100', '101', '110', '111']
```

Alternatively, we can map the range to have negative numbers in the second half, starting with –1 at the end and going backward to the half-point. Note that the second half of the binary range starts with the digit 1:

```
[k for k in range(2**(n-1))] + [k-2**n for k in range(2**(n-1), 2**n)]
```

The output is

```
[0, 1, 2, 3, -4, -3, -2, -1]
```

The second half of the list entries are the original values minus the size of the range. For example, we subtract 8, the size of the range, from 4, the original value of the string, to get –4. Another way to look at this is to imagine that we're counting our position from the end of the list rather than the beginning. In fact, Python lists allow negative indexing that works exactly this way (i.e., index –1 is the last value in the list).

A.2 Using complex numbers to represent amplitudes

We can visualize the numbers 0 through 7 as binary strings in a circle. Let's wrap the list clockwise around a circle, as shown in figure A.7. The numbers whose binary representation starts with 0 are in the top half of the circle, and those that start with 1 are in the bottom half.

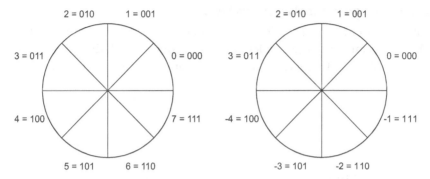

Figure A.7 Binary strings of length three for encoding nonnegatives (left) and negatives (right)

We will see that this encoding appears naturally when using quantum operations. We are already used to using both negative and nonnegative angles on the unit circle (i.e., $7 \cdot 2\pi/8$ is equivalent to $-2\pi/8$). This technique is known as *Two's Complement* in computer science.

> **Two's Complement: Why the name?**
> Computing professionals are used to describing the Two's Complement technique in terms of its mechanical application inside a computer. The procedure to get the negative representation of a number can be summarized as follows:
>
> 1. Write the number's absolute value in binary form.
> 2. Flip each bit to get the *complement* of each digit (changing all 0s to 1s and all 1s to 0s).
> 3. Add 1 to the result.
>
> We do not need to use this complex procedure. The description in this section is all we need to encode negative numbers.

A.2 Using complex numbers to represent amplitudes

The state of a quantum system consists of amplitudes that can be visualized as arrows that exist in two dimensions. There is one amplitude for each possible outcome. An amplitude is like a force that determines the probability of its corresponding outcome.

From a computational point of view, complex numbers are a very convenient way to represent amplitudes. Before we discuss them, let's look at the vector, or arrow, representation of amplitudes. Later in the section, we'll provide a brief overview of complex numbers.

> **NOTE** An amplitude is like a force that determines the probability of its corresponding outcome.

A.2.1 Amplitudes as arrows inside the unit circle

Vectors can show the magnitude (strength) and direction of a force, as shown in figure A.8. The sum of the squared lengths (magnitudes) of all the amplitudes of a state must be equal to 1. This means any single amplitude arrow can be no longer than 1.

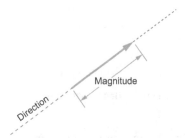

Figure A.8 A vector defined by a magnitude and a direction

The unit circle is a circle with a radius of 1, centered at the point where the x axis and y axis meet (the origin). If we position the start of an amplitude vector at the origin of the plane, the vector will be inside the unit circle, as shown in figure A.9. Also, because we know where the vector starts, we don't need to mark its end with an arrow. Brian Cox, the well-known physicist, sometimes refers to amplitudes as "clocks"; when we visualize an amplitude inside a unit circle, it is easy to see why.

Figure A.9 A "clock" representation of a quantum amplitude inside the unit circle

A.2.2 Amplitudes as complex numbers: The algebraic form

The coordinates (x, y) of the endpoint of a vector that starts at the origin define a *complex number* $z = x + iy$, as shown in figure A.10. Here, i is the *imaginary unit*, a number with the special property that its square is -1: $i^2 = -1$. In this form, called *algebraic*, x is the real part of z, and y is the imaginary part.

A.2 Using complex numbers to represent amplitudes

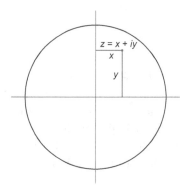

Figure A.10 The (x, y) coordinates of the endpoint of a vector define a complex number z = x + iy.

Using the algebraic form of complex numbers, we can add and multiply amplitudes in a straightforward way. Take two amplitudes $z_0 = x_0 + iy_0$ and $z_1 = x_1 + iy_1$. To find their sum, we can add them as complex numbers:

$$z_0 + z_1 = (x_0 + x_1) + i(y_0 + y_1)$$

To compute their product, we multiply them

$$z_0 z_1 = (x_0 x_1 - y_0 y_1) + i(x_0 y_1 + x_1 y_0)$$

taking into account that $i^2 = 1$.

Python represents the imaginary unit, i, in a complex number with the symbol j. The following creates a complex number in Python:

```
z = 0.2 + 0.3j
print(type(z))
```

The output is

```
<class 'complex'>
```

We can get the real parts with the built-in real and imag attributes:

```
print(z.real, z.imag)
```

The output is

```
0.2 0.3
```

The magnitude of a complex number in algebraic form, $z = x + iy$, is $|z| = \sqrt{x^2 + y^2}$. We can get the magnitude (absolute value) of the complex number defined previously using the abs function:

```
abs(z)
```

The output is

0.36055512754639896

A.2.3 Amplitudes as complex numbers: The trigonometric (polar) form

Instead of using the coordinates of a vector's endpoint, we can represent the vector by its magnitude and direction. In geometric terms, the magnitude is the distance from the origin to the point, denoted by r. The direction is the angle from the x axis, denoted by θ. We can restrict θ to the interval $[0°, 360°]$ or $[-180°, 180°]$.

When dealing with direction, we need to understand some basic trigonometry concepts.

> **Revisiting trigonometry basics**
>
> A point on the unit circle corresponds to an angle θ between 0 and 360 degrees. We measure the angle from the positive side of the x axis in a counterclockwise direction. We can also use negative angles measured in a clockwise direction. This point's x coordinate is the cosine of the angle ($\cos\theta$), and its y coordinate is the sine of the angle ($\sin\theta$).
>
>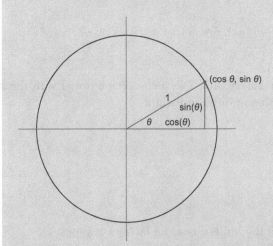
>
> **A point on the unit circle and its coordinates**
>
> This is how the cosine of the acute angles of a right triangle is defined: the ratio of the side next to the angle over the hypotenuse. The sine is the ratio of the side opposite the angle over the hypotenuse.

Given the magnitude r and direction θ of an amplitude, we can calculate the coordinates of its endpoint by using the expressions $x = r\cos\theta$ and $y = r\sin\theta$. The corresponding complex number can be written as $z = r(\cos\theta + i\sin\theta)$. This alternative representation is the trigonometric, or *polar*, form of complex numbers.

A.2.4 Conjugates of complex numbers

The *conjugate* of a complex number is the number you get when you change the sign of the imaginary part. For example, a complex number $z = x + iy$ has a conjugate of $x - iy$, denoted by $\bar{z}$. In polar form, $z = r(\cos \theta + i \sin \theta)$ has a conjugate of $r(\cos \theta - i \sin \theta) = r(\cos(-\theta) + i \sin(-\theta))$. This means the conjugate $\bar{z}$ is the same number but with the opposite sign of its direction. Also, note that $z\bar{z} = \bar{z}z = r^2$.

In Python, we can get the conjugate of a complex number using the following code:

```
z = 0.2 + 0.3j
z.conjugate()
```

The output is

```
(0.2-0.3j)
```

A.2.5 Combining amplitude pairs

The most basic operation of quantum computing recombines two amplitudes into two new ones. This operation preserves the sum of the amplitudes' squared magnitudes. The process is best explained by using two-by-two matrices of complex numbers, even though we will not use this representation in code. We structure the pair of amplitudes as a column matrix (or vector of complex numbers):

$$\begin{bmatrix} z_0 \\ z_1 \end{bmatrix}$$

Now assume that we have a two-by-two matrix of complex numbers:

$$\begin{bmatrix} a & b \\ c & d \end{bmatrix}$$

The value of the entries depends on the operation definition.

In Python code, we can represent this matrix with nested lists:

```
[[a, b], [c, d]]
```

The new amplitude values are computed with the following formulas:

$$z_0 \leftarrow az_0 + bz_1$$
$$z_1 \leftarrow cz_0 + dz_1$$

> **Do we need matrix multiplication?**
>
> The formulas we used to transform amplitudes z_0 and z_1 happen to also be the definition of multiplying the two-by-two matrix with the quantum state column vector:
>
> $$\begin{bmatrix} a & b \\ c & d \end{bmatrix} \begin{bmatrix} z_0 \\ z_1 \end{bmatrix} = \begin{bmatrix} az_0 + bz_1 \\ cz_0 + dz_1 \end{bmatrix}$$
>
> We are not relying on matrix multiplication to understand quantum gates. Instead, we use simple formulas in our simulation code. Standard computing data structures are enough to express quantum computations and are usually more efficient than matrix multiplication.
>
> We will sometimes make connections between related concepts and their matrix forms for readers who are familiar with advanced mathematics.

As we see in the formulas, the values in the first row of the matrix tell us how to recombine the pair of amplitudes to create the first new amplitude. The second row does the same for the second amplitude. Another way to view the matrix is that a column tells us how we split an amplitude. The first column in the matrix contains the factors we use to split the first amplitude into two parts; each part goes to one of the new amplitudes. The second column does the same for the second amplitude.

NOTE If you are familiar with the butterfly operation in the fast Fourier transform (FFT) algorithm, combining pairs of amplitudes is very similar. The quantum version of the Fourier transform is discussed in chapter 7.

A.2.6 Amplitudes as colored bars

As we discussed, we can plot a complex number in its polar form. Each amplitude of a quantum state will have a magnitude less than or equal to 1. This tells us we can plot amplitudes within the unit circle.

Now we are going to use these properties of amplitudes to visualize them with colors. We overlay the unit circle with a color wheel, as shown in figure A.11.

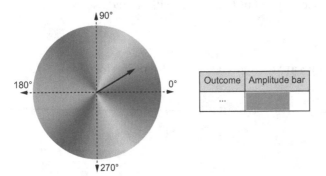

Figure A.11 Mapping an amplitude to a colored bar

A.2 Using complex numbers to represent amplitudes

The color of the bar indicates the direction of the amplitude. Draw a bar with this color, and set the saturation to the highest level for visibility. The length of the bar should match the magnitude of the amplitude.

We can use this method to visualize a quantum state using a color bar chart. The bar can be either horizontal or vertical, depending on the context. Figure A.12 shows a colored bar visualization of a three-qubit system's state. The example state is the result of applying a quantum phase estimation algorithm. We will talk about this algorithm in more detail in a later chapter.

Outcome	Binary	Amplitude	Direction	Magnitude	Amplitude bar
0	000	0.10 + 0.04i	20.2°	0.11	
1	001	0.07 + 0.07i	42.8°	0.10	
2	010	0.05 + 0.11i	65.2°	0.12	
3	011	0.01 + 0.16i	87.8°	0.16	
4	100	−0.13 + 0.35i	110.3°	0.37	
5	101	0.58 − 0.63i	−47.2°	0.86	
6	110	0.19 − 0.09i	−24.7°	0.21	
7	111	0.13 − 0.01i	−2.2°	0.13	

Figure A.12 A tabular representation of the state of a three-qubit quantum system using colored bars

appendix B
More about quantum states and gates

B.1   The Bloch sphere

A qubit (and, more generally, a pair of amplitudes) can be illustrated using the three-dimensional Bloch sphere, shown in figure B.1. In this book, we do not rely on the Bloch sphere for visualizing single-qubit states. However, you may find it helpful for building intuition.

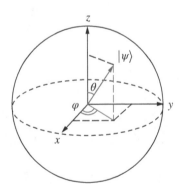

Figure B.1 The Bloch sphere

A single-qubit state with probability $p = \cos^2 \theta/2$ of the outcome 0 can be written in Ket notation as

$$|\psi\rangle = \cos\frac{\theta}{2}|0\rangle + e^{i\phi}\sin\frac{\theta}{2}|1\rangle$$

where $0 \leq \phi < 2\pi$.

We can get to this form by starting with a state in the general form:

$$\sqrt{p}(\cos\theta_0 + i\sin\theta_0)|0\rangle + \sqrt{1-p}(\cos\theta_1 + i\sin\theta_1)|1\rangle$$
$$= \sqrt{p}e^{i\theta_0}|0\rangle + \sqrt{1-p}e^{i\theta_1}|1\rangle$$
$$= e^{i\theta_0}\left(\sqrt{p}|0\rangle + \sqrt{1-p}e^{i(\theta_1-\theta_0)}|1\rangle\right)$$

Using an angle $0 \leq \theta < \pi$ such that $p = \cos^2\theta/2$, and therefore $1 - p = \sin^2\theta/2$, we arrive at this expression:

$$e^{i\theta_0}\left(\cos\frac{\theta}{2}|0\rangle + e^{i(\theta_1-\theta_0)}\sin\frac{\theta}{2}|1\rangle\right)$$

This is the same as the Bloch sphere representation, which ignores the factor $e^{i\theta_0}$, called a *global phase*.

Let's use a Bloch sphere to visualize the example single-qubit state where the probability of outcome 0 is $p = 0.35$ and the directions of the amplitudes are $\theta_0 = 60° = \pi/3$ and $\theta_1 = 120° = 2\pi/3$. We can express the state with the following equation:

$$|\psi\rangle = e^{i\frac{\pi}{3}}\left(\cos\frac{\theta}{2}|0\rangle + e^{i(\frac{2\pi}{3}-\frac{\pi}{3})}\sin\frac{\theta}{2}|1\rangle\right) = e^{i\frac{\pi}{3}}\left(\cos\frac{\theta}{2}|0\rangle + e^{i(\frac{\pi}{3})}\sin\frac{\theta}{2}|1\rangle\right)$$

Referencing this equation, we know that $\phi = \pi/3$ and $\sqrt{p} = \cos\frac{\theta}{2}$, and therefore $\theta = 2\arccos(\sqrt{p})$.

B.2 Building any gate from Hadamard and phase gates

All other single-qubit gates can be built from Hadamard and phase gates. In fact, most quantum computers take advantage of this fact in one form or another. Gate identities can also be used to simplify quantum circuits.

B.2.1 Example: The Z gate

It is easy to see that the Z gate is the same as $P(\pi)$ because changing the sign of a complex number is the same as adding 180°, or π radians, to its direction. Let's define an example single-qubit state and simulate applying a Z gate:

```
state = [0.2958+0.51235j, -0.40311+0.69821j]
state = [state[0], -state[1]]
state

[(0.2958+0.51235j), (0.40311-0.69821j)]
```

Now let's use the same state and apply a phase gate with angle π:

```
state = [0.2958+0.51235j, -0.40311+0.69821j]
state = [state[0], cis(pi)*state[1]]
state

[(0.2958+0.51235j), (0.40311-0.69821j)]
```

We express this equivalence of gate applications with the identity $Z = P(\pi)$.

B.2.2 Example: The X gate

To implement the X gate, we can first use a Hadamard gate to convert a pair of amplitudes into their sum and difference (divided by the square root of 2). Then we can change the sign of the difference with a Z gate (which is the same as $P(\pi)$) and apply another Hadamard gate to arrive at the original amplitudes, swapped. Let's simulate applying an X gate to an example single-qubit state:

```
state = [0.2958+0.51235j, -0.40311+0.69821j]
state = [state[1], state[0]]
state

[(-0.40311+0.69821j), (0.2958+0.51235j)]
```

Now let's apply an H gate followed by a Z gate and then another H gate to the same example state:

```
state = [0.2958+0.51235j, -0.40311+0.69821j]
state = [sqrt(0.5)*(state[0]+state[1]), sqrt(0.5)*(state[0]-state[1])]
state = [state[0], -state[1]]
state = [sqrt(0.5)*(state[0]+state[1]), sqrt(0.5)*(state[0]-state[1])]
state

[(-0.40311+0.69821j), (0.2958+0.51235j)]
```

We express this equivalence of gate applications with the identity $X = HZH = HP(\pi)H$.

> **More gate identities**
>
> We will not derive the representations of the other gates in terms of the H and P gates, but we provide them here as a reference. You may find it useful to spend time justifying these identities. The code base contains unit tests to verify them. Throughout

B.2 Building any gate from Hadamard and phase gates

the book, we will use code assertions on random states rather than formal proofs; you are encouraged to justify them more rigorously.

$$Z = P(\pi)$$
$$X = HZH = HP(\pi)H$$
$$R_Z(\theta) = XP\left(-\frac{\theta}{2}\right)XP\left(\frac{\theta}{2}\right) = HP(\pi)HP\left(-\frac{\theta}{2}\right)HP(\pi)HP\left(\frac{\theta}{2}\right)$$
$$R_X(\theta) = HR_Z(\theta)H = P(\pi)HP\left(-\frac{\theta}{2}\right)HP(\pi)HP\left(\frac{\theta}{2}\right)H$$
$$R_Y(\theta) = P\left(\frac{\pi}{2}\right)R_X(\theta)P\left(-\frac{\pi}{2}\right) = P\left(-\frac{\pi}{2}\right)HP\left(-\frac{\theta}{2}\right)HP(\pi)HP\left(\frac{\theta}{2}\right)HP\left(-\frac{\pi}{2}\right)$$
$$Y = P(\pi)R_X(\pi) = HP\left(-\frac{\pi}{2}\right)HP(\pi)HP\left(\frac{\pi}{2}\right)H$$

appendix C
Outcome pairing strategies

C.1 Additional strategies for pair selection in Python

In chapter 4, we explain one way of selecting outcome pairs. Following are two additional methods, which may perform better depending on the context.

C.1.1 Recognizing pairs by checking the digit for the target qubit

Given a target qubit position t, we can traverse through all outcomes and select pairs by finding the "0 side" of a pair and adding 2^t to find the "1 side." Given n qubits, we know the decimal forms of the outcomes are 0 to $2^n - 1$. For each possible outcome, we check whether the target qubit in the binary form is 0 using the `is_bit_set` function. If the target qubit is 0 in the binary form, we find the second item in the pair by adding 2^t.

Listing C.1 Traverse-and-check method for selecting pairs

```
def is_bit_set(m, k):
    return m & (1 << k) != 0

def pair_generator_check_digit(n, t):
    distance = int(2 ** t)

    for k0 in range(2**n):
        if not is_bit_set(k0, t):
            k1 = k0 + distance
            yield k0, k1
```

- The difference between pairs, or distance, is 2t.
- range(2**n) iterates through the outcomes in decimal form.
- Checks whether the target qubit is 0 (not 1) in the decimal form of the outcome
- Adds the distance to get the second item in the pair

Let's take the example of three qubits (n = 3) and target qubit 0 (t = 0) and generate the pairs using this method:

```
for (k0, k1) in pair_generator_check_digit(3, 0):
    print(k0, k1)

0 1
2 3
4 5
6 7
```

The pairs match the highlighted rows discussed previously and shown in figure C.1.

Outcome	Binary
0	000
1	001
2	010
3	011
4	100
5	101
6	110
7	111

Outcome	Binary
0	000
1	001
2	010
3	011
4	100
5	101
6	110
7	111

Outcome	Binary
0	000
1	001
2	010
3	011
4	100
5	101
6	110
7	111

Outcome	Binary
0	000
1	001
2	010
3	011
4	100
5	101
6	110
7	111

Figure C.1 The pairs of outcomes for applying a single-qubit gate to a three-qubit system with a target qubit in position 0

C.1.2 Generating pairs by concatenating the prefix, target, and suffix

Given n qubits and a target qubit t, the binary string outcomes will have t digits after the target digit and $n - t - 1$ digits before it. We will call the digits before the target digit the *prefix* and the digits after the target digit the *suffix*. We can generate prefixes and suffixes to assemble pairs.

Each prefix will be a binary string of length $n - t - 1$, so there will be 2^{n-t-1} possible prefixes. Each suffix will be a binary string of length t, so there will be 2^t possible suffixes. We can generate pairs by taking each possible prefix, appending 0 in the target position, and then appending each possible suffix.

For example, for four qubits ($n = 4$) and target qubit 1 (t), the prefix will have $n - t - 1 = 2$ digits. Therefore, the possible prefixes are '00', '01', '10', and '11'. The suffix will have one digit, so the possible values are 0 and 1. For each possible prefix, we append 0 and 1 in the target position. Starting with the prefix '00', we append 0 to get the 0 side of the pair, '000', and 1 to get the 1 side of the pair, '001'. Then we append each possible suffix. By appending the suffix 0, we get the first pair: '0000' and '0010'. And by appending the suffix 1, we get the second pair: '0001' and '0011'. If we repeat this process for each of the three other prefixes, we can generate all eight pairs.

If we think about the prefix and suffix values in decimal form, appending 0 in the target position is equivalent to multiplying the prefix value by 2×2^t. Appending the suffix is equivalent to adding the decimal value of the suffix. Once we have the 0 side of the pair, we can use the distance to get the second item in the pair.

In the code, we will use decimal values. In Python, we can use nested `for` loops to generate the pairs.

Listing C.2 Generating pairs by concatenating the prefix, target, and suffix

```
def pair_generator_concatenate(n, t):
    distance = int(2 ** t)              # The difference between pairs, or distance, is 2t.
    suffix_count = int(2 ** t)          # Gets the number of digits
    prefix_count = int(2 ** (n - t - 1))# in each prefix and suffix

    for p in range(prefix_count):       # Iterates through the
        for s in range(suffix_count):   # decimal form of each
            k0 = p * suffix_count*2 + s # possible prefix
            k1 = k0 + distance
            yield k0, k1
```

Let's generate all the pairs for the previous example (n = 4 and t = 1):

```
for (k0, k1) in pair_generator_concatenate(4, 1):
    print(k0, k1)

0 2
1 3
4 6
5 7
8 10
9 11
12 14
13 15
```

The generated pairs consist of outcomes that differ by $2^t = 2^1 = 2$. If we looked at the four-digit binary form of each of these pairs, we would find that they differ only in position 1.

index

A

abs function 40, 42, 329
action_on_progress function 301
amplitude amplification 133–152
   algorithm 30
   Grover iterate 144–150
   inversion operator 139–152
   oracles 135–136
amplitude bar 36
amplitude estimation 242–249
   estimating number of good outcomes with quantum counting 245–247
   estimating probability of good outcomes with amplitude estimation 247–249
amplitudes 12, 24–27, 36, 161
analog encoding 18, 160
anatomy of a computation of multiple quantum bits
   measuring a qubit-based quantum system 14
   state evolution 14–16
   state of qubit-based quantum system 13
ancillary qubit 122
append method 117–118
applications of single-qubit computations 65–67
arrows, amplitudes as arrows inside unit circle 328
assert statement 199, 216, 267
atan2 function 36, 41, 80

B

bad outcomes 136
Bell states 76
Bernoulli distribution, encoding in single-qubit quantum state 64–65
binary optimization 20
binary strings 322–327
   adding digit to 324–325
   converting between binary and decimal values 322–323
   encoding negative integers 326–327
   joining and splitting with prefixes and suffixes 325–326
   outcomes as 22–24
   visualizing with binary trees 325
binomial probability distribution 103
bit oracles 113, 115–117, 122–123
bit quantum oracles
   converting between phase and bit quantum oracles 124–128
   converting from phase quantum oracles 124–126
   converting to phase quantum oracles 126–128
bits
   classical, computing with single 10
   quantum 11–16
butterfly pattern 312–315

C

c_append method 118, 125, 307
c_transform function 94–95
central maximum, defined 187
choices function 62, 96
circuit_params dictionary 287, 294
circuits, single-qubit 60
cis expression 46, 200
cis function 46, 165, 169
classical bits, computing with single 10

INDEX

colored bars 332–333
combinatorial optimization problems 318–321
    Shor's factorization algorithm 320–321
complex numbers 12, 34, 36, 327–333
    amplitudes as arrows inside unit circle 328
    amplitudes as colored bars 332–333
    amplitudes as complex numbers 328–330
    combining amplitude pairs 331–332
    conjugates of 331
complex sinusoid 164
composite sound waves 161
computational bases 178
controlled quantum transformations 92–96
    simulating controlled gate transformations in Python 94–95
    simulating multicontrol gate transformations in Python 95–96
control qubit 92
cos function 162
CPBO (constrained polynomial binary optimization) 318–321

D

DFT (discrete Fourier transform) 160, 171–174
diffraction 187
digital encoding 17
discrete sinc, as sequence of coin flips 205–207
discrete sinc function 187, 189
discrete sinc quantum states, encoding periodic signal 189–204
    numerical forms of frequency encoding pattern 198–201
    phase-to-magnitude frequency encoding 195–198
    reversed qubit implementation of phased discrete sinc quantum states 202–204
divmod function 182
dot products 137

E

eigen_circuit parameter 237–238
eigenstates 228
eigenvalues 228
eigenvectors 228
encoding
    encoding an integer as a frequency 196–198
    polynomial functions 272–275
    polynomials with noninteger coefficients 319
estimating probability of specific outcomes 18
estimation register 232

F

factorization algorithms, Shor's 320–321
FFT (fast Fourier transform) 4, 173, 306, 332
fft package 173
fib_circuit function 130
Fibonacci numbers, selecting outcomes with oracles 128–132
flow_state dictionary 287
for loops 71, 175, 234, 261
fourier_basis function 175
frequency, defined 161
functions
    encoding function inputs and outputs 254–268
    encoding in quantum states 253–275
    linear function of binary variables 28–29, 260
    polynomial functions, finding zeros of 272–275
    polynomial of binary variables 263

G

GAS (Grover adaptive search) algorithm 277–281
gates 15, 44
    simulating changing amplitudes with 57–60
generate_state function 116, 125
geometric distribution 107
geometric sequence 165, 167
geom function 165–166
global phase 335
golden ratio, selecting outcomes with oracles 128–132
good outcomes 136
grid_state function 258–259, 267, 280
Grover's algorithm 133, 155–157
Grover iterate 135, 144–155
Grover operator 135
Grover optimizer 277, 283–297
    solving knapsack problem with 297–303

H

Hadamard gates 49–50
    building from X and Z gate 335–337
    converting from phase to magnitude encoding with 169–171
Hoeffding Inequality 242
Hume
    simulator 32
    swapping between Qiskit and 308
hybrid algorithm 277

I

icft function 175
imag attribute 329
imaginary unit 36, 328
init_state function 44, 57, 83
initial_circuit_params dictionary 287
initialize method 126
initializing multi-qubit states 83
inner function 138–139, 172
instance parameter 309
inverse method 154
inversion 134
  by the mean 134, 139, 143
  operator 135, 139–154
IQFT (inverse quantum Fourier transform) 174–178, 185–186, 219, 254, 307
  quantum circuits for 179–183
  simulating with classical code 174–175
is_bit_set function 94
is_close function 44
iterations parameter 155

J

joining, binary strings with prefixes and suffixes 325–326

K

ket notation 25, 39, 82, 193, 231
key register 254
knapsack problem 19–33
  encoding function inputs and outputs 259–262
  optimization problems 20–21
  overview of 20–21
  problem setup 21
  quantum solution to 27–31
  solving with Grover optimizer 297–303
  tools for programming quantum solutions 31–32

L

last_good_outcome_results dictionary 287
linear interpolation 225
lists
  comprehensions, building state tables with 79–83
  encoding multi-qubit states with list of complex numbers 78–79
  encoding two-qubit states with list of complex numbers 72–73
  programmatically encoding single-qubit states with 39–43

M

magnitude amplification 134, 152–157
  Grover's algorithm 155–157
  Grover iterate 155
  inversion operator 154
  quantum oracle 153
math
  binary strings 322–327
  complex numbers 327–333
  library 36, 41
mc_transform function 95
mcp method 119
mcp (multi-control phase gate) 264
measure_all method 310
measurement, simulating single-qubit states 61–64
measurement counts 70
measure method 221
MLE (maximum likelihood estimation) 227
monomial 263
multi-qubit quantum systems, encoding uniform distribution in 90–92
multi-qubit states 78–83
  building state tables with Python list comprehensions 79–83
  encoding with list of complex numbers 78–79
  general form of 78
  simulating in Python 83

N

n_key parameter 285
negative integers, encoding 326–327
negative values, representing 267–268
neg parameter 259
noninteger coefficients 319
numpy package 138, 173

O

one_digits function 256
optimization problems 20–21
oracle_circuit parameter 127
oracle functions 280, 294
oracles
  amplitude amplification 135–136
  selecting outcomes with golden ratio and Fibonacci numbers 128–132

outcomes
  as binary strings 22–24
  selecting with oracles, golden ratio and Fibonacci numbers 128–132
  selecting with quantum oracles, quantum implementation of oracles 117–123

P

pair_generator function 87
parallelism 70
periodic signal 160
  encoding using discrete sinc quantum states 189–204
phase, defined 161
phased discrete sinc state 199, 220
phase estimation, alternative implementation of phase estimation circuit without qubit swaps 239–241
phase gates 48–49
  building from X and Z gates 335–337
phase oracles 113–115, 119–121
phase quantum oracles
  converting between phase and bit quantum oracles 124–128
  converting from bit quantum oracles 126–128
  converting to bit quantum oracles 124–126
phase-to-magnitude frequency encoding 195–198
  encoding integer as frequency 196
  encoding non-integer as frequency 196–198
pitch (Y) 55
plot_histogram function 311
polar area chart 14
polar form 38, 330
poly function 285
polynomial functions, finding zeros of 272–275
polynomials
  complexity of polynomial-encoding circuits 266–267
  encoding function inputs and outputs 263–266
  encoding with noninteger coefficients 319
postulates 24
predicate function 114, 136
prefixes 325–326
prepare_binomial function 157
prepare_state function 44, 57, 79
printing states 58
print parameter 285
probabilistic bit 11
probabilities, quantum state and 24–27

probability amplitude 24
probability distribution 61
  sampling from 17, 71
process_outcome function 294, 300
process_pair function 87
prod function 199
programming, encoding single-qubit states with lists 39–43
progress function 289–290, 293–294
Python
  implementing single-qubit quantum computing simulator in 43–45
  pair selection in 86–87
  simulating controlled gate transformations in 94–95
  simulating multicontrol gate transformations in 95–96
  simulating multi-qubit states in 83
simulator, understanding quantum computations with 71
single-qubit states 35–45

Q

QAOA (quantum approximate optimization algorithm) 318
QFT (quantum Fourier transform) 186–217
  classical to quantum Fourier transforms 171–178
  encoding trigonometric distributions in quantum states 208–216
  periodic patterns in sound waves and quantum states 160–169
  quantum circuits for 179–183
  simulating with classical code 176–178
  single-slit experiment 187–189
QFTs (quantum Fourier transforms) 305
Qiskit, swapping between Hume and 308
qiskit-ibm-runtime package 309
QPE (quantum phase estimation)
  algorithm for 232–237
  alternative implementation of phase estimation circuit without qubit swaps 239–241
  amplitude estimation and quantum counting 242–249
  circuit-level implementation of quantum phase estimation algorithm 237–238
  estimating frequency of periodic quantum state 219–228
  quantum circuits as rotations with eigenstates and eigenvalues 228–232
quantum advantage 305

INDEX

QuantumCircuit class 99–101, 117, 124–126, 180, 221, 307–309, 315, 317
quantum circuits 34
    as rotations with eigenstates and eigenvalues 228–232
    creating from building blocks 117–119
    for QFT and IQFT 179–183
    simulating 96–108
quantum computations
    knapsack problem 27–31
    outcomes as binary strings 22–24
    patterns of 17–18
    steps of 22–27
    tools for programming quantum solutions 31–32
    understanding with simple Python simulator 71
quantum computing
    anatomy of 10–16
    programming quantum computers 3–18
    simulator in Python 43–45
quantum counting 242–249
    amplitude estimation 243–245
    estimating number of good outcomes with 245–247
    estimating probability of good outcomes with amplitude estimation 247–249
quantum dictionary 253
quantum gates 27, 34
    building from Hadamard and phase gates 335–337
    butterfly pattern and 312–315
quantum optimization, search-based
    Grover optimizer 283–297
    solving knapsack problem with Grover optimizer 297–303
quantum oracles 153
    converting between phase and bit quantum oracles 124–128
    describing outcomes with bit and phase oracles 113–117
    quantum implementation of 117–123
quantum parallelism 92
quantum readiness 305
QuantumRegister class 98, 308
quantum registers 24
quantum search, amplitude amplification 134–152
quantum search and probability estimation, magnitude amplification 152–157
    Grover's algorithm 155–157
    Grover iterate 155

inversion operator 154
quantum oracle 153
quantum software
    building and running on real quantum computers 306–312
quantum states 24–27, 69–108
    as images 315–317
    Bloch sphere 334–335
    changing amplitudes with quantum transformations 84–92
    complex numbers 72–83
    computing with more than one qubit 70–71
    controlled quantum transformations 92–96
    encoding function inputs and outputs 254–268
    encoding functions in 253–275
    visualizing evolution of 317
quantum systems 22
    qubit-based 13–16
QuantumTransformation entries 99
quantum transformations 84–92
    pair selection in Python 86–87
    selecting pairs of amplitudes based on target qubit 84–85
    simulating amplitude changes 87–90
qubits
    computing with multiple 12–16
    computing with single 11–12
QUBO (quadratic unconstrained binary optimization) 318

R

raised cosine distribution 209–213
random_circuit function 248
random_transformation function 151
random package 62, 73, 96, 221
real attribute 329
report() method 156, 196
resonant frequency 161
roll (X) 55
roots of unity 168–169
rose chart 14
rotation, single-qubit gates 45–46
run_and_yield method 317
RY gate 54–55, 103–104, 231
RZ gate 50–54

S

sampler object 310
sampling, from probability distribution 17, 71
schedule sequence 294

search-based quantum optimization 276–303
  Grover adaptive search 277–281
  Grover optimizer 283–297
  solving knapsack problem with Grover optimizer 297–303
searching, for specific outcomes 17–18
selecting with quantum oracles, quantum implementation of oracles
  bit oracle 122–123
  creating quantum circuits from building blocks 117–119
  phase oracle 119–121
Shor's factorization algorithm 320–321
shots 18
shots parameter 221
show_probs parameter 259
signal, defined 160
SIMD (single instruction, multiple data) processing 90
simulating
  implementing Bell states 106–107
  multi-qubit states in Python 83
simulating quantum circuits 96–108
  encoding Binomial distribution in multi-qubit state 103–106
  implementing Bell states 106–108
  measurement of multi-qubit states 96–97
  quantum registers and circuits in code 97–102
  reimplementing uniform distribution with registers and circuits 102–103
simulators, single-qubit quantum computing simulator in Python 43–45
sinc function 189
single-qubit circuits 60
single-qubit gates
  basic 46–55
  changing amplitudes with 45–57
  general form of 52–53
  single-qubit gate inverses 55–57
single-qubit states 35–45
  applications of single-qubit computations 64–67
  changing amplitudes with single-qubit gates 45–57
  encoding uniform distribution in 63–64
  general form of 38–39
  implementing single-qubit quantum computing simulator in Python 43–45
  pair of complex numbers 35–45
  programmatically encoding with lists 39–43
  simulating changing amplitudes with gates 57–60
  simulating measurement of 61–64
  transforming 58–59
  visualizing with tables 35–38
single-slit experiment 187–189
  discrete sinc function 189
sinusoids 161
size parameter 98
solve_knapsack function 29
splitting binary strings with prefixes and suffixes 325–326
starting_result 294
state
  preparation 208
  tables 25
  vector 34, 72
states
  printing 58
  transforming 58–59
  visualizing 58
stopping_condition function 294
successive division method 182
suffixes 325–326
superposition 14
swap parameter 239, 244

T

table comprehension 79
tables, visualizing single-qubit states with 35–38
tag bit 115
target qubit 84
target register 232
terms list 285
test_ry_phase_estimation function 241
theta parameter 190
to_qiskit function 32
transform function 59, 87–88
transforming, single-qubit states 58–59
trees, binary 325
trigonometric distributions, encoding in quantum states 208–216
  other trigonometric functions 213–216
  raised cosine distribution 209–213
trigonometric form 330
trigonometric functions 213–216
Two's Complement 327
two-qubit states 72–78
  Bell states 76–78
  composing state from two independent single-qubit states 73–76
  encoding with list of complex numbers 72–73
  general form of 72

U

unary implementation 106
uniform distribution 63–64, 71
uniform function 103, 118, 156, 245
unit circle 328
update_circuit_params function 291–292, 294, 301

V

value register 254
variable-bias coin 11
vdot (vector dot product) function 138
visualizing
   binary strings with binary trees 325
   single-qubit states with tables 35–38
   states 58
von Neumann, John 78

W

weight function 262

X

X gate 46–47, 232
   building from Hadamard and phase gates 336–337

Y

yaw (Z) 55
Y gate 51–52

Z

Z gate 47–48
   building from Hadamard and phase gates 335–336

RELATED MANNING TITLES

Quantum Computing in Action
by Johan Vos

ISBN 9781617296321
264 pages, $49.99
January 2022

Learn Quantum Computing with Python and Q#
by Sarah C. Kaiser and Cassandra E. Granade

ISBN 9781617296130
384 pages, $59.99
May 2021

Quantum Programming in Depth
by Mariia Mykhailova

ISBN 9781633436909
276 pages (estimated), $69.99
May 2025 (estimated)

Machine Learning Algorithms in Depth
by Vadim Smolyakov

ISBN 9781633439214
328 pages, $79.99
July 2024

For ordering information, go to www.manning.com

The Manning Early Access Program

Don't wait to start learning! In MEAP, the Manning Early Access Program, you can read books as they're being created and long before they're available in stores.

Here's how MEAP works.

- **Start now.** Buy a MEAP and you'll get all available chapters in PDF, ePub, Kindle, and liveBook formats.

- **Regular updates.** New chapters are released as soon as they're written. We'll let you know when fresh content is available.

- **Finish faster.** MEAP customers are the first to get final versions of all books! Pre-order the print book, and it'll ship as soon as it's off the press.

- **Contribute to the process.** The feedback you share with authors makes the end product better.

- **No risk.** You get a full refund or exchange if we ever have to cancel a MEAP.

Explore dozens of titles in MEAP at www.manning.com.

Hands-on projects for learning your way

liveProjects are an exciting way to develop your skills that's just like learning on the job.

In a Manning liveProject, you tackle a real-world IT challenge and work out your own solutions. To make sure you succeed, you'll get 90 days of full and unlimited access to a hand-picked list of Manning book and video resources.

Here's how liveProject works:

- **Achievable milestones.** Each project is broken down into steps and sections so you can keep track of your progress.
- **Collaboration and advice.** Work with other liveProject participants through chat, working groups, and peer project reviews.
- **Compare your results.** See how your work shapes up against an expert implementation by the liveProject's creator.
- **Everything you need to succeed.** Datasets and carefully selected learning resources come bundled with every liveProject.
- **Build your portfolio.** All liveProjects teach skills that are in demand from industry. When you're finished, you'll have the satisfaction that comes with success and a real project to add to your portfolio.

Explore dozens of data, development, and cloud engineering liveProjects at www.manning.com!